KITCHENER'S
ARMY

KITCHENER'S
ARMY

THE RAISING OF THE NEW ARMIES
1914-1916

Pen & Sword
MILITARY

First published in Great Britain in 1988 by
Manchester University Press
Reprinted in 2007 by

PEN & SWORD MILITARY
an imprint of
Pen & Sword Books Ltd
47 Church Street
Barnsley
South Yorkshire
S70 2AS

ISBN 978 1 84415 585 9

Printed and bound in Great Britain
By Biddles Ltd

Pen & Sword Books Ltd incorporates the Imprints of
Pen & Sword Aviation, Pen & Sword Maritime, Pen & Sword Military,
Wharncliffe Local History, Pen & Sword Select,
Pen & Sword Military Classics and Leo Cooper.

For a complete list of Pen & Sword titles please contact:
PEN & SWORD BOOKS LIMITED
47 Church Street, Barnsley, South Yorkshire, S70 2AS, England
E-mail: enquiries@pen-and-sword.co.uk
Website: www.pen-and-sword.co.uk

Contents

Acknowledgements

It is impossible to thank adequately all those who have helped me in the preparation of this book. However, I must acknowledge the considerable debt of gratitude which I owe to the Trustees of the Imperial War Museum and to the two Directors under whom I have worked, Dr Noble Frankland and Dr Alan Borg, for giving me both the opportunity and the time to undertake the necessary research and to complete the manuscript. Robert Crawford, the Deputy Director and Head of the Research and Information Office, has also offered me valued support at every stage of the project.

Of my many colleagues in the Museum who have helped and encouraged me throughout, I wish to extend my special thanks to Roderick Suddaby and the staff of the Department of Documents, to Dr Gwyn Bayliss and the Department of Printed Books, to Jane Carmichael and the Department of Photographs and to Margaret Brooks and the Department of Sound Records. Others who have been of great assistance to me include Laurie Milner, Mark Seaman, Christopher Dowling, Michael Hibberd, Chris McCarthy, Jan Mihell, Michael Moody and David Penn. Outside the Museum, Dr Ian F. W. Beckett has taken a close interest in the project from the beginning and has done much to smooth the path towards publication. I am no less indebted to Dr M. J. Allison, Professor Brian Bond, Stephen Brooks, Malcolm Brown, Dr Patrick Callan, Dr Peter N. Farrar, Dr David French, Michael Houlihan, Clive Hughes, Dr Keith Jeffery, David L. Jones, John Keegan, Peter Liddle, Dr Patricia M. Morris, Gary Sheffield, Keith Simpson, Dr Edward M. Spiers and Dr J. M. Winter. All have given generously of their time and expertise. I am, of course, solely responsible for any errors of fact or interpretation that remain.

I am most grateful to the following for granting me access to manuscript collections of which they are the owners or custodians and, where requested, for permission to quote from documents whose copyright they control: Lord Bonham Carter; the Earl of Derby; the Viscount Esher; the Earl Haig; Mr M. A. F. Rawlinson; the Earl of Selborne; Mrs Joan Simon; the Trustees of the Imperial War Museum; the Trustees of the Beaverbrook Foundation; the Trustees of the British Library Board; the Master, Fellows and Scholars of Churchill College, Cambridge; the Trustees of the Liddell Hart Centre for

Military Archives, King's College, London; the Clerk of the Records and the House of Lords Record Office; the Trustees of the National Library of Scotland; the Trustees of the National Library of Wales; the National Library of Ireland; the Public Record Office; the Chelmsford and Essex Museum; the National Army Museum; the University of Birmingham Library; the Bodleian Library; the University of Newcastle upon Tyne Library; Nuffield College, Oxford; Bristol Central Library and Record Office; the Essex Record Office; Leeds City Library; Liverpool City Libraries; Manchester Central Library; Westminster City Libraries; and the Labour Party Archives, Transport House. Extracts from Crown copyright material held in the Public Record Office and elsewhere are reproduced by permission of the Controller of Her Majesty's Stationery Office.

For permission to quote directly from documents deposited in the Imperial War Museum I must thank Miss Joan Ashley; Lieutenant-Colonel C. C. Aston; Mr A. M. Bickerton; Miss Daphne Bird; Mr D..M. A. Cain; Mr Charles Cameron; Colonel John Christie-Miller; Mr O. D. H. Clauson; Mr W. N. Collins; Mr Julian Colyer; Mr E. A. Crane; Mr A. W. Day; the Reverend Christopher Drummond; Mrs R. A. Du Cane; Mr J. N. Dykes; Miss Mary Fraser; Mrs Barbara Gamble; Mrs Fay Gjester; Mrs Edith Gordon; Mr David M. Griffiths, Mrs A. L. Hemming; Mr Brian Hunt; Mr Paul Jones; Mr Peter Kirkpatrick; Dr W. B. D. Maile; Mrs J. M. Ockleshaw; the Reverend Raymond Patston; Mrs R. J. Pearson; Mrs L. G. Perkins; Mr A. E. Perriman; Sir Richard Pilditch, Bt.; Captain R. C. Read; Miss Enid M. Roberts; Mrs Phyllis Robinson; Mrs E. Scullin; Mrs J. E. Sharp; Mrs C. Sheard; Mrs J. J. H. Swallow; Mr Leslie F. Taylor; Mr C. F. J. Thompson; Mrs S. M. Vischer; Mrs Margaret Williams; and Mr A. I. Winstanley.

My thanks are also due to the following individuals, publishers and literary agents for allowing me to quote from books whose copyright they hold: Basil Blackwell Ltd for *Letters of Arthur George Heath* (1917); Lady Bliss for *As I Remember* by Sir Arthur Bliss (Faber, 1970); Buchan and Enright Ltd for *A Passionate Prodigality* by Guy Chapman (Buchan and Enright, 1985; originally published by Ivor Nicholson and Watson, 1933); Constable and Co. Ltd for *At Suvla Bay* by John Hargrave (1916) and *Experiences of a Dug-out* by Major-General Sir C. E. Callwell (1920); Eyre and Spottiswoode Ltd for *In London during the Great War* by Michael MacDonagh (1935) and *Make me a Soldier* by Arthur Behrend (1961); Grafton Books Ltd for *Disenchantment* by C. E. Montague (Chatto and Windus, 1922); the Hamlyn Publishing Group Ltd for *The World Crisis, 1911–1914* by Winston S. Churchill (Thornton Butterworth, 1923); Harrap Ltd for *The Life of John Redmond* by Denis Gwynn (1932); David Higham Associates Ltd. for *My Political Life* by L. S. Amery (Hutchinson, 1953–55), *The Supreme Command, 1914–1918* by Lord Hankey (Allen and Unwin, 1961) and *Lloyd George: A Diary by Frances Stevenson*, edited by A. J. P. Taylor (Hutchinson, 1963); Hodder and Stoughton Ltd for *An Autobiography* by R. B. Haldane

(1929); C. S. Kendall and the Lancashire Evening Post for H. Cartmell's *For Remembrance* (Toulmin, 1919); William Kimber and Co. Ltd (Thorsons Publishing Group) for *Schoolboy into War* by H. E. L. Mellersh (1978), *Johnny Get Your Gun* by John F. Tucker (1978) and *The Anger of the Guns* by John Nettleton (1979); Macmillan Publishers Ltd. for *Life of Lord Kitchener* by Sir George Arthur (1920); Methuen and Co. Ltd for *Great Britain and the War of 1914–1918* by Sir Llewellyn Woodward (1967); John Murray Ltd for *The Weary Road* by Charles Douie (1929) and *Inside Asquith's Cabinet*, edited by Edward David (1977); the National Library of Wales and David Higham Associates Ltd for *Lloyd George Family Letters, 1885–1936*, edited by Kenneth O. Morgan (University of Wales Press, 1973); A. D. Peters and Co. Ltd for *The Life of Lord Carson* by Ian Colvin (Gollancz, 1934–36); Regimental Headquarters, The Royal Green Jackets for *The Oxfordshire and Buckinghamshire Light Infantry Chronicle* (1914–15); The Rifle Brigade Club for *The History of the Rifle Brigade in the War of 1914–1918* by Reginald Berkeley (1927); Routledge and Kegan Paul Ltd for *Enlistment or Conscription* by A. M. B. Meakin (1915); Sidgwick and Jackson Ltd for *The 23rd (Service) Battalion Royal Fusiliers (First Sportsman's)* by F. W. Ward (1920); Arthur H. Stockwell Ltd. for *Soldier's Luck* by Percy Croney (1965); Unwin Hyman Ltd for *Society at War, 1914–1916* by Caroline E. Playne (Allen and Unwin, 1931); A. P. Watt Ltd on behalf of the Executors of the Estate of Robert Graves for *Good-bye to all That* (Cape, 1929); Dennis Wheatley Ltd for *Officer and Temporary Gentleman, 1914–1919* by Dennis Wheatley (Hutchinson, 1978); and H. F. and G. Witherby Ltd. for *Roundabout* by Viscount Buckmaster (1969). Every effort has been made to trace and acknowledge the holders of all copyright material, but some have proved elusive. I trust that anyone whose copyright I have unwittingly infringed will accept my sincere apologies.

Finally I must express my gratitude to Jean Lucas and Rosemary Sharman for their help with the typing; to Annette Musker for her work on the index; and, last but not least, to my wife Jane, my daughter Catherine and my mother Peggy for supporting me in so many ways. I am only sorry that my late father did not live to see the publication of a book in which he took such a lively interest.

Peter Simkins
Imperial War Museum, May 1988

Abbreviations

Used in the text

ASC	Army Service Corps
BEF	British Expeditionary Force
CID	Committee of Imperial Defence
CIGS	Chief of the Imperial General Staff
CO	Commanding officer
DCLI	Duke of Cornwall's Light Infantry
GHQ	General headquarters
GOC	General Officer Commanding
ILP	Independent Labour Party
MP	Member of Parliament
MT	Mechanical Transport
NCF	No Conscription Fellowship
NCO	Non commissioned officer
OTC	Officers' Training Corps
PRC	Parliamentary Recruiting Committee
RE	Royal Engineers
RSM	Regimental sergeant-major
TUC	Trades Union Congress
UDC	Union of Democratic Control
UPS	University and Public Schools' Brigade
UVF	Ulster Volunteer Force
WAC	Welsh Army Corps
WNEC	Welsh National Executive Committee

Used in the notes

AC	Austen Chamberlain papers
AO	Army Order
BBC/GW	BBC Great War Series correspondence
BL Add. Mss	British Library Additional Manuscripts

BT	Board of Trade papers
CAB	Cabinet papers
DA	Department of Art (Imperial War Museum)
DER	Derby papers
DPB	Department of Printed Books (Imperial War Museum)
ERO	Essex Record Office
FO	Foreign Office papers
GOC-in-C	General Officer Commanding-in-Chief
HLRO	House of Lords Record Office
HMSO	His (Her) Majesty's Stationery Office
IWM	Imperial War Museum
KCL	Liddell Hart Centre for Military Archives, King's College, London
LRO	Liverpool Record Office
MH	Ministry of Health papers
MUN	Ministry of Munitions papers
NATS	Ministry of National Service papers
NLS	National Library of Scotland
NLW	National Library of Wales
OC	Officer commanding
PP	Parliamentary Papers
PRO	Public Record Office
RECON	Ministry of Reconstruction papers
WAC	Welsh Army Corps papers
WEWNC	War Emergency Workers' National Committee papers
WO	War Office papers

Illustrations

Introduction

The performance of Field-Marshal Lord Kitchener as Secretary of State for War from August 1914 to June 1916 has of late come to be regarded with a rather more benevolent eye than was once the case. For years historians followed the example of Lloyd George's *War Memoirs* in criticising Kitchener both as a strategist and as an administrator. Even such perceptive modern scholars as John Gooch judge his appointment in August 1914 a grave mistake, and others continue to regard his handling of the munitions problem unfavourably in comparison with Lloyd George's accomplishments as Minister of Munitions after May 1915.[1] American and Canadian-based historians have led the way in revising this long-established interpretation. In *Kitchener: Architect of Victory*, published in 1977, George H. Cassar argues that only Kitchener could have persuaded the Cabinet and the nation in August 1914 that Britain must prepare for a long war. The creation of his New Armies, despite incredible obstacles, ranks, according to Cassar – using the words of Winston Churchill – as 'among the wonders of the time'.[2] Cassar also maintains that Kitchener's efforts to expedite munition supplies resulted in an unprecedented increase in output and laid the foundation for the later production figures for which Lloyd George unjustly claimed sole credit.[3]

Peter Fraser similarly dismisses Lloyd George's attempts to conceal Kitchener's achievements in this direction. Sources now available, writes Fraser, 'reveal Kitchener more as a lone and thwarted advocate of full-scale national war effort which was the real question at issue in May 1915'.[4] Another scholar, Keith Neilson, suggests that Kitchener's strategic ideas were not capricious but founded on a shrewd understanding of the two-front nature of the war and the relative strengths of Britain and her allies. In particular, Neilson attributes many of Kitchener's decisions to his appreciation of the value of Russia as an ally and to his belief that the war would be a long one.[5] The British historian Dr David French, in his book *British Economic and Strategic Planning, 1905–1915* (1982), endorses the current premise that the blame for the muddles which arose during the simultaneous reorganisation of the army and of munitions production in 1914–15 rests not just on the shoulders of Kitchener but on the Liberal government as a whole for its reluctance, before the war, to accept the full implications of a Continental commitment.

Most writers are agreed, however, that, having inherited a Continental commitment, Kitchener's greatest achievement was to give Britain an army capable of meeting it. In numerical terms the army which he expanded eventually became the biggest in the country's history. Some 5,704,000 men served in the army during the First World War, compared to 3,788,000 between 1939 and 1945. The army of 1914–18 was also the largest and most complex single organisation created by the British nation up to that time.[7] Perhaps its most remarkable feature was that nearly half those who filled its ranks between August 1914 and November 1918 were volunteers. By the end of 1915, in fact, 2,466,719 had voluntarily enlisted in the army. As will be emphasised later on, this was a higher total than the country was able to obtain by conscription in 1916 and 1917 combined, while the number of men secured by compulsory means in 1918 was only 30,000 more than the number of volunteers who were attested in September 1914 alone.[7]

When one considers the magnitude of the national effort required to improvise a mass army in the midst of war, it is astonishing that the story of its creation has received such scant treatment from historians. Indeed, with the exception of a somewhat romantic account by V. W. Germains, published in 1930 under the title of *The Kitchener Armies*, no significant study of the subject appeared between the end of the First World War and the late 1970s. Kitchener's most recent biographers have, admittedly, dealt with some aspects of the expansion of the army but devote no more than one or two chapters each to the topic.[8] It is encouraging to note that, in the past seven or eight years, a number of scholars have begun to probe, in increasing depth, this hitherto relatively unexplored area of Britain's participation in the Great War. Here one should single out for mention Dr J. M. Osborne's valuable study *The Voluntary Recruiting Movement in Britain, 1914–1916*, which was published in the United States in 1982; the research carried out by Clive Hughes and Patrick Callan on recruiting in Wales and Ireland respectively; and the work undertaken by Dr Ian Beckett, Dr Patricia Morris, Gary Sheffield and others on individual Territorial and New Army units. Nevertheless, useful as all this work has been, there still appears to be a need for an historical overview of the raising of Britain's first-ever mass citizen army during Kitchener's term of office. Dr Osborne's study, for instance, concentrates primarily on the progress of the recruiting campaign in the early part of the war, with special reference to enlistment in the city of Bristol, and does not seek to examine in detail the impact of the rapid expansion either on the army as an institution or on the men who joined it. Part of the object of the present book, therefore, is to fill some of these gaps in the historiography of the First World War.

In trying to reduce such a multi-faceted subject to manageable proportions, and to bring the most important aspects of the story into sharper relief, I have adopted a thematic rather than a chronological approach. Again, in order to help the reader follow the broader themes more easily, I have divided the text into two main parts. The first half of the book describes how Kitchener's New Armies were actually raised and reviews the principal political, economic and social effects of the recruiting campaign of 1914 and 1915. The second part, from chapter 6 onwards, is much more concerned with the experiences and impressions of the officers, NCOs and men who made up the New Armies. Apart from analysing their motives for joining the army, this half of the book also records how they were fed, housed, equipped and trained before leaving for active service on the Western Front and elsewhere. Whenever appropriate, evidence from officers and men of the Territorial Force is included, for, although not strictly belonging to Kitchener's New Army formations, the Territorials underwent expansion at the same time as the New Armies were being raised and many of the problems encountered in the early months were common to both. Certainly the distinctions between Kitchener men and Territorials became more and more blurred as the war went on. The book stops at the point where the Kitchener divisions went overseas, as, notwith-standing that the military operations of the war are already well covered, any fresh examination of the performance of the New Armies on the field of battle would require at least one and probably several additional volumes.

If one salient conclusion emerges from this particular study it is that, partly because Britain entered the war with no systematic contingency plans for a major expansion of the army or the full mobilisation of her industrial resources, and partly because Kitchener and the War Office lost their grip on the recruiting boom in the early autumn of 1914, much of the work involved in raising, housing and even equipping the New Armies was carried out by civilians at a local rather than a national level. Some historians have claimed that, in the years immediately before the 1914–18 conflict, industrial unrest, the activities of the Suffragettes and the possibility of armed resistance by the Ulster Unionists to Home Rule were all signs that 'Liberal Britain' was beginning to break up and that the country was 'approaching the threshold of civil war'.[9] The evidence presented in this book, however, tends to refute such a thesis. Clearly the gigantic feat of constructing a Continental-scale army in wartime could not have been achieved without a considerable measure of underlying social cohesion, given all the extra stresses which the task imposed. It may be true that by 1914 society was becoming increasingly polarised and that men and women of all classes were more willing to resort to violent behaviour as a means of realising their political, social or economic ends, but the bonds holding that society together were still far stronger than the forces of disruption. The similarities between the revival of the Volunteer movement in 1859 and the raising of the Pals battalions in 1914, for example, suggest continuity in attitudes and response to crisis rather than revolu-tionary change. Grave though some of its pre-war political and social problems were, British society in 1914, as this study illustrates, was still a long way from being on the brink of disintegration.

Notes

1 John Gooch, *The Plans of War: The General Staff and British Military Strategy, c. 1900–1916*, Routledge and Kegan Paul, London, 1974, p. 299; see also R. J. Q. Adams, *Arms and the Wizard: Lloyd George and the Ministry of Munitions, 1915–1916*, Cassell, London, 1978; and John Grigg, *Lloyd George: from Peace to War, 1912–1916*, Methuen, London, 1985.
2 George H. Cassar, *Kitchener: Architect of Victory*, Kimber, London, 1977, p. 486; Winston Churchill, *The World Crisis, 1911–1914*, Thornton Butterworth, London, 1923, p. 236.
3 Cassar, *Kitchener*, pp. 359–60.
4 Peter Fraser, 'The British "Shells Scandal" of 1915', *Canadian Journal of History*, Vol. XVIII, No. 1, 1983, p. 86.
5 Keith Neilson, 'Kitchener: a Reputation Refurbished', *Canadian Journal of History*, Vol. XV, No. 2, 1980, p. 207.
6 Correlli Barnett, *Britain and her Army 1509–1970: a Military, Political and Social Survey*, Allen Lane, London, 1970, p. 392.
7 *Statistics of the Military Effort of the British Empire during the Great War, 1914–1920*, HMSO, London, 1922, p. 364.
8 See, for example, Cassar, *Kitchener*, pp. 195–212; Trevor Royle, *The Kitchener Enigma*, Michael Joseph, London, 1985, pp. 251–79.
9 Arno J. Mayer, 'The domestic causes of the First World War', in Leonard Krieger and Fritz Stern (eds.), *The Responsibility of Power*, Macmillan, London, 1968, p. 288; see also George Dangerfield, *The Strange Death of Liberal England*, Constable, London, 1935, *passim*.

Prologue

I

The last twenty years or so have seen a marked upsurge of scholarly interest in the First World War, not least among British historians. Serious study has been greatly facilitated by the opening for research of the huge mass of British official records of the conflict. Of parallel importance are the achievements of institutions such as the Imperial War Museum, Churchill College and the Liddell Hart Centre for Military Archives, and of individuals like Peter Liddle at Sunderland Polytechnic, in assembling and making available major collections of relevant private papers. The growing acceptance of military history as an academic discipline has, of course, also led to a corresponding increase in opportunities for postgraduate research in the field.

Inevitably many aspects of the background to the war, and of Britain's participation in it, have come under fresh scrutiny. Much has been written since the early 1960s on the causes of the war, military and naval reforms prior to 1914, civil–military relations, war aims, the influence of new technology and the impact of the war on British society as well as the more customary subjects of strategy, tactics and the actual nature and conduct of the fighting on land, at sea and in the air. Moreover, the quest for what James Joll has called the 'unspoken assumptions' which determine men's actions has induced students of the conflict to venture beyond the traditional paths of research and explore the wider social and cultural framework within which the decision-makers of 1914 operated.[1] As Dr Zara Steiner has commented, for example, no one currently studying the origins of the war would now confine his or her research to official government archives: 'Schoolbooks and speech-day orations, rifle corps and cadet groups, newspaper leaders and popular novels, Navy League pamphlets and military drill instructions . . . have all become source materials for the serious investigator.'[2]

The approach of British historians, like that of their colleagues elsewhere, has been profoundly affected by the furious historical debate which has raged since the appearance in 1961 of Fritz Fischer's *Griff nach der Weltmacht*, first published in English in 1967 as *Germany's Aims in the First World War*, and

4th R. Sussex Regt. Arundel Camp 1912

D.69

of his later work *Krieg der Illusionen,* translated into English as *War of Illusions* in 1973. Fischer's thesis, reviving the idea of Germany's prime responsibility for the outbreak of the war, has not aroused the same violent controversy in Britain as it has in Germany but the prominence given by the Fischer school to the influence of the 'military party' in Berlin has encouraged historians to reconsider the role of the professional heads of Britain's armed forces in the years before 1914. Earlier commentators, including David Lloyd George and Basil Liddell Hart, traced the origins of the appalling British casualties on the Western Front back to those pre-war strategic decisions which steered Britain into a disastrous Continental commitment. In particular, these commentators saw the appointment of the Francophile Brigadier-General Henry Wilson to the post of Director of Military Operations in 1910 as a key factor in the shift towards involvement in mass Continental warfare. Now, thanks to the opening of the records and to the work of such historians as Brian Bond, Dr John Gooch and Dr Neil Summerton, several aspects of this interpretation have been significantly amended.

Brian Bond's excellent study *The Victorian Army and the Staff College* and Dr Gooch's equally illuminating book *The Plans of War* have added greatly to our knowledge of the emergent General Staff in the decade before 1914. These authors show, as Michael Howard remarks in his foreword to John Gooch's book, that the policies advocated by Henry Wilson and his colleagues were based not on prejudice 'but on hard and, within its limits, clear thinking, after careful examination of possible alternatives'.[3] It has also been shown that Wilson inherited, rather than initiated, the policy of direct military assistance to France in the event of an attack on the latter by Germany. Most scholars would probably now agree with Samuel R. Williamson that the preliminary signs of a gradual drift towards a Continental involvement actually preceded the Anglo-French staff talks which began early in 1906 in the wake of the first Moroccan crisis. Gooch has described how the playing in 1905 of a war game which envisaged both a German violation of Belgian neutrality and British action to defend it reinforced this new direction in strategy. A Canadian historian, Professor John McDermott, goes even further in suggesting that the change of course coincided with the efforts in 1904 to establish the General Staff and was, in part, designed to serve the army's interests by providing the army with the role it lacked and by breaking the monopoly of India in British strategic thinking. Thus, although the international crisis of 1905 did give additional impetus to this policy, the army had in fact embarked on an anti-German course before the Kaiser set foot in Morocco. In Brian Bond's view, Henry Wilson did not question the strategy of British intervention in the European theatre but merely undertook a rigorous examination of the feasibility of existing plans.[4]

In his later years Lord Hankey, the former Secretary of the Committee of Imperial Defence, claimed that the CID was the centre of strategic planning in Britain prior to the war, but, as Nicholas d'Ombrain demonstrates in his detailed analysis of that body, it was precisely the failure of the CID to integrate the policies of the army and Royal Navy that left the two service departments free to pursue their own incompatible strategies.[5] Other scholars, notably Ruddock F. Mackay and Dr Paul Haggie, have argued that the Royal Navy was prevented from offering a viable alternative strategy by Admiral Sir John Fisher's fierce opposition to all attempts to establish a Naval War Staff during his initial term of office as First Sea Lord.[6] Today the majority of historians accept that this was one of the principal reasons for the inadequate performance of the Admiralty representatives at the crucial CID meeting of 23 August 1911 when, in the aftermath of the second Moroccan crisis, the General Staff's case triumphed and an official imprimatur was placed upon Continental involvement. Both Zara Steiner and Samuel Williamson submit, moreover, that the navy's poor showing at the meeting helped to conceal the weaknesses in the army's own proposals. Williamson maintains that one of the major disadvantages of the secret Anglo-French staff conversations was that very few soldiers and civilians were aware of the exact nature of the likely commitment. He observes that, apart from a cross-examination at the CID meeting of 23 August 1911, Henry Wilson never had to defend either his unfounded belief that the war would be short or his exaggerated confidence in the impact of the British Expeditionary Force in the opening stages of a Franco-German conflict. In addition, Wilson's forceful claims for the BEF diverted attention from what were the logical corollaries of a Continental commitment – the necessity of raising a mass army and the corresponding need of a blueprint for industrial mobilisation to keep that army supplied. Williamson therefore concludes that at least part of the genesis of many British problems on the Western Front 'lay in the nature and illusions of the military conversations'.[7]

For all the influence that Wilson and his colleagues may have exerted, historians generally concur that, throughout the pre-1914 period and in the July crisis, it was the politicians and not the soldiers who kept control of the diplomatic machinery and preserved the right to decide between peace and war. Dr Paul M. Kennedy, a prolific writer on the background to the First World War, contends that the Anglo–French staff talks were more decisive in establishing what sort of war Britain would fight if she came in than in settling the question of whether she had to enter the war. If politicians such as Asquith and Grey were ignorant of strategic realities, failed to grasp the full implications of a Continental involvement and underestimated the extent to which Britain had become morally obliged to support France, the CID meeting of August 1911 had illustrated that civilians in Britain could probe military and naval plans in some detail if they so wished. Kennedy reaffirms that it was out of a sense of obligation to defend Belgium and the balance of power rather than as a result of a binding agreement with France that the Cabinet and Parliament voted to go to war.[8] But, as Dr Steiner stresses, the ultimate decision was made by a civilian Cabinet: 'Right up until 5 August, there was no final assurance that an expeditionary force would be sent, how many divisions would be committed or whether they would land in the appointed places.'[9]

II

The army reforms instituted by R. B. Haldane as Secretary of State for War between 1905 and 1912 have also been the subject of renewed attention in the past few years. Until the 1970s the consensus of historical opinion was that Haldane, aware of the possible ramifications of the Anglo–French staff conversations, immediately endeavoured to create an army capable of fighting against Germany in Europe and that all his reforms followed from the need to organise an expeditionary force for that purpose. The seeds of this interpretation may be traced back to Haldane's own writings, for he declared in his memoirs that, on coming to office, he both foresaw and provided for the demands of a Continental war.[10] However, this orthodoxy too has recently been challenged by a number of scholars whose research suggests that the role of the expeditionary force was not seen in quite such a clear light in 1906 as some members of the government of the day, and many historians, subsequently claimed.[11]

Shortly after taking up the reins of the War Office, Haldane asserted that Britain needed 'a highly-organised and well-equipped striking force which can be transported, with the least possible delay, to any part of the world where it is required'.[12] He elaborated on this theme two months later, on 8 March 1906, when presenting his first Army Estimates to Parliament. Accepting the strategic assumption of the previous Conservative administration of Arthur Balfour that 'our coasts are completely defended by the Fleet', Haldane stated that Britain's army 'is wanted for purposes abroad and overseas', but he insisted that, in order to judge the proper size of that army, clear and scientific thought was vital. He observed that it must necessarily be a professional army of high quality and maintained that 'we could not get such an army by conscription'. In his view, Britain's striking force existed to protect the 'distant shores' of the empire from the attacks of an invader:

We want therefore an Army which is very mobile and capable of rapid transport. For fighting which has to be at a distance and cannot be against large masses of men it ought to be on a strictly limited scale, and perfect rather in quality than in expanded quantity. . . . If the Army is something which is not wanted for Home Defence then its size is something which is capable of being calculated. The size of the striking force is the principal ingredient in the present cost of the Army. . . .

In laying emphasis on the 'strictly limited scale' of the striking force, Haldane did not neglect the fact that the army might have to be enlarged at some future date. 'I do not think you will ever satisfactorily reduce your striking force,' he said, '. . . unless you provide some power of expansion behind it in this country.' His remarks in this connection contained an oblique reference to the role that might be played here by the Territorial Force, plans for which were already forming in Haldane's mind. It might be possible to shrink the 'vast and costly organisation' of the army, he noted, 'if that skeleton of expansion of which I have spoken is lying behind, which will become a very real expansion in time of national emergency, and which, until a time of national emergency, need not be made a real expansion.' Nevertheless, he correctly reasoned that the size and purpose of the army were not questions which should or could be answered by the War Office alone. The Foreign Office, the Colonial Office, the India Office and the Admiralty were also involved in shaping the overseas policy which, in the end, governed the size of the army and the level of expenditure on it.[13] Although the Anglo–French staff talks were already in progress when Haldane made these statements in the House of Commons, a European commitment for the army was still only one possible role among several. A memorandum circulated early in January 1906 by Major-General J. M. Grierson, then Director of Military Operations, referred to four strategic situations, other than a war in alliance with France against Germany, that might call for the despatch of a large expeditionary force. One was a Boer rebellion in South Africa, necessitating the deployment of 62,000 troops; the second was a war against France, requiring an expeditionary force of 100,000; the third was a war with the United States in defence of Canada, for which 140,000 men or more might be needed; and the fourth was a war with Russia over India.[14]

The menace to India, it is true, now appeared less serious in the light of recent Russian defeats in the war against Japan and the current improvement in Anglo–Russian relations. India no longer dominated strategic enquiries as it had under Balfour's administration from 1902 to 1905. On the other hand, Haldane could not yet afford to disregard this area completely in planning his reforms and fixing the size of the expeditionary force. For example, India had to be taken into account while Haldane was considering the problems of mobilisation, for in the first half of 1906 there remained marked differences between the organisation of the home forces and those on the sub-continent, differences which, as Haldane commented in February 1906, 'must prove detrimental in war should the two armies ever be required to act together'.[15] In the home-based forces the army corps of between 30,000 and 40,000 men had survived from the late nineteenth century as a standard formation for mobilisation purposes. The army corps consisted of three divisions, each of which contained two infantry brigades. The brigade, in turn, comprised four battalions, each made up of eight small companies. The war establishment of an infantry division under this system was approximately 10,000 men. The Indian Army, in contrast, had not adopted the army corps and was organised instead in large divisions, each containing three brigades with battalions composed of four strong companies. With ancillary services, a 'great' division of this type had an establishment of 18,000–20,000 men.

The army corps system had been partly copied from Europe, where such formations were usually based in a particular territorial district and kept in a state of readiness for rapid mobilisation. The existence of permanent corps staffs eliminated the need for hasty improvisation if an assortment of individual divisions had to operate together in an emergency. Given that the army might now have to fight in Europe and that Grierson and others had made out a strong case for speedy intervention in such a war, the army corps still appeared to possess some advantages. Its main drawback was that it was much less suitable for an army with widespread imperial responsibilities and which, in peacetime, had to maintain a constant flow of reliefs and drafts for colonial garrisons. Sir William Nicholson, the Quartermaster-General, wrote in March 1906 that, because of the uncertainty about the calls which could be made upon the army, he was 'hardly prepared to admit that our war organisation should be based on one contingency only, namely, a possible intervention in a Continental struggle, or that it would be wise closely to imitate the war organisation of Continental armies, the peace organisation of which is fundamentally different from that of our Regular Forces, being based on universal service, and the territorialisation of units'.[16]

Throughout the spring of 1906 the Military Members of the Army Council continued to study the relationship between organisation and mobilisation and to assess which system would best enable the Regular army to meet the varied demands likely to be made upon it in the foreseeable future. As the discussions on the topic ran on into May and June, Haldane significantly refrained from taking sides. The majority of members of the Army Council, however, eventually opted for the 'great' divisions rather than army corps. The former, it was thought, would provide more intermediate-level commanders should the army be required to assemble bigger forces, and most agreed with Nicholson's opinion that it would be easier to combine rather than divide formations when the need arose. Seeing it as 'more flexible for tactical purposes, and also more analogous with the organisation of the Indian Army', the Army Council, on 21 June, formally established the 'great' division of 18,000–20,000 men as a standard formation for the Regular army.[17] The reorganisation of the home-based forces into larger divisions was one of the most important of the reforms introduced during Haldane's term as Secretary of State for War, yet this part of the scheme was fashioned more by the Military Members of the Army Council than by Haldane himself and stemmed as much from an appreciation of Indian and imperial needs as from any premeditated effort to construct an army able to fight in Europe.

A similar set of factors dictated the actual size of the expeditionary force. As a peacetime Secretary of State for War presiding over an army with imperial commitments Haldane had to keep the units abroad supplied with drafts and reliefs and was therefore fully aware that the scale of the expeditionary force would depend upon how many divisions could be formed from the home-based battalions. He later told the Cabinet that the two considerations which dominated the whole question of army organisation were, in order of priority: '(*a*) The necessity for finding drafts in peace for units in India and in colonial garrisons. (*b*) The mobilisation as an organised field force of the units which are maintained at home in view of (*a*).'[18] Behind these considerations lay the question of cost, a matter which was never far from the minds of Victorian and Edwardian statesmen. Social reform was accorded a higher priority than army reform in the programme of the new Liberal government and, in submitting any proposals to the Cabinet and Parliament, Haldane was compelled to demonstrate that he had made a genuine attempt to effect economies. Thus, apart from strategic and organisational factors, the size and composition of the expeditionary force hinged, above all, upon what could be achieved within the agreed military budget, which, for most of Haldane's term of office, had a ceiling of £28 million. Outlining his plans in a general statement in the Commons on 12 July 1906, and in a memorandum on army reorganisation published at the end of that month, Haldane explained that the expeditionary force would consist of six 'great' infantry divisions and four brigades of cavalry, with artillery and a full complement of ancillary services – or around 150,000 men in all. On 12 January 1907 the War Office issued a Special Army Order instituting the new organisation for the Regular army in much the same form as Haldane had described it in the Commons six months earlier.[19]

It would, of course, be wrong to argue that a European role for the expeditionary force played no part in Haldane's thinking when he was drawing up his army reforms. He was too astute a politician to underestimate the importance of recent international developments. But the shift towards a Continental strategy for the army was a gradual process, being much less sharply defined in 1906 than it was by the time Haldane left the War Office in 1912. Furthermore, it has already been noted that Continental requirements were not the sole determinants of the structure of the expeditionary force. As Dr Edward Spiers puts it in his penetrating study of the Haldane era, far from 'perceiving a strategic objective and simply providing the wherewithal in men, arms and organisation to meet it, Haldane had set a mandatory financial limit and had hoped that the existing forces, if better organised, would fulfil the strategic requirements'.[20]

The other main component of Haldane's reforms was the reorganisation of the auxiliary forces – the Militia, Yeomanry and Volunteers – into a more efficient second-line army. In his 'Preliminary Memorandum' of 1 January 1906 he discerned that an adequate Reserve would be necessary to maintain the strength of an expeditionary force in war and saw this role as being filled by the Militia, which alone could furnish the requisite numbers.[21] Taking his ideas a stage further in his 'Second Memorandum' of 1 February, he now envisaged that, besides supplying drafts to Regular line units in the initial phases of a war, the Militia and Yeomanry might also provide the striking force with many of its ancillary services. To cater for possible expansion during a war, a 'Territorial Army' could be built from the Volunteer Force and those elements of the Militia and Yeomanry which were not earmarked for service with the striking force. Even at this early stage, however, Haldane was taking a long-term view. The 'education and organisation of the Nation for the necessities of Imperial defence' were the principal objects of his scheme, he declared:

Consequently the basis of our whole military fabric must be the development of the idea of a real national army, formed by the people and managed by specially organised local Associations. The Army must be capable of evolution with the least possible delay into an effective force of all arms should serious danger threaten the Empire. It might be styled the Territorial Army'.[22]

On 25 April, in his 'Fourth Memorandum', Haldane returned to the theme of a two-line military organisation which would 'have its foundations in the nation itself' and would possess 'the distinctive character of being a natural development from a nation truly in arms'. The Territorial Army would be created for a very different purpose from that of the Volunteer Force, which, wrote Haldane, existed almost entirely 'on the basis of a theory of Home defence which has now been displaced'. In essence, he visualised the Territorial Army as a kind of partially trained second reserve for the striking or expeditionary force. With the Royal Navy protecting Britain against invasion, it could be brought up to full efficiency by a period of more rigorous training when embodied on the outbreak of war. A vital ingredient in the scheme was the proposal that the Territorial Army would be raised and administered by local associations, themselves partly elected. With the co-operation of the education authorities, the local associations would be expected to foster military drill and physical training in cadet corps, miniature rifle clubs and schools and to provide financial assistance where appropriate, so helping to inspire boys to enlist in the Territorial Army when they reached the age of nineteen. Haldane appreciated that all this would take some years to bear fruit but he was sure that such a scheme would eventually give Britain a military structure with a greater capacity for expansion than it had at present.[23]

Haldane knew that, before introducing the necessary legislation, he must consult the leaders of the auxiliary forces and, if possible, win their blessing for his scheme. He therefore convened an unofficial Territorial Army Committee, which included representatives from the Militia, Yeomanry and Volunteers and which first met on 17 May 1906, when some thirty members were in attendance to hear what he proposed. With proper training for war, Haldane told them, the Territorial Army would provide the means for the expansion of the regular forces in the field. Mindful of potential anxieties about the powers of the county associations, as they were to be called, he stressed that, while these bodies would raise and administer the Territorial Army, the command of local forces would remain vested in the Crown and the general officers commanding-in-chief. He was also at pains to point out that the associations would not come under the control of county councils but would be chaired by the Lords Lieutenant of the counties and would include *ex officio* members from local Territorial forces in addition to elected representatives from the county and borough councils. The projected reforms, he felt, would make the whole army structure more efficient and economical and would help to bring it closer to the people.[24]

Haldane's hopes of securing the early agreement of the auxiliary forces were quickly squashed. Yeomanry and Volunteer leaders were hostile to the concept of the county associations, one of the chief bones of contention being Haldane's plan to separate command from administration. Commanding officers feared that, if financial powers were handed over to the new associations, they would lose much of their present personal control over their own units. The intransigence of the auxiliary forces threatened, for a time, to throw the whole of Haldane's scheme for an integrated army structure back into the melting pot. However, in October his closest advisers, particularly Lord Esher, persuaded him that the Volunteers could be appeased by minimising the elective element in the associations and by ensuring that they were composed mainly of Volunteer and Yeomanry representatives, with certain other *nominated* members.[25] By heeding this advice Haldane was able to preserve the proposed administrative and financial responsibilities of the associations, though in sacrificing their elected element, even before the parliamentary battle had been joined, he had effectively cast aside one of the cornerstones of his earlier vision of a 'nation in arms'.

By November 1906 Haldane had refined many of his ideas on the organisation and training of the Territorial Army. Major-General Douglas Haig, who, as Director of Military Training, was helping to work out the details of its organisation, had advocated that a Territorial Army of 900,000 men should be raised in twelve months and maintained in the field for five years, but this proposal was now shelved and, instead, Haldane decided to aim initially for a more realistic target of 300,000. He believed that this figure was 'well within the reach' of the existing auxiliary forces. The Territorial Army would comprise fourteen large infantry divisions, including field artillery and ancillary services, while Yeomanry units would provide the force with a mounted arm of fourteen cavalry brigades. Looking ahead, Haldane hoped that 'the organisation proposed will render a much larger force available than we have now'. He was also more specific about the role of the Territorial Army than hitherto, stating quite categorically that it would be recognised as 'the main means of home defence on the outbreak of war, both for coast defence strictly and for repelling possible raids', and as 'the sole means of support and expansion of the professional army' in any war involving the whole of that army 'and lasting more than six months.' He forecast, a trifle prematurely, that between a sixth and a quarter of all Territorials would volunteer for foreign service if asked.[26]

The final draft of the Territorial and Reserve Forces Bill was ready early in the new year and was approved by the Cabinet. When Haldane presented his second Army Estimates to the House of Commons on 25 February 1907 he seized the opportunity to unveil many of the Bill's main points. Acknowledging that the Territorial Army – or the Territorial Force, as it was now beginning to be called – would be enlisted for home service, Haldane, on this occasion, made no secret of its possible wider role. If the country became involved in an overseas conflict and the expeditionary force went abroad, the Territorials would be embodied and receive six months' systematic training. Haldane believed that, at the end of this period:

... not only would they be enormously more efficient then the Volunteer or Yeomanry Force is at the present time, but they would be ready, finding themselves in their units, to say – 'We wish to go abroad and take our part in the theatre of war, to fight in the interests of the nation and for the defence of the Empire' . . .[27]

None of the proposed reforms would be much use unless Haldane acted to remedy the current shortage of 4,000 Regular and 6,000 auxiliary officers. The previous August he had set up a War Office committee, chaired by Sir Edward Ward, the Permanent Under-Secretary of State for War, to consider the problem. At Haldane's request the committee published an interim report, dealing principally with the supply of Regular officers, on 22 February 1907, in time for his Estimates speech. The report recommended the establishment of a Supplementary List of Regular officers, made up of men who had received a year's preliminary training and who would be liable to recall until they reached the age of thirty-five, undergoing a fortnight's additional training at least once every two years during that time. They could qualify as Reserve officers by completing one year's continuous service with a Regular unit, though possession of certificates of military proficiency could enable a candidate to reduce this term of service. Certificate A, awarded to those who had spent two years as a public school cadet, gained them four months' exemption, while candidates who also obtained Certificate B from a university corps would be exempt from eight of the stipulated twelve months of qualifying service with the Regulars. The committee proposed that, to administer the system, an Officers' Training Corps should be created, with a Senior Division in the universities and a Junior Division based on the cadet corps in the schools. The OTC would report direct to the War Office and would be supervised by specially chosen instructors. Because all its branches would receive financial aid from army funds, the school and university cadet corps would no longer be totally dependent on local military units for help and encouragement. Ward and his colleagues admitted that their scheme would not transform the situation immediately, estimating that it might produce 2,000 Supplementary List officers for the Regulars and 5,000 for the auxiliary forces after eight years; but they foresaw that there would be others of military age, either still serving in a school or university corps, or who had completed a cadet course, who might be willing to take a commission on the outbreak of war.[28]

Haldane welcomed these recommendations and referred to them in his Estimates speech on 25 February, informing the House that their implementation was high on his list of priorities. He agreed with the committee that the universities and public schools alone could supply officers from among 'young men of the upper middle class, who are the usual source from which this element is drawn'. To those who might be worried that the OTC scheme would increase militarism in the public schools he explained that 'the spirit of militarism already runs fairly high both there and at the universities. What we propose to do in our necessity is to turn to them and ask them to help us by putting their militarism to some good purpose.'[29] However, the voices of dissent from the Labour benches in the ensuing debate provided a foretaste of the opposition still to come on this issue. James Keir Hardie, the leader of the Parliamentary Labour Party, protested that the proposals 'would result in the training of officers from the ranks of the rich and well-to-do to the practical exclusion of the capable sons of the working classes', while John Ward, the MP for Stoke, contended that Britain would only have a successful 'national army' if opportunities were given to the rank and file to obtain commissions.[30]

The Territorial and Reserve Forces Bill was introduced by Haldane in the Commons on 4 March. Under its terms the Militia, in its old form, would disappear and the task of providing drafts for the expeditionary force would now fall to a new creation known as the 'Special Reserve', which was to be a semi-professional force consisting of seventy-four battalions designed to support the corresponding seventy-four pairs of linked regular line battalions. Early in Haldane's speech, however, it became clear just how far his previous proposals relating to the county associations had been modified to make them 'more agreeable' to the commanding officers of the auxiliary forces. At least half the members of every association would be officers drawn from the various branches of the Territorial Force raised in the county. The Army Council, after consulting the parties concerned, would also appoint nominated representatives of the county and borough councils, and from the local universities if these existed. The association itself could appoint a number of co-opted members to represent the interests of employers and workmen. An association would be entrusted with the organisation and administration of the Territorial units in its area at all times except when they were called out for training, embodied or required for actual military service, but it would be responsible for the recruitment of local Territorial formations both in peace *and* in war. The associations were empowered to provide and maintain rifle ranges, buildings, camp sites and magazines; to secure the use of special areas for manoeuvres; to establish and help rifle clubs and cadet corps; to negotiate with employers so that men could be given time off for training; to pay separation allowances to the families of Territorials when the need arose; and to supply all the horses, arms and equipment required by their units on mobilisation. The Army Council would grant the associations, out of money voted by Parliament, such sums as were deemed necessary to cover the expenditure incurred. Any man recruited for the Territorial Force would serve for four years and could re-enlist at the end of that time, although anyone wishing to leave the force before completing his service could obtain a discharge by giving three months' notice in writing and paying a sum of up to £5. During his term of service a Territorial soldier was expected to undergo annual training in camp for not less than eight and not more than fifteen days, and to attend a prescribed number of drills at the discretion of his commanding officer.

Haldane's speech on 4 March also suggested that his views on the function of the Territorial Force had suddenly changed. In this regard the whole emphasis of his opening statement was quite different from that of his Estimates speech only eight days before. The 'primary purpose' of the Territorial Force, he now declared, was 'to defend our shores'. He announced that the government would leave it open for individuals and units to volunteer for foreign service in a national emergency, yet he avoided imposing any statutory obligation on Territorials to serve overseas. 'They can go abroad if they wish,' he added, 'but the scheme and provision is for a force for home defence; and it is upon that basis that the Bill is framed.'[31] As Dr Spiers has observed, Haldane's rapid retreat from his earlier position may well have been prompted by the tactical necessity of forestalling criticism from the Radical members of his own party, who were suspicious of the 'expeditionary' element of his reforms. By stressing home defence Haldane might also entice more Volunteers into the ranks of the Territorial Force.[32] But, in making such fundamental changes so early in the Bill's progress, Haldane had patently overestimated the strength of his parliamentary opponents. As it happened, the Bill aroused little excitement in the Commons and passed both its second and third readings by large majorities.

Despite the weakness of the opposition in the Commons, Haldane felt obliged to make other concessions before the Bill became law. One of these stemmed from Radical and Labour objections to the Bill's original clause relating to the support of cadet corps by the county associations. During the second reading, on 23 April, Ramsay MacDonald led the Labour attack on Haldane's concept of a 'nation in arms', arguing that the Secretary of State wished to impose 'a form of militarism which did not now correspond to the industrial condition of the country'. The military education of youths, claimed MacDonald, would poison 'the springs of politics at the very source'.[33] As a sop to Radical and Labour sentiment Haldane moved an amendment in committee which added the proviso that no financial help should be given by an association 'in respect of any person in a battalion or corps in a school in receipt of a Parliamentary grant until such person has attained the age of sixteen'.[34] In the House of Lords on 9 July, however, Lord Methuen accused the government of bowing to pressure from 'people who seemed to recognise militarism in every proposal of this kind', and Haldane's proviso was rejected. A clash between the two Houses on the issue was averted by a compromise amendment, moved by Lord Esher on 19 July, whereby associations could support cadet corps for boys under sixteen, 'provided that no financial assistance out of money voted by Parliament shall be given'.[35] Once this had been accepted by the Commons the Bill was ratified on 30 July and, three days later, on 2 August, it received the Royal Assent.

Haldane's achievement in steering the measure through Parliament should not be underrated. Succeeding where several of his predecessors had failed, he had at last rationalised the organisation of the auxiliary forces, integrating them more closely with the Regular formations in a two-line army, while improving the draft-finding system and providing an additional avenue of possible future expansion through the new County Associations. By creating a proper divisional structure for the Territorial Force, with staff, artillery and a whole range of ancillary services, and by separating command from administration, Haldane also gave the auxiliaries a better chance of reaching a higher level of overall military efficiency. But the concessions which he had made in the process weakened the impact of his reforms. In deciding, at the crucial moment, to emphasise the home defence role of the Territorial Force rather than its potential for overseas service or its capacity for support and expansion, he deprived the proposed six-month training period on mobilisation of much of its logic and rendered it less likely that Territorials would commit themselves in advance to foreign service. In diluting the cadet corps clause and removing the elective element from the County Associations he had virtually abandoned two of the main features of his original conception of a 'nation in arms' and had partly negated his own programme for the military education of the young.

It is easy to understand why Haldane allowed short-term tactical considerations to override his long-term objectives. He had seen for himself how parliamentary pressure groups had sabotaged previous reform schemes and how the Conservatives could use their majority in the Lords to reject or impose drastic changes on Bills which they found unacceptable, thus making it all the more essential to keep the Liberal Party, including the Radical wing, solidly behind him. He knew too that he must not totally alienate the Volunteers, as he would soon be dependent upon their co-operation to make the Territorial Force work. At the same time, he seems to have attached more weight to the wishes of the Volunteer lobby than was justified by its strength in the Commons. He could also, perhaps, have obtained more political leverage than he did from the trump cards which he held: his scheme, based on the voluntary system, was infinitely preferable to conscription in the eyes of many; it offered a more efficient army without increasing the military budget; and, when the Bill was passed, the Liberals could devote greater attention to social reform. In other words, he had failed to exploit all the factors on his side and conceded more than was necessary. At the end of the day the Territorial and Reserve Forces Act, like the creation of the expeditionary force, was shaped as much by political expediency as by foresight or 'clear and scientific thought' about military requirements.

III

The Territorial Force officially came into existence on 1 April 1908. Its initial progress gave Haldane good cause for optimism. On 7 April he noted that 'the Volunteers are pouring in' and ventured to suggest that 'the new Army is going to be a real success'. To gain War Office recognition, a unit had to reach 30 per cent of its nominal establishment. In less than five weeks this was achieved by 174 infantry battalions out of 204, forty-eight Yeomanry regiments out of fifty-six, 287 artillery units out of 369 and sixty-nine engineer units out of 117. Apart from the Territorial horse artillery batteries, many of which were entirely new formations, nearly all these were directly descended from former Volunteer or Yeomanry units. By 1 June 1908 the Force numbered 144,620 officers and men, and after another month its overall strength had risen to 183,000. That summer 4,765 officers and 99,982 other ranks attended annual training in camp for the full fifteen days.[36]

The early growth of the Territorial Force was undoubtedly stimulated by the concurrent rise in public concern about the nation's defences. In 1906 the launching of HMS *Dreadnought*, a revolutionary type of 'all-big-gun' battleship, had inaugurated a new and more dangerous phase of Anglo–German naval rivalry. The Germans had quickly responded by starting to construct their own dreadnoughts and, in February 1908, an amendment to the German navy law of 1900 increased the number of new battleships to be laid down each year. The intensification of the naval race fuelled the anxieties already caused and reflected by a steady flow of fictional and often lurid accounts of German invasion, one of the latest of which – William Le Queux's *The Invasion of 1910* – had been serialised in the *Daily Mail* in 1906. At the beginning of 1909 Haldane announced that each Territorial unit had been assigned a specific role either in coastal defence or as part of a central force. But public concern about invasion reached fresh heights in the first half of that year. In January Guy du Maurier's play *An Englishman's Home*, a dramatised account of an invasion, was an overnight sensation in London. A recruiting booth was set up in the theatre foyer and Lord Esher, as chairman of the London Territorial Force Association, received a cheque for £10,000 from Lord Northcliffe as well as the support of the *Daily Mail* for Territorial recruiting in the capital. A delighted Haldane reported to his mother that 300 men had enlisted in London on 5 February alone. The simultaneous naval scare in the spring of 1909 was also of advantage to the Territorial Force. The acceleration of German naval building led to considerable agitation in the British press, and in Parliament, for the immediate construction of eight dreadnoughts instead of the four which the government had originally planned in the programme for 1909–10. Public opinion rallied to the cry 'We want eight and we won't wait', a slogan coined by the Conservative MP George Wyndham. Territorial recruiting flourished in this atmosphere. At the beginning of June the Force numbered 268,776 officers and men, and by 1 October its strength had topped 270,000.[37]

This was the high-water mark of the Territorial Force in the years before the First World War. Concern about invasion subsided after the government's announcement in July 1909 that the extra dreadnoughts would be built without prejudice to the 1910–11 programme. A constitutional crisis – hastened by the rejection of Lloyd George's 'People's Budget' in the House of Lords – led, in 1910, to two general elections which, together with the death of King Edward VII, a wave of industrial unrest and the mounting violence of the campaign for women's suffrage, further diverted the thoughts of the public away from home defence. The Territorial Force itself came in for increasing censure inside and outside Parliament. Criticisms were made of the Force's standards of training and musketry, the level of attendance at annual camp and the delays in providing drill halls and ranges for individual units. More and more serving Territorials began to seek discharges and there was a perceptible fall in the rate of recruiting. Instead of attaining its target establishment of just over 312,000 men, the Force declined slightly in strength to 267,096 by October 1910. George Wyndham in the Commons and Esher in the Lords both speculated that voluntary recruiting for the Territorials had already reached its limits. Esher repeated his views in an article published in September 1910 in the *National Review*, a journal edited by the pro-conscriptionist Leo Maxse. Certain that the Territorial Force would not obtain its required annual intake of 60,000 recruits, Esher remarked that the electorate would have to choose between 'leaving the forces of the country below the minimum admitted by everyone to be necessary and imposing by law upon our children the duty to bear arms in its defence'. Haldane was hurt and incensed by these damaging comments from his close friend and adviser, particularly as Esher was also chairman of the London Territorial Association.[38]

The decline of the Territorial Force continued during the remaining years of peace. Over 197,000 Territorials failed to attend annual camp for the full fifteen days in 1911. Haldane left the War Office in the summer of 1912 to become Lord Chancellor, but his successor as Secretary of State for War, J. E. B. Seely, lacked the ability and the personal commitment needed to stop the rot. By September 1913 the overall strength of the force had fallen to 245,779 and it was now 1,893 officers and 64,778 other ranks short of establishment. Forty thousand of its men were under the age of nineteen, while 80 per cent of its strength had seen less than four years' service. Although there had been an influx of 67,205 recruits in 1912–13, as against 57,946 in 1911–12, 67,978 had taken their discharge compared with 34,585 the previous year, many of these being men who were not prepared to re-enlist on completion of their first four-year term of service. The annual rate of wastage in the Territorial Force stood at 12·5 per cent compared with 7 per cent in the Regular army. Moreover, the emphasis Haldane placed on the home defence role of the force when guiding his Bill through Parliament had given the Territorials little incentive to volunteer in advance for overseas service. In 1910 members of the force had been invited to accept a liability to go abroad in the event of mobilisation, but only 1,090 officers and 17,788 NCOs and men – or scarcely 7 per cent of the Force – had taken this Imperial Service obligation by September 1913.[39]

The Territorials had other problems besides those of dwindling numbers. Territorial infantrymen were still armed with the old long Lee Enfield rifle, while the artillery was equipped with equally obsolete fifteen-pounder field guns and five-inch howitzers. The infantry battalions of the Force retained the eight-company organisation which had long since been discarded by Regular battalions, making effective training harder for those units whose individual companies were scattered throughout a relatively wide geographical area. An officer of the 4th Battalion of the Green Howards in Yorkshire noted that, under this system, companies 'hardly ever see each other' in time of peace.[40] The attitude of employers did not always help when it came to releasing men for the annual training camp. Lieutenant-General E. C. Bethune, the Director-General of the Territorial Force, complained in December 1913 that 'if we could overcome the business difficulties which are raised by employers and foremen we should get more men to stay out for fifteen days'.[41] A sub-committee of the Committee of Imperial Defence which had been convened in 1913 to examine the dangers of invasion was highly critical of the Territorial Force when it issued its report in April the following year. Territorial officers were described as 'the weakest point' of the force. The NCOs were also seen as 'a weak point', the period of training was thought to be 'too short' and the standards of musketry were judged 'very low'. The sub-committee concluded, as had a similar invasion inquiry in 1908, that a major invasion was impracticable as long as Britain possessed naval supremacy, but its poor opinion of the Territorial Force led it to repeat another of the 1908 recommendations, namely that the equivalent of at least two of the six divisions of Regular troops should be held back at home on mobilisation. The strength of the Territorial Force increased slightly to 268,777 officers and men by July 1914, though only 18,683 had accepted the Imperial Service obligation and many connected with the force had already become disillusioned and demoralised. In April 1913 no fewer than seventeen County Associations had declared their support for a resolution proposed by the Essex Association which contained a barely disguised demand for some form of compulsory service.[42]

Recruiting problems were not restricted to the Territorial Force. The Regular army, for instance, required an annual intake of some 35,000 recruits, yet from 1908–09 to 1912–13 it only twice succeeded in attracting more than 30,000 men, and its average intake during these years was 29,626. In May 1914 it was nearly 11,000 men, or around 6 per cent, below its nominal peacetime establishment. Similarly the Special Reserve never managed to reach its establishment of 74,166 before the outbreak of war. A significant number of former Militiamen refused to transfer to it, and in the early spring of 1914 the Reserve was still 13,699 men below strength, with approximately 29 per cent of its existing members under twenty years of age. Emigration was regarded as one of the central causes of these shortfalls in manpower. Official figures showed that, during 1913, over 178,000 male British subjects had emigrated and even though it was recognised that few of them could have been expected to enlist, it was also argued that they had nevertheless left vacancies for jobs at home which might each be filled 'by one who in other circumstances would have entered the Army'.[43] Despite improvements in conditions and terms of service the Regular army had failed to widen its social composition and, as in the nineteenth century, continued to draw the largest proportion of its rank and file from the unskilled and unemployed. The officer corps too still relied heavily on its own traditional sources of supply. The peerage, the gentry and military families – and to a lesser extent, the clergy and the professions – furnished the vast majority of officers. Comparatively few came from commercial and industrial families. Most young officers, however, had been to a public school.[44] Before leaving the War Office, Haldane had to concede that the Officers' Training Corps scheme, which was largely based on the public school cadet corps, had not yet produced the desired results. Reviewing its progress in May 1912, he revealed that while nearly 18,000 cadets had already left the OTC after completing some form of military instruction, only 283 of them had so far taken commissions in the Special Reserve.[45] Even so, Haldane was hopeful that the OTC would show its value if war was declared:

... it is not too much to expect that, in the event of a supreme national emergency, feelings of patriotism would, as has always been the case in the past, induce a certain number of gentlemen to come forward and take commissions ... many of whom would have had the advantage of the improved training now given in the Officers' Training Corps.[46]

The events of 1914 would prove that Haldane's instincts were right. As several recent studies indicate, public school boys in late Victorian and Edwardian Britain had been educated in a gentlemanly tradition of honour, loyalty, chivalry, patriotism and leadership, preparing them implicitly for the challenge of war. The public school cult of organised games helped them to develop not only personal fitness but also physical courage, self-discipline and team spirit – attributes which were of obvious value in a military context.[47] Yet such ideas and principles spread far beyond the public schools themselves. Popular newspapers, novels and plays, as well as the boys' magazines which proliferated around the turn of the century, contributed in full to the dissemination of patriotic sentiment and public school codes of behaviour. Following W. E. Forster's Education Act of 1870, a newly literate population eagerly swallowed colourful accounts of invasion, espionage and deeds of daring on the frontiers of the empire. A subsequent Education Act in 1902 further widened the system of elementary and secondary education, with many State secondary schools openly imitating the style and organisation of the public schools by creating 'houses' and bodies of prefects. Public school stories figured prominently in the literary diet even of working-class boys. Robert Roberts, who grew up in the slums of Salford, later recalled how such tales, over the years, moulded the attitudes of a whole generation: 'The public school ethos, distorted into myth and sold among us weekly in penny numbers, for good or ill, set ideals and stadards.'[48]

The same ethos was reflected in the youth movements, such as the Boys' Brigade, the Church Lads' Brigade and the Boy Scouts, which sprang up in the late nineteenth and early twentieth centuries. Founded at a time of increasing social and economic uncertainty and of growing external threats, these youth movements represented, above all, an attempt by an anxious middle class to arrest what it saw as symptoms of national decline. While embracing elements of a variety of currently influential concepts, including imperialism, Social Darwinism and the quest for 'national efficiency', they were not predominantly militaristic in intent, aiming, as much as anything, to instil in the young habits of order, good conduct and respect for the established social structure. Indeed, in 1910–11, when Haldane tried to incorporate the various youth movements into a homogeneous national cadet force, to be administered by the County Associations, both the Boys' Brigade and the Boy Scouts rejected the invitation, even though it meant losing some privileges in the form of financial help and the provision of camping equipment. Nevertheless, all the major youth organisations adopted the military trappings of drill and rudimentary uniforms and they certainly played a part in nurturing military virtues and patriotism among the young. It has been estimated that, by 1914, up to 41 per cent of all male children and adolescents may have belonged to one or other of these youth movements.[49]

When examining the level of military preparedness in the British Isles on the eve of the First World War one must not forget that, in Ireland, there existed two large paramilitary forces which had been created for purposes which were entirely different from those of the OTC or the youth movements. The Protestants of Ulster had long since declared their hostility to the idea of Home Rule, having no wish to become part of even a semi-independent Ireland in which they would be dominated, and possibly discriminated against, by the Catholic majority in the south. Such opposition had hardened in the face of Gladstone's two abortive Home Rule Bills of 1886 and 1893 and, although anti-Home Rule agitation had diminished in the intervening years, the nucleus of organised resistance had remained intact, an Ulster Unionist Council having been formed in 1905 to unite all the Unionist associations and provide a central body to decide Unionist policy in Ulster. The Irish question once more came to the forefront of politics after the two general elections of 1910 left the Liberal government, under Herbert Asquith, dependent upon eighty-four Irish Nationalist MPs for the maintenance of its parliamentary majority. At the same time the passing of the Parliament Act in 1911 greatly weakened the power of the Conservative and Unionist majority in the House of Lords, for the upper House could no longer permanently veto Bills approved by the Commons. Now any Bill passed by the Commons in three successive sessions of Parliament automatically became law even if rejected three times by the Lords. The Prime Minister, Asquith, recognised that the moment had arrived for a significant measure of Home Rule. The Bill he introduced in April 1912 was by no means extreme in its objectives. It aimed to set up an Irish legislature and executive for purely domestic Irish affairs, but upheld the supremacy of the Imperial Parliament at Westminster in all matters affecting the Crown, the armed forces and international affairs, and sought to impose safeguards and checks to limit Irish autonomy in the spheres of finance, education and law. The Royal Irish Constabulary, for example, was to stay under British control for a period of at least six years. Restricted as the measure was, it sufficed to sting the Ulster Protestants into renewed and more vigorous action, pushing them further along the path towards armed resistance and bringing Ireland to the verge of civil war.

The course which Ulstermen were likely to take under their new leader, Sir Edward Carson, had already become evident in November 1910 when the Ulster Unionist Council opened an armament fund.[50] On 23 September the following year, still over six months before the third Home Rule Bill was presented to Parliament, a big demonstration took place at Craigavon, near Belfast. Craigavon was the home of Captain James Craig, one of the most active members of the Ulster Unionist Council, who has been described as the 'real organiser' of Ulster resistance.[51] Among the 50,000 or so men from the Orange lodges and Unionist clubs who paraded on that day was a group from Co. Tyrone who had been drilling on their own initiative and who impressed everyone with their marching and smart appearance. Within a short time Orange lodges throughout Ulster were striving to emulate them. This was made easier by the discovery of a legal loophole which allowed any two Justices of the Peace to authorise drilling in their district, as long as it was intended to help citizens protect their rights and liberties while maintaining the established constitution of the United Kingdom. As the Liberals had permitted the Peace Preservation Act to lapse in 1907, it was also legal to import firearms for the purpose, provided the individual owner obtained a firearms licence for 10*s* from a post office. From the beginning of 1912 licences for drilling were being issued in ever increasing numbers. Not until December 1913 were two Royal Proclamations published prohibiting the importation of arms and ammunition into Ireland.[52]

Once the Home Rule Bill had been introduced the movement gained extra momentum. On 28 September 1912, and in the days that followed, over 218,000 men in Ulster signed a 'Solemn League and Covenant' pledging themselves to use 'all means which may be found necessary to defeat the present conspiracy to set up a Home Rule Parliament in Ireland'. Nearly 229,000 women signed a similar declaration in their support. With groups of volunteers now busy drilling all over the province, the Ulster Unionist Council decided, in January 1913, to form them into a single body called the Ulster Volunteer Force. It would consist of 100,000 men who had recently signed the Covenant and were aged between seventeen and sixty-five. The organisation of the Ulster Volunteer Force was based on the network of Orange lodges and Unionist clubs, the nine counties of Ulster being split into various divisions and districts, each county division raising a number of regiments in proportion to the strength of its volunteers. The regiments would be divided into battalions, companies and sections. Belfast was to contribute a regiment from each of its four parliamentary constituencies. By the end of February 1914 the UVF totalled approximately 90,000 men, of whom some 30,000 belonged to the twenty battalions organised in Belfast. County Down and County Antrim provided the next largest contingents, both with around 11,000 men, while the smallest regiments were from Cavan and Monaghan, where each had a little over 2,000. The efficiency of the organisation was emphatically demonstrated on 25 April 1914 when, covered by specially mobilised detachments of the UVF, over 24,000 rifles and some 3 million rounds of ammunition, which had been secretly purchased in Germany, were landed at Larne and Bangor and distributed throughout the province.[53]

Not unexpectedly, the creation of the Ulster Volunteer Force led to demands for a rival organisation in southern Ireland. A body known as the Irish National Volunteers, designed to counterbalance the UVF, was formally founded at a huge public meeting at the Rotunda in Dublin on 25 November 1913. Only 10,000 had been enrolled at the end of the year but the political developments of 1914 caused a rapid rise in membership and by May its strength equalled – and may even have exceeded – that of the Ulster Volunteer Force. On the other hand, though drilled by ex-British army instructors, the Irish National Volunteers possessed few rifles and did not yet match the degree of proficiency attained by the UVF.[54]

As both sides became more firmly entrenched a peaceful solution to the Irish question seemed as remote as ever in 1914, and civil war remained a distinct possibility until the greater crisis engulfed Europe. The British army had itself become seriously entangled in the web of Irish politics. In March 1914 Brigadier-General Hubert Gough and some sixty officers of the 3rd Cavalry Brigade, stationed at the Curragh near Dublin, threatened to resign rather than be employed by the Liberal government to coerce Ulster into accepting Home Rule. Gough managed to secure a written guarantee from J. E. B. Seely, the Secretary of State for War, that the army would not be used for this purpose. The guarantee, however, was repudiated by Asquith and the Cabinet, forcing Seely himself to resign, together with Field-Marshal Sir John French, the Chief of the Imperial General Staff, and Lieutenant-General Sir John Spencer Ewart, the Adjutant-General. The Curragh incident had several other unfortunate effects. It undermined morale and discipline in the army, soured civil–military relations and was bad for recruiting, besides paralysing the government's policy towards Ireland and inducing a kind of fatalistic acquiescence in the continued existence of the sectarian paramilitary organisations.[55] These were problems the government and the army could well have done without on the eve of a European war.

Taking the bodies of volunteers in Ireland into account, it can be said, then, that literally hundreds of thousands of young men in the British Isles had acquired some experience of drill and military discipline outside the army or had been conditioned by their education and upbringing to respond positively to their country's call in a national emergency. But this does not mean that Britain was a militarised nation in the summer of 1914. Patriotism, pride in the empire and an appetite for military pageantry and stories of adventure had not been translated into improved recruiting returns or widespread public support for a larger army. The average voter was loath to bear extra burdens of taxation for the sake of an expanded army in peacetime. It was the Royal Navy, the traditional guardian of Britain's security, that generally gained most from the recurrent invasion scares and international crises. No one could predict exactly how big or how effective the response of the nation's manhood would be if and when a situation arose in which Britain required a sudden and massive increase in the size of her army.

There were, of course, many who were not satisfied with the vague hope that voluntary methods of recruiting would somehow produce the required numbers when the time came. The National Service League, founded in February 1902, had been actively campaigning for some form of compulsory military service for over a decade and had more than 96,000 members by 1913.[56] Leading soldiers like Henry Wilson favoured conscription, and even Lloyd George, when considering the need for a coalition government as a way out of the constitutional crisis of 1910, flirted briefly with the idea of compulsory training for home defence. However, the League always suffered from the divergence of views among its members, some merely seeking compulsory training for boys while others wanted full-scale adult male conscription as on the Continent. Of the five separate compulsory service Bills which were placed before Parliament between 1908 and 1914, only one was officially sponsored by the League, this exception being the National Service (Training and Home Defence) Bill, introduced by the League's president, Lord Roberts, in the Lords in July 1909. Its content mirrored the efforts of the League to present a moderate programme which, by steering clear of extremes of opinion on the issue, was more likely to be politically acceptable and win popular backing. The Bill, making clever use of Haldane's Territorial scheme, proposed that all males between eighteen and thirty should be liable for service in the Territorial Force for the purposes of home defence. This would have involved four months' continuous recruit training for infantry and up to six months for other branches, as well as fifteen days' annual training in each of the ensuing three years. But the Bill was defeated, as were the four others introduced before the war. The main obstacle lay in the fact that, although the League's membership was predominantly Conservative and middle-class and several prominent Conservative politicians – including Lord Curzon, Lord Lansdowne and Andrew Bonar Law – sympathised with its aims, compulsory service was a political millstone. As Lloyd George noted in 1910, 'No Party dare touch it, because of the violent prejudices which would be excited even if it were suspected that a Government contemplated the possibility of establishing anything of the kind.' Failing an inter-party agreement, which was never forthcoming in the years before the war, compulsory service simply could not be pushed through Parliament. According to Dr Allison, each of the major parties believed – no doubt correctly – that the British people would be averse to any form of military compulsion in peacetime, and they therefore drew back from any step which might have a disastrous effect on their future electoral prospects. In short, 'national service was a victim of the near-impossibility in a democratic society of implementing – or even discussing fully on its merits – a measure which is electorally unpopular'.[57]

The truth was that Britain was as dependent as ever on what W. S. Hamer has described as the system of 'decision by crisis'. Fundamental decisions about defence matters, especially if they were likely to lead to higher expenditure, tended to be taken only when the international situation was sufficiently menacing to alarm the country as a whole and when the government of the day therefore felt that the weight of public opinion was behind it.[58] Thus the precarious parliamentary balance after 1910 inhibited the Liberal government's desire and ability to extend the scope of its earlier military reforms. Until the Germans invaded Belgium in August 1914 and public opinion was mobilised in favour of a greatly expanded army, a wide gulf existed between Britain's military strategy and her actual military resources.

Notes

1 The title of the inaugural lecture given by Professor Joll at the London School of Economics and Political Science in April 1968; reprinted in H. W. Koch (ed.), *The Origins of the First World War: Great Power Rivalry and German War Aims,* Macmillan, London, 1972, pp. 307–28.
2 Zara S. Steiner, *Britain and the Origins of the First World War,* Macmillan, London, 1977, p. 2.
3 Foreward by Michael Howard in John Gooch, *The Plans of War: the General Staff and British Military Strategy,* c. 1900–1916, Routledge & Kegan Paul, London, 1974, p. x.
4 Samuel R. Williamson, *The Politics of Grand Strategy: Britain and France*

Prepare for War, 1904–1914, Harvard University Press, Cambridge, Mass., 1969, p. 369; Gooch, *The Plans of War,* p. 280; John McDermott, 'The revolution in British military thinking from the Boer War to the Moroccan crisis', *Canadian Journal of History,* Vol. IX, No. 2, 1974, p. 1972; Brian Bond, *The Victorian Army and the Staff College, 1854–1914,* Eyre Methuen, London, 1972, p. 257.

5 Nicholas d'Ombrain, *War Machinery and High Policy: Defence Administration in Peacetime Britain, 1902–1914,* Oxford University Press, 1973, pp. 74–114.

6 See Ruddock F. Mackay, *Fisher of Kilverstone,* Oxford University Press, 1973, pp. 354–5, 420–2; Paul Haggie, 'The Royal Navy and war planning in the Fisher era', *Journal of Contemporary History,* Vol. 8, No. 3, 1973, pp. 113–31.

7 Steiner, *Britain and the Origins of the First World War,* pp. 194–210; Williamson, *The Politics of Grand Strategy,* pp. 187–204, 369.

8 Paul M. Kennedy (ed.), *The War Plans of the Great Powers, 1880–1914,* Allen & Unwin, London, 1980, p. 14.

9 Steiner, *op. cit.,* pp. 213–14.

10 See, for example, Haldane's *Before the War,* Cassell, London, 1920, pp. 29–33.

11 Williamson, *op. cit.,* p. 92; see also Edward M. Spiers, *Haldane: an Army Reformer,* Edinburgh University Press, 1980, pp. 11–28, 48–73, 78–91, 192–200; and John Gooch, 'Mr Haldane's army: military organisation and foreign policy in England, 1906–7' in *The Prospect of War: Studies in British Defence Policy, 1847–1942,* Cass, London, 1981, pp. 92–112.

12 R. B. Haldane, 'A Preliminary Memorandum on the present Situation. Being a rough note for consideration by Members of the Army Council', 1 January 1906, Haldane papers, NLS 5918.

13 *Parliamentary Debates, House of Commons, 1906,* CLIII, cols. 663–76.

14 Grierson, 'Memorandum upon the Military Forces required for Oversea Warfare', 4 January 1906, WO 106/44.

15 Haldane, 'Second Memorandum', 1 February 1906, Haig papers, NLS Vol. 32a; Spiers, *Haldane,* p. 82; John Gooch, 'Haldane and the "National Army" ', in Ian F. W. Beckett and John Gooch (eds.), *Politicians and Defence: Studies in the Formulation of British Defence Policy, 1845–1970,* Manchester University Press, 1981, pp. 75–6.

16 Minute from Nicholson to General Sir Neville Lyttelton, Chief of the General Staff, 22 March 1906, WO 32/1043/79/1000.

17 *Minutes of Proceedings and Précis prepared for the Army Council,* 77th meeting, 21 June 1906, Précis No. 278, 'Proposed Divisional Organisation of Troops at Home', WO 163/11.

18 Haldane, 'Considerations governing the peace strength of the Regular Army', 1 February 1907, CAB 37/86/11.

19 Colonel John K. Dunlop, *The Development of the British Army, 1899–1914,* Methuen, London, 1938, p. 261; *Parliamentary Debates, House of Commons, 1906,* CLX, cols. 1077–114; *Memorandum by the Secretary of State for War on Army Reorganisation: dated 30 July 1906,* PP, 1906, LXVII, Cd 2993.

20 Spiers, *Haldane,* p. 73.

21 Haldane, 'Preliminary Memorandum', 1 January 1906, Haldane papers, NLS 5918.

22 Haldane, 'Second Memorandum', 1 February 1906, Haig papers, NLS Vol. 32a.

23 Haldane, 'Fourth Memorandum', 25 April 1906, Haig papers, NLS Vol. 32a.

24 'Address by the Secretary of State to the Territorial Army Committee', 17 May 1906, Haig papers, NLS Vol. 32a.

25 Esher to Haldane, 19 October 1906, see M. V. Brett (ed.), *Journals and Letters of Reginald Viscount Esher,* Nicholson & Watson, London, 1934–38, II, pp.

195–7; Spiers, *Haldane,* pp. 104–5.

26   Haldane, 'Memorandum embodying a General Statement on the subject of the organisation and training of the Territorial Army', 23 November 1906, Esher papers, 16/8; Hugh Cunningham, *The Volunteer Force: a Social and Political History, 1859–1908,* Croom Helm, London, 1975, pp. 142–3.

27   *Parliamentary Debates, House of Commons, 1907,* CLXIX, cols. 1286–301.

28   *Interim Report of the War Office Committee on the provision of officers (a) for service with the Regular Army in war, and (b) for the Auxiliary Forces,* PP, 1907, XLIX, Cd 3294.

29   *Parliamentary Debates, House of Commons, 1907,* CLXIX, cols. 1320–4.

30   *Ibid.,* CLXX, cols. 307–11 and CLXXII, cols. 266–73.

31   *Ibid.,* CLXX, cols. 503–24.

32   Spiers, *Haldane,* p. 112; see also A. J. Anthony Morris, 'Haldane's army reforms, 1906–8: the deception of the radicals', *History,* Vol. 156, No. 186, 1971, pp. 17–34.

33   *Parliamentary Debates, House of Commons, 1907,* CLXXII, cols. 1597–601.

34   *Ibid.,* CLXXIV, cols. 1575–80.

35   *Parliamentary Debates, House of Lords, 1907,* CLXXVII, cols. 1298–9, and CLXXVIII, cols, 813–15.

36   Haldane to his mother, 7 April 1908, Haldane papers, NLS 5979; *Army Debates, Session 1908,* cols. 1240, 1271, 1722; Dunlop, *The Development of the British Army,* p. 286.

37   *The Scotsman,* 8 January 1909; Brett (ed.), *Journals and Letters,* II, pp. 369–71; Haldane to his mother, 6 February 1909, Haldane papers, NLS 5981; H. R. Moon, 'The Invasion of the United Kingdom: Public Controversy and Official Planning, 1888–1918', unpublished Ph.D. thesis, London, 1968, pp. 398–406; *The Annual Return of the Territorial Force for the Year 1910,* PP, 1911, XLVI, Cd 5482.

38   *The Times,* 28 February 1910; *The Annual Return of the Territorial Force for the Year 1910,* PP, 1911, XLVI, Cd 5482; *Parliamentary Debates, House of Commons, 1910,* XVIII, cols. 701–2, and *House of Lords, 1910,* VI, col. 265; Lord Esher, 'The voluntary principle', *National Review,* Vol. LVI, No. 331, September 1910, pp. 41–7; M. J. Allison, 'The National Service Issue, 1899–1914', unpublished Ph.D. thesis, London, 1975, pp. 232–3.

39   Spiers, *Haldane,* p. 182; *The Annual Return of the Territorial Force for the Year 1913,* PP, 1914, LII, Cd 7254; Ian F. W. Beckett, 'The Territorial Force', in Ian F. W. Beckett and Keith Simpson (eds.), *A Nation in Arms: a Social Study of the British Army in the First World War,* Manchester University Press, 1985, p. 129.

40   Notes by 'M.L.B.' in *The Green Howards Gazette,* Vol. XXII, No. 263, February 1915, p. 215.

41   Minute from Bethune to H. J. Creedy, 6 December 1913, WO 32/11242.

42   See 'Invasion: Report of a Sub-committee appointed by the Prime Minister to reconsider the question of Oversea Attack', 22 October 1908, CAB 3/2/1/44–A; 'Attack on the British Isles from Oversea: Report of Standing Sub-committee', 15 April 1914, CAB 38/26/13; H. R. Moon, 'The Invasion of the United Kingdom', p. 413; Beckett, 'The Territorial Force', *op. cit.,* p. 130; Allison, 'The National Service Issue', pp. 205–6.

43   *Parliamentary Debates, House of Commons, 1914,* LIX, cols. 1245, 1256, and LXIII, col. 37; *The General Annual Report on the British Army for the Year ending 30 September 1913,* PP, 1914, LII, Cd 7252, pp. 7–10; Edward M. Spiers, *The Army and Society, 1815–1914,* Longman, London, 1980, p. 279, and 'The regular army in 1914', in Beckett and Simpson (eds.), *A Nation in Arms,* p. 44.

44   Spiers, *The Army and Society,* pp. 1–29; Keith Simpson, 'The officers' in Beckett

and Simpson, *A Nation in Arms*, p. 65; see also C. B. Otley, 'The Origins and Recruitment of the British Army Elite, 1870–1938', unpublished Ph.D. thesis, Hull, 1965; and Ian Worthington, 'Antecedent education and officer recruitment: the origins and early development of the public school–army relationship', *Military Affairs*, Vol. XLI, No. 4, 1977, pp. 183–9.

45 *Parliamentary Debates, House of Commons, 1912*, XI, cols. 984–6.

46 *Ibid.*, col. 989.

47 Peter Parker, *The Old Lie: the Great War and the Public School Ethos*, Constable, London, 1987, *passim*; Geoffrey Best, 'Militarism and the Victorian public school', in Brian Simon and Ian Bradley (eds.), *The Victorian Public School*, Gill & Macmillan, London, 1975, pp. 131–7; Spiers, 'The regular army in 1914', *op. cit.*, p. 42.

48 John Gooch, 'Attitudes to war in late Victorian and Edwardian England', in *The Prospect of War, op. cit.*, pp. 35–51; David French, 'Spy fever in Britain, 1900–1915', *Historical Journal*, Vol. 21, No. 2, 1978, pp. 355–70; Colin Nicolson, 'Edwardian England and the coming of the First World War', in Alan O'Day (ed.), *The Edwardian Age: Conflict and Stability, 1900–1914*, Macmillan, London 1979, pp. 163–8; Steiner, *op. cit.*, pp. 154–63; Robert Roberts, *The Classic Slum: Salford Life in the First Quarter of the Century*, Pelican edition, London, 1973, p. 161.

49 John Springhall, *Youth, Empire and Society: British Youth Movements, 1883–1940*, Croom Helm, London, 1970, pp. 14–16, 29–30, 37–46, 53–64, 124–6; P. Wilkinson, 'English youth movements, 1908–30', *Journal of Contemporary History*, Vol. 4, No. 2, 1969, pp. 3–24; M. D. Blanch, 'Imperialism, nationalism and organised youth', in J. Clarke, C. Critcher and R. Johnson (eds.), *Working Class Culture*, Hutchinson, London, 1979, pp. 103–20; Ian F. W. Beckett, 'The nation in arms, 1914–18', in *A Nation in Arms*, pp. 4–5; Allison, *op. cit.*, pp. 209–12.

50 *Freeman's Journal*, 30 November 1910.

51 A. T. Q. Stewart, *The Ulster Crisis: Resistance to Home Rule, 1912–14*, Faber, London, 1967, p. 41.

52 *Ibid.*, pp. 69–72, 107.

53 *Ibid.*, pp. 70, 128, 196–212, 244–9.

54 Robert Kee, *The Green Flag: a History of Irish Nationalism*, Weidenfeld & Nicolson, London, 1972, pp. 497–8; see also *Parliamentary Debates, House of Commons, 1914*, LXIII, col. 764.

55 Ian F. W. Beckett (ed.), *The Army and the Curragh Incident, 1914*, Bodley Head for the Army Records Society, London, 1986, pp. 26–9; Esher to Balfour, 26 April 1914, see Brett and Esher, *Journals and Letters*, III, pp. 163–5; *Parliamentary Debates, House of Commons, 1914*, LXII, col. 1272.

56 Allison, 'The National Service Issue', p. 127, n. 3.

57 *Parliamentary Debates, House of Lords, 1909*, II, cols. 255–468; Lloyd George, Confidential Memorandum on Coalition Government, dictated at Criccieth, August 1910, Lloyd George papers, HLRO Ll.G. C/16/9/1; Allison, *op. cit.*, pp. 127, 141–5, 151–8, 164, 171–2, 245.

58 W. S. Hamer, *The British Army: Civil–Military Relations, 1885–1905*, Clarendon Press, Oxford, 1970, pp. xi, 213–22.

Part I
The recruiting campaign

1

Kitchener and the call to arms

On 4 August 1914, at the very moment when Britain became directly involved in a general European conflict for the first time in nearly a century, there was no permanent head of the War Office, the higher direction of the army being subject to a curious form of divided responsibility. Ever since the resignation of J. E. B. Seely at the end of March that year, over his mishandling of the Curragh incident, Asquith had deferred the appointment of a new Secretary of State for War, combining the office with that of Prime Minister. With the coming of war, however, it was obvious that this state of affairs could not be allowed to continue, as the overall burdens of government would leave Asquith with precious little opportunity to look after the War Office. 'It was quite impossible for me to go on, now that war is actually in being,' he told his confidante, Venetia Stanley, on 5 August; 'it requires the undivided time and thought of any man to do the job properly, and as you know I hate scamped work.'[1]

Asquith's first thought was to give to Haldane, then Lord Chancellor, the task of supervising the military machinery which the latter had largely created and perhaps best understood. 'I am finishing my judicial work tomorrow,' Haldane explained to his sister on 3 August, 'and then take over the war office – remaining chancellor and Asquith remaining war minister and delegating the work to me.'[2] In fact this makeshift arrangement was never put to the test. The news that Haldane was returning to the War Office aroused an immediate, if unjustified, storm of protest in the press. A typical reaction was that voiced by the *Daily Express,* which declared on 5 August, 'This is no time for elderly doctrinaire lawyers with German sympathies to play at soldiers.'[3] As Grey, Asquith's Foreign Secretary, later observed, it was widely felt that Haldane's known interest in German philosophy must make him pro-German, while his earlier work at the War Office, though admired by Cabinet colleagues and soldiers alike, 'was not in the knowledge of, or at any rate not present to, the public mind'.[4]

The outburst against Haldane coincided with a swelling chorus of demands

YOUR KING & COUNTRY NEED YOU

A CALL TO ARMS

An addition of 100,000 men to His Majesty's Regular Army is immediately necessary in the present grave National Emergency.

LORD KITCHENER is confident that this appeal will be at once responded to by all those who have the safety of our Empire at heart.

TERMS OF SERVICE

General Service for the period of the war only.
Age on Enlistment, between 19 and 30.
Height, 5 ft. 3 in. and upwards. Chest, 34 in. at least.
Medically fit.
Married Men or Widowers with Children will be accepted, and will draw Separation Allowance under Army conditions.

MEN ENLISTING FOR THE DURATION OF THE WAR

will be discharged with all convenient speed, if they so desire, the moment the war is over.

HOW TO JOIN

Men wishing to join should apply at any Military Barrack or at any Recruiting Office; the addresses of the latter can be obtained from Post Offices or Labour Exchanges.

GOD SAVE THE KING

for the appointment to the War Office of Field-Marshal Earl Kitchener of Khartoum, who happened to be in England on leave from his post as British agent and consul-general in Egypt and whose name, by 1914, stood as a symbol of achievement and victory. Born near Listowel in County Kerry on 24 January 1850, Horatio Herbert Kitchener had passed out of the Royal Military Academy at Woolwich in December 1870, having qualified creditably, but without distinction, for a commission in the Royal Engineers. While waiting to be gazetted, he saw service in the Franco-Prussian War, enlisting as a private in General Chanzy's First Army of the Loire, although his first taste of battle was cut short by a bout of pneumonia. On his return to England he was reprimanded by the Commander-in-Chief, the Duke of Cambridge, for a breach of discipline but still received his commission in the Royal Engineers. After a few years of routine service at home, he was engaged by the Palestine Exploration Fund in 1874 to carry out survey work in the Holy Land, and thus established a close connection with the Middle East which was to endure almost for the rest of his life.

Kitchener joined the Egyptian army in 1883, attracting wider recognition for his reconnaissance and intelligence work during the Gordon relief expedition of 1884–85. Then, following two years as Governor-General of the Eastern Sudan, he became first the Adjutant-General of the Egyptian army and then, in 1892, its Sirdar or commander-in-chief. He transformed the Egyptian army into an effective fighting force, his period of command culminating in the reconquest of the Sudan and the victory of Omdurman in 1898. His next appointment, as Governor-General of the Sudan, lasted less than a year, for in December 1899 he was sent to South Africa as Chief of Staff to Field-Marshal Lord Roberts, succeeding him as Commander-in-Chief in South Africa in November 1900. Kitchener countered the guerilla tactics of the Boers by setting up lines of blockhouses across the country, and from these bases he organised a series of drives against the elusive enemy by mounted troops. Here, as in the Sudan, Kitchener's successes stemmed more from painstaking planning and an understanding of the problems of transport and supply than from any genuine tactical flair, but his policy of attrition ultimately wore the Boers down and he played a conciliatory role in the peace settlement of 1902.

As Commander-in-Chief in India from 1902 to 1909 he became embroiled in a long dispute with the Viceroy, Lord Curzon, over the system of dual control under which the Military Member of the Viceroy's Council had come to assume an authority which challenged that of the Commander-in-Chief. In forcing Curzon's resigation on this issue in 1905, Kitchener re-established the supremacy of the Commander-in-Chief and confirmed his own power and influence into the bargain. He also instituted several overdue reforms in the Indian Army, including the organisation and grouping of standardised divisions to meet the threat of external aggression rather than that of internal rebellion. In addition, he modernised training methods, improved the

machinery for mobilisation and stimulated military education by founding a
staff college. After leaving India he set off on a tour of the Far East, Australasia and the United States, during which he was asked to advise the
governments of Australia and New Zealand on their respective defence
organisations. He was appointed British agent in Egypt in 1911, devoting his
attention there mainly to social reforms and the development of the Sudanese
and Egyptian economies.

Although his impressive list of achievements had made him a national hero,
Kitchener had a number of serious weaknesses which grew more pronounced
as his career prospered. His intolerance of interference and opposition, his
seemingly boundless capacity for hard work and his constitutional inability
to delegate responsibility all encouraged him to disregard normal procedures
and to act as his own chief of staff and military secretary. Henry Rawlinson
wrote, after the Battle of the Atbara in 1898, 'He is an absolute autocrat, does
exactly what he pleases, and won't pay any attention to red-tape regulations,
or to the keeping of records of telegrams and letters.'[5] This tendency to
over-centralise was fostered by years of independent command on the frontiers of the empire, and Kitchener had always avoided entering the War
Office, preferring posts in which his personal authority would be given freer
rein. 'If there is a war and they want me,' he once told Leo Amery, 'I'll take a
house well away from the War Office and run the war from there.'[6] Indeed,
his remoteness from Whitehall undoubtedly helped to nurture the Kitchener
legend but, having spent most of his life abroad, he was correspondingly
ignorant of conditions at home. 'I don't know Europe; I don't know England,
and I don't know the British Army,' he confessed to Sir Edward Carson.[7]
While his autocratic traits did not matter too much in the context of a limited
and independent field command, they caused major difficulties when he was
required to serve within the framework of a complex and highly organised
administration.

In spite of these shortcomings, Kitchener could offer the government a
priceless quality in August 1914. In the words of one of his biographers, he
inspired the British people 'with a confidence which the strenuous attempts of
three administrations to effect a root-and-branch reform of the army failed to
impart between 1902 and 1914'.[8] On 3 August, as Kitchener was getting
ready to return to Egypt, Colonel Repington, the military correspondent of
The Times, spoke for many when he urged the nomination of a Secretary of
State for War whose time was not fully occupied with other affairs. Repington pointed out that 'Lord Kitchener is at home, and his selection for this
onerous and important post would meet with warm public approval.'[9] J. A.
Spender, editor of the *Westminster Gazette,* felt it necessary to convey to 'the
proper quarter' a warning that, should Kitchener be permitted to depart,
'there would tomorrow be such an uproar against the Government as had not
been known in our time'.[10]

At this point the Prime Minister still favoured Haldane for the War Office and when he recalled Kitchener from Dover on 3 August Asquith merely informed him that 'with matters in their present critical position, I was anxious that you should not get beyond the reach of personal consultation and advice'.[11] The prospect of Kitchener becoming Secretary of State for War was apparently viewed with misgiving on both sides. Kitchener asked Asquith on 4 August 'if there is any objection now to my making arrangements to leave for Egypt on the P. and O. next Friday', while Haldane confided to Sir Ian Hamilton that he had taken over the War Office himself rather than let Kitchener have it.[12] Even so, by 5 August Asquith and Haldane were convinced that the appointment of Kitchener would ensure public support for the Cabinet and that, as a soldier outside politics, he would bring a non-party element into the government at a time when national unity was of paramount importance. Walter Runciman, the President of the Board of Trade, commented that Asquith no doubt foresaw 'the political convenience of having the unattackable K. at the War Office and at his board'.[13]

On 5 August Kitchener was finally persuaded to accept the post. Asquith recorded that 'K. was, to do him justice, not at all anxious to come in, but when it was presented to him as a duty he agreed', though the Prime Minister revealed his own lack of enthusiasm by adding, 'It is a hazardous experiment, but the best in the circumstances, I think.'[14] Kitchener's sentiments were reflected in a remark to Sir Percy Girouard: 'May God preserve me from the politicians.'[15] The majority of people, however, had no such reservations, and the news of Kitchener's acceptance was greeted with universal relief. Asquith's daughter later recalled that 'The psychological effect of his appointment, the tonic to public confidence, were instantaneous and over-whelming.'[16]

Kitchener dominated the Cabinet in the opening weeks of the war. He at once assumed a place in the government hierarchy second only to Asquith, his position being emphasised by the fact that he sat next to the Prime Minister at Cabinet meetings.[17] His massive reputation prompted his Cabinet colleagues to hand over to him almost total responsibility for the conduct of the war. According to Lloyd George, who, as Chancellor of the Exchequer, had himself been Asquith's principal lieutenant up to the outbreak of war:

In 1914 he was practically military dictator and his decisions upon any questions affecting the war were final. The Members of the Cabinet were frankly intimidated by his presence because of his repute and his enormous influence amongst all classes of the people outside. A word from him was decisive and no one dared to challenge it at a Cabinet meeting.[18]

Together with Asquith and Winston Churchill, the First Lord of the Admiralty, Kitchener formed part of a triumvirate which few in the Cabinet were prepared to challenge. Between Kitchener and Asquith there was a special relationship, as Kitchener needed the Prime Minister's guidance in political matters while Asquith relied heavily on Kitchener's military judgement. As Arthur Balfour observed in a letter to the Conservative leader

Andrew Bonar Law on 26 September, 'I doubt whether he [Asquith] possesses any influence with either K. or Churchill in military matters, or whether, if he does possess such influence, he would care to exert it.'[19]

On the other hand, Kitchener was ill suited to the Cabinet system of government and to parliamentary methods. Walter Long noted that 'he shrank from them with positive dislike'.[20] Accustomed to making his own decisions, he found it difficult to adapt to the concept of collective responsibility. Lloyd George wrote that 'His main idea at the Council table was to tell the politicians as little as possible of what was going on and get back to his desk at the War Office as quickly as he could decently escape.'[21] Kitchener's innate distrust of politicians was increased by the suspicion that his Cabinet colleagues could not keep secrets. 'I cannot tell them everything,' he admitted to Maurice Hankey in September 1915, 'because they are so leaky . . . If they will only all divorce their wives I will tell them everything!'[22] Consequently Kitchener displayed a tendency to block or evade questions during Cabinet meetings. Charles Hobhouse, the Postmaster-General until May 1915, regarded him as 'quite remarkably astute and untruthful, in all matters big and small', and the First Commissioner of Works, Alfred Emmott, wrote in his diary, 'He is never frank and tells lies if he does not want to tell at all.'[23]

The crushing burden of responsibility placed on Kitchener's shoulders in 1914 was itself an indication of the government's unpreparedness for the type of war it now faced, but the extended powers granted to him rested on insecure foundations, since they were delegated to him informally and personally by the Cabinet and remained largely undefined. The problems surrounding the central direction of the war effort were also aggravated by the fact that he was the senior field-marshal on the active list. His military rank complicated his relationship with his professional advisers and made it harder for him to provide that link of mutual interpretation between the army and the Cabinet which normally resulted from appointing a politician Secretary of State for War.

Many of these problems might have been eased if Kitchener had made greater use of the machinery to hand, but he was reluctant to alter his style of administration to meet his new circumstances. It is true that, in some ways, this had beneficial effects. Major-General C. E. Callwell, who was called out of retirement to serve as Director of Military Operations, wrote:

Within the War Office itself he certainly made things hum. In pre-war, plain-clothes days, those messengers of distinguished presence – dignity personified in their faultlessly-fitting offical frock-coats and red waistcoats – had lent a tone of respectability to the precincts, compensating for the unfortunate impression conveyed by Adjutant-Generals and such like who perambulated the corridors in grimy, abandoned-looking 'office jackets' . . . But . . . I have seen those messengers tearing along the passages with coat-tails flying as though mad monkeys were at their heels, when Lord K. wanted somebody in his sanctum.[24]

By the same token, Kitchener's appointment had less desirable repercussions.

When he entered the War Office he was unfamiliar with, and prejudiced against, its existing organisation. Lord Midleton, himself a former Secretary of State for War, found in 1913 that 'Kitchener condemned the system adopted in 1904 . . . and ignored the new Board'.[25] Haldane too remarked to Sir Almeric Fitzroy, on 9 August 1914, that Kitchener had 'some difficulty in recognising that he has not to begin the organisation of the army *de novo,* but merely takes over a highly perfected system, which he is asked to make the best of'.[26] His long-standing indifference to accepted procedures unquestionably created unnecessary administrative difficulties, and Asquith noted with concern on 12 August 1914 that 'Lord K. has rather demoralised the War Office with his bull in the china shop manners and methods'.[27] An interesting account of Kitchener's administrative failings has been left by Orlo Williams, who worked at the War Office as a civilian for seven months in 1914 and 1915:

He *was* the War Office, and all the vital decisions emanated from the Secretary of State's own room, often in the form of autograph telegrams written in pencil on pieces of notepaper. Also, when one of these autograph telegrams was sent, its circulation within the War Office was extremely limited, with the result that important executive branches were often in the dark as to the policy in which they were involved.[28]

This situation was made worse when most of the leading members of the General Staff departed for France with the British Expeditionary Force, leaving Kitchener with a team of subordinates who were unlikely to stand up to him or to check his tendency to concentrate all authority in his own hands. General Sir Charles Douglas, who stayed as Chief of the Imperial General Staff, was described by Lord Esher as a conscientious but unimaginative soldier, though Esher scarcely encouraged opposition to Kitchener's methods by informing others that the Secretary of State 'has been given by the Government absolute authority, and there is really nothing more to be said'.[29] Douglas died in October 1914 and was succeeded by Lieutenant-General Sir James Wolfe Murray, an officer whose unsuitability for the job was revealed by his own admission that he sometimes left meetings of the War Council 'with a very indistinct idea of any decision having been made at all'.[30] Kitchener complained more than once that he could never get Wolfe Murray to give him an opinion.[31] Major-General Sir Stanley von Donop, the Master-General of the Ordnance, was competent and hard-working but his cold manner and barely concealed contempt for politicians made him unpopular with the Cabinet. His refusal to acknowledge that anyone other than a professional soldier was qualified to speak about the technical aspects of munitions supply soon earned him a great deal of criticism, particularly from Lloyd George. Before the war was more than twelve weeks old, Sir George Riddell, the newspaper proprietor, had commented on von Donop's narrowness of vision.[32] The Adjutant-General, Lieutenant-General Sir Henry Sclater, remains a shadowy figure, for hardly anything has ever been written about him, but, if somewhat colourless, he was certainly loyal and efficient, and his appetite for work and attention to detail fitted him admirably for the role he was to play in the expansion of the army in 1914. The one truly outstanding officer on the Army Council was Major-General Sir John Cowans, the Quartermaster-General. The fact that he was the only member of this group still in his post at the end of the war testifies to his ability. Callwell called him 'a wonderful organiser with a genius for getting things done', while Sir Charles Harris, the Assistant Financial Secretary at the War Office, wrote of him:

I do not think I ever saw him really rattled . . . When Kitchener first came to the War Office in August 1914, and began to give everybody impossible orders about everybody else's business, Cowans (who had the advantage of having served under him in India) said to me, 'That's his way; we must give him what he wants if we possibly can, but don't take any notice if he gives wrong orders about the things he doesn't understand' . . .[33]

Kitchener rarely saw his senior advisers as a body, preferring to consult them individually, and although the Military Members of the Army Council assembled nearly every day in the opening months of the war, their meetings often had no other purpose than to record decisions already made by Kitchener and to discuss how best to act upon them. It therefore became virtually impossible for the Military Members to present him with a firm collective opinion. By allowing the Army Council and General Staff to drift into abeyance, Kitchener abetted the growth of a system in which political considerations and the ideas of amateur strategists outweighed professional counsel.

II

As Secretary of State for War Kitchener did not directly instigate any fundamental shift in British strategy. When he took office the British Expeditionary Force was already committed to serving in France, and operations on the Western Front quickly assumed a form which was to endure until 1918 and which Kitchener himself could do little to change. From the start he believed that Britain should stand firm alongside France, but where he differed from most of his leading political and military colleagues was in his estimate that the war would last at least three years and that Britain's full military strength could not be deployed until 1917. In August 1914 he was almost alone among the country's principal soldiers and statesmen in predicting that the war would be a protracted and costly business. This was not a sudden 'flash of instinct' on his part, as Grey has implied, for in the autumn of 1911 Kitchener had told Esher that a general conflict would be ended and victory achieved only by 'the last million' of men that Britain could throw into the scales.[34] Kitchener's views on the likely duration of the war and the need for a greatly expanded army were remarkably similar, in several respects, to those expressed by Haig at the first meeting of the War Council on 5 August 1914, a meeting which Kitchener attended. On that occasion Haig also argued that Britain must organise her resources for a war of several years and 'must at once take in hand the creation of an army. I mentioned one million as the number to aim at immediately, remarking that that was the strength originally proposed for the Territorial Force by Lord Haldane.'[35] But it was Kitchener, above all, who convinced the government and the people that they must prepare for a prolonged struggle. It was in providing the vital impetus for the mobilisation of national resources that he made his most significant contribution to the war effort.

In his opinion the existing military organisation was wholly inadequate for anything more than a war of limited liability. On 6 August, in the course of his first morning at the War Office, his private Secretary, Sir George Arthur, handed him a pen with which to give his signature for the official stamp. The pen did not work. 'Dear me,' muttered Kitchener, 'what a War Office! Not a scrap of army and not a pen that will write!'[36] He instantly took steps to expand the army. Later that day, parliamentary approval was sought for the size of the Army to be increased by 500,000 men, and the following morning Kitchener's preliminary 'call to arms' was published in the newspapers. Under the heading 'Your King and Country Need You' it was announced that 'an addition of 100,000 men to His Majesty's Regular Army is immediately necessary in the present grave National Emergency. Lord Kitchener is confident that this appeal will be at once responded to by all who have the safety of our Empire at heart.' Men aged between nineteen and thirty were asked to enlist for general service 'for a period of three years or until the war is concluded', thus providing the public with an early indication that the possibility of a long struggle was now seriously contemplated.[37]

A few hours after his appeal had appeared in the press, Kitchener outlined his proposals to the Cabinet. Declaring that the war could not be won solely by the exercise of sea power, he insisted that Britain must be ready to place armies of millions in the field and to sustain them there for several years. Churchill later wrote that these 'inspiring and prophetic truths' were received by the Cabinet in silent assent.[38] Kitchener summed up his own thinking at the outbreak of war in a speech which he made to Members of the House of Commons on 2 June 1916, three days before his death:

. . . I was convinced that, not only had we got to feed the existing Expeditionary Force. and maintain an adequate garrison here and in India, but, further, we had to produce a new army sufficiently large to count in a European war. In fact, although I did not see it in detail, I must ask Gentlemen of the House of Commons to recognise that I had, rough-hewn in my mind, the idea of creating such a force as would enable us continuously to reinforce our troops in the field by fresh divisions, and thus to assist our Allies at the time when they were beginning to feel the strain of the war with its attendant casualties. By this means we planned to work on the up-grade while our Allies' forces decreased, so that at the conclusive period of the war we should have the maximum trained fighting army this country could produce.

Such an idea was contrary to the theories of all European soldiers. Armies, it had

always been argued, could be expanded within limits, but could not be created in time
of war. I felt, myself, that, though there might be some justice in this view, I had to take
the risk and embark on what may be regarded as a gigantic experiment. I relied on the
energy of this country to supply deficiencies of previous experience and preparation,
and set to work to build a series of new armies, complete in all their branches.[39]

Being largely ignorant of British politics, Kitchener was willing to defer to the
judgement of Asquith and the Cabinet that the introduction of compulsory
military service might endanger national unity at a critical moment in the
country's history. Accordingly, he resolved to raise his new formations by the
traditional system of voluntary enlistment. What Kitchener envisaged was
essentially an expansion of the Regular army through the normal recruiting
channels under the Adjutant-General's Department of the War Office rather
than through the County Associations which recruited and administered the
Territorial Force. It was more than a coincidence that the First New Army
was originally termed the 'New Expeditionary Force'.[40]

On 11 August the Army Council agreed on the details of the proposed
organisation of the First New Army, and these were announced in the press
the next day. Six of the eight regional commands, into which Britain was
militarily divided, were each to provide an infantry division based on the
pattern of those of the BEF, complete with artillery, engineers, mounted
troops, signal companies and field ambulance units. Aldershot Command
and the London District were the two commands not required to furnish a
division under the scheme. As in the BEF, the standard division was to contain
three infantry brigades, each of four battalions. To make up these new
divisions, at least one fresh battalion was to be recruited for every line
regiment. These 'Service' battalions, as they were called, were numbered
consecutively after existing battalions of the parent regiment. Thus in the
Royal Berkshire Regiment, for example, the 1st and 2nd Battalions were
Regular units, the 3rd Battalion formed part of the Special Reserve, the 4th
Battalion belonged to the Territorial Force and the 5th (Service) Battalion
was raised for the First New Army. Instead of a 'Southern' Division, however,
there was to be a 'Light' Division, formed by adding one or more extra
battalions to light infantry and rifle regiments.[41] Finally, an infantry battalion was attached to each division for general duties as Army Troops, thereby
giving the standard division thirteen battalions in all.

As will be shown later, by mid-August Kitchener was thinking of raising
four New Armies, making a total of thirty divisions in the field, including
those of the BEF. However, the pressure of events caused the gradual upward
revision of this target, first to fifty divisions and ultimately to seventy divisions.

III

Probably no other aspect of Kitchener's policy in August 1914 has been subjected to such severe criticism, from both contemporaries and historians alike, as his decision to raise his new formations outside the framework of the Territorial Force, which many saw as offering the best and most obvious means of achieving a rapid expansion of the army. 'I was unable to prevail upon him to adopt or even to make much use of, the Territorial organisation I had provided,' wrote Haldane. 'He would not raise troops through the medium of the County Associations, on whom, under the existing arrangements, the duty of recruiting and supplying the troops would have devolved automatically.'[42] To evaluate these criticisms, it is therefore worth examining, in detail, the possible motives for Kitchener's decision to by-pass the Territorial organisation.

Some writers have suggested that Kitchener was influenced by his memories of the poor performance of Chanzy's ill trained citizen soldiers of the Garde Nationale at Le Mans during the Franco-Prussian War. Churchill has related how Kitchener 'dwelt on this incident to me on several occasions, and I know it created fixed impressions in his mind'.[43] Similar claims have been made that Kitchener was far from enthusiastic about some of the Volunteer units which served under him in the South African War. Sir George Arthur argued that Kitchener distrusted the Territorial Force because it was 'only partially under War Office direction and administration, and largely in the hands of local associations in which the civilian element predominated, and in which local influences prevailed and would be sure to assert themselves'.[44] Others felt that, since Kitchener had spent most of his life abroad, he failed to grasp the wider implications of Haldane's reforms and also underrated the quality of the Territorials. Haig recorded in his diary on 5 August 1914 that Kitchener did not appreciate 'the progress made by the Territorial Army towards efficiency', while Lloyd George wrote that on the evening after war was declared Kitchener was 'full of jest and merriment' at the expense of the Territorial Force and 'thought of it in terms of the Volunteers who were the joke of the Regulars – a few hundred thousand young men officered by middle-aged professional men who were allowed to put on uniform and play at soldiers'.[45]

There is little doubt that Kitchener's attitude to the Territorial Force was coloured by prejudice against non-professsional soldiers. Grey reported that he called it a 'Town Clerk's Army'.[46] 'I prefer men who know nothing to those who have been taught a smattering of the wrong thing,' Kitchener once told Violet Asquith, and on his first morning at the War Office he informed Sir Charles Harris that he 'could take no account of anything but Regular soldiers'.[47] Nevertheless, it would be a gross oversimplification to ascribe Kitchener's decision merely to prejudice and ignorance. There were more solid reasons for his reluctance to build the New Armies on the foundations laid by Haldane.

We have already seen that the strength of the Territorial Force on mobilisation was well below establishment and that its degree of training fell short of the ideal. The statutes of the Force recognised the part-time nature of Territorial service under peacetime conditions and provided for six months of training on mobilisation to bring units up to the required standard. Although Haldane had envisaged the Territorial Force as a base for expansion and as a reserve for the field if the need arose, its primary role had come to be regarded, by 1914, as that of home defence, but even to perform this role properly it first had to recruit up to establishment and train the new men. It was therefore reasonable to assume that, if the Territorial units were swamped by masses of raw recruits at the beginning of the war, they might be rendered temporarily incapable of carrying out any function at all. The military correspondent of *The Times* pointed out the dangers on 11 August 1914, when he forecast that it would take months for Kitchener's new units to become efficient. 'It will not be advisable,' he said, 'in any way to diminish the value of our Reserve or Territorial formations for the benefit of a force which will take so long to create.'[48]

The need to maintain a viable home defence force was constantly in Kitchener's mind during the early months of the war and was a major factor in shaping his policy for the expansion of the army. If, with the advantage of hindsight, we now know that fears of a German invasion in 1914 were groundless, it must not be forgotten that many, including Kitchener, viewed it as a very real possibility at the time. The frequent 'spy scares' and the hostility shown by British people towards aliens in the autumn of 1914 were symptoms of this anxiety. Such fears also help to explain why, on 6 August, the War Council accepted Kitchener's recommendation to delay the departure for France of two of the BEF's six infantry divisions, a proposal which Asquith also favoured because the 'domestic situation might be grave, and colonial troops or territorials could not be called on to aid the civil power'.[49] Once again, Kitchener's address to Members of the House of Commons on 2 June 1916 offers an insight into his thinking on this issue at the beginning of the war:

... the efficiency of the Home garrison was a matter of vital importance, for a raid of a desperate nature, though obviously doomed to failure as an attempt at conquest might certainly have paralysed our industrial powers ... The necessity for keeping these Territorial Divisions intact and at their war stations in day and night readiness for an emergency is a point which I think it well to mention now, as it is one apt to be overlooked by those whose attention is riveted on the actual points of enemy contact. My problem was therefore to produce a force independent of those forces which had formed a part of pre-war calculations'.[50]

The threat of invasion, or at least of raids, was still being taken seriously two or three months after the outbreak of war. Kitchener was frequently plied with scornful arguments discounting the practicability of a German descent on Britain's coasts. 'I am only prepared,' was his habitual reply, 'to rule out the feasibility of an invasion if I can learn that the Germans regard it as an impossible operation.'[51] His chief worry was that an operational lull on the

Western Front might enable the Germans to detach a substantial force for a raid or invasion while the High Seas Fleet kept the Royal Navy occupied elsewhere. On 20 October he wrote:

We have been buoyed up with the hope that a serious invasion of these shores was impossible, but we must remember that that has never been the opinion of German army and navy experts ... As soon, therefore, as men are available the German project of invasion of these shores will, in all probability, be tested. Their information of our military defences through spies may be considered to be absolutely complete, and the German opinion is that, once a considerable force is landed in England, they would have a fair chance of defeating the defensive forces still kept in this country. The one deterrent that they have always felt would have made invasion impossible – our fleet – has now been removed to such a distance by their action that the opportunity is probably now considered by them a favourable one.[52]

Kitchener was not mollified by Churchill's assurances that the Admiralty's policy was to maintain a force which was capable of defeating the entire German navy and that there was no question of dispersing or dividing the Grand Fleet.[53] At a Cabinet meeting on 21 October Kitchener insisted that the Admiralty should take more specific precautions against a German landing. Churchill retorted that the function of the Grand Fleet was not to prevent the landing of an invading force but to strike at and destroy the enemy's covering fleet.[54] Even so, invasion fears began to permeate the Admiralty itself and Churchill found it necessary to alter his stance, noting:

From 1st Nov. begins the maximum danger period for this country, ending during January when new armies and territorials acquire real military value. During this period, very likely deadlock on land enabling Germany to economise troops for an invasion. If ever to be attempted, this is the time. I am confident of our ability to inflict military punishment if it is tried, but no precaution must be neglected.[55]

When nothing happened, the invasion issue receded into the background for a while, but revived again with the bombardment of Scarborough and the Hartlepools in December 1914. Thus while Kitchener may have greatly overestimated the desire and the capacity of the Germans to mount an invasion, it is clear that the requirements of home defence were never completely absent from his thoughts during the time when most of the key decisions affecting the expansion of the army were being taken.

Another point to consider is that, in the critical early weeks of the war, Kitchener was by no means certain how far the Territorials could be relied upon to undertake active service abroad. There was no statutory obligation for its members to fight overseas and anyone who had completed his term of service could take his discharge even though the war was in progress. If Kitchener had reservations about the idea of using Territorials for foreign service he does not appear to have entertained them for long, once he had taken office. On 9 August the Military Members of the Army Council noted his decision that if any Territorial units volunteered *en bloc* for foreign service their offer would be accepted.[56] Two days later the Army Council agreed that 'units volunteering for service abroad from the Territorial Force will, as far as possible, be grouped together so as to maintain their existing Territorial connection. Units, all of whose members cannot volunteer, will be arranged so that complete units of those volunteering can be formed, the residues being re-formed into complete units for the Home Defence Force.'[57] Lord Esher observed on 13 August that Kitchener 'realises that he will be forced to make use of the Territorials for foreign service, while his new armies are in course of formation; of course, he knows nothing of the organisation of our home armies, but he is learning.'[58]

In view of all the subsequent criticism of Kitchener's treatment of the Territorial Force, it is interesting to note that the immediate response to the call for foreign service volunteers was somewhat mixed. On 14 August *The Times* published a letter from man whose son, a private in the 6th West Yorkshire Regiment, had been asked to undertake such service:

This is very serious news for parents with sons in the Territorials, and is not quite playing the game. The Territorials were formed for the distinct and only purpose of defending our country from invasion, and every man was enlisted on this understanding; on any other understanding the great majority would not have joined, nor would parents have allowed them to do so. I am proud that my son should have entered the Service, and I am fully prepared for whatever this may entail in the fulfilment of his accepted duties and the defence of his country. But compulsory foreign service is another matter . . . When men under such circumstances are 'asked' to volunteer it is impossible to refuse and the request becomes a command.[59]

Lloyd George's own complaints about Kitchener's attitude to the Territorials also look less convincing in the light of a letter which he wrote to his wife on 11 August concerning their son Gwilym, then serving in a Welsh Territorial unit:

. . . They are pressing the territorials to volunteer for the war. We mustn't do that just yet. We are keeping the sea for France – that ought to suffice here for the moment especially as we are sending 100,000 men to help her to bear the first brunt of the attack. That is all that counts for Russia will come in soon. I am dead against carrying on a war of conquest to crush Germany for the benefit of Russia. . . . I am not going to sacrifice my nice boy for that purpose. You must write Wil telling him on no account to be bullied into volunteering abroad.[60]

These sentiments were sufficiently common to persuade the War Office to issue a long statement attempting to clarify Kitchener's intentions with regard to the employment of the Territorial Force. The statement, which was published in the press on 15 August, pointed out that Kitchener was fully aware that many Territorials might have very good reasons for wishing to remain at home. He was anxious that those who felt unable to volunteer for foreign service should not be forced to do so and he certainly did not want them to leave the Territorial Force. The statement went on to say that:

. . . certain units should be designated for home service and receive all those who cannot volunteer for foreign service into their ranks, whilst those who have not such important ties at home should be passed from units remaining for home defence into units of the Territorial Force who have selected to volunteer for foreign service. Lord

Kitchener would then be able to organise both forces for the respective roles they will have to perform . . . Homogenous units for foreign service should take up continuous training, and endeavour by every means in their power to make themselves thoroughly efficient for service in the field. The fact of a Territorial unit having volunteered for foreign service, and being, by this arragement, full up with men who can give their entire time to the Service, does not imply that such units will be employed abroad until they reach a standard of efficiency which would enable them to do credit to the British Army . . .[61]

In the days immediately following the circulation of this statement there was still some hesitation within the ranks of the Territorial Force on the question of active service abroad. On 17 August C. P. Burnley, then a private in the Honourable Artillery Company, wrote in his diary, 'Volunteered for the front, as also did 48 per cent. Not very good.' When the commanding officer of the 12th London Regiment (The Rangers) addressed his battalion in camp at Bullswater Common and asked for foreign service volunteers 'the first response was not as good as those who had their country's defence at heart could wish'. A similar appeal to men of the Cheshire Brigade produced 'only fairly satisfactory results'. Ralph Thompson has described the reaction in the Civil Service Rifles (15th London Regiment):

The response to the Colonel's appeal was not generous. The majority of the men were in well-paid jobs; not a few of them being in Government employ did not feel prepared to damage their prospects by entangling themselves in complicated military ventures. The Colonel was advised of the attitude of the men and he promised to make appropriate representation to the proper quarters. A few days later we were again harangued by the Colonel who told us that all employers would be urged by the Government to keep situations open for men volunteering for active service. In addition, soldiers who were in Government employment would receive full salary less the amount of their Army pay. Moreover they would not forfeit any seniority while on active service. As a result of this information, approximately 50 per cent declared their readiness to sign for foreign service. But half a battalion could not be sent abroad as a complete unit. The powers that be therefore resolved to send us for training to Bedmond in Hertfordshire while the requisite 50 per cent was made up from new recruits.[62]

Such hesitation was by no means universal and even in the units where the call for foreign service volunteers was not immediately successful the required numbers soon came forward. Nevertheless, it would appear that for a few days, at the very time when Kitchener was trying to determine how the army should be expanded, there was an element of doubt about the extent to which the Territorial Force could be called upon to fight overseas. It needed more than a pen to transform a home service force into a foreign service army. In the event, Kitchener allowed the Territorials to continue recruiting, to complete their training as far as possible and to volunteer for active service alongside his New Armies, or relieve Regular units in overseas garrisons. By 25 August Kitchener was able to announce that over seventy Territorial battalions had already volunteered to serve abroad.[63] Orders issued on 21 and 31 August, and reiterated on 21 September, gave County Associations general authority to form a second-line Territorial unit for every battalion accepted for foreign service, and in November instructions were issued that, when a unit went abroad and was replaced at home by a second-line formation, a reserve or third-line unit should be raised, thereby releasing even second-line battalions for the front in due course.[64] By the end of 1914 twenty-three Territorial battalions had gone to the Western Front, while three divisions left for India and one for Egypt to replace Regular formations on garrison duty.

In all, 318 Territorial battalions saw front-line or garrison service abroad during the war, as against 404 of the battalions raised for Kitchener's own New Armies. The Territorial Force mustered 692 battalions in all during the war, compared with 404 Service battalions and 153 reserve battalions in the New Armies.[65] The statistical evidence alone gives the lie to criticisms that Kitchener neglected the Territorial Force. In fact he was able to weld the Force into the national army without dislocating it or totally destroying its original character. His policy permitted it to retain its place in the home defence structure but also to reinforce the BEF at a critical juncture in 1914–15, even if considerable waste and duplication of effort resulted from allowing two organisations to exist side by side.

Notes

1   Asquith to Venetia Stanley, 5 August 1914, see Michael and Eleanor Brock (eds.), *H. H. Asquith: Letters to Venetia Stanley,* Oxford University Press, 1982, p. 157.
2   Haldane to his sister, 3 August 1914, Haldane papers, NLS 6012.
3   *Daily Express,* 5 August 1914.
4   Viscount Grey of Fallodon, *Twenty-five Years, 1892–1916,* Hodder & Stoughton, London, 1925, II, p. 68.
5   Major-General Sir Frederick Maurice, *The Life of General Lord Rawlinson of Trent,* Cassell, London, 1928, p. 34.
6   L. S. Amery, *My Political Life,* Hutchinson, London, 1953, I, p. 217.
7   Ian Colvin, *The Life of Lord Carson,* Gollancz, London, 1934–36, III, p. 79.
8   Sir Philip Magnus, *Kitchener: Portrait of an Imperialist,* Murray, London, 1958, p. 175.
9   *The Times,* 3 August 1914.
10 J. A. Spender, *Life, Journalism and Politics,* Cassell, London, 1927, II, p. 63.
11 Asquith to Kitchener, 3 August 1914, Kitchener papers, PRO 30/57/76.
12 Kitchener to Asquith, 4 August 1914, Kitchener papers, PRO 30/57/76; Ian B. M. Hamilton, *The Happy Warrior: a Life of General Sir Ian Hamilton,* Cassell, London, 1966, p. 266.
13 Runciman to Sir Robert Chalmers, 7 February 1915, Runciman papers.
14 H. H. Asquith, *Memories and Reflections, 1852–1927,* Cassell, London, 1928, II, p. 24.
15 Girouard to Austen Chamberlain, 9 December 1929, Chamberlain papers, AC 14/2/6.
16 Violet Bonham Carter, *Winston Churchill as I knew Him,* Eyre, Spottiswoode and Collins, London, 1965, p. 316.
17 Edward David (ed.), *Inside Asquith's Cabinet: from the Diaries of Charles*

    Hobhouse, Murray, London, 1977, p. 229.
18 David Lloyd George, *War Memoirs,* Nicholson & Watson, London, 1933–36, I, p. 499.
19 Balfour to Bonar Law, 26 September 1914, Balfour papers, BL Add. Mss 49693.
20 Viscount Long of Wraxall, *Memories,* Hutchinson, London, 1923, p. 224.
21 Lloyd George, *op. cit.,* I, p. 76.
22 Lord Hankey, *The Supreme Command, 1914–1918,* Allen & Unwin, London, 1961, p. 221.
23 David (ed.), *Inside Asquith's Cabinet,* p. 231; Emmott Diary, 13 June 1915, Emmott papers.
24 Major-General Sir C. E. Callwell, *Experiences of a Dug-out,* Constable, London, 1920, p. 55.
25 The Earl of Midleton, *Records and Reactions, 1856–1939,* Murray, London, 1939, p. 156.
26 Sir Almeric Fitzroy, *Memoirs,* Hutchinson, London, 1927, II, p. 564.
27 Asquith to Venetia Stanley, 12 August 1914, see M. and E. Brock (eds.), *op. cit.,* p. 168.
28 Orlo Williams, 'The War Office from the inside', *National Review,* July 1919, pp. 735–6.
29 M. V. Brett and Viscount Esher (eds.), *Journals and Letters of Reginald Viscount Esher,* Nicholson & Watson, London, 1934–38, III, p. 178.
30 Lieutenant-General Sir James Wolfe Murray to Dardanelles Commission, 10 October 1916, Minutes of Evidence, CAB 19/33.
31 Sir George Arthur to Dardanelles Commission, 1 May 1917, Minutes of Evidence, CAB 19/33.
32 Lord Riddell, *War Diary,* Nicholson & Watson, London, 1933, pp. 35–6.
33 Major Desmond Chapman-Huston and Major Owen Rutter, *General Sir John Cowans: the Quartermaster-General of the Great War,* Hutchinson, London, 1924, II, p. 18.
34 Grey, *op. cit.,* II, p. 69; Viscount Esher, 'Lord K.', *National Review,* July 1916, p. 686.
35 Haig Diary, 5 August 1914; 'Secretary's Notes of a War Council held at 10, Downing Street', 5 August 1914, CAB 41/1/2; John Terraine, *Douglas Haig: the Educated Soldier,* Hutchinson, London, 1963, pp. 73–4; Robert Blake (ed.), *The Private Papers of Douglas Haig, 1914–1919,* Eyre & Spottiswoode, London, 1952, p. 69.
36 Sir George Arthur, *Life of Lord Kitchener,* Macmillan, London, 1920, III, p. 7.
37 *Parliamentary Debates, House of Commons, 1914,* LXV, col. 2082; *The Times,* 7 August 1914.
38 Winston Churchill, *The World Crisis, 1911–1914,* Thornton Butterworth, London, 1923, p. 235.
39 Speech to Members of Parliament, 2 June 1916. The full text is given in Sir George Arthur, *Life of Lord Kitchener,* III, pp. 326–42.
40 Minutes of meeting of the Military Members of the Army Council, 9 August 1914, WO 163/44.
41 Minutes of Proceedings of the Army Council, 1914: 11 August 1914, WO 163/21.
42 R. B. Haldane, *An Autobiography,* Hodder & Stoughton, London, 1929, pp. 297–8.
43 Churchill, *op. cit.,* p. 236.
44 Arthur, *op. cit.,* III, p. 308.
45 Blake, *The Private Papers of Douglas Haig,* p. 69; Lloyd George, *op. cit.,* pp. 391–2.

46 Grey, *op. cit.*, II, p. 68.
47 Violet Bonham Carter, *op. cit.*, p. 319; Sir Charles Harris, letter to *The Times*, 28 August 1928.
48 *The Times*, 11 August 1914.
49 Minutes of meeting of the War Council, 6 August 1914, CAB 43/1/3.
50 Speech to Members of Parliament, 2 June 1916, quoted in Arthur, *op. cit.*, pp. 329–30.
51 *Ibid.*, III, p. 10.
52 Memorandum by Kitchener on an Admiralty paper 'Notes on Mining', 20 October 1914, CAB 37/121.
53 Churchill to Kitchener, 19 October 1914, Kitchener papers, PRO 30/57/72.
54 Asquith to Venetia Stanley, 21 October 1914, see M. and E. Brock, *op. cit.*, p. 281.
55 Churchill to Battenberg and Sturdee, 23 October 1914, see Arthur J. Marder, *From the Dreadnought to Scapa Flow: the Royal Navy in the Fisher Era, 1904–1919*, 5 vols., Oxford University Press, 1961–70, II, p. 63.
56 Minutes of meeting of the Military Members of the Army Council, 9 August 1914, WO 163/44.
57 Minutes of Proceedings of the Army Council, 1914: 11 August 1914, WO 163/21.
58 Brett and Esher (eds.), *op. cit.*, III, pp. 177–8.
59 *The Times*, 14 August 1914.
60 Lloyd George to his wife, 11 August 1914, see Kenneth O. Morgan (ed.), *Lloyd George Family Letters, 1885–1936*, University of Wales Press, Cardiff, 1973, p. 169.
61 *The Times*, 15 August 1914.
62 Diary of Lieutenant C. P. Burnley, 17 August 1914, IWM 73/130/1; Captain A. V. Wheeler-Holohan and Captain G. M. G. Wyatt, *The Rangers' Historical Records: from 1859 to the Conclusion of the Great War*, Harrison, London, 1921, p. 20; Lieutenant-Colonel W. A. V. Churton, *The War Record of the 1/5th (Earl of Chester's) Battalion the Cheshire Regiment, August 1914–June 1919*, Phillipson & Golder, Chester, 1920, p. 4; Captain R. J. Thompson, *Adventure Glorious: the Diary of a British Soldier in France, 1914–1918*, unpublished account, *c*. 1925, IWM 78/58/1.
63 *Debates on Army Affairs, House of Lords, 1914*, col. 452.
64 Ian F. W. Beckett, 'The Territorial Force', in Ian F. W. Beckett and Keith Simpson (eds.), *A Nation in Arms: a Social Study of the British Army in the First World War*, Manchester University Press, 1985, p. 132.
65 These figures have been compiled from the details given in Major A. F. Becke, *History of the Great War: Order of Battle of Divisions*, Parts 1 to 4, HMSO, London, 1935–45; and Brigadier E. A. James, *British Regiments, 1914–1918*, Samson, London, 1978.

2

The recruiting boom, August–September 1914

I

By the time Kitchener issued his first appeal Britain was already being swept by a rising tide of patriotism, and the recruiting offices were filled with eager volunteers. In fact the recruiting boom had begun a few hours before the declaration of war. On Saturday 1 August only eight men had been attested at the principal recruiting office of the London District in Great Scotland Yard and the following two days were a Sunday and a bank holiday, yet when the recruiting officer arrived on the moring of 4 August he was confronted with a mass of volunteers waiting to enlist. Even with the help of a score of policemen it took him some twenty minutes to force his way inside, after which both he and his medical staff worked without a break for the rest of the day.[1] Hundreds more presented themselves for enlistment on 5 August, despite the heavy rain which fell during the afternoon, and the next day 700 men were still outside when the office closed at 4.30 p.m. Recording the scene at Great Scotland Yard on 7 August, the day on which Kitchener's appeal was published, *The Times* noted that:

. . . the crowd of applicants was so large and so persistent that mounted police were necessary to hold them in check, and the gates were only opened to admit six at time . . . There was no cheering and little excitement, but there was an undercurrent of enthusiasm, and the disappointment of those who failed to pass one or other of the tests was obvious.[2]

Between 4 and 8 August the total number of men attested over the whole country was 8,193, an average daily intake of around 1,640 men. On Sunday 9 August 2,433 enlisted.[3] These figures, of course, represented a considerable increase on pre-war recruiting returns but they were less encouraging than they might have been, for while Kitchener's call led immediately to a further upsurge of recruiting in the capital, the provinces were slower to respond. For example, approximately one-third of all the men who enlisted in Britain on 8 August were enrolled at Great Scotland Yard alone, and on 9 August London produced 1,100 recruits, or almost half the national total for that day.[4]

It can be argued that the returns for the first week were not a true reflection

of the national response, as, throughout the country, men had turned up at recruiting offices only to be condemned to a long and fruitless wait in the street outside. Although Britain was as yet barely awake to the army's needs, the flow of volunteers, even at this stage, was greater than the recruiting offices could handle. This was hardly surprising, since the peacetime flow of recruits for the Regular army had comprised 30,000 men annually, or less than 100 per day over the entire United Kingdom. Nevertheless, within a few days of the outbreak of war it was becoming evident that the full potential of the voluntary system would not be realised until the recruiting machinery itself had been expanded and overhauled.

One solution was to increase the number of recruiting stations. A start was made in London as early as 7 August, when additional offices were opened in the boroughs of Battersea, Camberwell, Fulham, Islington and Marylebone. More were established the following day at New Cross, Peckham, Stratford and Woolwich.[5] Several of these were housed in schools, which were conveniently empty because of the summer holidays. On 11 August a marquee was erected on Horse Guards Parade to reduce the crush at Great Scotland Yard, where recruits were now being sworn in at the rate of 100 per hour.[6] Such measures were not confined to London. Recruiting offices were opened for the first time on 12 August in places as far apart as Nelson in Lancashire and Attleborough in Norfolk.[7]

However, there were other problems besides those of accommodation. Large numbers of clerks and doctors had to be found to augment the existing recruiting staffs, while the latter also had to be persuaded to shake themselves free from the ordered routine of peacetime enlistment. Leo Amery, the Conservative MP for Birmingham South, perceived how plodding this routine could be when he went to that city at Kitchener's personal request to stimulate recruiting. At one recruiting office on 8 August he discovered a huge crowd of men standing patiently in pouring rain, waiting to be let in one at a time. Inside, each man was expected to have a cold bath in the single bathroom before being examined by the only doctor and then taken laboriously through the questions on the official attestation form by the sole recruiting sergeant present. To make matters worse, the supply of attestation forms was nearly exhausted. Acting in Kitchener's name, Amery at once went to see the Deputy Mayor, Alderman W. H. Bowater, and after obtaining permission to use the Town Hall as a recruiting station, he engaged a keen Territorial officer, Colonel Ludlow, to help him in his task:

We rang up the leading doctors and arranged for an ample panel of medical officers to be available for any possible number of recruits. We got Messrs Avery's to send round a dozen or more weighing machines. We went round to an office which someone had opened for National Reservists, i.e. for ex-reservists who had registered their names as willing to re-enlist in an emergency. We found a couple of hundred of these crowding round, and soon collected a score of old sergeants with recruiting experience, telling them to be at the Town Hall early on Monday. I then went back to the recruiting officer and told him to dismiss the crowd and tell them to report on Monday at the

Town Hall. Seizing one of the last of the precious attestation forms I took it round to the *Birmingham Post* and got them to print off 20,000 copies over the weekend.

Contrary to Amery's later assertions, it took three or four days before these methods began to have any real effect, but by the end of the following week 388 recruits were attested in Birmingham in one day, and from then until November the recruiting returns in that city never totalled less than three figures on any weekday.[8]

Amery's experiences in Birmingham underlined the fact that the Regular recruiting organisation, which had worked smoothly enough in peacetime, was ill equipped to deal with the sudden influx of volunteers. In the absence of new instructions, individual recruiting officers were still acting in accordance with pre-war procedures and submitting requests for standard items like attestation forms through normal channels instead of exploring sources of supply closer to hand. This rigid adherence to peacetime methods inevitably produced bottlenecks and delays at all levels. To overcome such difficulties much greater flexibility was required, particularly at the lower end of the structure, and something akin to the Territorial recruiting system would therefore have to be adopted. As Amery had demonstrated, good results could be achieved by making more extensive use of the apparatus of local government and by securing the co-operation of local politicians and businessmen, who possessed precisely the kind of knowledge and experience of regional conditions which the War Office lacked.

That Kitchener quickly grasped these lessons was shown by his immediate appointment of Amery as Director of Civilian Recruiting for Southern Command. Working under the supervision of Sir Henry Rawlinson, then Director of Recruiting at the War Office, Amery and Rawlinson's Assistant Director, Major-General H. B. Jeffreys, set off on 11 August for a whirlwind tour of the cities and towns in the Command. Their aim was to induce local authorities and political organisations to form civilian recruiting committees and arrange public meetings in their respective areas, thereby sharing some of the load currently borne by the War Office and the staff of the Command. In three days Amery and Jeffreys managed to visit Salisbury, Bristol, Rugby, Coventry, Warwick, Birmingham and Worcester. They observed in several places that, in spite of Kitchener's appeal for volunteers and his simultaneous plea to the Territorial Force County Associations for assistance in raising them, the main effort of patriotic citizens was devoted to hospital and relief work or the formation of makeshift local defence corps rather than to recruiting for the army. Having done what they could to rectify this during their brief stay in each place, Amery and Jeffreys lost no time in reporting their findings to Kitchener on their return to London. 'It was clear to us,' Amery remarked later, 'that what was needed was a systematic scheme for enlisting public opinion and civilian drive behind recruiting over the whole country'.[9] In recognising this need, if not its full implications, the War Office was taking the first step along a path which led directly to the creation of the

Parliamentary Recruiting Committee and the mushroom growth of the Pals movement at the end of the month.

In his memoirs, published some forty years after the event, Amery gives the impression that he originated most of the key proposals which caused the War Office to enlarge the base of its recruiting organisation so early in the campaign. Although he may have exaggerated his overall influence on recruiting policy, his successes in certain areas undoubtedly helped to convince Kitchener and Rawlinson of the advantages to be gained from devolution. In Bristol, for instance, an extra recruiting station had been opened in Old Market Street in an attempt to alleviate the congestion at the Colston Street office, but the problems continued to multiply. Then, following Amery's arrival in the city, the Lord Mayor, Alderman John Swaish, convened an emergency meeting at the Royal Hotel on 12 August at which it was decided to form a committee of leading citizens to run a large recruiting office in the Colston Hall. Alderman Swaish, as chairman, delegated his duties to Sir Herbert Ashman, a former lord mayor, and as their recruiting officer the Bristol Citizens' Recruiting Committee appointed Lieutenant-General W. E. P. Burges, who had retired in 1913 after five years in command of the 3rd (Special Reserve) Battalion of the Gloucestershire Regiment. A staff of clerks and voluntary assistants was also chosen, all this being done with such speed that recruiting got under way at the Colston Hall on 15 August. The medical services were organised by Barclay Baron, who arranged for up to a dozen fellow doctors to be in attendance daily from 8 a.m. to 8 p.m., while local firms supplied all the necessary stationery and essential equipment such as weighing machines. By 26 August over 1,000 men had enlisted at the Colston Hall, and on the last day of the month the new office was able to process nearly 600 recruits.[10] Thus in Bristol, as in Birmingham, the problems created by the initial rush to the colours were greatly eased once the civilian recruiting authorities became closely involved in the recruiting campaign.

As the war entered its second week there were signs that the recruiting campaign was beginning to gather momentum. The strongest evidence of this was the significant rise in recruiting returns. 43,354 men enlisted between 9 and 15 August, the highest figures to date being recorded on Thursday 13 August when 8,023 volunteers were attested.[11] At the same time, local authorities were giving increasing support to the War Office. In London more and more public buildings were being made available for recruiting. By 15 August they included the town halls in East Ham, Lambeth, Shoreditch, Southwark and Walthamstow; the Canning Town Public Hall; the Catford labour exchange; the offices of the Poor Law Guardians in Chelsea and South Kensington; and schools in Greenwich, Holloway, Limehouse and Westminster. Three days later it was announced that the mayors of all twenty-eight metropolitan boroughs had offered to place their town halls and their staffs at the disposal of the War Office.[12]

Another indication that the nation was getting more solidly behind the recruiting campaign could be seen in the growing wave of patriotic meetings being organised throughout the country. Typical of these was an open-air meeting at Deal in Kent on 13 August at which the Mayor presided. Well over 2,000 people assembled in South Street to hear the speeches and thirty-seven men had volunteered for the army before the proceedings came to an end.[13] Several recruits also came forward at a crowded meeting held the same evening in a park at Burgess Hill in Sussex.[14] The importance of these gatherings lay not so much in the number of men which each one produced as in the cumulative effect on recruiting figures and in the fact that, at this juncture, they were being organised spontaneously by local citizens rather than at the direct behest of the War Office. Even so, the results were sometimes extremely disappointing. A big meeting in the Market Place at Boston in Lincolnshire on 12 August yielded only four recruits, although a few more joined later in the day. Indeed, Boston, with a population of over 16,000, provided Kitchener with only fifty recruits in the first three weeks.[15]

The relatively poor response from many areas at a time when the national recruiting figures were showing a distinct upward swing may be attributed in part to the continuing dispersal of civilian effort among a multitude of patriotic causes, a problem which Amery had identified on his tour of Southern Command. For example, on 15 August a Patriotic Association was formed in the Northamptonshire parish of Eye, near Peterborough, but only one of the eleven sub-committees subsequently appointed by the association was primarily concerned with recruiting, the others dealing with matters ranging from nursing and relief work to war savings schemes.[16] The proliferation of irregular local forces also tended to divert attention away from the official recruiting campaign. A meeting of Newcastle businessmen on 6 August had led to the formation of a Citizens' Training League on Tyneside, and drilling was soon in progress in the grounds of the Royal Grammar School.[17] Similarly, a training corps was organised at Hyde in Cheshire for the male employees of Ashton Brothers' Mills, the largest firm in the town. The Ashton Brothers Training Corps ultimately reached a strength of several hundred men. A rifle range was set up in one of the firm's sheds and dummy rifles and bayonets were made in the workshops for drill purposes. A second local defence force came into existence on 18 August when the Hyde branch of the Junior Unionist Association met 'to consider the starting of a junior section of a civilian army, to assist the authorities in any crisis which is likely to arise'. Some forty-five members, aged between seventeen and twenty-five, were at once enrolled and began drilling under a former Volunteer sergeant and an officer of the Boys' Brigade.[18] Admittedly, these and other local defence corps provided their members with a useful grounding in drill and military discipline and eventually furnished many men for the army, yet, for the time being, their very existence had an adverse effect on recruiting. As Lord Leconfield argued at a meeting of the Sussex Territorial Force Association on 10 August, the patriotism of the organisers of these *ad hoc* formations was to be admired but, in his opinion, 'it would be infinitely better that they should confine themselves to raising the men that Lord Kitchener asked for'.[19]

Lord Leconfield was not alone in judging that, despite the massive upsurge in recruiting, a more concentrated effort was needed to provide the numbers for which Kitchener had called. On 12 August, in a leading article entitled 'Recruiting and the rich', *The Times* pointed out that it would be necessary to maintain the flow of volunteers for some time to come and urged all those who had men of 'suitable age and vigour' in their employ to release them for military service. These remarks were addressed chiefly to private citizens retaining men in 'unproductive domestic occupations' namely as valets, footmen, grooms and gardeners. Many of these citizens, *The Times* commented, 'may not perhaps have realised yet how large a reserve of the national manhood is represented by those who serve their personal comforts and gratifications'.[20] While no one could afford to be complacent, Kitchener and the Army Council at least had reason to believe that the confusion of the first week had been brought under control. Most Territorial units had reached full strength within a few days of mobilisation and, although men were still required to replace those who had declined to volunteer for foreign service, the County Associations were now in a better position to meet Kitchener's request of 7 August and relieve the pressure on the Regular recruiting organisation. By 15 August the Army Council had enough confidence in the recruiting arrangements to issue a statement through the Press Bureau, acknowledging that severe problems had been encountered at the start:

On account of the enthusiasm engendered at the outbreak of war the greatest difficulty was experienced in dealing with the number of men who rushed to enlist in the Army . . . Large additions to the staff as well as to recruiting agencies had to be at once devised. These additions have now been made, and the machinery is beginning to cope satisfactorily with the requirements of the situation. It is hoped that all those for whom facilities were not at once available will again respond to the call to arms and come forward to serve their country by now applying to one of the many recruiting offices which have since been opened and are now in working order, both in London and in every large town, as well as throughout the country districts.[21]

The events of the following week appeared, in some respects, to justify the Army Council's guarded optimism. In particular, the returns from the big industrial centres began to show a dramatic improvement. On 20 August it was reported that Glasgow was producing between 200 and 300 recruits per day, nearly 600 of the city's tramway workers having already joined the army.[22] In Birmingham a huge barometer outside the Town Hall registered the fact that 2,000 men had enlisted there by 20 August, and this was only one of several recruiting stations now open in the city.[23] On Merseyside Lord Derby, the chairman of the West Lancashire Territorial Association and a figure of considerable influence in the political and commercial life of the north-west, associated himself with the work of raising the first Service battalion of the King's (Liverpool) Regiment. In a letter published in the local newspapers on Wednesday 19 August Derby indicated various ways in which the people of Liverpool could help. It was suggested that motorists should make their vehicles available to the recruiting authorities, that 'the proprietors of picture palaces' should publicise the appeal at their performances and that 'employers should tell their employees that if they answer their King's call their places shall be kept open for them'. The letter was accompanied by a list of recruiting offices in the Greater Liverpool area. Apart from the regimental depot at Seaforth Barracks, these included the town halls at Bootle and Southport; the Corn Hall, Ormskirk; Warbreck House at Aintree; and a technical school in Garston. 'I am sure,' Lord Derby predicted, 'that if the military authorities can receive the help I now ask from all classes of the community, we shall be able on Friday evening to tell Lord Kitchener that not only is the battalion full, but full to overflowing.'[24] The raising of the battalion actually took three days longer than anticipated but the unit, designated the 11th King's (Liverpool) Regiment, had the required number of recruits by the evening of 24 August. Liverpool therefore claimed the distinction of being the first city to enrol a complete battalion for Kitchener's army, although the 10th Royal Fusiliers, recruited in the City of London, reached establishment early the next day.[25]

The methods adopted in Liverpool were symptomatic of the trend towards increased civilian participation in all aspects of recruiting. Guildford and Portsmouth were just two of the places where civilian committees were created to promote recruiting during the second and third weeks of the war. The composition of the committee at Guildford provides an excellent illustration of the variety of organisations and institutions now identifying themselves with Kitchener's call. Of its thirteen members, only Colonel W. J. Perkins, a local solicitor who had served for thirty-five years in the old Volunteers and was a former commanding officer of the 5th Queen's Royal West Surrey Regiment, had well defined military connections. Besides the Mayor and three or four Corporation officials, the others comprised representatives from the Castle and Friary breweries, the Guildford Gas Company, the Royal Surrey County Hospital, the Guildford Rifle Club, the Chamber of Trade and a local firm of printers.[26] Against all this, the enlistment figures for the week ending 22 August fell some way short of expectations. 49,982 men joined the army over the seven-day period, certainly the highest weekly total so far but only 6,628 above the figure for the previous week. Moreover, although a new record for a single day was set on Tuesday 18 August, when 9,699 enlisted, the returns for the last three days of the week were in each case lower than those of the previous Thursday, Friday and Saturday.[27]

There were several reasons for this failure to maintain the earlier rate of acceleration in recruiting. Many men, particularly those who were married and held a good job, needed time to settle their affairs and make sure their families would be cared for before joining the army, however patriotic they

may have been. Others were waiting to be given some guarantee that their
jobs would be kept open for them until they returned. The fear of unemployment remained the working man's most constant worry, and this anxiety
did not simply disappear overnight with the declaration of war. In addition,
while there was mounting evidence of civilian involvement in the recruiting
campaign, such support was still somewhat patchy. The majority of major
towns and cities had yet to follow the lead of places like Bristol and create
civilian recruiting committees of their own.

The feeling was also growing that recruiting regulations were being applied
too rigorously in some areas. Admiral Sir William Kennedy wrote to *The
Times* complaining that his butler, a fine shot, had been rejected as too old at
the age of thirty-two.[28] Another man, signing himself 'Not Wanted', made a
similar complaint:

I am 6 ft 1 in., 38 in. round the chest, have been pronounced medically fit by two
doctors, have served in the Artillery . . ., have won several prizes for shooting. But the
Army won't have me because their ranks are full! Does England want men like me or
doesn't it?[29]

Of all those who voiced their opinions in the correspondence columns of the
national and local press, Sir Henry Morris, the eminent surgeon, perhaps
came the nearest to diagnosing the main problem. Writing on 27 August, he
suggested that it was not indifference but ignorance of the consequences of
defeat 'that is the cause of Lord Kitchener's appeal to the country having been
less completely and energetically responded to than it has been'.[30] Certainly,
many people were not yet fully aware of the nature of the emergency or the
magnitude of the task facing the country. The initial flush of patriotic
enthusiasm was already beginning to wear off, and the majority of men still
had to be persuaded that their services were required. The public had not
properly understood what Kitchener's appeal meant, a state of affairs for
which the government was largely to blame. Arthur Lee, the Conservative
MP for Fareham, pointed this out in the House of Commons on 26 August.
'There is a prevalent impression,' he said, 'that 100,000 men are required,
and that when they are obtained more are not necessary.' Asquith replied that
this was a mistaken impression. 'We want all the recruits we can get,' he
declared.[31] However, the Prime Minister's statement, while confirming the
need for men, also amounted to a confession that the government had not
made its intentions sufficiently clear in the first place.

Even as these opinions were being expressed, events at the front had
imparted a new urgency to the situation. The first news of the Battle of Mons
reached the public on the morning of Tuesday 25 August. A headline in *The
Times* referred to the 'British Army's Stern Fight' two days before, and an
editorial summary of the principal facts began with the sober admission: 'The
battle is joined and has so far gone ill for the Allies.' A leader in the same issue
stated ominously, 'Yesterday was a day of bad news, and we fear that more

must follow.' In these circumstances, *The Times* urged, it was vital to cut through the 'excessive regard for red tape in accepting recruits. No doubt it was necessary to begin cautiously, but minute insistence on details may easily degenerate into wasteful pedantry.'[32]

Reports of the battle, and of the subsequent withdrawal of the BEF from Mons, had an immediate impact on the recruiting figures. The mood of the nation altered perceptibly, and people everywhere were roused to fresh heights of patriotic energy. On 25 August itself 10,019 men enlisted, the first time a five-figure total had been achieved in a single day. The totals for the following four days were 10,251, 11,396 and 12,789 respectively, the overall figure for the week exceeding 63,000.[33] The contributions of individual cities were equally impressive. Between 23 and 29 August London produced 10,334 recruits, Birmingham 3,516, Manchester 3,141, Glasgow 2,220, Newcastle 2,126, Cardiff 1,544 and Liverpool 1,469. In contrast, only 398 joined in Dublin. Outside London, Birmingham had the highest total for any one day, 709 enlisting there on 29 August.[34]

By 25 August, in his maiden speech as a Minister of the Crown, Kitchener was able to announce in the House of Lords that the 100,000 recruits 'for which, in the first place, it has been thought necessary to call have been already practically secured'. However, he added a note of warning:

I cannot at this stage say what will be the limits of the forces required, or what measures may eventually become necessary to supply and maintain them. The scale of the Field Army which we are now calling into being is large and may rise in the course of the next six or seven months to a total of thirty divisions continually maintained in the field. But if the war should be protracted, and if its fortunes should be varied or adverse, exertions and sacrifices beyond any which have been demanded will be required from the whole nation and Empire, and where they are required we are sure they will not be denied to the extreme needs of the State by Parliament or the people.[35]

In effect Kitchener was hinting that, if sufficient recruits were not forthcoming, some form of compulsory service might have to be introduced. Others were more outspoken. As the country was galvanised into action by the news from across the Channel the demand for conscription suddenly intensified. Commenting on Kitchener's speech, *The Times* observed that the rest of the nation had no right to shelter behind those who had left their homes and businesses to answer the call of duty. It argued that the present age limit of thirty for recruits was too low, noting that the Continental nations were calling up men years older. It also drew attention to 'the great army of shirkers' who preferred to go to cricket matches and the cinema rather than serve Britain in her hour of need: 'It is a national scandal that the selfish should get off scot-free while all the burden falls on the most public-spirited section of our available manhood; and if the voluntary system can do no better it will have to be changed.'[36]

The views expounded by the Northcliffe press undoubtedly echoed the sentiments of a large number of people at the time. Over the next week or so, newspapers in all parts of the country were inundated with letters in favour of compulsory recruiting. Many older correspondents burned with indignation at the seeming apathy of the nation's youth. In Sussex 'A British Matron' proposed that every Englishwoman should learn to use a revolver: 'As I see hundreds of cowardly young male curs (I cannot call them men) perambulating the streets daily, apparently ignoring their obligations to their country, and oblivious to the danger that is daily coming nearer to us, I think it would be wise for women to try and help themselves, so that when England is invaded by a horde of German barbarians they could at least account for one foe the less and save their own honour.'[37] Writing from the Reform Club on 26 August, the dramatist Henry Jones also made a special appeal to women: 'The English girl who will not know the man – lover, brother, friend – that cannot show an overwhelming reason for not taking up arms – that girl will do her duty and will give good help to her country.'[38] Before the end of the month women in Folkestone were handing out white feathers as a symbol of cowardice to young men still in civilian clothes.[39]

In the excitement and partial panic caused by the German advance through Belgium and France it was almost inevitable that there would be a revival of the demand for compulsion and that the case for it would be overstated. Allied reverses were bound to arouse serious concern about the maintenance of the supply of recruits. On the other hand, anti-conscriptionists could claim that the British people were only just beginning to recognise the gravity of the situation and that the voluntary system had not yet been fully tested. The government, indeed, was willing to defend the voluntary system as long as it produced the required numbers of men. In the House of Commons on 26 August two Conservative MPs asked the Prime Minister whether the government intended to secure the safety of the United Kingdom by bringing in a measure of compulsory service. Asquith tersely replied that the answer was in the negative and referred his questioners to Kitchener's speech of the previous day.[40] For the moment, the opposition was reluctant to break the recently established political truce and so refrained from forcing the issue.

As it was, the wind was at once removed from the sails of the conscriptionists by a gigantic recruiting drive in the last week of August. By 27 August Kitchener had informed the Army Council of his decision to call for a further 100,000 volunteers, and his appeal duly appeared in the press the following day. The upper age limit was extended to thirty-five for new recruits, forty-five for ex-soldiers and fifty for certain ex-noncommissioned officers. The appeal also pointed out that married men or widowers with children would be accepted and would draw separation allowances at army rates.[41] At this point, it seems, Kitchener had no immediate plans for the formation of another six divisions on the lines of those created earlier in the month. The second 100,000 men were to be used, in the first instance, to bring all Special Reserve battalions up to a strength of 2,000, the balance being kept for training at the regimental depots.[42]

On the same day as Kitchener launched his second appeal the Prime Minister, sensitive as ever to changes in the political climate, at last took a personal hand in the recruiting campaign. He wrote to the Lord Mayors of London, Cardiff and Dublin, and the Lord Provost of Edinburgh, informing them that 'the time has now come for combined effort to stimulate and organise public opinion and public effort in the greatest conflict in which our people has ever been engaged'. Asquith proposed that a start should be made by holding meetings throughout the United Kingdom 'at which the justice of our cause should be made plain, and the duty of every man to do his part should be enforced'.[43]

The creation of the Parliamentary Recruiting Committee provided the government with the machinery it needed to draw together all the diverse strands of the recruiting campaign and to monitor and direct civilian effort more systematically at a local level. According to the minutes of a preliminary meeting held in the Liberal Chief Whip's office in the House of Commons on 27 August, the committee grew out of the desire 'strongly expressed by Ministers and Members of both Houses, irrespective of Party, that their services should be fully utilised, and to the best advantage, in order that the grave issues of the War should be fully comprehended by the people, and thereby to give a powerful impetus to recruiting'. The meeting was attended by the Chief Whips of the major political parties, together with Arthur Steel-Maitland, the chairman of the Conservative Party. Rawlinson was also present and, on Kitchener's behalf, 'gave his hearty approval to the proposal and an assurance that the War Office would welcome and facilitate the work of such a Committee in every possible way'.[44] A second meeting took place on 28 August and three days later the Parliamentary Recruiting Committee was officially constituted. Asquith, Bonar Law and Arthur Henderson were its joint presidents, Henderson having become leader of the Parliamentary Labour Party earlier in the month when Ramsay MacDonald resigned in protest against Britain's entry into the war. The full committee comprised thirty-two members and included eleven Conservative, seven Liberal and four Labour MPs as well as other party officials. From the House of Lords came Lord Colebrooke for the Liberals and the Duke of Devonshire for the Conservative peers. The War Office was represented by Rawlinson and by Major A. B. Gosset, the Deputy Adjutant-General and Chief Recruiting Staff Officer for the London District.

It was at the meetings of 28 and 31 August that the foundations of the committee's future activities were laid. It was decided that, in any given area, the effort of the party organisations and the recognised recruiting authorities should be co-ordinated, with the Parliamentary Recruiting Committee helping individual civilian recruiting committees to obtain distinguished speakers for public meetings. Local autonomy was to be encouraged. For example, local political associations were to determine whether a few large recruiting meetings or a whole series of smaller gatherings would be likely to produce the best results in their own constituencies. There was general agreement concerning the importance of keeping the press fully informed about the intentions and scope of the committee's work and of producing recruiting literature to supplement that prepared by the War Office. A special Publicity and Publications Sub-department was therefore set up to orchestrate recruiting propaganda throughout the country. Furthermore, a scheme was devised whereby party workers would canvass for recruits in much the same way as they normally canvassed for votes.

Of all the schemes put forward by the Parliamentary Recruiting Committee, this last proposal was the most far-reaching in its ramifications. In every constituency, party agents would be instructed to organise their sub-agents, canvassers and volunteer workers to deliver recruiting circulars to all male citizens on the electoral register. Each circular would be accompanied by a stamped, addressed card upon which the elector was invited to enter details of his age and marital status, to indicate his willingness to come forward as a recruit if called upon by the War Office or, alternatively, to state any 'qualifications or reservations' which might affect his availability for military service. Canvassers were to go round within three to five days of delivery to find out whether the card has been sent in and, if not, to follow the matter up. Completed cards would be sorted and classified by the political agents, then handed over to the local recruiting officer.[45]

The project was discussed at some length on 31 August but it was decided to hold it in reserve 'until Lord Kitchener deemed such action necessary'. However, the very fact that the scheme was drawn up less than a month after the declaration of war showed how far and how quickly the initiative in recruiting had passed from the military to the civil authorities. Designed as it was to make full use of the extensive network of local political organisations, the canvassing plan reflected a growing awareness of the need for a more precise method of assessing Britain's potential military manpower than was offered by the traditional forms of census. It can therefore be seen as the first tentative move towards the efficient mobilisation of the nation's manpower resources by the government and also as a precursor of the National Registration Act and the Derby Scheme of 1915.

Although the emergence of the Parliamentary Recruiting Committee marked the point at which responsibility for the direction and administration of the recruiting campaign began to be transferred from the War Office into the hands of the politicians, it is doubtful whether anyone, least of all Kitchener, viewed it in those terms at the time. For one thing, the MPs and party officials most closely connected with the committee's formation were motivated by a desire to assist the War Office, not to usurp its authority. For another, Kitchener himself was no doctrinaire in questions of recruiting and was willing to accept constructive offers of help from almost any quarter. It must be re-emphasised that when Kitchener first set out to increase the size of the army he did not know exactly how many extra divisions would be required and had little more than an outline plan as to how they were to be raised. In this respect his policy for the expansion of the army evolved gradually, being shaped and modified by events rather than proceeding along predetermined lines towards a fixed goal. His main problem throughout the early months was that of continually striking the right balance between the demands of the British Expeditionary Force in France and Belgium and those of the home defence forces and new units training in the United Kingdom. Kitchener's views on this issue were made clear when he wrote to Sir John French on 27 August, immediately after the battles of Mons and Le Cateau, explaining why it was necessary to retain the 6th Division at home pending the formation of the 7th and 8th Divisions from Regular battalions then being withdrawn from overseas garrisons:

When the Defence Committee and the General Staff decided on sending a force abroad, it was laid down that the Sixth Division, though kept quite in readiness, should not leave England until the Territorial Force had had time to do some training. If this Sixth Division had gone, you know what Regular forces would have been left here; besides which there would only be immobile Reserve Battalions in Coast Defences, and the unfit and untrained Territorials . . . We are all determined to support you to the utmost, and to see that, as soon as possible, you shall be provided with an adequate force, which will increase as we go on . . . But pray do not increase my troubles by the thought that if the Divison had been with you, some of your men's lives might have been saved. Do remember that we shall have to go through much more fighting before we are out of the war, and that by prematurely putting all our eggs in one basket we might incur far greater losses. Believe me, had I been consulted on military matters during the last three years, I would have done everything in my power to prevent the present state of affairs in which this country finds itself.[46]

Apart from the situation in France, three main problems appeared to occupy Kitchener's attention as August drew to a close. First, it was vital to keep the flame of national enthusiasm burning fiercely and therefore to explore every conceivable method of making the public aware of the urgent need for men. Secondly, it was now more important than ever to decentralise and to spread the burden of raising, housing and equipping the new formations, since the understaffed War Office could not make adequate provision for the numbers of volunteers coming forward. Thirdly, some way had to be found of incorporating the remarkable but isolated recruiting efforts of various local authorities into a co-ordinated scheme of expansion. The War Office was thus caught in something of a vicious circle, for as more and more men were called upon to enlist, the harder it became to deal with them.

The influence of these considerations on Kitchener's policy in the latter half of August may be detected in the active support he gave to the formation of Pals battalions, now being raised by the mayors and corporations of large cities or by self-appointed committees of local dignitaries, industrialists and private citizens. The same factors weighed heavily on his decision to authorise the raising of a reserve, or second-line, formation for each original Territorial unit in which 60 per cent of the men had volunteered for service abroad. The

story of the Pals movement will be examined in more detail in the next
chapter. It is sufficient to point out here that these developments at once
changed the patterns of enlistment by increasing the opportunities for individual communities to express their patriotism in a specific form and to raise
units with a strong local identity. This not only injected a new sense of
purpose and pride into local recruiting efforts but also enabled the War Office
to delegate a much greater proportion of its work to civilian bodies.

If a further shock was required to jolt the conscience of the people, it was
provided by the so-called 'Amiens dispatch', which appeared in *The Times* on
30 August. This highly coloured and somewhat inaccurate account of the
retreat from Mons was written by Arthur Moore, who arrived on the line of
march of the British 4th Division on 28 August, encountering scattered
fragments of that formation. His subsequent dispatch referred to the BEF as a
'broken army' which had been 'forced backwards and ever backwards by the
sheer unconquerable mass of numbers of an enemy prepared to throw away
three or four men for the life of every British soldier . . . Our losses are very
great. I have seen the broken bits of many regiments . . .' As published, the
report concluded:

We have to face the fact that the British Expeditionary Force, which bore the great
weight of the blow, has suffered terrible losses and requires immediate and immense
reinforcement. The British Expeditionary Force has won indeed imperishable glory,
but it needs men, men, and yet more men.[47]

By the time the 'Amiens dispatch' was printed the failure of the Germans to
pursue II Corps had given the BEF the chance to stabilise the situation and
repair much of the damage it had suffered. Thus, even though publication of
the dispatch had been authorised by F. E. Smith, the head of the Press Bureau,
the War Office issued two statements on 31 August in an attempt to 'restore
the necessary perspective to the recent operations' and warning that reports
such as that written by Moore 'should be received with extreme caution'. The
Daily Telegraph alluded to 'highly alarmist stories . . . not justified by the
facts', and the *Daily Express* complained that the *The Times* had 'made
hearts stand still'.[48] The same day, in an angry adjournment debate in the
House of Commons, F. E. Smith accepted responsibility for having passed the
article in the form in which it appeared and even confessed that, to help
Kitchener, he had suggested the inclusion of the passage calling for recruits to
reinforce the BEF.[49] Nevertheless, for all these disclaimers and explanations,
Moore's dispatch had made its impact on the public at large.

All these elements combined to produce a kind of recruiting fever which
raged throughout the country during the last week of August and the first two
weeks of September, inspiring extraordinary deeds of personal and collective
patriotism. The effects of the fever were visible at every turn. Many London
taxis now carried recruiting placards and people were urged only to engage
cabs bearing these notices. Illuminated tramcars adorned with recruiting

slogans nightly toured the streets of Leeds and Glasgow. In Guildford recruits for the Queen's Royal West Surrey Regiment were paraded through the town, with the Stoughton Band at their head and with Boy Scouts acting as torch bearers. The local Conservative MP, Edgar Horne, booked a whole page in the *Surrey Advertiser* of 5 September, filling it with the names of Guildford men who had enlisted, as an incentive to others to follow suit. A few days earlier the committee of Blackheath Rugby Football Club had resolved to cancel all fixtures for the new season, solemnly declaring that 'every Rugby footballer of the present day comes within the scope of Lord Kitchener's appeal'.[50]

Employers too were probably more prepared to make public-spirited gestures during this period than at any other stage of the war. The owners and directors of most of the large ironworks and shipbuilding firms in Middlesbrough agreed that the family of each man who enlisted should receive half his normal pay every week so long as he was in the army, while many of the workers who remained behind consented to a levy of 3*d* in the pound from their wages to help support the dependants of soldiers. Some firms mixed patriotism with advertising. Aquascutum, the sporting outfitters, announced in *The Tatler,* 'We shall be pleased to pay half his present salary to any of our present employees while serving and will keep his situtation open for him on his return. In the event of a parent or parents being dependent on the volunteer, full salary will be paid him during his service.' At Beaconsfield, in Buckinghamshire, Lord Burnham offered a bonus of £10 to every man on his estate who joined the army. An engineering firm in Dartford advertised that they would not take on any unmarried men who were eligible for enlistement, and this served to convince the bulk of the single men already at the works that they should also volunteer. A similar case was reported in South Wales when all the unmarried men employed at a steelworks in Neath presented themselves in a body for enlistment in Cardiff. The enrolling of servants of wealthy people was a feature of the day at Great Scotland Yard on 3 September. 'Several ladies well known in society came in their motor-cars with excellent recruits from their households,' noted *The Times.* In Gloucestershire, on 4 September, the Stroud Brewery Company held a dinner for employees who had joined up, paying each man a £4 bonus. That week more than fifty men from the nearby Dudbridge Ironworks Company left their jobs to enlist. Small wonder that, in the prevailing excitement, many firms suddenly lost a substantial part of their work force. By 12 September, for instance, thousands of male employees had disappeared from the big London stores, including 400 from Harrods, 350 from Waring and Gillow, 200 from John Barker and 200 from Selfridges.[51]

The recruiting returns for the week 30 August to 5 September were the highest for the whole of the war. 174,901 men were attested over the seven days, thus nearly trebling the figures for the previous week. The daily totals topped 20,000 for the first time on Monday 31 August, and two days later

31,947 men enlisted. The highest total ever for a single day was recorded on Thursday 3 September, when 33,204 men joined the army.[52] On that day alone 3,521 enlisted in London, 2,151 in Manchester, 1,653 in Birmingham, 1,131 in Preston, 1,084 in Cardiff, 1,014 in Glasgow and 935 in Sunderland. Once again Dublin fell far behind, with only 114 recruits on 3 September, a total well below those recorded at places like Derby, Leicester, Northampton, Sheffield and Hull, all of which had much smaller populations.[53]

II

The first six divisions of Kitchener's army had begun to assemble at their training centres a fortnight or more before the recruiting boom reached its peak. Batches of men were posted daily to the new battalions from the regimental depots at an increasing rate after 21 August, the date on which these six divisions officially came into existence. The battalions were organised initially around small cadres of Regulars drawn from the units of the BEF, the command being given, in many cases, to the Regular majors who had been left in charge of the depots on mobilisation. For instance, the 5th (Service) Battalion of the King's Shropshire Light Infantry, part of the Light Division, started life with a nucleus of two captains, one second lieutenant and thirty other ranks from the Regular 1st Battalion at Tipperary. The 5th Battalion was formed at Blackdown Camp, Aldershot, towards the end of August, under Major H. M. Smith, who had been in command of the depot at Shrewsbury at the outbreak of the war.[54] The 5th Oxfordshire and Buckinghamshire Light Infantry, in the same division, was commanded by Lieutenant-Colonel C. H. Cobb, who was at home on leave from the 1st Battalion in India when war was declared. Cobb reached Deepcut Barracks near Aldershot on 23 August and, like most commanding officers of the new Service battalions, discovered that his unit consisted of little more than a bewildered mob of civilians. His account of the battalion's early days provides a graphic illustration of the problems which had to be overcome:

On arrival at the barracks I found Captain R. O. Logan and Lieut. B. C. T. Paget (1st Battalion) in command of about 150 men of the new Battalion, having come from Oxford three days before; and on the following day I took over this party. Then I began to get busy. I was ordered to draw camp equipment, blankets, etc., for 1,000 men, and to move to Old Dean Common (near Camberley), where I was to pitch a camp. I had no quartermaster, but with the aid of my car we managed things between us. I interviewed several people of the Ordnance, A.S.C., and Transport, and though I found everyone working at high pressure and nearly off their heads, still they readily rose to the occasion and did all they could for me . . .

That evening three more officers arrived, including a captain from the 21st Punjabis and another from the 1st Battalion. On 25 August the party marched to Old Dean Common:

The men were fully armed and equipped, but were absolutely raw and new, and, the weather being hot, they felt even this short march very much. Then came a real difficulty – pitching camp with men who had never seen a tent before. The officers and the few NCOs did most of the work, but gradually the recruits picked it up, and we got a camp going. On the following day . . . the men had their first experience of a wet camp, for it rained all day. However, we had to be busy, trying to get things into shape, and in the evening Lieut. Hanbury-Williams (2nd Battalion) arrived with 100 more men, who came in plain clothes, as the stock of uniforms at the Depot had become exhausted.

Feeding the men presented Cobb with one of his greatest difficulties, because only the 150 men of the original party had mess tins and later arrivals had no utensils from which to eat or drink:

We were obliged to have meals in relays, using the same mess-tins, and this was a serious handicap, in that it wasted time and delayed work a good deal. But it was only one of the many discomforts with which my new soldiers had to put up.[55]

The handful of officers and NCOs striving to organise the battalions of the first six divisions were fortunate in as much as the recruits for these units were sent to the training centres in successive drafts over several days rather than all at once. From its nucleus of 150 men on 23 August, the 5th Oxfordshire and Buckinghamshire Light Infantry was completed by two drafts of 500 men each on 5 and 7 September, and a smaller batch of sixty-four recruits on 8 September. In the case of the 5th Royal Berkshire Regiment, assembling at Shorncliffe as part of the 12th (Eastern) Division, the first draft arrived on 26 August, the second on 28 August, and two more – of 400 and 200 men respectively – on 4 and 5 September, bringing the battalion strength to a total of 990 men at that point.[56] From the very beginning the War Office was determined that the training of all units in the first six divisions should be maintained at the same level and ordered the GOCs-in-C of the regional commands to ensure that 'the formation of all the Service battalions should be proceeded with simultaneously'. This task, however, was complicated by the fact that a few regiments had been directed to contribute more than one battalion. The Royal Scots and the Highland Light Infantry, for example, were to provide two battalions each for the 9th (Scottish) Division; the 10th (Irish) Division was to include two battalions each from the Royal Munster Fusiliers, Royal Dublin Fusiliers, Royal Irish Fusiliers and Royal Inniskilling Fusiliers; and there were to be two battalions of the Royal Fusiliers in the 12th (Eastern) Division. The Adjutant-General's Department therefore issued instructions that, in these regiments, the formation of the second Service battalion should be undertaken as soon as 100 recruits had been allotted to the first battalion. When the second unit also had 100 recruits, succeeding drafts were to be sent to each unit in approximately equal numbers.[57]

On 29 August, the day after Kitchener's second appeal, the Adjutant-General was asked to draw up proposals for the raising of another series of six divisions. From that date the Army Council also began to describe the first six divisions collectively as the First New Army or 'K 1'.[58] It was now becoming imperative for the Army Council to proceed with considerable haste, for men were pouring into the regimental depots from the recruiting offices at a much faster rate than the depleted depot staffs could process them and post them to the training centres or Special Reserve battalions. Returns submitted to the War Office on 29 August showed that many depots, designed to accommodate between 250 and 500 men, were bursting at the seams. Indeed, fifteen depots contained well over 1,000 recruits and one, the depot of the South Staffordshire Regiment at Lichfield, was crammed with 2,408 men.[59] Only three days before, the War Office had decreed that recruits should remain at the depots for forty-eight hours at most, or just long enough to receive their uniforms and regimental numbers, but on 30 August depot commanders were directed to dispatch recruits to their battalions without delay, whether clothing was available or not.[60]

Sclater was ready with his proposals by 1 September. As soon as the battalions of the 8th to the 13th Divisions were complete to war establishment, i.e. to 1,100 all ranks, and the Special Reserve battalions had reached a strength of 2,000, duplicate divisions, numbered from 14th to 19th, were to be formed. The infantry battalions of the new divisions were to correspond, as nearly as possible, to those of the 8th to 13th Divisions, but service battalions whose depots were unable to furnish the requisite numbers of men were to be filled up by volunteers from neighbouring depots where recruits were abundant. In a further effort to clear the serious overcrowding at most depots, Sclater also ordered that, pending the actual formation of these latest battalions, recruits for them should be attached to the battalions of the 8th to 13th Divisions.[61]

The recruiting boom was now at its height and volunteers were swarming in at a pace which defeated all attempts by the War Office to bring order to the situation. In particular the congestion at the depots grew steadily worse during the first few days of September. By 12 September 68,727 men were at infantry depots throughout the country, as against 43,720 on 29 August, and the total for all arms at depots was a staggering 312,360. Six infantry depots contained more than 2,000 recruits each, and the depot of the Cheshire Regiment at Chester had as many as 3,052. Moreover, instead of reducing this congestion, Sclater's decision to attach recruits to the battalions of the first six divisions merely meant that the overcrowding spread to the training centres. According to returns made on 5 September, some battalions of the First New Army were three or four times over establishment. The 8th Cheshire Regiment at Tidworth then had 4,042 other ranks but only ten officers. Another unit in the 13th (Western) Division, the 7th Gloucestershire Regiment, had 3,953 men and 12 officers, and the 6th Duke of Cornwall's Light Infantry, part of the Light Division at Aldershot, had twelve officers and 3,034 other ranks.[62]

It was, perhaps, at this juncture, rather than a week later, that the government should have applied the brake to recruiting. The 'Second Hundred Thousand' had been raised in under a week and on 4 September, in a speech at the Guildhall, Asquith stated that although Kitchener had asked for 200,000 men, between 250,000 and 300,000 had answered the call, of whom London alone had provided 42,000. On 10 September Asquith announced in the House of Commons that of the 500,000 men authorised as an increase to the Regular army a month ago, 439,000 had been attested, exclusive of enlistments into the Territorials. The same day Parliament was asked to sanction the raising of a further 500,000 men.[63] The recruits themselves were by now paying a stiff price for such rapid expansion. On every side there were acute shortages of accommodation, uniforms, weapons, personal equipment, blankets, bedding and even rations but, despite all the evidence of a major breakdown in the machinery for handling recruits, the War Office still pressed ahead with its plans. In view of the army's desperate need for men, it would be unjust to blame Kitchener for trying to secure as many recruits as he could while the tide of national enthusiasm was running high; on the other hand, it must be said that most of the early problems faced by the New Armies were the direct result of his failure to impose some sort of ceiling on enlistments until the War Office was in a position to cope with the influx of volunteers.

These broader issues notwithstanding, the flow of men was sufficient by 9 September to persuade Kitchener to authorise the formation of two more series of divisions, bringing the total of New Army divisions to twenty-four. These were quite apart from the Pals units being raised by private citizens and municipalities, for which no clear scheme of organisation had yet emerged. The plan to form a Regular 8th Division from battalions on garrison duty was finalised, and so the divisions of the First New Army were renumbered 9th to 14th, with the Light Division, originally designated as the 8th, becoming the 14th Division. The second series of six divisions, which had been authorised on 1 September, were numbered 15th to 20th and became known collectively as the Second New Army or 'K 2'. The Third New Army, consisting of the 21st to 26th Divisions, was to be raised immediately, while the Fourth New Army would be formed in due course from the surplus recruits who had been sent to the Special Reserve battalions from 27 August onwards.[64]

The work of organising the battalions of the 15th to 20th Divisions by duplicating those of the 9th to 14th Divisions was already in hand when the Second New Army was formally created by Army Order XII of 11 September 1914.[65] The speed with which the new battalions sprang into existence may be illustrated by citing the example of the 9th Black Watch. The 8th Battalion, part of the 9th (Scottish) Division, had assembled at Aldershot and was at full strength on 3 September but, in accordance with the Adjutant-General's directive, further drafts were posted to it over the next few days, including one of 200 men on 6 September. Three days later, therefore, approval was given to form these surplus drafts into a separate unit, the 9th Battalion, which was to join the 15th (Scottish) Division in the Second New Army.[66] The process was even more rapid in the case of the 20th (Light) Division. On

11 September the huge battalions of the 14th Division were paraded at
Aldershot and company officers were simply told to fall out half their men to
form the new battalions for the 20th Division. Captain C. E. Jesser-Davis,
who had returned from Ceylon to join the Rifle Brigade, wrote:

At about 6 p.m. I was drilling with 'D' Company of the Eighth Battalion when I was
sent to take command of 'C' Company of the Eleventh Battalion. I found three
hundred and twenty men and boys in every variety of civilian attire, mostly rather
shabby (although one man was in possession of a white collar) waiting in the road
with their newspaper parcels under their arms, and had to get them into the very
limited accommodation allotted to me – one barrack-room and two or three bell
tents.[67]

The territorial basis on which the First and Second New Armies had been
organised proved impossible to maintain when the Third New Army was
created on 13 September. The great reserves of manpower were in the
industrial areas of Scotland, South Wales, the Midlands, the north of England
and in London, not in the rural counties or in southern Ireland. Thus, whereas
there were eventually nineteen Service battalions of the Northumberland
Fusiliers, including Pals units, the Devonshire Regiment could contribute
only three Service battalions to Kitchener's New Armies. Even in the first two
New Armies some battalions from predominantly agricultural counties had
to be filled up with recruits from the bigger population centres. The 9th
Devonshire Regiment, which was attached to the 20th (Light) Division,
contained a mere eighty native Devonians, the remainder coming mostly
from London and Birmingham. The 6th Wiltshire Regiment in the 19th
(Western) Division also had a preponderance of London and Birmingham
men. In the Third New Army the 7th Royal Berkshires, part of the 26th
Division, included a platoon of Welsh miners as well as a large number of men
from the Midlands.[68] The situation was worse still in Ireland. The 6th
Leinster Regiment, a battalion of the 10th (Irish) Division in the First New
Army, began recruiting in August but failed to attract the requisite number of
men from its own area in King's County, Queen's County and Meath, and
was strengthened in September by a draft of 600 men from Bristol. The
Leinster Regiment, in fact, managed to form only two Service battalions. In
the 16th (Irish) Division of the Second New Army one battalion, the 7th
Royal Inniskilling Fusiliers, was nearly 500 men short of establishment as late
as April 1915.[69] Some Irish units solved the problem by 'poaching' recruits
from English depots. In September 1914 Captain Godfrey Drage was posted
from Tralee for duty at the depot of the York and Lancaster Regiment at
Pontefract and, acting on his own initiative, seized the opportunity to obtain
men for the 6th and 7th Royal Munster Fusiliers. Drage's impromptu and
purely unofficial appeal to a vast crowd of recruits produced an amazing
response:

. . . I realised that I had very little idea how many men the Munsters could possibly
absorb. However a thousand seemed a good round number and so I announced 'I'm

only authorised to take a thousand of you.' Then I made them strip to the waist and walked down the ranks feeling each man's biceps and asking him what he was in civil life. If he said 'I'm a miner' I took him without more ado. So far I'd got away with everything but, by the time I'd five hundred lined up, the Adjutant of the depot heard about my goings-on and came running up – 'Here I say, Captain Drage, you can't do that! You're taking all my best men.' I thought I'd better not ride my luck too far and so I saluted very subserviently and replied – 'Yes sir, certainly sir, would you like to choose the rest yourself, sir?' He did so and you can imagine what the next five hundred were like. Anyway, I'd got my draft and thought I'd better be off while the going was good . . .[70]

The unauthorised poaching of recruits persisted into 1915. In February that year General Mackinnon, the GOC Western Command, received reports that an officer of the Ulster Division was trying to enlist men in Liverpool. Mackinnon therefore issued an immediate order that 'no recruiting parties are to be sent to recruit outside their own areas, unless leave has first been obtained'. This order halted the activities of the officer in question, but Mackinnon felt it necessary to reassure Lord Derby, 'There will, no doubt, still be men who will only enlist in Irish regiments, and those will be attested in Liverpool, and sent to their depots in the ordinary course, but no recruiting agent from Ireland will be allowed in Liverpool.'[71]

A brief comparison of the contributions of different regions and counties in terms of infantry battalions for the first three New Armies will serve to underline the uneven nature of recruiting patterns in the opening months of the war. For example, Lancashire, with thirty-three Service battalions, Scotland, with thirty, and Yorkshire, with twenty-five, together provided more than a third of the overall total of 250 battalions. In contrast, the four counties of south-west England (Devon, Dorset, Cornwall and Somerset) provided only eleven battalions between them. Southern Ireland, having furnished eight battalions for the First New Army and seven for the Second, did not contribute any to the Third New Army. Because of this variation in response, the titles 'Light', 'Eastern', 'Northern' and so on were dropped from the divisions of the Third New Army, and instead of brigades being composed of four battalions from four different regiments, as usually happened in the first two New Armies, it now became increasingly common for two battalions or more from the same regiment to serve side by side in a brigade.[72]

The most significant feature of the first three New Armies, however, was that they were drawn from a much wider span of society than the pre-war Regular army. Within two or three weeks the social composition of the army had changed almost beyond recognition. Following Kitchener's appeal, men who had previously regarded service in the ranks as the final refuge of the unemployed and unemployable now rushed to enlist as privates. The 5th Cameron Highlanders, for instance, contained a whole company from the Glasgow Stock Exchange, and the regiment's 6th Battalion included a large body of students from Glasgow University. In the 27th Field Ambulance, a unit of the 9th (Scottish) Division, there were architects, farmers, under-graduates, miners and bricklayers. Lieutenant-Colonel Cobb recalled some of those who served under him in the 5th Oxfordshire and Buckinghamshire Light Infantry:

There were a great many from most respectable homes and businesses. Some gentlemen, many indoor servants, grooms, gardeners, chauffeurs, gamekeepers, well-to-do tradesmen, hotel-keepers, clerks etc., etc., to say nothing of the engineers, fitters and hands from the great works in Birmingham and Coventry. All these men had left good, comfortable homes, with good wages, and had come voluntarily out of a sheer sense of duty. They were brought suddenly face to face wtih every sort of discomfort on Old Dean Common – discomforts which were absolutely unavoidable, because of the impossibility of supplying the wants of 500,000 recruits at a moment's notice. Yet they faced it all in a splendid way . . . and with never a murmur.[73]

III

Cobb's men may have refrained from complaining but it could not be concealed that, by the beginning of September, the recruiting boom was getting out of hand. Besides having to deal with the congestion and confusion at the depots and training centres, the War Office also had to act swiftly to avert another crisis at the recruiting offices, which were again becoming swamped by the flood of volunteers. In some places it was physically more difficult to enlist than it had been early in August. A survey by *The Times* on 2 September revealed that, at many of the forty-two recruiting stations in London, men were waiting up to eight hours to enlist, even though most recruiting offices now had large clerical staffs and teams of doctors working in relays. Consequently 'thousands of young men had to be temporarily dismissed with their desire to enrol in the service of their country as yet unsatisfied'.[74]

The desperate efforts of recruiting staffs to speed up the enlistment process and clear the bottlenecks during this period resulted in a general lowering of standards, particularly on the medical side. Large numbers of civil prac-titioners who had never previously examined recruits and who were ignorant of the physical requirements of the army were now being asked to carry out the medical examinations at the recruiting centres. Because of the pressure on the recruiting offices, many of these civilian doctors attempted to inspect far more men than they could examine properly in the time available. The fact that civil practitioners were paid a fee of 2s 6d for every recruit examined provided them with a further incentive to handle as many as they could in a day. The inevitable outcome was that medical examinations were often extremely superficial. Disabilities such as varicose veins, bad teeth, hernia, defective eyesight, middle-ear disease and even lameness, all of which should easily have been detected, were either missed or deliberately overlooked.[75] According to Lietenant-Colonel H. Clay, at one time the Chief Recruiting Staff Officer, London District, some men avoided the medical examination altogether:

The system was this: 600, 700 or 1,000 men went to the depot. The recruiting officer went outside and fell in the party and called the roll, and the party was put under the command of an officer, an NCO, or a civil policeman, whoever was handy, and marched off to go to, say, the 9th Surreys at Shoreham. Bill Jones in the back row said, 'I don't want to go to Shoreham.' Other men said the same, and before the party had marched off 20 to 30 had changed places with other men who had not been medically examined.[76]

These shortcomings in the enlistment system were not immediately apparent but in the following months, as the numbers of unfit men being discharged from the army grew progressively larger, the Army Council was compelled to tighten up the arrangments for the medical examination of recruits. The indiscriminate recruiting of the opening weeks also had serious long-term effects on industry, for the many skilled men who joined the army at that time could not always be replaced later in the war.

In the short term the government faced increasing criticism, even from its own supporters, over the treatment of recruits. In the first week of September Kitchener's senior colleagues at the War Office persuaded him to institute a scheme of deferred enlistment under which recruits, once attested, would pass into the reserve and would be allowed to return home with a subsistence allowance of 6*d* a day until the army was ready to take them. By adopting this scheme it was hoped that, while the recruiting campaign proceeded at full throttle, the War Office could call up the attested men in successive quotas, thus regulating the rate of flow into the depots and training centres.[77] The trouble was that no attempt was made to announce this change in the press and many who had given up their jobs to enlist now found themselves unemployed and with only a paltry daily allowance.

That week, on 4 September, Kitchener also reluctantly agreed to sugge-sions made by Leo Amery and by Lord Midleton that the Territorial Force County Associations might share at least part of the burden of housing, clothing and training New Army recruits. A committee, chaired by Midleton, was immediately formed to co-ordinate the activities of the County Associa-tions in this respect, and the Duke of Buccleuch gave up Montague House so that it could serve as the committee's headquarters. The Midleton Com-mittee, which included Amery, Lord Esher and Lieutenant-General Sir Robert Baden-Powell among its members, met at Montague House on 7 September and worked tirelessly over the next few days to instruct the County Associations about their additional responsibilities and to suggest to them how they could be most helpful. According to Amery, the Midleton Committee 'discovered accommodation in all sorts of unexpected places' as well as unearthing new sources of supply for cloth, boots and various items of equipment.[78]

However, when Parliament reassembled on 9 September a lengthy attack on the recruiting policy of the government and War Office was launched by

Major-General Sir Ivor Herbert, the Lord Lieutenant of Monmouthshire and Liberal MP for Monmouthshire South. Having described the poor conditions at the depots and training centres, Herbert accused the War Office of lack of foresight in the arrangements for the reception of recruits, saying:

... I have had a staff of thirty or forty ladies or gentlemen doing the work of recruiting, making out registration papers and so on during all that time, without demanding a single penny of money. That is the patriotic spirit that has been shown in the county, and the response made by the Department over which the right hon. Gentleman presides is that the men who come up are to have sixpence a day, after they have lost their employment and, in many cases, broken up their homes. . . . I can only say that if this is to be the beginning, God help us before we are through with what has to be done! If this is to be an example of the organisation now at the War Office, it is time that the Secretary of State, who has the reputation of being a good organiser, should vindicate that reputation.[79]

The attack impelled the government to increase the subsistence allowance at once to 3s per day, although the way in which the decision was taken caused some disagreement inside the War Office. Rawlinson, who appears to have instigated the proposal, recorded in his journal on 10 September:

Rather a fuss in the office today, as there was a misunderstanding about my proposal of an allowance of 3s a day for the recruits sent to their homes. Sclater told me that it had been agreed, so I thought he had submitted it to K. I therefore told Illingworth (the Liberal Chief Whip), who told the Prime Minister, who announced it to the Cabinet. K. knew nothing about it, and was furious so I got it in the neck! K. threatened to resign if politicians interfered with him in his work, and I wrote to the Prime Minister to say there had been a misunderstanding.

Rawlinson delivered the letter to Asquith in person and explained the situation. The Prime Minister at once sent a note to Kitchener, saying that he thought it essential that he should be able to tell the House of Commons 'what is the provision to be made for the men for whom accommodation cannot be found'. Kitchener was therefore finally induced to agree to the new allowance and Asquith announced the increase in the House later that day.[80]

Meanwhile, the Army Council had been pressing Kitchener to take more positive steps to control the recruiting flood. Here too Kitchener was reluctant to alter his policy, telling Sir Stanley von Donop, the Master-General of the Ordnance, 'I have held up my finger, and the men are flocking to me in thousands; how can I now hold up my hand, and tell them to go back?'[81] Sir Charles Harris met with much the same reaction at first:

I went to him and said that only a slackening of the rush could enable us to . . . clear up the muddle. He drew me over to the window looking on Whitehall and, pointing to a gang of men at work, said, 'You ask me to slack off recruiting. The British public has taken charge, and if you and I get in the way we shall be hanged on the lamp post those men are putting up' . . .

Harris, however, continued to urge that a brake should be put on recruiting 'by putting up the physical standards, till we can get straight again'.[82] As on the question of the subsistence allowance, Kitchener eventually yielded to the pressure. On Friday 11 September the War Office announced through the press that the minimum height requirement for all recruits other than ex-soldiers enlisting in the infantry would henceforth be raised to 5ft 6in. Simultaneously, the minimum chest measurement was increased to 35½in.[83] Unfortunately for the Army Council, this step had a more profound effect than anticipated, for it gave the impression that the War Office felt free to pick and choose men and might not need so many recruits as it had originally suggested. Moreover, some 10,000 recruits who had enlisted shortly before 11 September, and who had left their jobs to join their new units, were now rejected as too small.[84]

Given that the accommodation problem was still far from being solved, it was odd that Kitchener should have chosen this very moment to dispense with the Midleton Committee. On 11 September its members received a message from Kitchener telling them that their services were no longer required. No official reason was supplied for this abrupt decision. Midleton felt that Kitchener, having been stung by Sir Ivor Herbert's criticisms in the House of Commons, was anxious to shift the blame to the committee. Amery thought that it was a consequence of the War Office measures to check the flow of recruits. He believed that, by raising the physical standards, Kitchener hoped somehow to be able to cope with enough men for the first three New Armies through the existing War Office system, without having to rely upon a Territorial organisation which he had unwillingly accepted but disliked as not being totally under his control.[85] Amery was probably nearer the truth, although it is equally likely that the success of the Pals movement in the first days of September had offered Kitchener an alternative means of spreading the administrative load without having to endure the potentially troublesome presence of men such as Amery and Lord Esher at his elbow.

12,527 men enlisted on 11 September but that was the last day on which a five-figure total was registered. The following week the daily average fell to 6,382.[86] The recruiting boom had come to an end, and the enlistment returns never again approached the high-water mark of the first week of September. Nevertheless, between 4 August and 12 September 478,893 men had joined the Army, 301,971 having enlisted in the fortnight after 30 August. The recruiting boom may have been comparatively short, climbing suddenly to a peak after a slow start, but, while it lasted, it had gone a long way towards providing Britain with the first mass army in her history.

Notes

1 *The Times*, 5 August 1914; V. W. Germains, *The Kitchener Armies*, Davies, London, 1930, p. 57.
2 *The Times*, 8 August 1914.
3 These figures are taken from the daily recruiting returns submitted to the Adjutant-General for the period 4 August–27 December 1914, Adjutant-General's papers, WO 162/3.
4 *Ibid.*, WO 162/3; *The Times*, 9 and 10 August 1914.

5   *The Times*, 7 and 8 August 1914.
6   *Ibid.*, 12 August 1914.
7   *The 'Leader' Local War Record, 1914–1915*, Coulton, Nelson, 1915, p. 22; Major J. H. Kennedy, *Attleborough in War Time*, London and Norwich Press, 1920, p. 18.
8   L. S. Amery, *My Political Life*, II, p. 26.
9   *Ibid.*, p. 28.
10 Amery, *My Political Life*, II, pp. 27–8; George F. Stone and Charles Wells (eds.), *Bristol and the Great War*, Arrowsmith, Bristol, 1920, pp. 108–9; Minutes of the Executive Committee of the Bristol Citizens' Recruiting Committee, 20 August 1914; *Western Daily Press*, 13 August and 1 September 1914; *Bristol Times and Mirror*, 27 August 1914. For a detailed analysis of recruiting in Bristol see J. M. Osborne, *The Voluntary Recruiting Movement in Britain, 1914–1916*, Garland, New York, 1982.
11 Daily recruiting returns submitted to the Adjutant-General, 9 to 15 August 1914, WO 162/3.
12 *The Times*, 16 and 18 August 1914.
13 E. C. Pain, *History of Deal, 1914–1953*, Pain, Deal, 1953, p. 8.
14 *Brighton Gazette*, 15 August 1914.
15 Martin Middlebrook, *Boston at War*, Kay, Boston, 1974, pp. 21–2.
16 The Rev. Lawrence P. Field, *The Souvenir Book of Eye, 1914–1919*, Eye Patriotic Association, 1920, p. 15.
17 Captain C. H. Cooke, *Historical Records of the 16th (Service) Battalion Northumberland Fusiliers*, Newcastle and Gateshead Chamber of Commerce, 1923, p. 1.
18 Randal Sidebotham, *Hyde in Wartime: Soldiers', Sailors' and Civilians' Deeds*, North Cheshire Herald, 1916, pp. 2, 17.
19 *Brighton Herald*, 15 August 1914.
20 *The Times*, 12 August 1914.
21 *Ibid.*, 16 August 1914.
22 *Ibid.*, 20 August 1914.
23 *Ibid.*, 21 August 1914.
24 *Liverpool Daily Post*, 19 August 1914.
25 *Extracts from the Diary of Brigadier-General the Hon. Robert White*, Dimbleby, Richmond, n.d., pp. 3–4.
26 William H. Oakley, *Guildford in the Great War*, Billing, Guildford, 1934, pp. 32–3.
27 Daily recruiting returns submitted to the Adjutant-General, 16 to 22 August 1914, WO 162/3.
28 *The Times*, 27 August 1914.
29 *Ibid.*, 28 August 1914.
30 *Ibid.*, 28 August 1914.
31 *Parliamentary Debates, House of Commons, 1914*, LXVI, cols. 38–9.
32 *The Times*, 25 August 1914.
33 Daily recruiting returns submitted to the Adjutant-General, 23 to 29 August 1914, WO 162/3.
34 Daily recruiting returns for cities, 23 to 29 August 1914, NATS 1/84.
35 *Debates on Army Affairs, House of Lords, 1914*, col. 453.
36 *The Times*, 26 August 1914.
37 *Brighton Herald*, 5 September 1914.
38 *The Times*, 1 September 1914.
39 *Daily Mail*, 31 August 1914.
40 *Parliamentary Debates, House of Commons, 1914*, LXVI, col. 43.

41 Minutes of meeting of the Military Members of the Army Council, 27 August 1914, WO 163/44; *The Times,* 28 August 1914.

42 Minutes of meeting of the Military Members of the Army Council, 27 August 1914, WO 163/44.

43 *The Times,* 29 August 1914.

44 Minutes of preliminary meeting of the Parliamentary Recruiting Committee, 27 August 1914, BL Add. Mss 54192.

45 Minutes of meetings of the Parliamentary Recruiting Committee, 28 and 31 August 1914, BL Add. Mss 54192.

46 Kitchener to French, 27 August 1914, quoted in Sir George Arthur, *Life of Lord Kitchener,* III, pp. 39–41.

47 *The Times,* 30 August 1914.

48 *Daily Telegraph,* 31 August 1914; *Daily Express,* 31 August 1914.

49 *Parliamentary Debates, House of Commons, 1914,* LXVI, cols. 494–8.

50 *The Times,* 26 and 29 August 1914; W. H. Scott, *Leeds in the Great War, 1914–1918,* Libraries and Arts Committee, Leeds, 1923, p. 13; Thomas Chalmers (ed.), *An Epic of Glasgow: History of the 15th Battalion the Highland Light Infantry (City of Glasgow Regiment),* McCallum, Glasgow, 1934, p. ix; W. H. Oakley, *op. cit.,* pp. 32–5.

51 William Robertson (ed.), *Middlesbrough's Effort in the Great War,* Jordison, Middlesbrough, n.d., pp. 6–7; *The Tatler,* 26 August 1914; *Stroud News,* 4 and 11 September 1914; *The Times,* 26 August, 2 September, 4 September and 12 September 1914.

52 Dailing recruiting returns submitted to the Adjutant-General, 30 August to 5 September 1914, WO 162/3.

53 Daily recruiting returns for cities, 3 September 1914, NATS 1/84.

54 Major W. de B. Wood (ed.), *The History of the King's Shropshire Light Infantry in the Great War, 1914–1918,* Medici Society, London, 1925, p. 123.

55 Lieutenant-Colonel C. H. Cobb, in *The Oxfordshire and Buckinghamshire Light Infantry Chronicle,* Vol. XXIV, 4 August 1914–31 July 1915, pp. 348–9.

56 F. Loraine Petre, *The Royal Berkshire Regiment (Princess Charlotte of Wales's),* Vol. II. *1914–1918,* The Barracks, Reading, 1925, p. 205.

57 Circular from Adjutant-General's Department to GOCs-in-C of Commands, 24 August 1914, WO 162/3.

58 Minutes of meeting of the Military Members of the Army Council, 29 August 1914, WO 163/44.

59 Note on the strengths of infantry depots, according to returns submitted to the Adjutant-General's Department on 29 August 1914, WO 162/4.

60 Circular from Adjutant-General's Department to GOCs-in-C of Commands, 30 August 1914, WO 162/3.

61 Minutes of meeting of the Military Members of the Army Council, 1 September 1914, WO 163/44; Circular from Adjutant-General's Department to GOCs-in-C of Commands, 2 September 1914, WO 162/24.

62 Note on the strengths of Service battalions of the First New Army, 5 September 1914, WO 162/4; Statement showing the strengths of infantry depots, 12 September 1914, WO 162/24.

63 *Parliamentary Debates, House of Commons, 1914,* LXVI, cols. 663–9; *The Times,* 5 September 1914.

64 Minutes of meetings of the Military Members of the Army Council, 9, 10 and 13 September 1914, WO 163/44.

65 Army Order XII of 11 September 1914 (AO 382 of 1914).

66 Major-General A. G. Wauchope (ed.), *A History of The Black Watch (Royal Highlanders) in the Great War, 1914–1918,* Vol. III, *New Army,* Medici Society,

London, 1926, p. 107.

67   Captain C. E. Jesser-Davis, in Reginald Berkeley, *The History of the Rifle Brigade in the War of 1914–1918*, Vol. I, Rifle Brigade Club, London, 1927, p. 108.

68   C. T. Atkinson, *The Devonshire Regiment, 1914–1918*, Eland, Exeter, 1926, pp. 54–5; Colonel N. C. E. Kenrick, *The Story of the Wiltshire Regiment (Duke of Edinburgh's), 1756–1959*, Gale & Polden, Aldershot, 1963, p. 147; Petre, *op. cit.*, p. 286.

69   Lieutenant-Colonel F. E. Whitton (ed.), *The History of the Prince of Wales's Leinster Regiment (Royal Canadians)*, Part II, *The Great War and the Disband-ment of the Regiment*, Gale & Polden, Aldershot, 1924, p. 97; G. A. Cooper-Walker, *The Book of the Seventh Service Battalion the Royal Inniskilling Fusi-liers: from Tipperary to Ypres*, Brindley, Dublin, 1920, pp. 1–11.

70   Commander Charles Drage, *Chindwin to Criccieth: the Life of Godfrey Drage*, Evans, Caernarvon, 1956, p. 100.

71   Western Command Orders, 13 February 1915, No. 4403; Mackinnon to Derby, 21 February 1915, LRO 920 DER(17)33.

72   Major A. F. Becke, *History of the Great War: Order of Battle of Divisions*, Part 3A, *New Army Divisions (9–26)*, HMSO, London, 1938, pp. 3–149.

73   *Historical Records of the Queen's Own Cameron Highlanders*, Vol. IV, Blackwood, Edinburgh, 1931, p. 47; Lieutenant-Colonel Norman MacLeod (ed.), *War History of the 6th (Service) Battalion Queen's Own Cameron High-landers*, Blackwood, 1934, p. 2; W. G. Cook, unpublished account, 1975, IWM 77/183/1; Lieutenant-Colonel Cobb, *op. cit.*, p. 350.

74   *The Times*, 3 September 1914.

75   Major-General Sir W. G. Macpherson, *Official History of the War: Medical Services, General History*, Vol. I, HMSO, London, 1923, pp. 118–20.

76   Evidence of Lieutenant-Colonel H. Clay, *Report of the War Office Committee of Enquiry into Shell-shock*, HMSO, London, 1922, p. 175.

77   Telegram from Adjutant-General's Department to GOCs-in-C of Commands, 4 September 1914, WO 159/18; Major-General Sir Frederick Maurice, *The Life of General Lord Rawlinson of Trent*, p. 99.

78   Midleton to St Loe Strachey, 10 September 1914, St Loe Strachey papers, HLRO S/24/2/18; Midleton to Bonar Law, 14 September 1914, Bonar Law papers, HLRO 34/6/44; Amery, *My Political Life*, II, pp. 29–31.

79   *Parliamentary Debates, House of Commons, 1914*, LXVI, cols. 607–15.

80   Maurice, *op. cit.*, p. 99; Asquith to Kitchener, 10 September 1914, Kitchener papers, PRO 30/57/76; *Parliamentary Debates, House of Commons, 1914*, LXVI, col. 668.

81   Speech by Sir Stanley von Donop to the Kitchener Scholars' Association, 5 December 1930, von Donop papers, IWM 69/74/1.

82   Sir Charles Harris, 'Contacts with Kitchener', Part II, *Yorkshire Observer*, 21 November 1939.

83   *The Times*, 12 September 1914; Telegram from Adjutant-General's Department to OCs Districts, 11 September 1914, WO 159/18; Recruiting Memorandum No. 72, 17 September 1914, WO 159/18.

84   Sclater to St Loe Strachey, 5 December 1914, St Loe Strachey papers, HLRO S/24/2/11; Amery, *op. cit.*, pp. 30–1.

85   Amery, *op. cit.*, pp. 31–2; Edward David (ed.), *Inside Asquith's Cabinet: from the Diaries of Charles Hobhouse*, p. 190.

86   Daily recruiting returns submitted to the Adjutant-General, 11 to 19 September 1914, WO 162/3.

3

The Pals battalions

We have seen that the inability of the War Office to cope with the recruiting flood of August and early September 1914 forced Kitchener to rely to an increasing extent upon civilian help in raising the New Armies. Before a month had elapsed Kitchener was only too pleased to accept offers of assistance from MPs, local authorities and leading citizens, who, throughout the country, lent or hired halls to accommodate bigger recruiting offices, collected civilian doctors and clerks to deal with the thousands of volunteers, and often housed and fed the men until they could be sent off to their training centres. The most striking manifestation of this surge of civilian effort, however, lay in the formation of the Pals battalions. These units were mainly raised by local authorities, industrialists or committees of private citizens and were generally composed of men who lived in a particular city or district or who shared a common social and occupational background.

In terms of infantry battalions alone, the Pals units ultimately comprised a substantial proportion of Kitchener's army and did much to give that army its distinct character. Whereas 250 Service battalions and eighty-two reserve battalions were produced by the normal machinery, 145 Service and seventy reserve battalions were locally raised. This meant that, excluding the new Territorial units formed during this period, 215, or 38 per cent, of the 557 Service and reserve battalions which came into existence between August 1914 and June 1916 were raised initially by bodies other than the War Office. The extent of the shift towards locally raised units can be recognised even more clearly if one examines the origins of the front-line Service battalions formed after September 1914. From 1 October onwards only nineteen Service battalions were raised by the War Office through the traditional channels for the first three New Armies, while eighty-four locally raised battalions were formed.[1] Thus, so far as the infantry was concerned, the War Office, less than two months after the outbreak of war, was already concentrating on recruitment for the Special Reserve battalions and reserve units of the First, Second and Third New Armies, leaving the raising of new infantry battalions

almost completely to local authorities and the Territorial Force County Associations.

The Pals battalions were, above all, a reflection of Edwardian civic pride and a product of the accelerated urbanisation which, by the first decade of the twentieth century, had transformed society. In the early 1870s there were only thirty-seven towns or cities in England and Wales with a population of more than 50,000, yet this total had doubled by 1901. Ten years later, in 1911, the five principal conurbations in England each had populations of well over one million, including Greater London, with 7,256,000, south-east Lancashire, with 2,328,000, the West Midlands, with 1,634,000, West Yorkshire, with 1,590,000 and Merseyside, with 1,157,000.[2] The rapid growth of the cities and towns caused urban poverty and overcrowding on a level unknown to the early Victorians but it also led to an immense increase in the power and influence of local government, symbolised by the proliferation of public offices, parks, museums, libraries, baths, schools, hospitals, waterworks, tramways and sewage farms. Creative municipal life flourished in late Victorian and Edwardian Britain, particularly in the provinces. As Sir Charles Petrie has observed, the influence of Whitehall was not then as marked as it was later to become, two world wars having resulted in a concentration of authority in the hands of the national government that would have seemed impossible to the vast majority of Edwardians.[3]

The provincial cities unquestionably allowed more room for the exercise of middle-class initiative and for a greater degree of independence and self-help among the working class than was attainable in the smaller towns and villages, where the social structure was more rigid. In their newspapers the big cities possessed an effective vehicle for the focusing of attention on local issues and enterprises. They also had large numbers of voluntary bodies, catering for a wide variety of specialised interests. Urban society in Edwardian Britain encompassed a huge network of organisations and clubs, ranging from unions, working men's institutes, churches, chapels and Sunday schools to Old Boys' Associations, the Boy Scouts, Boys' Brigade and Church Lads' Brigade, cricket, rugby, football and cycling clubs and many more. For all the variations in wages and living conditions within an urban area, these organisations helped to give people a sense of community and nurtured a shared pride in their own city which frequently overrode class consciousness. When the stresses of war fused local pride with national patriotism, the mixture proved irresistible, as the raisers of the Pals battalions were quick to perceive in the autumn of 1914. As Malcolm Brown has pointed out, it was therefore 'entirely natural that local communities should sponsor the founding of locally based battalions precisely intended to preserve the companionship of peace in the circumstances of war'.[4]

There was nothing essentially new in the Pals concept as it emerged in 1914. Many first-line Territorial units and, before them, Volunteer battalions had contained whole companies of men drawn from the same community or work place. Indeed, it can be argued that the Volunteer and Territorial Forces had been built on that very foundation. The chief difference in 1914 was that, with the appearance of the Pals battalions, the concept was applied on a significant scale for the first time to the raising of units for active service abroad rather than home defence.

Lord Derby is usually given the credit for translating this basic idea into a scheme whereby local authorities would be allowed to raise battalions which men might be encouraged to join on the promise that they could serve with their friends, neighbours and workmates. Derby certainly discussed such a proposal with Kitchener on 24 August and secured the latter's consent for the raising of a battalion from among the business houses of Liverpool.[5] However, there is some evidence to indicate that the scheme actually originated inside the War Office. On 19 August, five days before Derby's meeting with Kitchener, Rawlinson lunched with Major the Hon. Robert White at the Travellers' Club in Pall Mall and informed him that Kitchener was anxious to get a further supply of recruits from London for the Royal Fusiliers. Rawlinson asked White to raise a battalion composed of men who worked in the City, and later that day he drafted a formal letter of confirmation which clearly hinted how White might proceed with the task. 'I understand,' Rawlinson wrote, 'that there are many City employees who would be willing to enlist if they were assured that they would serve with their friends, and I suggest that you collect names and addresses of those who would be willing to serve in the Service Battalion of the Royal Fusiliers in Lord Kitchener's new Army.'[6] White spent the whole of the next day addressing letters to City firms and talking to representatives from Lloyd's and the Baltic Exchange, as well as consulting the chairman of the Stock Exchange. A recruiting office was opened in Throgmorton Street on 21 August and 210 men were enrolled in the first few hours. By 27 August the Stockbrokers' Battalion, as it was popularly known, was 1,600 strong. Parading in all sorts of clothing from silk hats and morning coats to caps and Norfolk jackets, the men were inspected in Temple Gardens by Lord Roberts on 29 August and then marched to the Tower, where they were sworn in as a body by the Lord Mayor of London. In another five days the unit, which shortly became the 10th (Service) Battalion of the Royal Fusiliers, was ready to leave for training at Colchester.[7]

The Bristol Citizens' Recruiting Committee was, in fact, also thinking along these lines during the last week of August. On 25 August the chairman had placed before the committee 'a form which he had drawn up in connection with the better class young men in Bristol, appertaining to a Citizens' Battalion'. Approval for such a unit was immediately sought but, although the War Office authorised its formation on 30 August, administrative problems caused the official reply to Bristol's request to be delayed for a few days. Meanwhile, on 3 September, the Bristol Citizens' Recruiting Committee, who were confident that permission would eventually be received, decided to proceed in any case and to make an announcement about the battalion the following day. The people of Bristol had therefore been among the first to suggest the raising of a local citizens' battalion even if other cities actually started recruiting their Pals units before them.[8]

Whoever was responsible for planting the seed of the Pals movement, it was in the cities of the industrial north that it really took root. Once Kitchener had sanctioned the raising of such a formation in Liverpool, Derby obtained approval for the command of the new battalion to be given to his own brother, Major the Hon. Ferdinand Stanley, who was then serving with the Grenadier Guards. A letter containing Derby's preliminary appeal appeared in the Liverpool newspapers on 27 August. The appeal was couched in terms very similar to those used by Rawlinson eight days before. 'It has been suggested to me,' Derby explained, 'that there are many men, such as clerks and others engaged in commercial business, who wish to serve their country and would be willing to enlist in the battalion of Lord Kitchener's new Army if they felt assured that they would be able to serve with their friends and not be put in a battalion with unknown men as their companions.' As if unsure what the response would be, Derby added that before starting on the work he would 'like to have some idea as to whether such an appeal would be a success' and invited all those who were interested to attend a meeting at the Territorial drill hall in St Anne Street the following evening.[9]

Lord Derby need not have worried. The local newspapers immediately gave the scheme their enthusiastic support. On 28 August the *Liverpool Daily Post* recorded that the heads of the commercial and shipping houses in the city had 'adopted the pressing persuasiveness of recruiting sergeants' and forecast that more than one 'battalion of friends' would be forthcoming: 'Liverpool, indeed, may set an example to other places in showing how readily office mates may become camp mates.'[10] That evening more than 1,500 men turned up at the drill hall in St Anne Street. The room set aside for the meeting was soon crammed to capacity, with hundreds standing in the aisles and balcony. The crowd soon became so dense that it was necessary to arrange a second meeting in a larger room downstairs. It was at the earlier of the two meetings that Lord Derby first publicly referred to the new unit as a 'battalion of pals', a term which was to be widely adopted in other northern cities over the next few days. Although he announced that no one would be attested until the following Monday, the men at both meetings voted *en masse* in favour of his proposals. Before midnight Derby was able to inform Kitchener by telegram that the battalion was already full.[11] Less than forty-eight hours later he was considering raising a second Pals unit on Merseyside. As he wrote to General Mackinnon on 30 August, 'I have many applications from outside districts who are not big enough to form battalions of their own and are exactly the same class of man who want to come in and therefore with very little difficulty I shall be able to get two battalions.'[12]

To prevent unnecessary congestion when the work of enlistment began at

St George's Hall on Monday 31 August, separate tables were allotted to the different branches of Liverpool's trade and commerce. These included the Cotton Association, the Corn Trade Association, the Stock Exchange, the provision and sugar trades, the seed, oil and cake trade, the timber trade, fruit and wood brokers, the Law Society and chartered accountants, the banks and insurance companies and the Cunard and White Star steamship lines. Recruits from various firms gathered at their respective trade exchanges or other pre-arranged points before marching to St George's Hall, 120 men coming from the Cunard offices and 218 from the Cotton Exchange. By ten o'clock in the morning 1,050 men had been attested, and more batches were arriving every few minutes. The process of attestation continued in this way throughout the week, and in five days the total of recruits reached 3,000, enough for three battalions. Since authority had been given for only one battalion, Rawlinson told Derby and his brother to rest content for the time being. Derby, in fact, was forced to take to his bed through overwork and became so ill that he had to be operated upon shortly afterwards. With the formation of the 1st, 2nd and 3rd City Battalions, later officially designated the 17th, 18th and 19th Battalions of the King's (Liverpool) Regiment, recruiting for the Liverpool Pals came to a temporary halt. However, a 4th City Battalion – the 20th King's (Liverpool) Regiment – was raised in October.[13]

Lord Derby was also associated with the raising of several Pals battalions in Manchester. On 28 August, the day after his appeal was published in the Liverpool press, a group of influential Manchester employers met at the Town Hall under the auspices of the Lord Mayor and resolved to recruit a battalion from the warehouses and offices in the city. The unit was to be known as the Manchester Clerks' and Warehousemen's Battalion. At the same meeting A. Herbert Dixon, the chairman of the Fine Cotton Spinners & Doublers Association, proposed that another battalion should be raised from men working in the engineering trades. The recruiting officer invited to attend the meeting was lukewarm about the proposals, believing that they might interfere with his duties. He 'seemed hardly able to grasp the main idea, namely, the better spirit obtained by those acquainted with one another working together', Arthur Taylor, a local cotton manufacturer, told Derby.[14] Nevertheless, an organising committee was formed and, before the meeting ended it was agreed to set up a special guarantee fund of some £15,000 to provide the troops with uniforms and equipment. A telegram was sent at once to the War Office offering to raise, clothe and equip a battalion of Manchester men entirely at the city's expense. Lord Derby was invited to become the unit's honorary colonel.[15]

By 1 September War Office approval had been received and recruiting was in progress. On that day the Lord Mayor swore in 800 men in a body, employees from large firms being put in the same companies and platoons wherever possible. Within twenty-four hours the ordinary channels of recruiting were blocked and the crowds of eager volunteers in Albert Square began to chafe at the delays. Emergency accommodation was found in the Free Trade Hall and in the Albert Hall, immediately opposite. The men were assembled in the gallery of the Free Trade Hall and, shepherded by the city police, were marched in groups of fifty across to the Albert Hall, where the medical examinations and attestations took place. On 3 September Arthur Taylor was able to let Lord Derby know that the flow of recruits was sufficient to ensure three battalions and that the raising committee intended to try for more. Even the previously unenthusiastic recruiting officer had 'undergone a process of regeneration and is working admirably – such is your Lordship's influence', Taylor added. The 3rd City Battalion was complete by 9 September and plans were made to recruit a fourth, which would contain men employed by various local authorities, including the Manchester Corporation, neighbouring County and Urban District Councils, Education Committees and Boards of Poor Law Guardians. The 4th City Battalion was itself up to strength by 16 September. Thus in just over a fortnight Manchester had raised four battalions, the equivalent of a brigade of infantry. Subscriptions to the guarantee fund soon totalled £26,701, the largest single contribution of £7,000 coming from the Gas Department of the Manchester Corporation. E. Tootal Broadhurst, a prominent member of the original committee, personally donated £1,000.[16]

Birmingham too was quick to follow Liverpool's lead. Here also the intention was to raise one battalion from the business and commercial classes. The scheme was introduced to local citizens in the *Birmingham Daily Post* on 28 August and the next morning Alderman Bowater, the deputy mayor, told Kitchener that the city was prepared to recruit and equip a battalion of young businessmen. Kitchener replied on 30 August that such a unit 'would be most acceptable and a valuable addition to His Majesty's forces'. The Birmingham Corporation, however, had profited from the experiences of the opening fortnight of the war and wisely decided to defer enlistment until its own recruiting machinery was properly organised. To prevent local enthusiasm from evaporating in the meantime, volunteers were invited to send in their names to the offices of the *Daily Post*, a list of those who had done so being published each day. By the end of the following week, 4,500 men had submitted their names. A large proportion of these were engaged in non-manual occupations, and included teachers and shop assistants as well as articled clerks and other office workers. Thus, before the special recruiting office had opened, permission was sought from Kitchener to raise a second battalion and there were still enough names on the *Daily Post*'s register to form a third.

Every effort was made by the authorities to allow friends to join up together and, to guide the officials who were to issue the 'calling up' notices, lists were compiled of all men who worked for a particular firm or who were members of the same Old Boys' Association. The recruiting clerks themselves were mainly corporation employees. In most cases the men on the lists were sent a postcard two days in advance telling them the time at which the recruiting office would be in a position to deal with them. When they had been attested, the men were permitted to return to their homes and jobs until they moved off to a training camp. Recruits were therefore not only spared the ordeal of a long wait at the recruiting office but also avoided the discomforts of the congested regimental depot. The enrolling of the 1st Birmingham Battalion began at the Art Gallery extension in Great Charles Street on 7 September and that of the 2nd Battalion a week later. Wise as the corporation's scheme of controlled enlistment was, some men tired of the delay and joined other units, so the enlistment of the 3rd Battalion took longer than expected. Meanwhile, following a joint appeal by the deputy mayor and the *Daily Post*, local firms and private citizens had contributed well over £10,000 towards an equipment fund for the new battalions, the sum ultimately rising to about £17,000. Individual donations ranged from the £1,000 subscribed by the Birmingham Small Arms Company to a shilling sent by an anonymous well-wisher.[17]

Originally, special funds of the type described above appear to have been intended more as a patriotic gesture than anything else, but before very long they became vital to the whole development of the Pals movement. It is clear that, by the beginning of September, Kitchener regarded the raising of Pals battalions by local authorities both as a means of relieving the pressure on the War Office recruiting organisation and as a way of easing some of the short-term financial problems created by the sudden expansion of the army. He therefore decided to sanction local battalions only when the raisers themselves were prepared to bear the bulk of the initial expenses. On 4 September the War Office informed the regional commands of Kitchener's hope 'that those large cities and private committees which are now raising or contemplate raising complete battalions will be able to make arrangements in connection with County Associations to find training grounds and housing or tentage and to clothe and feed the men on a contract scale fixed by the War Office, until they can be taken over by the military authorities'.[18] Eight days later, members of the Army Council were given to understand that this was now a firm policy.[19] The basic costs incurred by the raising committees were subsequently refunded, mostly in the summer of 1915, but while they were being fed, housed, clothed and equipped by bodies other than the War Office the Pals battalions were virtually private citizen armies and remained so for several months. In the case of the 1st County of Durham Battalion, recruited in Darlington, the Hartlepools, Middlesbrough, Stockton, Sunderland and Durham itself, the raising committee under the Earl of Durham declined to accept the War Office grant of £10,000 when the time came in August 1915. The unit was therefore, in essence, a gift to the nation.[20]

The conditions imposed by Kitchener did not slow down the growth of the Pals movement. On the contrary, during the first fortnight of September, Pals battalions sprang into existence in towns and cities throughout the British Isles. By the end of the month fifty battalions were complete or in the process of formation. So quickly did they become part of the established social and military scene that any sizeable town or city without its own Pals battalions soon felt itself to be somehow less patriotic than its neighbours. Civic and community pride thus provided a powerful motive force for the creation of these units.

Several other communities besides Liverpool, Manchester and Birmingham managed to produce more than one battalion. One of the most notable achievements was that of Hull, where four battalions were raised in little over eleven weeks by Lord Nunburnholme, the Lord Lieutenant of the East Riding and president of the East Riding Territorial Force Association. Nunburnholme had been instructed by Kitchener on 29 August to form a Service battalion in Hull and two days later posters were printed and put up calling on 'clerks and others, engaged in commercial business' to join the new unit at Wenlock Barracks from 1 September onwards. Like so many of the early Pals battalions, this unit was middle-class in origin and social composition, as the *Hull Daily Mail* explained, somewhat defensively, on 1 September:

Today has seen the commencement of recruiting for the middle-class, clerks, and professional men, or the 'black-coated battalion'. It must not be thought there is a desire for class distinction, but just as the docker will feel more at home amongst his every day mates, so the wielder of the pen and drawing pencil will be better as friends together.[21]

The Hull Commercials (10th East Yorkshire Regiment) had almost reached their full complement after only four days and although recruiting for the battalion closed on 7 September, two others were raised the same month. These were the Hull Tradesmen (11th East Yorkshire Regiment), who set up their headquarters at the cricket pavilion in Anlaby Road, and the Hull Sportsmen and Athletes (12th East Yorkshire Regiment), based initially at the Artillery Barracks in Park Street. A fourth battalion (13th East Yorkshire Regiment) followed in November, the men of this unit, for want of an alternative title, being known simply as 'T'others'. Subsequently the four battalions together formed a complete infantry brigade, the 92nd Brigade, in the 31st Division.[22]

Glasgow contributed three Pals battalions during this period. At a meeting in the Municipal Buildings in George Square on 3 September the corporation decided to raise at least two battalions. One, the 15th Highland Light Infantry, was recruited entirely from among the drivers, conductors, mechanics and labourers of the corporation tramways, thanks largely to the initiative of James Dalrymple, the manager of the Tramways Department. When he heard that the municipal authorities intended to form two infantry units, Dalrymple telephoned the tramcar depots at 5 p.m. that evening and asked for the names of those who were willing to join a Tramways Battalion. On arriving at his office at 9 a.m. the next morning, he found a list of 1,100 names awaiting him. Recruiting began at the Coplawhill tram depot on Sunday 13 September:

Hundreds of young men in their early twenties and older, moustached men about the thirties or more, were gathered under the high iron-girded roof . . . some seated in the ranked tramcars. Many of them formed jocular groups around the walls. The building rang with bustle and laughter. At one end were a table and weighing machine. Beside them stood the attesting officer, two doctors, and a man who turned out to be a Justice of the Peace. . . . 'Well,' one of these men remarked cheerfully, 'who has enough change in shillings for all this lot when we pass them?' . . .[23]

The second of Glasgow's municipal units, the 16th Highland Light Infantry, was officered and manned to a considerable extent by current and former members of the Glasgow Battalion of the Boys' Brigade. The third was raised not by the corporation but by the Glasgow Chamber of Commerce, and became the 17th Highland Light Infantry. One of its four companies was composed mainly of students from the Royal Glasgow Technical College, another contained ex-pupils of the Glasgow Academy and high schools, while the remaining two companies were drawn from the city's business houses and offices.[24]

No area of Britain answered the call for recruits more enthusiastically than Tyneside. Here the Newcastle and Gateshead Incorporated Chamber of Commerce played the leading role in raising new local battalions during the weeks when the Pals idea was first taking hold. It was on 2 September that the council of the Chamber of Commerce resolved to seek War Office approval to recruit and equip a battalion of infantry from the young men working in businesses on the Newcastle Quayside, and a Military Committee was immediately appointed to set things in motion. Four hundred men were enrolled provisionally by 7 September but, as no formal authority had yet been received from the War Office, a detachment of 250, calling themselves the Quayside Company, left Newcastle to join a non-Pals unit, the 9th Northumberland Fusiliers, then training in Dorset. However, the War Office sanctioned the Newcastle Commercial Battalion the following day and the required numbers were secured within eight days. Two more battalions, the 1st and 2nd Tyneside Pioneers (18th and 19th Northumberland Fusiliers) were raised by the Chamber of Commerce before Christmas.[25]

The work of the raisers in Newcastle and elsewhere was not restricted to recruiting, nor did it cease when the Pals units were taken over by the War Office. The organisation behind the Newcastle Commercials and the 1st and 2nd Tyneside Pioneers, for example, included as many as six different sub-committees at any one time, all operating under the general supervision of the main Military Committee of the Chamber of Commerce. The Clothing Committee was responsible for the procurement and supply of uniforms and equipment amounting to some £50,000 in value, while the Billeting and Camp Committee not only arranged for the construction of a hutted camp at Alnwick to house the Newcastle Commercials but also drew up billeting schemes for the Tyneside Pioneers at Morpeth and Rothbury. As soon as recruiting began, a Dependants' Committee was formed to ensure that wives and families of soldiers in the battalions would be looked after. The assistance given was supplementary to the official separation allowances and was intended to relieve distress whenever the grants provided by the government proved inadequate to sustain individual families. At one stage there were 1,500 cases on the books, involving a weekly outlay of £240, or over £12,000 a year. The total expenditure of this committee was about £38,000, the money coming from the guarantee funds subscribed by members of the Chamber of Commerce and others. The guarantee funds were administered in turn by a Finance Committee. When the battalions proceeded overseas a Comforts Committee arranged for a regular supply of magazines and newspapers to be sent to the men in the trenches, and a Ladies' Working Party produced 37,426 pairs of hand-knitted socks for the troops. Finally, an Entertainments Committee organised garden parties and river trips during the summer, and concerts at local theatres in the winter, for wounded soldiers undergoing treatment at military hospitals in the Newcastle area.[26]

Bristol, in common with several other cities, was eager to attract middle-class recruits into the ranks of its own battalion. The Bristol Citizens' Recruiting Committee had resolved, at the end of August, that its appeal should be aimed at 'athletic, mercantile, and professional' young men and circulated details to political, social and sports clubs, insurance offices, banks, manufacturers and retailers. Application forms for enlistment in the battalion were supplied to the Colston Hall and the Stock Exchange as well as to clubs and businesses. Applicants were expected to be between nineteen and thirty-five years old, single and engaged in 'mercantile or professional work', but they did not necessarily have to be public school men. When recruiting opened on 4 September, however, the response was steady rather than spectacular and a large proportion of the applicants were later rejected for various reasons. The raisers were therefore obliged to open the battalion to recruits from elsewhere in the West of England and to drop the restriction that applicants should be unmarried. It was not until 1 October that the number of men attested reached 1,000 and recruiting for the battalion was halted. The unit was designated the 12th (Service) Battalion of the Gloucestershire Regiment but was more familiarly known as 'Bristol's Own'.[27]

Other cities and towns, like Bristol, found that it took longer to raise their battalion than anticipated, but chiefly because of the competition they faced from their larger neighbours. A committee headed by Montague Barlow, MP, began to recruit the 1st Salford Battalion (15th Lancashire Fusiliers) in mid-September 1914 but, as many Salford men had already joined other Lancashire units, including the Manchester Pals, it was late November before the battalion attained full strength. The 2nd and 3rd Salford Battalions (16th and 19th Lancashire Fusiliers), which were raised between December 1914 and March 1915, both contained companies recruited principally in Eccles and Swinton, and although Barlow and his colleagues ultimately succeeded in raising a fourth battalion, this was not up to establishment until the end of July 1915.[28] The Oldham Comrades (24th Manchester Regiment), formed at the beginning of November, were still short of men a month later and the commanding officer was authorised by the Mayor and his Executive Committee to offer a bonus of 5s to members of the battalion for every extra recruit they obtained.[29] The Accrington Pals Battalion (11th East Lancashire Regiment) was complete in less than a fortnight, yet only half the men were drawn from Accrington itself, three platoons coming from Burnley, another three from Chorley and two from Blackburn.[30] Barnsley, however, provided two Pals battalions before the end of May 1915, a remarkable performance considering that Leeds and Bradford, which had bigger populations than Barnsley, could also furnish no more than two Pals-type units each, while Sheffield produced just one City Battalion.

A few battalions owed their existence to the efforts of small groups of private citizens rather than to the initiative of local government officials or prominent businessmen. In August 1914 a handful of old boys of the Wintringham Secondary School at Grimsby approached their former headmaster, Captain E. J. Stream, with a suggestion that he should form an infantry company from ex-pupils of the school. The idea was formally adopted during a meeting at the school on 1 September, and fifty-two recruits were secured that evening. At the end of the first week the Grimsby Chums, as they immediately styled themselves, numbered over 200 and they offered their services to the 5th Lincolnshire Regiment, a Territorial unit. When told that this battalion had all the men it needed, Captain Stream persuaded the Mayor of Grimsby and his colleagues on the local recruiting committee to seek permission to organise a complete battalion from the borough. The old boys of Wintringham School were quickly joined by others from Humberstone Grammar School, St James's Choir School, Louth Grammar School and Worksop College, as well as by bank clerks, civil servants and young businessmen. By the beginning of November the Grimsby Chums, afterwards designated the 10th (Service) Battalion of the Lincolnshire Regiment, were over 1,000 strong.[31]

Several units had a predominantly industrial background. One was the North Eastern Railway Battalion (17th Northumberland Fusiliers), raised entirely from employees of the company during the latter half of September 1914. Another was the Miners' Battalion (12th King's Own Yorkshire Light Infantry), which was offered to Kitchener by the West Yorkshire Coal Owners' Association, a body representative of practically all the colliery proprietors in the West Riding. Nearly one-third of the men in this battalion came from pits in the Featherstone district.[32] A further variation on the Pals theme was provided by the 11th Battalion of the Border Regiment, recruited by the Earl of Lonsdale and an Executive Committee on a regional basis. Two of its companies were raised in north and east Cumberland, one in west

Cumberland and one in Westmorland.[33]

Strangely, London produced only one municipally raised battalion up to December 1914, namely the 22nd (Kensington) Battalion of the Royal Fusiliers, though eight other units of the Pals type were formed by different bodies in the capital during this period. Among the earliest of these was the Empire Battalion (17th Royal Fusiliers), which was raised by the British Empire Committee between 31 August and 12 September, taking its recruits from West End banks and insurance offices, the Stock Exchange and the theatrical world, together with a sprinkling of veterans of the old Imperial Light Horse.[34] Most of the London-based battalions were unashamedly elitist in their recruiting. In September Mrs E. Cunliffe-Owen, a well known sportswoman, obtained special permission from Kitchener to raise a battalion of upper and middle class men up to the age of forty-five. The India Room at the Hotel Cecil was used as a recruiting headquarters and volunteers were asked not only for the usual personal details concerning their age, employment and marital status but also about their sporting activities. The unit, which became known as the First Sportsman's Battalion (23rd Royal Fusiliers), was complete in four weeks.

The first nominal roll of the Sportsman's Battalion included authors, artists, clergymen, engineers, actors, archaeologists, big-game hunters, footballers, cricketers and oarsmen. Patsy Hendren and Andrew Sandham, the England cricketers, served as privates in the battalion, as did Jerry Delaney, the Lightweight boxing champion of England. Another private had once been Mayor of Exeter. A member of the unit later described the men of one hut in the battalion's camp at Hornchurch:

In this hut the first bed was occupied by the brother of a peer. The second by the man who formerly drove his motor-car. Both had enlisted at the same time at the Hotel Cecil. . . . Other beds in this hut were occupied by a mechanical engineer, an old Blundell School boy, planters, a mine overseer from Scotland, . . . a photographer, a poultry farmer, an old sea dog who had rounded Cape Horn on no fewer than nine occasions, a man who had hunted seals, . . . a bank clerk, and so on. It must not be thought that this hut was an exceptional one. Every hut was practically the same, and every hut was jealous of its reputation.[35]

A Second Sportsman's Battalion (24th Royal Fusiliers) was formed in November and the two battalions eventually served side by side in the 99th Brigade of the 33rd Division.

Five battalions consisted almost entirely of men who had been educated at public schools. One of these, the 16th (Public Schools) Battalion of the Middlesex Regiment, was organised by a small committee working from an office in St James's Street. A parallel effort on a much bigger scale resulted from a meeting at the Hotel Cecil in August when it was proposed to form various units for ex-public school men who wished to make some contribution to home defence. On 26 August a letter appeared in *The Times,* signed by 'Eight Unattached' who had been disappointed to find that the organisers of the Hotel Cecil meeting 'only required grey-haired, spare time veterans'. The 'Unattached' therefore invited all public school men of similar age and qualifications to themselves to attend a second meeting to 'discuss the formation of a "Legion of Marksmen" with a view of offering its services *en bloc* to one of the new battalions now being formed'.[36] This second meeting took place at Claridge's Hotel on 27 August, the hundreds of men present finally agreeing to a scheme put forward by Mr H. J. Boon for the raising of 5,000 volunteers between the ages of eighteen and forty, with the object of forming a corps representative of public school men as a class. Enlistment was to be open to all who had been to schools mentioned in the *Public Schools' Year Book*. It was hoped to secure the 5,000 recruits within a fortnight. A committee was elected with H. J. Boon as its chairman and on 28 August a letter was forwarded to the Under-Secretary of State for War, who arranged that Boon should meet Kitchener on the evening of Monday 31 August. In the meantime the committee decided that recruiting should not be confined to London but should embrace the whole of the United Kingdom.

Parliamentary duties prevented Kitchener from meeting Boon at the agreed hour, so the latter was deputed by the committee to call at the Secretary of State's private residence. Here he saw Sir George Arthur, to whom he gave a copy of the letter already sent to the War Office. Arthur returned after a few minutes with a message from Kitchener, saying, 'Go ahead, and if you can raise 10,000 men I shall be all the better pleased.' That night a recruiting poster was drawn up and a circular letter sent to the mayors and provosts of over fifty towns and cities. Next day the opening of the recruiting campaign produced 300 applicants and on 2 September 1,200 men were medically examined and attested. 5,000 had been enlisted by 12 September, many of whom were enrolled by recruiting agents in the provinces. 1,023 men were attested in Manchester, over 300 in Derby, 250 in Cardiff, 150 in Durham and 120 in Birmingham. All the work of enlisting and attesting was done by volunteer helpers. 25,000 forms had to be filled up, 10,000 index cards filed and many hundreds of letters answered daily.

While the work was in full swing, the Chief Recruiting Officer in Whitehall declared that the whole process was invalid, since Kitchener's approval had been given verbally through a third party. Boon once again hurried round to Kitchener's house, where Sir George Arthur explained that the Secretary of State was tired out but promised that the matter would have his first attention the following morning. Thus, early on 9 September, the corps received official sanction. The four battalions raised by Boon and his colleagues became the 18th, 19th, 20th and 21st (Service) Battalions of the Royal Fusiliers, known collectively as the University and Public Schools' Brigade. The 20th Royal Fusiliers was formed largely from the men who had enlisted in Manchester.[37]

The highly selective recruiting policy of many of the raisers of Pals battalions incurred a fair amount of criticism in the autumn of 1914, both in the national and the local press. In the socialist *Labour Leader* on 29 October,

A. W. Humphrey complained that class distinctions were being perpetrated by these units:

The middle-class and professional classes form exclusive companies, they do not hasten away to the nearest recruiting office, for fear they should rub shoulders with their less polished fellow-beings. Their patriotism does not run to that.[38]

Earlier that month the *Leeds and District Weekly Citizen* had suggested that the drop in the overall recruiting figures was caused by the snobbery attached to the raising of battalions like the Leeds Pals:

When the workers see that they are really the producers, and that they are a back number every time, they will change things. The boom over the 'Pals' was all very nice and full of esteem and goodwill, but it froze the stream of recruits right off. It was the sharp contrast that did it, and potential recruits felt something they could not express, and stayed at their work . . .[39]

III

Although most of the raising bodies had little trouble in obtaining War Office authority for their battalions, those attempting to form units with a strong national flavour experienced much greater difficulties. In Ireland the problems were mainly political. The Ulster Volunteer Force, as Kitchener realised, was an obvious source of recruits. About half its members were of the right age for the army, and many of them already had some knowledge of drill and weapons, if not up to the standards of Regular soldiers. On 7 August Kitchener sent for Colonel T. E. Hickman, a Member of Parliament and president of the British League for the Defence of Ulster, and told him, 'I want the Ulster Volunteers.' Hickman replied that Kitchener should consult the Ulster Unionist leader, Sir Edward Carson, and his chief lieutenant, Captain James Craig. Through Hickman a meeting was soon set up at which, after some preliminary sparring, Kitchener consented to the Ulster Volunteers joining the army not as scattered recruits but in their own units. Hitherto, Kitchener observed, the word Ulster had not figured in the list of British regiments, yet he would allow the volunteer battalions to keep their names as subtitles to their new official designations and would also let them wear the Red Hand of Ulster on their badges.[40]

At first Kitchener appears to have been modest in his demands, aiming at a formation of brigade strength from the UVF, but he was informed at a later meeting that a whole division could be recruited in the province. Hickman and Craig were therefore appointed as chief recruiting officers for the Ulster area. The force was not raised immediately, however, for the entire issue of recruiting in Ireland was still clouded with uncertainty as to the government's intentions concerning the introduction of a Home Rule Bill. On the one side, John Redmond and the Irish Nationalists were reluctant to give their full support to the recruiting campaign until some measure of Home Rule was assured; on the other, Carson and the Ulster Unionists, despite their loyalty to the Crown, had misgivings about committing the UVF unless the government promised to shelve the Home Rule question, at least until after the war. Carson told Asquith on 10 August:

Now that it is believed that the Home Rule controversy is to be revived, the indignation in Ulster is extreme. They think they have been betrayed, and I am placed in the position that I must either resign the leadership of Ulster or go over to Belfast and throw in my lot with my people there in any action they may feel bound to undertake. . . . All this difficulty could be avoided by simply postponing the controversy, and if it were postponed Captain Craig informs me that he is in a position to offer Kitchener at once two divisions of trained men . . . with all their equipment for immediate service abroad; and in addition a similar number for home service in Ulster. If the controversy goes on of course none of these men will be available, much to my regret.[41]

As usual, the Prime Minister sought a compromise, suggesting in the House of Commons that further debate on the question should be adjourned until 26 August, when the government hoped to make proposals which might meet with something like general acquiescence.[42] The delay only made the heart-searchings of the Ulster Loyalists all the more painful. Many did not wait and enlisted in units of the 10th (Irish) Division or crossed to England and Scotland to join up. At Omagh, Captain A. St Q. Ricardo, of the Reserve of Officers, expecting the formation of an Ulster Division, had begun to recruit men from the Tyrone Volunteers for a battalion of the Royal Inniskilling Fusiliers. One Loyalist from County Tyrone summed up the feelings of these men in a letter to Carson on 18 August: 'We decided today at our meeting to hold all we can back till 26th when we should know yea or nay, but Home Rule won or lost, we must go in then for King and Country. . . . Some of the Omagh men will go in spite of us on Thursday and Ricardo told me today that he got forty yesterday from Belfast.'[43]

On 31 August Asquith moved the adjournment of the House of Commons until 9 September, but by then the reverses suffered by the allies in France and Belgium had helped Carson to make up his mind regarding the course which Ulster must take. On 28 August Augustine Birrell, the Chief Secretary for Ireland, had reported to Redmond that Kitchener had received an unconditional offer from Carson to put all his Ulster Volunteers at the disposal of the War Office for drilling and that 35,000 of them were willing to enlist and serve abroad.[44] Carson's offer was formally approved by the Ulster Unionist Council at a meeting in Belfast on 3 September. 'We do not seek to purchase terms by selling our patriotism,' Carson said in his speech on that occasion. 'England's difficulty is not Ulster's opportunity; England's difficulty is our difficulty.' He declared that 'we have a scheme which we can confidently commend to our men and which will keep them together as old comrades accustomed to do their military training together. If we get enough men they will go under the War Office as a division of their own.' He appealed to the Ulster Volunteers to 'Go and help to save your country and to save your Empire. . . . Go and win honour for Ulster and for Ireland,' promising them that 'We are quite strong enough to take care of ourselves even after the men who come within the limits of enlistment have all enlisted.'[45]

Next day Carson and Craig inspected 800 men of the North Belfast Battalion, who then marched in a body to enlist at the Old Town Hall. On 5 September the North Belfast Battalion provided another contingent, with the Belfast Young Citizens' Battalion and the East, South and West Belfast Battalions following suit. Before the end of the month the Belfast district had recruited some 12,000 men, and other districts of Ulster over 20,000 more.[46] In addition to the five Belfast battalions there were two from County Down, two from Antrim and one each from Tyrone and Derry. The Donegal and Fermanagh detachment of the UVF also combined to produce one battalion, with the Armagh, Monaghan and Cavan Volunteers doing likewise. Together, these battalions formed the 36th (Ulster) Division, which became one of the finest in Kitchener's army.

Whereas Kitchener had smoothed the path for the creation of the Ulster Division, he was not quite so co-operative in the case of the proposed Welsh Army Corps. The idea of a separate Welsh formation over and above the existing Welsh Territorial Division was first mooted by Lloyd George on 19 September at a meeting in the Queen's Hall, London, which was attended by leaders of all Welsh organisations and denominations in the capital. Having suggested in his speech that a battalion of London Welsh should be raised, Lloyd George went on to say:

I should like to see a Welsh Army in the field. I should like to see the race who faced the Normans for hundreds of years in their struggle for freedom, the race that helped to win the battle of Crecy, the race that fought for a generation under Glendower against the greatest captain in Europe – I should like to see that race give a good taste of its quality in this struggle. And they are going to do it.[47]

Two days later a number of prominent Welshmen, including the Earl of Plymouth, Lord Kenyon, Lord Mostyn and Major-General Sir Ivor Herbert, met Lloyd George at 11 Downing Street and formed a Provisional Committee to launch the scheme. In his *War Memoirs* Lloyd George claims that when the proposal came before Kitchener 'he promptly vetoed it', but it is probable that Lloyd George was either confused about the date of the approach or was exaggerating Kitchener's opposition at this particular stage, for on 23 September it was publicly announced that the Secretary of State had 'given his sanction to the formation of a Welsh Army Corps' and that a representative National Conference was to be held in Cardiff on Tuesday 29 September for the purpose of carrying out the project'.[48] Invitations to the Conference were to be sent to the Lords Lieutenant, Welsh peers, MPs, mayors, chairmen of County and Urban District Councils, chairmen and secretaries of Territorial Force Associations, employers, trade unionists and religious leaders.[49] Some observers saw dangers lurking ahead. Writing to Kitchener on 24 September, H. A. Gwynne, editor of the *Morning Post*, pointed out:

If this scheme of recruiting is persisted in we shall have the new armies clamouring to be divided into more or less local Army Corps. . . . This method . . . would tie your hands to such an extent that if . . . you wished to alter your scheme . . . you would find yourself faced by those national and semi-national forces which you would not be able to break up without arousing a considerable amount of local feeling.[50]

There can be little doubt that Kitchener did entertain some reservations about the reliability of Welsh troops. He told Asquith privately that no purely Welsh regiment was to be trusted, that they were 'always wild and insubordinate' and that they ought to be stiffened by an infusion of English and Scottish troops.[51] But while Kitchener invariably viewed proposals for national and semi-national formations with a great deal of caution, he was generally prepared to authorise them – as he did with the Welsh Army Corps – once he was sure that they would fit into the established framework of the army and would not remain as separate entities on their own. Hence Pals battalions and similar units were always given an official designation and numbered consecutively after other battalions of existing line regiments, even if they were permitted to retain their unofficial names as subtitles. In the case of the Welsh Army Corps there was an additional reason for conflict between Kitchener and Lloyd George, and that was a basic misunderstanding about the extent to which the new formation would embrace units recruited in Wales up to the end of September 1914. When this is also taken into account, many of the subsequent statements made by Kitchener, Lloyd George and others on the Welsh Army Corps question make much more sense.

On the day before the big meeting in Cardiff relations between Kitchener and Lloyd George were strained by a dispute in the Cabinet on the matter of sending Nonconformist chaplains to the front. Kitchener felt that it was impossible to cater for all the minor denominations in the army, but Lloyd George, knowing that the recruitment of the Welsh Army Corps depended on Nonconformist support, replied that they should be accorded the same privileges as Indian troops, who were accompanied by priests of their own faith. 'If you intend to send a Church of England army to the front, say so!' he told Kitchener, 'but you cannot fight with half a nation.'[52] Kitchener conceded the point grudgingly, asking Lloyd George to write down a list of the denominations concerned.

At the conference at the Park Hall, Cardiff, on 29 September, a National Executive Committee under the Earl of Plymouth was appointed to organise the Welsh Army Corps, and the scale of the proposed force was firmly set at two divisions, then the normal size for a formation designated as an army corps.[53] The Executive Committee, which met for the first time on 2 October, did not find it easy to secure the required numbers of recruits, as the scheme had been inaugurated when the enlistment boom was past its zenith. It was estimated that, up to 30 September, 50,000 had joined the services in Wales and, quite apart from Territorial and reserve units, the principality had so far contributed twelve battalions to the first three New Armies, including a

Cardiff Commercial Battalion (11th Welsh Regiment). The position of the Executive Committee was complicated by the fact that, on 10 October, when the War Office formally approved the raising of a Welsh Army Corps of two divisions, the letter of authority decreed that 'every effort must be made to complete existing Welsh units to establishment before recruits are encouraged to enlist in the new units of the Welsh Army Corps'.[54] The War Office was willing to allot to the Welsh Army Corps three Pals battalions then in process of formation: the 1st North Wales Battalion (13th Royal Welsh Fusiliers); the 14th Welsh Regiment, recruited in Swansea and district; and the 1st Rhondda Battalion (10th Welsh Regiment), orginally destined for the Third New Army but now diverted at the Executive Committee's request. Permission was refused to incorporate other Welsh units, including the series of battalions which the War Office was organising from the surplus recruits who had earlier been posted to the Special Reserve. Though they added a 2nd Rhondda Battalion (13th Welsh Regiment) by the end of October, the raisers of the Welsh Army Corps were thus compelled to mark time until their own organisation had taken shape and the precise limits of their recruiting activities had been settled with the War Office.

The air was cleared after a stormy Cabinet meeting on 28 October when, in the Prime Minister's words, Kitchener and Lloyd George 'came to very high words, and it looked as if either or both of them wd. resign'.[55] The ostensible cause of the clash was an order issued to men of the 2/1st Denbighshire Yeomanry, a Territorial cavalry unit, not to speak Welsh in their billets. On 27 October Lloyd George warned Kitchener that he would raise the matter in the Cabinet on the morrow and press for a withdrawal of the order. Kitchener sent a calm and conciliatory reply the same day, commenting that this isolated case had not been connected with the Welsh Army Corps and that it had resulted from the action of a 'Territorial idiot . . . who thought that muttering in Welsh was a means of using insubordinate language'. Kitchener confirmed that the War Office did not endorse the order and was merely concerned that Welsh should not be recognised as the language to be spoken on parade: 'It would be difficult if we had to have all the orders translated into Welsh, and even in India we have to carry out the same principles and use English words of command.'[56] Nevertheless, the question was brought up at the Cabinet meeting the next day and developed into an argument about the Welsh Army Corps. According to Charles Hobhouse, who was present:

Ll.G. raised the recruitment of the Welsh Army Corps; the WO had only left Lord Plymouth and the Committee raising it some 5,000 men out of 16,000. About 40,000 Welsh recruits, enlisted before the WAC was mooted, had been formed into 30 new units incorporated into other Divisions, and the balance had been taken to maintain the 3 Welsh Regts, at the front. K. refused to form any of these units into the WAC and was obstructive as possible. Ll.G. argued his case with skill and patience, K. saw no reason in grouping the Welshmen together etc.[57]

Lloyd George felt it necessary to remind Kitchener that he was not a dictator and that 'he was only one among nineteen, and must stand criticism in the same way as any other member of the Cabinet'.[58] The Chancellor also wrote to Churchill that afternoon to thank him for his support at the meeting:

I am in despair over the stupidity of the War Office. You might imagine we were alien enemies who ought to be interned at Frimley until we had mastered the intricacies of the English language sufficiently to be able to converse on equal terms with an East End recruit. I enclose copy of the order issued by the WO about the Welsh Army Corps. Under these conditions further recruiting is impossible. Does K. want men? If he does not let him say so then we will be spared much worry and trouble. Why cannot he give us eighteen battalions out of the thirty new battalions already formed in Wales? We could then send another division.[59]

Kitchener revealed similar impatience when he remarked to Sir Edward Grey, 'I am afraid I cannot go on if the army that has to fight is to be run as a political machine.'[60] Lloyd George believed that he had won the argument, and in the sense that the Welsh Army Corps Executive Committee was henceforth permitted to recruit without further official hindrance, he had. Moreover, within two days, Kitchener had offered to promote Lloyd George's protege, Owen Thomas, to be brigadier-general in command of the North Wales Brigade, a gesture which led Lloyd George to admit that Kitchener was 'a big man' and to write to the latter thanking him for the 'wholehearted and generous way' in which he had met him over the Welsh Army Corps question that morning (30 October) and for his recognition of the 'national susceptibilities of the Welsh people'.[61]

Whatever Lloyd George believed, Kitchener had not given way on the key question of allowing the previously formed Welsh units to be attached to the Welsh Army Corps. In the end only one of the two divisions proposed came into being. 10,000 men had been recruited by the end of December and 20,000 by the beginning of March 1915, but it was well into the spring of 1915 before some of the division's units were complete. As ultimately constituted the 38th (Welsh) Division contained the standard three infantry brigades. The 113th Brigade comprised three battalions raised in North Wales (13th, 14th and 16th Royal Welsh Fusiliers) and a battalion of London Welsh (15th Royal Welsh Fusiliers). The 114th Brigade had the two Rhondda battalions, recruited in the mining villages of South Wales, the battalion raised by the Swansea Corporation (14th Welsh Regiment) and a battalion recruited by a Carmarthenshire County Committee (15th Welsh Regiment). In the 115th Brigade was the Cardiff City Battalion (16th Welsh Regiment), two battalions recruited in Monmouthshire, known as the 1st and 2nd Gwent (10th and 11th South Wales Borderers), and another unit from North Wales (17th Royal Welsh Fusiliers).[62]

Kitchener's cautious attitude towards semi-nationalist formations also delayed the realisation of the full recruiting potential of the Tyneside area. Until the second week of October proposals to recruit Scottish and Irish units on Tyneside were turned down by the War Office, but Lord Haldane, following a visit to Newcastle on 10 October, persuaded Kitchener to change his mind, and five days later the necessary authority was given. Thereafter a race began between the raisers of the respective units, each trying to be the first to produce a formation of brigade strength. A donation of £10,000 from Joseph Cowen of Stella Hall provided sufficient funds for both raising committees to start work. The Tyneside Scottish battalions were in fact open to all, whereas the Tyneside Irish sought recruits only from among Irishmen living in Northumberland and Durham. Units were formed at a staggering speed. A complete Tyneside Scottish Brigade of four battalions was raised by 16 November, while the Tyneside Irish Brigade reached establishment on 12 January 1915. The Tyneside Scottish Committee commented:

During the whole period of enrolment so great was the pressure of crowds at the Chief Recruiting Office . . . that street traffic was constantly being held up . . . and there could be no more moving spectacle than that afforded by bodies of men marching into Newcastle from outlying villages for enlistment in the Brigade; one group of about ninety miners so marching some nine or ten miles into the city, headed by some of their number playing mouth organs'.

These successes did not totally dispel Kitchener's reservations. The Tyneside Scottish Brigade committee, for instance, was of private, not municipal, origin, but in December it transpired that the War Office would recognise only the Lord Mayor of Newcastle as the official raiser, a development which caused some ill feeling, since the committee saw no good reason why they should not remain in direct communication with the War Office. However, the committee decided not to pursue the matter, since 'each member felt that the need of the country was too great, and the success of the movement should not be imperilled by wasting time over a side issue'.[63]

Of course, not everyone joined Pals battalions in the autumn of 1914. The Territorial Force too had its attractions for men wishing to enlist with their friends in a local unit, and the creation of the second-line Territorial units from the latter half of August onwards gave them further opportunities to do so. 235,195 men volunteered for the Territorial Force in the first quarter of the war, and an additional 129,224 between 11 November 1914 and 3 February 1915. In October 1914 thirty-six out of eighty-three recruiting districts in the United Kingdom recorded a higher total of enlistments for the Territorial Force than for Kitchener units and the Special Reserve, and ten of these districts, mainly in Ireland, had no Territorial formations.[64] Taking Pals and Territorial units together, as many as 643 out of the 994 infantry battalions formed during Kitchener's term of office were raised by local effort outside the direct War Office recruiting channels.

Notes

1   Major A. F. Becke, *History of the Great War: Order of Battle of Divisions*, Parts 1 to 4, HMSO, London, 1933–45; Brigadier E. A. James, *British Regiments, 1914–1918*, Samson, London, 1978, pp. 42–118.

2 *Census of England and Wales 1901: General Report, with Appendices,* Cd 2174 (1904); *Census of 1911: General Report,* Cd 8491 (1917).
3 Sir Charles Petrie, *Scenes of Edwardian Life,* Eyre & Spottiswoode, London, 1965, p. 80.
4 Malcolm Brown, *Tommy goes to War,* Dent, London, 1978, p. 35.
5 Brigadier-General F. C. Stanley, *The History of the 89th Brigade, 1914–1918,* Liverpool Daily Post, 1919, pp. 3–4.
6 Rawlinson to Major the Hon. Robert White, 19 August 1914. A copy of the letter can be found in the papers of Captain P. M. Sharp, IWM 78/69/1.
7 *Extracts from the Diary of Brigadier-General the Hon. Robert White,* Dimbleby, Richmond, n.d., pp. 3–4; H. C. O'Neill, *The Royal Fusiliers in the Great War,* Heinemann, London, 1922, pp. 9–10.
8 Minutes of the Executive Committee of the Bristol Citizens' Recruiting Committee, 27 August 1914; *Bristol Times and Mirror,* 31 August and 2 September 1914; *Western Daily Press,* 3 and 4 September 1914.
9 *Liverpool Daily Post,* 27 August 1914; Stanley, *op. cit.,* p. 4.
10 *Liverpool Daily Post,* 28 August 1914.
11 *Ibid.,* 29 August 1914; Stanley, *op. cit.,* pp. 5–8.
12 Derby to Mackinnon, 30 August 1914, Derby papers, LRO 920 DER (17) 33.
13 Stanley, *op. cit.,* pp. 10–14; *Liverpool Daily Post,* 31 August 1914.
14 Arthur Taylor to Derby, 29 August 1914, Derby papers, LRO 920 DER (17) 14/2.
15 Brigadier-General F. Kempster and Brigadier-General H. C. E. Westropp, *Manchester City Battalions: Book of Honour,* Sherratt & Hughes, Manchester, 1917, p. xiii; Taylor to Derby, 29 August 1914, LRO 920 DER (17) 14/2.
16 Kempster and Westropp, *op. cit.,* pp. xiv–xxii; Lieutenant-Colonel H. L. James (ed.), *Sixteenth, Seventeenth, Eighteenth, Nineteenth Battalions, the Manchester Regiment: a Record, 1914–1918,* Sherratt & Hughes, Manchester, 1923, pp. 5, 107, 185, 281; Arthur Taylor to Derby, 3 September 1914, and Deputy Town Clerk of Manchester to Derby, 9 September 1914. LRO 920 DER (17) 14/2.
17 *Birmingham Daily Post,* 28 August 1914; J. E. B. Fairclough, *The First Birmingham Battalion in the Great War, 1914–1919,* Cornish, Birmingham, 1933, pp. 1–4; Sir William Bowater (ed.), *Birmingham City Battalions: Book of Honour,* Sherratt & Hughes, London, 1919, pp. 1–4.
18 Telegram from Adjutant-General's Department to GOCs-in-C of Commands, 4 September 1914, WO 159/18.
19 Minutes of meeting of the Military Members of the Army Council, 12 September 1914, WO 163/44.
20 Lieutenant-Colonel W. D. Lowe, *War History of the 18th (Service) Battalion, Durham Light Infantry,* Oxford University Press, 1920, p. 13.
21 *Hull Daily Mail,* 1 September 1914.
22 Captain C. I Hadrill (ed.), *A History of the 10th (Service) Battalion the East Yorkshire Regiment (Hull Commercials), 1914–1919,* Brown, London, 1937, p. 1; Peter N. Farrar, 'Hull's New Army, 1914', *Journal of Local Studies,* Vol. 1, No. 2, 1981, pp. 32–3.
23 Thomas Chalmers (ed.), *An Epic of Glasgow: History of the 15th Battalion the Highland Light Infantry (City of Glasgow Regiment),* McCallum, Glasgow, 1934, p. 2.
24 Thomas Chalmers (ed.), *History of the 16th Battalion the Highland Light Infantry,* McCallum, Glasgow, 1930, pp. 1–3; J. W. Arthur and I. S. Munro (eds.), *The Seventeenth Highland Light Infantry (Glasgow Chamber of Commerce Battalion): Record of War Service, 1914–1918,* Clark, Glasgow, 1920, pp. 14–15.

25   Captain C. H. Cooke, *Historical Records of the 16th (Service) Battalion Northumberland Fusiliers*, Newcastle and Gateshead Incorporated Chamber of Commerce, 1923, pp. 1–2, 223.
26   *Ibid.*, pp. 223–6.
27   Minutes of the Executive Committee of the Bristol Citizens' Recruiting Committee, 31 August and 14 September 1914; *Western Daily Press*, 4, 8, 23 and 25 September 1914; Stone and Wells (eds.), *Bristol and the Great War*, p. 55.
28   Sir C. A. Montague Barlow (ed.), *The Lancashire Fusiliers: the Roll of Honour of the Salford Brigade*, Sherratt & Hughes, Manchester, 1920, pp. 23–30.
29   Herbert Wilde (ed.), *The Oldham Battalion of Comrades: Book of Honour*, Sherratt & Hughes, Manchester, 1920, pp. 11–12.
30   Major-General Sir C. Lothian Nicholson and Major H. T. MacMullen, *History of the East Lancashire Regiment in the Great War, 1914–1918*, Littlebury, Liverpool, 1936, p. 519.
31   Major-General C. R. Simpson (ed.), *The History of the Lincolnshire Regiment, 1914–1918*, Medici Society, London, 1931, pp. 51–2.
32   Lieutenant-Colonel J. Shakespear, *A Record of the 17th and 32nd (Service) Battalions Northumberland Fusiliers (NER) Pioneers, 1914–1919*, Northumberland Press, Newcastle, 1926, pp. 1–2; Captain R. Ede England, *A Brief History of the 12th Battalion King's Own Yorkshire Light Infantry (Pioneers): the Miners' Battalion*, Borough Press, Wakefield, n.d., p. 20.
33   'V.M.', *Record of the XIth (Service) Battalion Border Regiment (Lonsdale) from September 1914 to July 1st 1916*, Whitehead, Appleby, n.d., p. 6.
34   Everard Wyrall, *The 17th (Service) Battalion Royal Fusiliers*, Methuen, London, 1920, p. 2.
35   F. W. Ward, *The 23rd (Service) Battalion Royal Fusiliers (First Sportsman's): a Record of its Services in the Great War, 1914–1919*, Sidgwick & Jackson, London 1920, pp. 17–18; Charles Perfect, *Hornchurch during the Great War*, Benham, Colchester, 1920, pp. 141–3.
36   *The Times*, 26 August 1914.
37   Anon., *The History of the Royal Fusiliers 'UPS': University and Public Schools Brigade (Formation and Training)*, Times Publishing Co., London, 1917, pp. 14–19.
38   *Labour Leader*, 29 October 1914.
39   *Leeds and District Weekly Citizen*, 2 October 1914.
40   Cyril Falls, *The History of the 36th (Ulster) Division*, M'Caw Stevenson & Orr, Belfast, 1922, pp. 3–4; Colvin, *The Life of Lord Carson*, III, p. 27.
41   Carson to Asquith, 10 August 1914, quoted in Colvin, *op. cit.*, III, p. 29.
42   *Parliamentary Debates, House of Commons, 1914*, LXV, col. 2297.
43   R. Stevenson to Carson, 18 August 1914, quoted in Colvin, *op. cit.*, III, p. 30.
44   *Ibid.*, III, p. 33.
45   *Ibid.*, III, pp. 33–4; *The Times*, 4 September 1914.
46   *The Times*, 5 September 1914; Monthly recruiting figures for cities and regimental districts for September 1914, NATS 1/85.
47   *The Times*, 20 September 1914; *South Wales Daily News*, 22 September 1914.
48   *The Times*, 23 September 1914; Lloyd George, *War Memoirs*, II, p. 754.
49   Circular letters from the Provisional Committee of the Welsh Army Corps, 24 September 1914, see *Welsh Army Corps: Report of the Executive Committee*, Cardiff, 1921, pp. 4–5.
50   H. A. Gwynne to Kitchener, 24 September 1914, Kitchener papers, PRO 30/57/73.
51   Asquith to Venetia Stanley, 30 October 1914, see M. and E. Brock (eds.), *Asquith: Letters to Venetia Stanley*, p. 298.

52 A. J. P. Taylor (ed.), *Lloyd George: a Diary by Frances Stevenson*, pp. 3–4.
53 *Welsh Army Corps: Report of the Executive Committee*, pp. 6–13.
54 Adjutant-General's Department to GOC-in-C Western Command, 10 October 1914, see *Welsh Army Corps: Report*, pp. 15–16.
55 Asquith to Venetia Stanley, 28 October 1914, see M. and E. Brock, *op. cit.*, p. 291.
56 Lloyd George to Kitchener, 27 October 1914, and Kitchener to Lloyd George, 27 October 1914, Creedy papers, IWM 71/22/1.
57 David (ed.), *Inside Asquith's Cabinet*, pp. 203–4.
58 A. J. P. Taylor (ed.), *op. cit.*, p. 7.
59 Lloyd George to Churchill, 28 October 1914, see Martin Gilbert, *Winston S. Churchill*, Vol. III, Heinemann, London, 1971, p. 143.
60 Kitchener to Grey, 28 October 1914, Grey papers, PRO FO 800/12.
61 Taylor, *op. cit.*, p. 8; Lloyd George to Kitchener, 30 October 1914, Kitchener papers, PRO 30/57/80.
62 *Welsh Army Corps: Report*, pp. 32–5, 40.
63 *Tyneside Scottish Brigade Committee: First Report of the Honorary Secretaries, September 1914–December 1915*, Newcastle, 1915, pp. 3–12; Felix Lavery (ed.), *Irish Heroes in the War*, Everett, London, 1917, pp. 84–112.
64 Monthly recruiting figures for cities and regimental districts for October 1914, NATS 1/85.

4

Recruiting in decline,
October 1914–May 1915

I

The formation of Pals battalions boosted the enlistment totals in individual areas during the late autumn of 1914, yet by the end of October the general recruiting situation was beginning to give the government some grounds for concern. In October 136,811 men joined the army, a huge drop from the figure of 462,901 recorded in the peak month of September. There was a slight improvement in November, when 169,862 enlisted, but the following month the national recruiting returns fell once more, this time to 117,860, the lowest monthly figure to date. Then, after another brief rise to 156,290 in January 1915, the total for February was a disappointing 87,896, this being the first occasion since the outbreak of war on which the monthly returns dropped below 100,000.[1] The totals for most towns and cities also reflected this downward trend. For example, in February 1915 Birmingham produced 1,513 recruits as against 19,160 the previous September, and Glasgow provided 1,801 compared with 17,890 in September. The average daily return for Manchester in February was ninety-four recruits as against 541 five months earlier, and in London it fell from 2,256 to 699 during the same period.[2]

There were many reasons for the sharp decline in recruiting after the boom of early September, some of which were directly related to the over-hasty expansion of the army in the first six weeks of the war. The widespread circulation of stories of congestion and discomfort at the depots and training centres unquestionably deterred large numbers of men from enlisting, and the raising of the height standard to 5ft 6in. on 11 September also had an immediate dampening effect on recruiting. These, however, were short-term problems which the government could and did take action to solve. By mid-October the overcrowding at the depots had eased sufficiently for the dam on recruiting to be lifted. Consequently, the minimum height for recruits was reduced to the normal standard of 5ft 4in. and the upper age limit was extended to thirty-eight. On 5 November the height standard was again reduced to 5ft 3in., a measure which contributed to the rise in enlistments

that month by bringing in men who had hitherto failed to meet the physical requirements of the army. Thus, while the height standard imposed in September and the publicity given to the poor treatment of recruits may have combined to cause the initial drop in enlistments, one must seek alternative explanations for the continuing decline in recruiting over the next few months.

A major factor in holding men back from the army, particularly those who were married, was the inefficiency of the machinery for paying separation allowances to the wives and dependants of soldiers. At the outbreak of war, the Commissioners of the Royal Hospital for Soldiers at Chelsea constituted the only official body charged with the administration of such benefits, and the actual allowances had not altered much since the South African War. In August 1914 the basic separation allowance granted to the wife of a private in the infantry was 7s 7d per week, with an additional 1s 2d for each girl under sixteen and each boy under fourteen years of age. From his pay the soldier himself also contributed a minimum of 3s 6d a week for his wife and 7d for each child. Thus a wife without children would receive 11s 1d a week, and a wife with two children 14s 7d. Any supplementary benefits came from charitable funds channelled through the Soldiers' and Sailors' Families Association or from the National Relief Fund.

Early in September agitation began for the allowances to be increased. On 10 September *The Times* published a letter from Lord Derby proposing that the basic allowance for a soldier's wife should be raised to 10s 6d, and that payments should be made weekly instead of monthly, since the majority of families were accustomed to weekly wages rather than a monthly salary.[3] A week later the Prime Minister announced that the standard allowance, inclusive of the compulsory allotment from the soldier's pay, would be increased from 11s 1d to 12s 6d, while the rate for a wife with two children would go up from 14s 7d to 17s 6d. These allowances were to be payable weekly through the Post Office as from 1 October.[4]

Even when the allowances were raised, there were often long delays before payments could be made. During the great rush to the colours in August and September, harrassed and inexperienced recruiting clerks had, in many cases, made out the official attestation forms incorrectly, while some men had managed to get into the army without going through the attestation process at all, thereby making it doubly difficult for the authorities to ensure that the proper allowances were issued to wives and dependants. Furthermore, within two weeks of the declaration of war the number of wives eligible for allowances jumped from 1,500 to around 250,000 and went on climbing in the following months. It is therefore hardly surprising that the machinery for administering payments, like the recruiting organisation itself, could not at first cope with the massive increase in the volume of work, and the voluntary organisations had to step in to fill the gap. Up to 31 December 1914 some 800 branches of the Soldiers' and Sailors' Families Association together dealt with

279,019 cases concerning wives' and 653,266 relating to children's allowances, involving a total expenditure of over £1 million from charitable funds for the relief of distress. Several Pals battalions also had their own welfare committees to assist in this work. A typical example was the Dependants' Aid Committee of the Tyneside Scottish Brigade, which alone investigated more than 300 cases of non-payment of allowances or applications for additional relief between December 1914 and May 1915.[5] The overall position did not noticeably improve until the introduction of the Naval and Military War Pensions Act in November 1915 and, in the meantime, the muddle over separation allowances continued to discourage large numbers of married men from volunteering.

Changes in the economic situation, both at a national and at a local level, also played a part in determining recruiting patterns in 1914 and 1915, although the economic factors governing enlistment were extremely complex and had varying effects on different regions and occupational groups at different times.[6] The first general effect of the war on industry was the creation of a feeling of uncertainty which in a few industries, notably cotton, exacerbated a trade decline which had started long before August 1914. In August the level of employment fell in most industries. Unemployment in the trade unions which submitted reports to the Board of Trade leapt from 2·8 per cent of the membership at the end of July to 7·1 per cent at the end of August. The number of people on the registers of the labour exchanges rose from 112,622 in mid-July to 194,580 on 14 August.[7] Board of Trade employment figures for September 1914 revealed that, since July, the number of males holding jobs had fallen by over 10 per cent.[8]

These figures do not reflect the full impact of the crisis, as in many industries the workers were put on short time instead of being laid off. In September 26 per cent of the labour force of two months before was on short time.[9] In the cotton hown of Todmorden five local mills had closed down indefinitely by 8 August and nine more were on short time. By 5 September 3,467 looms had stopped and 18,762 were working for two or three days a week. Only 1,383 looms were then operating at full capacity.[10] Wherever this occurred there was a decrease in the earnings of workers. In Birmingham, where August was always a bad time for local trades, around 78 per cent of all volunteers that month came from the same classes from which the army traditionally recruited in peacetime.[11] The government, in fact, instituted positive measures to induce the unemployed to enlist. On 20 August local charity commissioners were told not to give relief grants to able-bodied men of military age.[12] Reports from employers in September indicated that nine out of every ten men laid off had volunteered or had been called up as reservists.[13] As we have already seen, local and national levels of unemployment were not the only factors shaping enlistment patterns for in Birmingham at the beginning of September – as in other places like Liverpool, Manchester, Leeds, Newcastle and Hull – the raising of Pals battalions with a strong appeal to the relatively secure middle classes also clearly contributed to the recruiting boom. Even so, it can be inferred that, during August and the early part of September at least, rising unemployment, short-time working and reductions in real wages did add to the upsurge in enlistments.

The link between enlistment and the economic situation is also suggested by the fact that the recovery of employment conditions in mid-September coincided with the sudden fall in the recruiting figures. Once the August panic had passed, readjustment took place in the majority of industries. Trade unions with 7·1 per cent of their members out of work on 31 August reported only 5·6 per cent unemployed at the end of September and 2·5 per cent in December, which was practically equivalent to conditions at the end of 1913.[14] One of the principal reasons for this recovery was the placing of government contracts, which not only created a demand for labour in those establishments receiving such orders but also caused a shifting of labour from other industries. In September the reports sent to the Board of Trade from various industries were far more optimistic than in the previous month. The engineering trades in the West Midlands declared that employment was now good, with 'much overtime being worked and men obtained from other districts'.[15] The woollen trade stated that, owing to government orders, 'employment during the month showed a very marked improvement. Of the total number of work people covered by the returns, under 20 per cent were working short time compared with 60 per cent a month ago.'[16] It was reported by the boot and shoe industry, and the hosiery trade, that, in Leicester, firms which had received contracts for the army were now working on Sundays and operating a system of double shifts on weekdays.[17] A similar trend was observed in Bristol and the South West, where, of the 16,400 people engaged in boot manufacture, nearly 57 per cent were on overtime at the end of September.[18]

The recruiting boom of August and September directly influenced employment conditions by depleting the numbers of men available to industry and changing a labour surplus into a labour shortage in many trades. The effects of military service in reducing unemployment were not felt everywhere at once. They were noticed first in agricultural areas, where, even in August, it was said that 'some temporary inconvenience was caused in certain districts through men being called to the Colours'.[19] After two months the Board of Trade recorded that enlistments had helped to cut unemployment by 1·5 per cent since July and by the end of the year the effects were becoming obvious in such industries as coal mining, iron and steel, glass and in the docks.[20] The official figures for February 1915 showed that only 6 per cent of the industrial labour force was now working short time, as against 26 per cent the previous September.[21] Reviewing the employment situation after twelve months of war, the Board of Trade *Labour Gazette* commented:

Owing to the larger number of enlistments the number of males available has greatly decreased. To meet this shortage of labour there has been a considerable transference from trades adversely affected by the war to other industries which were rendered abnormally active; in addition there has been, wherever possible, a growing improvement in the direction of substituting female for male labour. The net result is that at the present time there is very little unemployment, except in a few luxury trades, while in a number of industries, notably coal mining, engineering, agriculture and transport, the demand for labour greatly exceeds the supply.[22]

The fall in unemployment was accompanied by a rise in wage rates. The increases usually took the form of bonuses granted for the duration of the war and were allowed on the grounds that they were necessary to compensate for the higher cost of living, but they were well above the average of those granted in previous periods of rising wages.[23] Accordingly, as the war progressed, better employment prospects and bigger wage packets made some men less eager to volunteer for the army. As one correspondent, signing himself 'Northumbrian', wrote in a letter to *The Times* in October 1914, 'Work is even more plentiful than usual and better paid . . . with plenty of work at 7½d an hour there is no inducement to the sturdy young men of the village to trudge away to lead the hard life of a recruit.'[24] In the wake of the recovery of local industries in Bristol the number of men enlisting there averaged barely fifty a week in December and the same factors may explain why, during one week in 1915, Leicester, which was busy with army boot contracts, provided only 124 recruits, as against 432 from nearby Nottingham.[25] It seems, therefore, that, by helping to create better employment conditions, the unrestricted recruiting policy in 1914 carried within it the seeds of its own decline.

It must be emphasised here that the response of different industries to the war, in terms of numbers volunteering, varied considerably, just as the impact of the war and recruiting on employment conditions in those industries was, in turn, uneven. Table 1 shows the enlistment response of different industries

Table 1

Distribution by sector of employment of men enlisting in the forces, August 1914–February 1916

Occupation	Men employed, July 1914 ('000)	Men who enlisted ('000)	Percentage of pre-war labour force enlisting
Manufacturing	6,165	1,743	28·3
(Mines and quarries)	(1,266)	(313)	(24·7)
Agriculture	920	259	28·2
Transport	1,041	233	22·4
Finance and commerce	1,249	501	40·1
Professions	144	60	41·7
Entertainment	177	74	41·8
Central government	311	85	27·3
Local government	477	126	26·4
All occupations	10,484	3,081	29.4

and occupational groups between August 1914 and February 1916.[26] These variations in response, which were by no means clear during the early rush to the colours, became more marked in 1915 and 1916 and merit some further investigation and explanation. It will be perceived, for instance, that the highest percentages of enlistment over the longer period were registered by the professions, men in commercial and clerical jobs and those working in branches of the entertainment industry (including hotels, restaurants, theatres, cinemas, etc.). An important factor in this was that the professions, commerce and the service and distributive trades had a more flexible work force than heavy industry, and a male employee in a shop or hotel could more easily be replaced by female labour than a man in shipbuilding. Many men from the professions were commissioned, while the commercial classes were a particular target for the raisers of Pals battalions. Moreover, trades like food, drink and tobacco had a younger labour force than, say, the railways or agriculture. Dr Dewey goes so far as to suggest that 'age was the largest single determinant of enlistment variations during the first year of the war'.[27] The official age limits for the army, of course, dictated that recruits would come predominantly from the lower age groups, and young men, with lighter domestic responsibilities and a greater spirit of adventure, were always likely to be among the first to enlist. Consequently, as time went on, those industries which had an older work force than others were bound to produce proportionally fewer recruits. However, this case should not be overstated. Employment statistics for February 1915 indicate that 15·6 per cent of the agricultural labour force had enlisted, as against 15·1 per cent of all industrial workers.[28] Even a year later, as the table illustrates, the overall enlistment rate from agriculture was still only just below the national average, in spite of the higher average age of the work force on the land.

Wages appear to have played a secondary part in shaping enlistment patterns during the opening weeks of the recruiting campaign, when patriotism was the predominant motive force, but thereafter their influence seems to have increased in some sectors of industry. Non-manual occupations and the higher-paid manual workers figured prominently in the first rush to the recruiting offices. Miners, who were among the better-paid workers, provide an interesting case study in this context. An official survey of the industry calculated that 115,000 members of the Miners' Federation of Great Britain enlisted in the early weeks. This total represented 15 per cent of the union's membership, the response of the industrial labour force as a whole during the first eight weeks being slightly over 10 per cent.[29] By the following summer 230,000 miners, or about 25 per cent of the work force in that industry, were in the army.[30] Their pre-war industrial militancy notwithstanding, the miners obviously possessed a fair share of patriotic enthusiasm for the war, although a desire to escape from the rigours of pit life may well have been an additional motive for many colliers. Yet, while the rates of wage increases in mining between August 1914 and July 1916 were high compared with most industries, the enlistment rate among miners was, by the latter date, nearly 5 per cent under the average for all occupations. This also applied to dock workers, who enjoyed similar rates of wage increases but fell even further below the average enlistment rate. Thus, if pre-war wage levels were a minor consideration in recruiting in the first few weeks, it could be argued that, after October 1914, relatively high rates of increase in earnings began to inhibit enlistment in certain industries.[31]

A different set of factors came into play in other sectors of the economy, particularly the railway and munitions industries, both of which had some form of official protection from enlistment. The continued efficiency of the railway system was, of course, vital to the war effort. As early as 4 September 1914 the Railway Executive Committee, the body which exercised general control over the industry, decreed, with War Office backing, that railwaymen who wished to volunteer had first to obtain the written consent of the company employing them. When recruiting figures dropped again in February 1915, Kitchener urged that the instruction should be withdrawn but, after representations from the Railway Executive Committee, agreed that it should remain in force.[32] These restrictions did not stop 17 per cent of railway workers from enlisting by February 1915, nor did it prevent the North Eastern Railway from raising its own Pals battalion. Nevertheless, despite comparatively high wage increases in the industry, the railways had one of the lowest percentages of enlistment throughout the voluntary recruiting period.[33]

Whereas the railway authorities had quickly attempted to regulate the flow of their workers into the army, the government failed to act equally promptly in the case of key industries connected with munitions output. By mid-1915 23·8 per cent of the male employees in the chemical and explosives industry had enlisted, as well as 23·7 per cent from electrical engineering, 21·8 per cent from the mines, 19·5 per cent from the engineering trades, 18·8 per cent from the iron and steel industry and 16·8 per cent from small arms manufacture.[34] At this stage the government's mounting awareness of the necessity of reinforcing the industrial labour supply, even at the expense of the army's manpower requirements, caused it to place extra restraints on recruiting.

The previous September the private armaments firm of Vickers proposed that war service badges should be given to employees to signify that they were engaged in essential munitions production, so offering them some defence against over-zealous recruiters. The idea was adopted by the Admiralty in December 1914 for workers in the Royal Dockyards and for Admiralty contractors. The War Office displayed less enthusiasm, mainly because the badging scheme was then still seen as a device which would militate against army recruitment. However, by March 1915 the War Office had come to recognise that one of the biggest reasons for delays in the deliveries of munitions was the labour shortage produced by its own indiscriminate recruiting policy. As a result, the War Office began to issue badges to skilled employees of the Royal Ordnance Factories and armaments firms working on government contracts, though the distribution was strictly monitored.

While the Admiralty had issued 400,000 badges by the end of July 1915, only 80,000 had received War Office badges, three-quarters of these being in the Royal Ordnance Factories and five armament firms.[35] Indeed, these men could not legally be prevented from enlisting, nor were recruiting officers always inclined to pay due attention to the badge. The story of badging, which in any event was no more than a palliative scheme, affords a good illustration of the government's lack of firmness in dealing with the man-power question as well as helping to throw light on the decline in recruiting. The effects of economic changes upon enlistment, then, were far from uniform. What held good for one industry did not necessarily apply to another. Age factors, high rates of wage increase, full order books, official protection, greater job security and differences in regional conditions probably all contributed to the decline in enlistments. But, even when all these variable factors have been taken into consideration, it is difficult to avoid returning to the simple explanation that, for the country at large, recruiting figures fell when employment and wage levels improved.

Within three or four months of the outbreak of war, variations in enlistments between different areas of the country also became more apparent. In a debate in the House of Lords on 8 January 1915 Lord Midleton called attention to the high percentage of recruits drawn from the predominantly industrial, as contrasted with the mainly agricultural, districts. Quoting figures supplied by the Parliamentary Recruiting Committee, he remarked that, up to 4 November 1914, southern Scotland had produced 237 recruits for every 10,000 people living there, while the Midland counties had furnished 196, Lancashire 178, London and the Home Counties 170, Yorkshire, Durham and Northumberland 150 and Ireland, including the Ulster counties and Dublin, Wicklow and Kildare, 127. By comparison, the West of England had provided only eighty-eight, the eastern counties eighty and the agricultural districts of southern Ireland as few as thirty-two recruits per 10,000 of the population.[36]

Recruiting in southern Ireland was plagued by a host of problems, not all of which were due to economic factors. Indeed, Kitchener himself did a lot to undermine such goodwill and enthusiasm as existed there at the start of the war. After the political crises over the Home Rule question in the spring and summer of 1914, culminating in the Howth gun-running episode on 26 July, when three people had been killed and thirty-eight wounded by a detachment of the King's Own Scottish Borderers in Bachelor's Walk, Dublin, the atmosphere had changed significantly on the very eve of war. In the House of Commons on 3 August John Redmond, the Irish Nationalist leader, had pledged support for Britain in her hour of need. 'I honestly believe,' he said, 'that the democracy of Ireland will turn with the utmost anxiety and sympathy to this country in every trial and every danger that may overtake it.' He also informed the government that they could safely remove their troops from Ireland at once and that the Irish coasts would be defended by the men of the National Volunteers together, he hoped, with the Ulster Volunteers in the north.[37]

Redmond, like many other Irishmen, was deeply stirred by the plight of neutral Belgium, an even smaller country than Ireland, in the face of the German invasion. He also saw that Ireland would be dishonoured if, just as the promised Home Rule Bill was about to pass into law, the Nationalists were to refuse to support Britain. Although his gesture had been inspired by a mixture of political motives and emotional attitudes, it was an accurate reflection of the mood of the bulk of the Irish people. In the following days and weeks, messages of endorsement reached Redmond from local government bodies and branches of the National Volunteers all over Ireland.[38] Yet when Redmond saw Kitchener at the War Office on 6 August the new Secretary of State for War did not give him a great deal of encouragement. 'Get me 5,000 men and I will say thank you,' Kitchener informed him. 'Get me 10,000 and I will take off my hat to you.'[39] Redmond, in fact, was shrewd enough to refrain from total commitment to the recruiting campaign until he was assured that Home Rule was actually forthcoming. On 7 August Percy Illingworth, the Liberal Chief Whip, told Kitchener that, once the Home Rule Bill had been passed, 'Redmond will undertake that you will get 100,000 or 200,000 or more recruits from Ireland'.[40]

For a month or so the government, though beset by a multitude of other considerations, seemed to be hesitating. No real attempt was made to take up Redmond's suggestion that the National Volunteers should be given the task of defending Ireland. As one correspondent wrote to the *Freeman's Journal*, '. . . A generous enthusiasm has been met by neglect. And another opportunity, greater perhaps than any before it, of treating Ireland with confidence and respect has been rejected.'[41] Even Sir Edward Carson, the Ulster Unionist leader, subsequently agreed that it had been a great mistake not to supply the National Volunteers with arms after Redmond's speech of 3 August.[42] However, in mid-September Asquith decided to put the Home Rule Act on the statute book immediately, and though the whole of the Conservative opposition walked out of the House of Commons in protest, the Act received the royal assent on 18 September. It was accompanied by a Suspensory Act which automatically postponed the enforcement of Home Rule for twelve months or until the end of the war, and was also subject to a new Amending Bill which the government proposed to introduce in due course to settle the problem of Ulster.

In spite of these qualifications, the passage of the Home Rule Act was a signal for rejoicing in southern Ireland. There were bonfires and street illuminations in most parts of the country and at Charleville, in County Cork, the words 'God Save the King' were uttered on a Nationalist platform for the first time within living memory.[43] Redmond, for whom this was a personal triumph, now threw himself with immense vigour into recruiting. In an impromptu speech to a parade of the East Wicklow Volunteers at Wooden-bridge on 20 September he declared that 'it would be a disgrace for ever to our country, and a reproach to her manhood, and a denial of the lessons of her history, if young Ireland confined her efforts to remain at home to defend the shores of Ireland from an unlikely invasion and shrunk from the duty of proving on the field of battle that gallantry and courage which has distinguished our race all through its history'.[44]

Support for Redmond was forthcoming from Asquith, who went to Ireland to help launch a recruiting appeal. In a speech at the Mansion House, Dublin, on 25 September, he made what appeared to be a clear pledge on behalf of the government that there would soon be a southern Irish formation of the army on the lines of the Ulster Division:

> ... I address myself for a moment particularly to the National Volunteers, and I am going to ask them all over Ireland – not only them, but I make the appeal to them particularly – to contribute with promptitude and enthusiasm a large and worthy contingent of recruits to the second new army of half a million which is now growing up, as it were, out of the ground ... I should like to see, and we all want to see, an Irish Brigade – or better still an Irish Army Corps. Don't let them be afraid that by joining the colours they will lose their identity and become absorbed in some invertebrate mass, or, what is perhaps equally repugnant, be artificially distributed into units which have no national cohesion or character.[45]

Having returned to London, Asquith wrote to Redmond confirming the pledge he had given in Dublin a few days before. 'I have spoken to Lord Kitchener,' he told Redmond, '... and he will have the announcement made that the War Office has sanctioned the formation of an Irish Army Corps.'[46] The way seemed to be open for Kitchener to offer the maximum backing to Redmond's efforts to persuade Irishmen to join the British army. However, the promised announcement was never made. Instead, Kitchener refused to acknowledge the advantages of giving an Irish Nationalist flavour to recruiting in the south and allowed every conceivable obstacle to be placed in the path of the formation of a specifically Irish Nationalist division like the one he had sanctioned for Ulster. When the 16th (Irish) Division was organised from new battalions of the existing Irish regiments of the British army, its commander, Lieutenant-General Sir Lawrence Parsons, bitterly opposed Redmond's wish that the division should be referred to under the nostalgic, if inaccurate, title of the 'Irish Brigade' and argued successfully for several months against the adoption of a distinctive Irish badge. It also became extremely difficult for Irish Catholics to obtain commissions in the division.[47] Kitchener's own prejudices may have stemmed partly from his childhood in County Kerry, where he had been taught to regard the Irish as a subject people. He also sympathised with Ulster Unionist aims and remained wary of the potential risks involved in arming the National Volunteers.[48] It is true that, throughout the period in which the New Armies were being raised, Kitchener consistently maintained that every fresh formation must be standardised to fit into the accepted framework of the army, but the reluctance of the War Office to make even minor concessions on the question of badges and titles undeniably had a counter-productive effect on Irish recruiting.

Provocative statements from Unionists in the north similarly tended to make Irish Nationalists think twice before enlisting. In September 1914 Carson assured Ulstermen who joined up that the Ulster Volunteers would be kept in being during their absence. 'We are not going to abate one jot or tittle of our apposition to Home Rule, and when you come back, you who go to the Front to serve your King and Country, you will come back just as determined as you will find us at home.'[49] The following month General Richardson, the commander of the Ulster Volunteer Force, reminded his audience at a recruiting meeting that the British army had come to the aid of Protestant Ulster in the Curragh incident that March and would do so again.[50]

As in the rest of Britain, economic factors added to the problems of recruiting in Ireland. A sparsely populated and chiefly agricultural country, from which many young men had emigrated before the war, Ireland had, in any case, a smaller reservoir of eligible men than England or Scotland.[51] The competing attractions of well paid jobs in British industry made the task of the recruiting authorities all the harder. In 1915 one recruiting official complained to John Dillon, the Irish Nationalist MP, that it was becoming difficult to get Irish recruits to fight in the trenches for a shilling a day when another government agency was offering them £2 10s a week for munitions work, with an assurance that they would not be asked to serve in the army.[52] In many respects, however, the recruiting authorities in Ireland had only themselves to blame, as they failed to see the danger signs in time. The fact was that the recruiting returns in the early months had been given an artificial gloss by the raising of the 36th (Ulster) Division. Dr Callan has pointed out that the Ulster Division, too, suffered the frustration of not being able to fill its reserve units when its enlistment rate settled down to the lower averages experienced elsewhere in Ireland, and English recruits had to be drafted in to swell these reserves.[53] There was no Irish equivalent of the Parliamentary Recruiting Committee until the end of April 1915. Even when this new co-ordinating body, called the Central Council for the Organisation of Recruiting in Ireland, was established it was 'never more than a superficial civilian profile to camouflage the military's control over recruiting matters'.[54] The Central Council stayed in existence for a few months but did little or nothing to improve the situation.

It would be misleading, however, to attribute the problems of Irish recruiting entirely to administrative muddle, to economic considerations or to War Office and Unionist intransigence. While Redmond commanded the support of a majority of Nationalists, anti-English sentiment in the south by no means disappeared with the outbreak of war. Following a review of some

2,000 National Volunteers in south Derry in mid-August, Louis Walsh, a Ballycastle solicitor, told a public meeting that, while they did not want a German invasion, 'they were not going to defend one tyranny against another'. They would defend their shores under Redmond and Green Flag, he said, but would not be turned into militiamen to be generalled by Kitchener.[55] The promise of Home Rule did not altogether stem this current of opinion. A leaflet was circulated in Waterford in October urging all Irishmen to refuse to join 'the demoralised, decadent, crimestained, blood-sodden British Army'. Home Rule, the message ran, 'is only a sop – the crumbs that fall from the table of the rich man England to the beggar Ireland'.[56] In November the Chief Secretary for Ireland, Augustine Birrell, presented the Cabinet with a balanced summary of the state of the country. He began by stating confidently that hostility towards England was no longer so marked as it had been before the war. 'The Irish have changed,' he said, 'and their attitude today, north, south, east and west, towards England in her tremendous struggle with Germany and Austria is, speaking of Ireland as a whole, one of great friendliness.' In the Irish Parliamentary Party there was not the slightest trace of sedition or opposition to the war. On the other hand, sedition was being disseminated through leaflets, in speeches and by newspapers like *Sinn Fein*, the *Irish Volunteer* and the *Irish Worker,* while a few outrageous orators were to be found among the ranks of the lower clergy.[57] This latter statement was based on reports submitted by the Royal Irish Constabulary. Though the bulk of the Catholic clergy backed Redmond, twenty-four priests came under investigation for making anti-recruiting and pro-German speeches in 1914, and forty-three for disloyal language or conduct the following year.[58]

The influence of anti-recruiting propaganda in Ireland should not be overestimated, for although only 23,015 men enlisted there between 16 December 1914 and 15 May 1915, compared with 40,439 between 4 August and 15 December 1914, the figures were also falling in the rest of Britain during this period. Nor was there any major difference between Catholic and Protestant enlistments. Of the total of 63,454 recruits up to 15 May, 33,440 were Catholics and 30,014 were Protestants. 16,185 came from the National Volunteers and 20,581 from the Ulster Volunteers.[59] Redmond's support for recruiting, however, created a split in the ranks of the National Volunteers. About 7 per cent of the total membership of 188,000 refused to identify themselves with Britain and formed a splinter group under John MacNeill. The main body under Redmond continued to be known as the Irish National Volunteers and the secessionists took the title 'Irish Volunteers' but were popularly called the 'Sinn Fein' Volunteers. It was some time before the real implications of this split were realised, yet, because the majority of recruits for the British army were drawn from the pro-Redmond faction, the more extreme nationalists and republicans under MacNeill and in James Connolly's small Irish Citizen Army gained ground as the strength of the official

National Volunteers was progressively weakened. To this extent Redmond's recruiting successes indirectly helped to foster the conditions in which the Easter Rising of 1916 became possible.

Opposition groups were, of course, active on the British mainland as well. Since these bodies represented diverse shades of political opinion, the reasons for their opposition to the war and to recruiting differed but there was a considerable amount of contact, cross-fertilisation and even common membership between the various groups. The three most important in 1914 and 1915 were the Union of Democratic Control (UDC), the Independent Labour Party (ILP) and the No Conscription Fellowship (NCF).

The Union of Democratic Control was founded in September 1914, mainly by radical Liberals who believed that the war was the result of ill judged foreign policies and secret diplomacy which had forged alliances merely for the sake of maintaining an illusory balance of power. Concentrating on this issue at first, the UDC demanded post-war parliamentary control over foreign policy and the abandonment of secret diplomacy, though by 1915 its leaders were also calling for a negotiated peace to be concluded at the earliest opportunity. The co-founders of the UDC included Arthur Ponsonby, from the pre-war Liberal Foreign Affairs Group, C. P. Trevelyan, who had resigned as Parliamentary Secretary to the Board of Trade when war was declared, Ramsay MacDonald of the Independent Labour Party, and Norman Angell, founder of the Neutrality League. They were supported outside the House of Commons by intellectuals such as J. A. Hobson and Bertrand Russell.

From the first, the Independent Labour Party was more outspoken in its opposition. On 6 August 1914 the ILP's journal, *Labour Leader,* urged, 'Workers of Great Britain, down with war. You have no quarrel with the workers of Europe. They have no quarrel with you. The quarrel is between the ruling classes of Europe. Don't make their quarrel yours. . . .'[60] While the Parliamentary Labour Party backed the government's recruiting campaign, the ILP objected to the pressure that was being put upon young men of the working class. In September 1914 its National Administrative Council declared:

In our view the operation of a sort of moral press-gang will be inequitable and unjust. We must also protest against all attempts to force men into the ranks by withholding assistance from them, or dismissing them from their employment. . . . Much as we detest universal military service, which we shall continue to oppose, that plan would be less discreditable than the general hunting and harrying of young men now taking place, often without knowledge of their individual circumstances and dependants.[61]

The ILP, however, was not completely pacifist. For instance, Ramsay MacDonald, who was furiously attacked by the patriotic press for his supposed anti-war sentiments, was certainly an anti-militarist, but he supported the call for recruits in Leicester, his own constituency, because he felt that it was necessary for the allies to achieve victory as a condition of peace. Once the

war had begun, in fact, most members of the ILP, whether they were moder-
ates like MacDonald or held more extreme views, looked to a negotiated
peace as advocated by the Union of Democratic Control, and relatively few
spoke in favour of an immediate end to the war. In the shorter term, the ILP
channelled its energies into defending the position of the dependants of
soldiers and workers. George Lansbury, the ILP Member from Bow, was
particularly active in the East End of London, where, with Sylvia Pankhurst
and her East London Federation of Suffragettes, he campaigned against the
privations caused among the poor by the government's failure to sort out the
muddle over separation allowances.

The majority of convinced pacifists gravitated towards the No Conscription Fellowship, which provided a rallying point for men who believed that
war was immoral and were determined to take no part in it. In the early
autumn of 1914 there was no single body to co-ordinate the views of such
men, so Fenner Brockway published a letter in the *Labour Leader* on 12
November suggesting joint action for mutual help and encouragement.
Brockway had no large organisation in mind, only some informal link, yet the
response to his proposal exceeded his expectations and later in the month the
No Conscription Fellowship was formed to gather together all those who had
decided to refuse to join the army in the event of compulsory military service
being introduced. The 300 original members elected a committee which
included Brockway himself, C. H. Norman and Clifford Allen, a pacifist and
socialist who was destined to become the NCF's guiding influence and most
outstanding individual figure. In the beginning Brockway's Derbyshire
cottage served as the NCF's headquarters but, as the size and enthusiasm of
the membership grew, it was found necessary to open a London office. The
NCF attracted the support of religous anti-war groups, especially the
Quakers, some Labour Party members such as Herbert Morrison, and intellectuals of the Bloomsbury Group, including Bertrand Russell. During the first
half of 1915 the No Conscription Fellowship was fairly subdued, though its
members were hard at work establishing branches throughout the country in
preparation for the struggle to come. It was in the second half of the year, as
the prospect of compulsory service greatly increased, that the NCF's voice
really began to be heard.

These pressure groups aroused much hostility, for their opinions were
contrary to those held by the mass of the people. With the exception of a
handful of socialist and pacifist weeklies, the press poured abuse and ridicule
on their activities, which were thought to be a threat to national unity and to
be sapping the country's will to fight. Anti-war campaigners were denounced
by newspapers like the *Daily Express* as traitors who were 'helping to stab the
Army in the back' and were 'fighting for Germany as usefully as the soldiers in
the German armies in France'.[62] Patriotic mobs frequently broke up meetings
organised by the Union of Democratic Control and the No Conscription
Fellowship. Such groups, then, represented only a small, if vocal, section of

the population. All the same, the fact they were sufficiently active to incur the wrath of the press and public suggests that their anti-war propaganda may have done something to slow down recruiting.

Outside these well organised and dedicated bodies of idealists, there were clearly substantial numbers of less articulate young men who held no deep-seated political or moral objection to military service but had purely personal excuses for remaining at home. In his book *Enlistment or Conscription*, published in 1915, A. M. B. Meakin related how a woman of his acquaintance decided to find out if there were still any potential recruits in the seaside town in which she was staying. She later sent a note of her experiences to a local newspaper, from which Meakin quotes:

I saw two young working men lounging against the railings, evidently unemployed. On my asking them why they did not enlist in Lord Kitchener's Army, they replied sheepishly as they sidled off that they had someone to care for. I then took the tramcar to the M——, and seeing a young man seated near me, asked if he was going to enlist. He replied sadly that he had been refused on account of his health; whereupon a strong-looking man of about forty said disapprovingly, 'The men are coming in quite fast enough.' On leaving the tramcar, I asked the able-bodied young conductor if he intended to serve his country. His reply was, 'I have three brothers in the Army; that's enough for me.' A little later, seeing a remarkably fine young man pushing a small laundry cart, I asked him the same question. He replied insolently, 'I don't want to be shot!'[63]

It was not unusual for men to put family before country. The Rev. E. H. L. Reeve, rector of Stondon Massey, in Essex, described the reaction of a young man in his village who was conscripted in 1916 after resisting all appeals to enlist under the voluntary system:

A lad who has done some useful work in the Rectory garden has now left as a recruit in the 3rd Essex Regiment. . . . He is stated to have said that he felt he owed a greater duty to his mother at home than to King George, for his mother had done much for him, whereas the King, so far as he knew, had not rendered him any service![64]

II

As the recruiting figures slumped, the government explored every possible method of raising new formations and of stirring up public enthusiasm. Parliamentary assent had first to be given for the proposed increases in the size of the army, and after the initial increase of 500,000 had been approved on 6 August, Asquith asked Parliament to sanction another 500,000 troops on 10 September and a further 1 million on 16 November, making a total of 2 million since the beginning of the war. Persuading this number to enlist was a different matter altogether, for by the end of November the enlistment figures had only just topped 1 million. This was a remarkable total by any previous standards but was obviously still a long way short of the target which the government had now set itself.

The success of the Pals movement earlier in the autumn led the War Office to encourage the formation of additional locally raised units during the coming months, often by making a direct plea to the mayor or Member of Parliament of a city or town where the reservoir of able-bodied men did not yet appear to have been exhausted. Some who had been refused permission to raise a local unit earlier were now asked if they wished to go ahead.[65] Particular attention was focused on the metropolitan boroughs of London, which had so far yielded surprisingly few municipally raised units. As a result, between November 1914 and July 1915 infantry battalions were produced by the boroughs of Battersea, Bermondsey, Islington, Lambeth, Lewisham, Shoreditch, St Pancras, Wandsworth and West Ham. The process was repeated elsewhere in the country. Manchester, for example, raised four more City battalions in this period and others were provided by Barnsley, Edinburgh, Middlesbrough, Nottingham, Salford and Sunderland.[66]

The new locally raised units which emerged during this period were not confined to infantry battalions. Among the towns and cities which provided artillery brigades for the New Armies were Aberdeen, Accrington, Blackburn, Glasgow, Handsworth, Huddersfield, Leicester, Nottingham, Rotherham, Wigan and York. In London other artillery brigades were raised by Camberwell, Deptford, East Ham, Fulham, Hackney, Hampstead, Tottenham, West Ham and Wimbledon. Places which produced Royal Engineers field companies included Barnsley, Cambridge, Coventry, Doncaster, Dundee, Leamington, Manchester, Norwich, Reading, Stockton on Tees and the Isle of Wight.[67]

Not every city, town or borough approached by the War Office was able or willing to respond in a positive way. The Recruiting Committee of the borough of Marylebone in London informed Kitchener in May 1915 that it was 'impossible to raise the necessary money or men for the formation of a battalion under present conditions'. It even went so far as to add that it was 'of the opinion that the only satisfactory method of dealing effectively with the situation is by some form of compulsory service and urges the authorities to take the necessary steps'.[68] Indeed, in terms of infantry battalions, the number of Pals-type units created each month mirrored the general pattern of recruiting. Whereas twenty locally raised battalions came into existence in November 1914, and ten in December, the total of new Pals battalions raised from January to July 1915 averaged only five per month.[69]

One idea which caught the public favour for a while was the creation of 'Bantam' battalions, composed of men between 5ft and 5ft 3in. in height. In October 1914 a Durham miner had walked from Durham to Birkenhead in a vain attempt to enlist. Although fit in all other respects he was repeatedly rejected as too small. Upon being turned down at Birkenhead, the disappointed man offered to fight anyone in the room and was removed from the recruiting office only with some difficulty. When he learned of the miner's story Alfred Bigland, the Conservative MP for Birkenhead, obtained special sanction from the War Office to recruit a Bantam battalion for the army. The response to Bigland's appeal was astonishing. Within a few days some 3,000 men from all quarters of Britain presented themselves for enrolment and were formed into the 1st and 2nd Birkenhead Bantams (15th and 16th Cheshire Regiment).[70]

Kitchener was quick to appreciate the possibilities afforded by the Bantam concept, and subsequently authorised the raising of similar units in other parts of the country, including two from south-east Lancashire, two from Glamorgan and one each from County Durham, East Anglia, Monmouthshire, North Wales and the West of England. Edinburgh, Glasgow, Leeds, Nottingham, Manchester and Salford also produced Bantam battalions. Twenty-four Bantam units were raised in all, ultimately comprising the whole of the infantry of the 35th (Bantam) Division and two-thirds of the 40th Division. When it was formed late in 1915 the 40th Division, in fact, had three complete brigades of Bantams but, by this time, many of the men being recruited for the Bantam battalions were patently unfit even for training at home. One battalion which joined the division at Aldershot over 1,000 strong was later reduced by medical rejections to little over 200 men. In consequence, four of the twelve battalions were disbanded in the spring of 1916 and replaced by non-Bantam units.[71]

Although local authorities continued to work hard to produce new formations there was a limit to what could be achieved by the isolated efforts of individual communities. The only real alternative was to mount a sustained and co-ordinated recruiting campaign on a national scale. Since it had been established for just such a purpose, the Parliamentary Recruiting Committee undertook this task, with the consent of the War Office, from mid-September onwards.

An important aspect of the committee's work was the organisation of public recruiting meetings up and down the country. Unpaid speakers were used as far as possible but the PRC's Finance Committee agreed to pay fees ranging from half a guinea to two guineas a day whenever necessary. For a meeting in a village the costs of advertising and printing were in the region of £1 10s, and for a mass meeting in a large town up to £15 was allowed.[72] In January 1915 it was reported that over 3,000 meetings had been held, and more than 6,000 speakers provided.[73] One member of the committee, the Duke of Devonshire, felt that too many speakers were being provided rather than too few.[74] It was open to question whether the numbers of recruits obtained by these gatherings were commensurate with the amount of work involved. As early as 7 November *The Times* observed that 'the meetings arranged by this body [the PRC] still go on nightly, but the speakers agree that the results are not as encouraging as they were'.[75]

On 21 October the Parliamentary Recruiting Committee decided that the time had come to proceed with the canvassing scheme which had been drawn up two months before. Curiously, neither Kitchener nor Major-General Jeffreys, the Director of Recruiting, had studied the proposals in detail up to this point, but Kitchener's approval was given five days later, by which time Major-General F. L. Campbell had succeeded Jeffreys.[76] After a fanfare of publicity the scheme was launched on 12 November in the area of south-east England covered by Eastern Command. An appeal signed by Asquith, Bonar Law and Henderson was distributed to all householders, who were asked to complete an enclosed form by giving particulars of men of military age who were living in the house and indicating whether or not they were willing to enlist. The initial response was satisfactory enough to induce the Parliamentary Recruiting Committee to extend the scheme to the Southern, Northern and Western Commands, and the forms had been distributed to 4,400,000 householders by 12 December. Two and a quarter million replies were received in the first six weeks.[77] Early in the new year Kitchener reported that the delivery of the 'Householder's Return' to country districts had now been completed, that distribution in the big cities and towns had begun and that some 218,000 names of men willing to enlist had already been registered.[78] The fundamental weakness of the scheme was that it was entirely voluntary. The government could not compel householders to fill in the forms and had no means of ensuring that those who promised to join the army actually did so. In the end the PRC's canvassing project was a failure. As Arthur Henderson revealed in July 1915, of the 8 million householders who received the forms, only 3,631,385 had taken the trouble to reply.[79]

Apart from these activities, the committee's main work lay in the production and distribution of pamphlets and posters. At the end of March 1915 it was estimated that the PRC had by then issued 20 million recruiting leaflets and some 2 million posters.[80] In the First World War posters were employed as a medium of propaganda on a scale hitherto unknown, and their impact on the urban landscape was vast. Michael MacDonagh of *The Times* described the scene in London on 3 January 1915:

Posters appealing to recruits are to be seen on every hoarding, in most windows, in omnibuses, tramcars and commercial vans. The great base of Nelson's Pillar is covered with them. Their number and variety are remarkable. Everywhere Lord Kitchener sternly points a monstrously big finger, exclaiming 'I Want You.' Another bill says: 'Lord Kitchener wants another 100,000 men.' ('My word,' remarked a lonely spinster according to a current joke, one would do me!') . . .[81]

Alfred Leete's famous design, which bore a portrait of a pointing Kitchener over the slogan 'Your country needs you', first appeared on the front cover of the magazine *London Opinion* on 5 September 1914. The following week, in answer to numerous requests for reproductions, the magazine offered postcard-size copies at 1s 4d per hundred.[82] The Parliamentary Recruiting Committee also obtained permission to use the design, with a slightly amended text which included, at Kitchener's insistence, the words 'God Save the King'. However, it was not until the end of September that the design began to be issued as a poster.[83] In view of the fact that it became arguably the best known poster in history, it is perhaps churlish to note that its widespread circulation in various forms did not halt the decline in recruiting.

Over two hundred different poster designs were issued by the Parliamentary Recruiting Committee and many others were produced by advertising agencies and local recruiting organisations. Eric Field, who worked for the Caxton advertising agency, which had prepared recruiting literature for the army since 1913, wrote, 'Pure patriotism as a recruiting appeal soon lost its initial force. . . . We ran the gamut of all emotions which make men risk their lives and all the forces which deter them from doing so.'[84] One of the most striking posters published by the PRC depicted a little girl asking her father, 'Daddy, what did *you* do in the Great War?' Robert Smillie, the Scottish miners' leader, is reputed to have said that his answer would be 'I tried to stop the bloody thing, my child.'[85] Large numbers of posters were aimed at women, inciting them to send their men into the army. 'Women of Britain say—go!' was the simple message on one, while another, directed at women in the capital, appealed 'To the young women of London. Is your best boy wearing khaki? If not don't *you think* he should be? . . . If your young man neglects his duty to his King and Country, the time may come when he will *neglect you*. Think it over – and then ask him to join the army – today.'[86]

An extraordinary product of the mass emotion surrounding the recruiting campaign was the disproportionate attention paid to footballers and their spectators. In October 1914 a *Punch* cartoon, later reproduced as a poster, showed Mr Punch addressing a professional footballer with the words 'No doubt you can make money in this field, my friend, but there's only one field today where you can get honour.'[87] Speaking in Tottenham on 7 November, J. H. Thomas, the Labour MP, said that if thousands of young men eligible for the army were able to attend football matches, 'either those young men did not understand the situation or they were cowards and traitors'.[88] Michael MacDonagh perceived in December that the sandwich boards carried by men outside Chelsea's ground no longer bore such messages as 'Repent, for the time is at hand' but now asked such questions as 'Are you forgetting that there's a war on?'[89] Special appeals were made to the players and supporters of particular clubs. To take just one example, the publicity department of the Central London Recruiting Depot issued a poster in November 1914 which read, 'Men of Millwall. Hundreds of football enthusiasts are joining the army daily. Don't be left behind. Let the enemy hear the 'Lions roar'.'[90] It became customary for recruiting sergeants to be in attendance at matches and for speakers to address the crowds. A Football Battalion (17th Middlesex Regiment) was raised in London in December by W. Joynson Hicks, the Conservative MP for Brentford, and another (23rd Middlesex Regiment) was formed the following June, but the idea was not copied elsewhere.

Women's organisations took a leading part in the recruiting effort. At the outbreak of war Emmeline and Christabel Pankhurst's Women's Social and Political Union and Mrs Fawcett's National Union of Women's Suffrage Societies had abandoned their militant campaign for the vote. Although Mrs

Pankhurst's more radical daughter, Sylvia, established her own Workers' Suffrage Federation and maintained a resolute opposition to the war, the majority of Suffragettes swung behind the government in the belief that they could best promote their case by demonstrating their patriotism in the national emergency and by supporting the call for recruits. Many women were active in the most fanatical of the unofficial recruiting bodies, the 'Order of the White Feather', which was inaugurated by Admiral Charles Penrose Fitzgerald from a bandstand in Folkestone in August 1914. Men out of uniform found it virtually impossible to avoid being handed a white feather, as a sign of cowardice, by these ever-vigilant women. MacDonagh wrote, 'The bellicosity of these females is almost as terrible to the young man who has no stomach for fighting as an enemy with banners and guns.'[91] While the receipt of a white feather certainly induced some men to enlist, the women distributing them were not always discerning in their choice of victims. Shortly after joining a Territorial unit in 1914, A. R. Kennewell, who had not yet been issued with a uniform, was given a white feather by a woman in Nottingham. He tersely suggested, 'If you have nothing better to do, why don't you go and help some of those women whose husbands have already gone?'[92] Carl Wehner, a young German internee, received one from a woman in a London park: 'The actual words spoken to me were "Young man, why aren't you in the army?" . . . My answer was, "I am a foreigner," but it did not seem to make any difference.'[93]

The rising hysteria characterised by the activities of the white feather women was also reflected in the frequent publication by the press of tales of German atrocities in France and Belgium. An early example was the story of a twenty-three-year-old nurse, Grace Hume, who according to the *Dumfries Standard* of 14 September 1914 had been serving in a camp hospital in Belgium when the Germans invaded. It was reported that the Germans had attacked the hospital, killing wounded men, and had then cut off Nurse Hume's right breast, leaving her to die in agony. Upon investigation it was discovered that Grace Hume was living in Huddersfield and had never been to Belgium. The entire story had been made up by her younger sister.[94] The lack of photographic or documentary evidence to substantiate such stories did not deter editors, however, and reports of the rape and mutilation of Belgian and French civilians continued to appear throughout 1915. Readers often questioned them after publication but many were accepted as fact. Robert Graves recalled, 'It never occurred to me that newspapers and statesmen could lie. I forgot my pacifism – I was ready to believe the worst of the Germans. . . . I discounted perhaps 20 per cent of the atrocity details as wartime exaggeration. That was not, of course, enough.'[95]

All this activity and emotion had very little effect on the recruiting figures. The best that can be said of both the official and unofficial recruiting drives during this period is that without them the enlistment totals would have been even lower than they were, but the immense effort poured into the campaign was never matched by any significant improvement in the returns. External factors appear to have exerted a greater influence than government exhortations. The brief upsurge in enlistments in November 1914 coincided with the most critical phase of the First Battles of Ypres and the second revival, in January 1915, came shortly after the German bombardment of Scarborough and the Hartlepools. In neither case was the improvement maintained. Only 113,907 recruits came forward in March 1915 and 119,087 in April.[96]

There is some justification for the view that, despite all the energy and resources devoted to recruiting, the government undermined its own campaign by refusing to acknowledge the shortcomings of the voluntary system. When W. F. Cotton, an Irish Nationalist MP, enquired in the House of Commons on 25 November 1914 whether any intimation had been given to the military authorities that conscription would be adopted if voluntary recruiting failed to improve, H. J. Tennant, the Under-Secretary of State for War, denied any such suggestion.[97] In the House of Lords on 8 January 1915 Lord Selborne predicted that if the voluntary system did not produce the men needed, compulsion would be necessary, as in the American Civil War, and stated that the whole problem of voluntarism against compulsory service required detailed study by the government. In reply Haldane said the the government had 'an open mind' on this great issue but claimed that, so far, there had been no reluctance to respond to the call for recruits and he could see no reason to anticipate a breakdown of the voluntary system:

In time of peace I have always told your Lordships that I thought to resort to compulsory service would be a bad thing, and at this time now I do not think it would be a good thing. Unless it becomes a final necessity, which it has not as yet, it should not be resorted to.... But at a time of national necessity any other consideration must yield to national interest and we should bar nothing in the way of principle if it should become necessary.[98]

Haldane's admission that the government was keeping its options open invited the pro-conscriptionists to launch a more vigorous attack on the policy of voluntarism. By this time, other politicians and civil servants were calling for a much more balanced manpower policy in which the needs of both the army and industry were fully taken into account. In a paper presented to the War Council early in January 1915 Arthur Balfour argued that indiscriminate recruiting should cease not only in industries such as munitions, mines and railways, which were of immediate importance to the war effort, but also in those which either produced goods for export or commodities for home consumption, like foodstuffs. Any system of enlistment which hampered such industries 'may, and indeed must, diminish our fighting efficiency', warned Balfour.[99] His stentiments were shared by senior officials in the Board of Trade. On 25 January the Permanent Secretary of the Board of Trade, Sir Hubert Llewellyn Smith, told the War Office that the only hope of extending recruiting to the extent which Kitchener wanted, without injuring the country's industrial and financial base, depended 'on a careful discrimination between industries in which it is desirable or undesirable to encourage recruiting for the time being'.[100] Llewellyn Smith also produced a memorandum for the Cabinet in which he calculated that, of Britain's remaining manpower resources, only another 1,100,000 could be recruited without crippling industry and an upper limit of 3 million men should therefore be imposed on the size of the army if the government wished to avoid serious damage to the economy. As Dr David French has commented, these proposals were significant because this was 'the first time anyone had looked into the future and tried to set a finite limit to recruiting for the New Armies'.[101]

Llewellyn Smith's memorandum was considered at a meeting of the Committee of Imperial Defence on 27 January 1915, but Kitchener refused to be swayed, maintaining that, to be victorious, Britain had to possess a great land force for which he would require at least a further 1,500,000 men by the end of the year. Recalling only too well how the 'stop–go' policy of the previous September had affected enlistments, Kitchener insisted that, even for the sake of the economy, 'it would be a dreadful thing at this stage to put a limit on recruiting'.[102] Kitchener's arguments won the day on this occasion, but the voices of dissent were not to be stilled. Leading members of the Conservative opposition were becoming disenchanted with the conduct of the war and were threatening to break the political truce established in August. In a long memorandum at the end of January Lord Curzon complained bitterly about the attitude of the government in general and Kitchener in particular:

The Secretary of State for War reads us exiguous memoranda of platitudes known to everybody, is acclaimed by the Liberal press as having delivered an almost inspired oration and scored off his impertinent antagonists, he interpolates a curt affirmative or negative to the solitary speech to which he deigns to listen, and he then marches out and leaves the rest of the debate to colleagues who either affect to know nothing or screen their silence behind his authority. The Parliamentary Recruiting Committee was started under the patronage of the Leaders and with the aid of the organisation of both political parties, but we are not allowed to hear anything about the results. . . . I' do not think that this state of affairs can continue indefinitely, both because the temper of our Party will not long stand it, and because in the interests of the nation, the position is both highly inexpedient and unfair.[103]

From this point on, parliamentary disapproval of the government's recruiting policy steadily mounted, although the critics still tended to concentrate their attention on the decline in the enlistment totals rather than on the pressing need for the government to re-examine its manpower priorities. On 8 February G. W. Currie, the Conservative MP for Louth, declared that no form of compulsion could be more tyrannical than 'the many appeals that will be possibly made if larger numbers of men are required to be raised'.[104] The government met all such challenges with bland assurances. On 1 March Asquith told the House that 'We have no reason to be other than satisfied with the progress of recruiting here at home' and on 11 March he said that it had not yet been found essential to carry out any investigation into conscription.[105] The matter came up again on 20 April, when Lloyd George, replying for the Prime Minister, stated, 'The government are not of the opinion that the war would be more successfully prosecuted by means of conscription.' He added, 'The Secretary of State for War is very gratified with the response which has been made to the appeal to the country for voluntary enlistment.'[106]

Optimistic statements like these did more harm than good, for the longer the government persisted in declaring itself content with the recruiting figures the more difficult it became to convince the country that a still greater effort was necessary. On 18 May Kitchener appealed in the House of Lords for an additional 300,000 volunteers.[107] The next day the age limit was raised to forty and the height standard for recruits other than those in Bantam units was reduced to 5ft 2in. The effects of this appeal on enlistment were minimal. The following account of a fourteen-day recruiting march carried out by the 3rd East Yorkshire Regiment shows how hard it was to persuade men to volunteer by the latter half of May 1915:

Our first stay was at Holme-on-Splading-Moor, where we stopped four days. The NCOs were sent out in pairs to visit the surrounding villages and farms. On Friday, 21st, we held a recruiting meeting in the village school. . . . We had fifty posters printed advertising this and we put most of them on the old farmers' gates and windows and doors, so as to attract attention. These may have caused annoyance, because many were pulled down directly they were put up. . . . After this meeting seven recruits offered their services; five, I am sorry to say, were ineligible. This meeting attracted many old ladies and children, but extraordinarily few men. . . . On the 22nd the party moved to Middleton-on-the-Wolds, where we stayed five days. Here we held an open-air meeting on the village green. About 100 young men attended, none of whom we influenced in the least. . . . We left Stamford Bridge on Monday, 31st, having been away a fortnight, and having got altogether eight recruits. . . .[108]

III

By failing to prepare a rational plan for the mobilisation of the nation's manpower at the beginning of the war the government had created a rod for its own back in later months. In the absence of such a blueprint, problems were tackled in piecemeal fashion as they arose, with the result that in May 1915 the country was faced with what appeared to be simultaneous crises in recruiting and munitions production. Some of the blame for this situation can be apportioned to Kitchener himself, for his consistent hostility to any form of extra-departmental interference hampered all attempts to establish a properly co-ordinated manpower policy in the first eight months of the war. He wanted men for his New Armies and also wished to enlarge and strengthen the armaments firms which were to equip them with weapons, but he did not consider that it was his task to ensure that a suitable compromise was struck between the requirements of the army and industry.

In August 1914 responsiblity for the supply of munitions to the army rested with the Master-General of the Ordnance, one of the four Military Members of the Army Council. To be fair, it must be said that both Kitchener and Major-General Sir Stanley von Donop, the Master-General of the Ordnance, immediately recognised the need for a substantial increase in munitions output and made energetic efforts to improve the supply. Kitchener informed the House of Lords on 17 September, at a time when recruits were still swarming in, that the chief difficulty confronting the New Armies was 'one of *matériel* rather than *personnel*'.[109] On the other hand, he showed few signs of understanding that, in an age of mass armies, any large-scale expansion embraced factors, such as the mobilisation of manufacturing resources and the distribution of labour, which transcended the normal bounds of War Office authority. His reluctance to accept alternative administrative machinery for the direction and supervision of munitions production made it harder to find an early solution to these broader problems and limited the ability of industry to respond in full to the demands of the war.

The first indications of unease in the Cabinet about the question of munitions manifested themselves at the beginning of October 1914, when Lloyd George, as Chancellor of the Exchequer, was disturbed to find that von Donop had chosen not to tell the major armament firms that the Treasury had made £20 million available to help them increase their production capacity.[110] Pressure from Lloyd George induced Asquith to set up a Cabinet Committee on Munitions on 12 October. Kitchener, Lloyd George, Churchill and Haldane were to serve on it, together with Reginald McKenna, then Home Secretary, Walter Runciman, President of the Board of Trade, and Lord Lucas, President of the Board of Agriculture. Meeting six times between 12 October and 1 January, the committee did much to expand the output of field guns, howitzers and rifles. In addition to placing large orders with American manufacturers, the committee persuaded the four biggest armament firms at home to increase their plant and facilities, although it was less successful in getting the private manufacturers to guarantee delivery' dates. Some headway was also made in breaking down the Ordnance Department's prejudice against manufacturers who were not on the official War Office list. An Armaments Firms Committee was formed from representatives of the government and companies on the War Office list to issue contracts for components among other engineering shops, and by May 1915 over 2,500 individual firms were engaged in some aspect of munitions production.[111]

Had the Cabinet Committee on Munitions carried on with its work in the first quarter of 1915 even more progress might have been achieved, but, after its sixth meeting on 1 January, it was allowed to lapse. The committee had always been something of an annoyance to Kitchener, and it was he who effectively killed it by claiming that he could no longer find time to attend its meetings. Over the next two months the government took little effective action to capitalise on the advances the committee had made. One of the main obstacles to progress was the attitude of the War Office on the question of spreading orders for munitions. The army's Director of Contracts, a man more at home with the elaborate procedures of peacetime, had been dismissed in the autumn of 1914 and replaced by U. F. Wintour, a brilliant organiser from the Board of Trade. Kitchener had subsequently tried to improve the organisation further by subordinating the Contracts Branch to von Donop, so giving the Ordnance Department the responsibility for assessing future requirements and placing the appropriate orders. But while the War Office was willing to permit its regular suppliers to sub-contract part of their work to other engineering firms, it was extremely reluctant to place whole orders for complete guns and shells to companies outside its recognised circle of manufacturers. In defence of the War Office, many of these outside firms lacked the experience, labour and equipment needed to produce finished guns, shells and fuses, and Kitchener and von Donop were afraid that dependence upon new suppliers would inevitably lead to sub-standard work and delays. Later deliveries of faulty shells and fuses showed that their fears were not entirely groundless. However, until the War Office altered its policy of organising production through the principal armaments firms, much of the country's engineering capacity was to remain unexploited.[112]

Though Treasury parsimony before 1914 had limited the ability of the armaments industry to expand rapidly in wartime, the Chancellor of the Exchequer, Lloyd George, was now convinced that only tighter State control of the nation's industrial capacity and manpower supply would suffice to guarantee that Britain had all the tools she needed to wage the war successfully. On 22 February he made his views abundantly clear in a memorandum to the Cabinet. 'All the engineering works of the country ought to be turned to the production of war material,' he argued. 'The population ought to be prepared to suffer all sorts of deprivations and even hardships whilst this process is going on.' He foresaw dire consequences if the government maintained its present approach to the problem:

If it turns out that my estimate errs on the side of pessimism the worst that happens will be that we shall spend a considerable amount of money, we shall have caused a considerable amount of inconvenience to the population. But all that is nothing compared with the disaster of having to face another year of war with inadequate preparation. This the public will never forgive after the warning we have received nor ought they be expected to forgive.[113]

The Conservatives supported Lloyd George's efforts to get the government to take a more positive line. 'The position seems to me to be most unsatisfactory,' Balfour told him on 5 March, 'and unless you will take in hand the organisation of the engineering resources of the country in the interests of military equipment, I do not see how any improvement is to be expected.'[114] That day the munitions issue was discussed at a meeting at 10 Downing Street which was attended by Kitchener, Lloyd George and von Donop. Lloyd

George was heartened by what he believed to be the main decision of the meeting, as he informed Balfour on 6 March, although he also complained about Kitchener's continuing intransigence:

An Executive Committee is to be set up for the purpose not merely of supervising existing work but for organising our engineering reserves for the purpose of increasing the output. Kitchener absolutely refuses to hand over the whole output of munitions of war for the Admiralty and War Office alike to the Executive. . . . He clearly means to retain control over this executive himself, and I fear he is on the lookout for a tame chairman who will carry out the directions of the War Office instead of acting on his own initiative. . . . Nothing can remedy this state of things except the placing at the head of this new Executive of an energetic, fearless man who will not be cajoled and bamboozled by von Donop nor bullied by anyone else'.[115]

Some time passed before the composition and duties of the new committee were worked out and, before it came into being, Kitchener made a determined bid to keep the control of munitions production in the hands of the War Office. On 15 March, in the House of Lords, Kitchener had admitted that the supply of war material at present and for the next two or three months was causing him very serious anxiety.[116] The following day he decided to set up his own Armaments Output Committee under the chairmanship of George Macaulay Booth, the Liverpool shipowner and industrialist, whose principal task was to find all the additional labour required by the established armaments factories. Booth really favoured a policy of spreading orders for munitions amongst all suitable private engineering firms, yet he agreed to do as Kitchener asked, hoping that, in the end, the War Office policy on contracts would be abandoned.[117] The creation of the Armaments Output Committee was not announced until 7 April but Booth himself started work at once.

In spite of Kitchener's attempt to safeguard the authority of the War Office on the munitions issue, the ground was shifting under his feet. He was not even invited to attend a meeting on 22 March at which Asquith discussed the matter with Lloyd George, Churchill, Balfour and Edwin Montagu, the Chancellor of the Duchy of Lancaster. On 23 March Asquith wrote to Kitchener to tell him that a new 'Committee on War Supplies' was to be established, under Lloyd George, to mobilise potential as well as existing sources of munitions supply. Because it was to derive its authority from the Cabinet rather than the War Office, this committee would have full power, after due consultation with the service departments, to 'enter into new contracts' in its own right. The Prime Minister tried to soothe Kitchener by assuring him that the decision would result in only 'the minimum of interference with the normal contract work of the Departments'.[118] Kitchener replied that he was certain that the committee under Lloyd George would be 'very helpful in finding new sources of output' but again insisted that it should not interfere with existing War Office contracts nor divert labour from firms which had been, or were about to be, registered as War Office suppliers and sub-contractors.[119] Asquith showed Kitchener's letter to Lloyd George, who lost no time in making his own feelings known to Kitchener, observing that if his committee was to be precluded from making any arrangements with War Office contractors to expedite 'the output of these works' it would impose 'a restriction upon the committee's activities which might paralyse their efforts'. He also added tartly, 'It was supposed that you and Churchill were so overwhelmed with other work that it would be a real assistance to you to have someone who would undertake this kind of work for you.'[120]

The dispute between Kitchener and Lloyd George soon took on the proportions of a 'truly royal row', as Asquith described it to Venetia Stanley on 28 March.[121] The Prime Minister strove to reinforce the authority of Lloyd George's committee by proposing, on 31 March, that it should have the power to examine new War Office contracts and that the War Office 'labour organisation' (i.e. Booth's Armaments Output Committee) should also come within its ambit.[122] A week later, on 8 April, Asquith finally announced the creation of the new Cabinet committee promised in March. With Lloyd George as chairman, the Munitions of War Committee, as it was called, was to include Balfour, Edwin Montagu and Arthur Henderson. Kitchener was not a member, the War Office being represented by von Donop and Booth. The object of the Munitions of War Committee was 'to ensure the promptest and most efficient application of all the available resources of the country to the manufacture and supply of Munitions of War for the Army and Navy'. Asquith confirmed that it had 'full authority to take all steps necessary for that purpose.[123]

In his customary fashion Asquith had tried to avert a head-on clash in the Cabinet by effecting a compromise but succeeded only in adding to the confusion, since, under the new system, neither Lloyd George nor Kitchener was wholly in control of munitions output. Matters were not helped by Kitchener's objections, on security grounds, to providing the Munitions of War Committee with details of the numbers of troops he intended to place in the field at given dates, information which was vital to Lloyd George if his committee wished to make accurate assessments of future munitions requirements.[124] The dynamic Booth, who, by force of circumstance, was now cast in the role of intermediary between Lloyd George and Kitchener, also attempted to find a way out of the *impasse* over contracts and labour. Booth suggested splitting the country into 'A' and 'B' areas. In the former, which were areas within twenty miles of government Ordnance factories or recognised War Office contractors, labour was to be concentrated in the existing munitions plants, even if this meant drafting in skilled labour employed on private contracts or less urgent munitions work. B areas were defined as districts where no direct War Office contracts or sub-contracts had yet been placed. Here manufacturers were to be encouraged to co-operate and pool their resources in plant and labour to tender for new contracts, though workers were to be available for transfer to A areas while their own engineering firms were converting to munitions production. Booth's scheme did have the advantage of setting more of the nation's unexploited engineering capacity to work on munitions, but the plan also had its weaknesses. One was that there was too little skilled supervision available for the B areas. Another was that the distribution of contracts among many small and widely separated firms was likely to be uneconomical. A third drawback lay in the proposal to allow the temporary transfer of men from B areas to A areas. The War Office would obviously suffer from this, because once an engineering firm in a B area had converted to munitions production and its old employees had returned, the War Office suppliers would again be left with a labour shortage.[125]

In mid-April Kitchener made a last effort to strengthen his hand by inviting Sir Percy Girouard, then managing director of Armstrong's at Elswick, to come to the War Office to advise on munitions problems. At Kitchener's urging, Girouard became an additional War Office representative on the Munitions of War Committee. Like Booth, Girouard had great respect and affection for Kitchener, but the plan he presented to the Munitions of War Committee on 26 April further undermined the War Office's position in the munitions debate. Girouard believed that the best way to exploit the country's engineering and manpower resources was to establish State munition factories in industrial areas rather than to spread production among many small firms. In his opinion, by concentrating the whole process of arms manufacture in such factories many of the problems of supervision, inspection and labour supply would be much easier to solve.[126] When Girouard's scheme was accepted by the Munitions of War Committee and recommended to the government, Kitchener gave more ground, authorising Booth and Girouard to carry the scheme into effect and 'to act without further reference to the Secretary of State'. He also conceded that in the event of 'any difference arising between them and any departments which cannot be mutually adjusted, the instructions of the Treasury Committee on Munitions of War are to be followed'.[127]

What Girouard had helped to identify, and Kitchener had at last acknowledged, was that the manufacture of munitions, with all its associated manpower issues, was too big a problem to be handled by the Ordnance Department of the War Office alone. The establishment of an independent Ministry to assume control of both the production and supply of munitions was the logical next step. The coming of such a Ministry was precipitated by two separate crises which shook the Liberal government in mid-May. On 14 May *The Times* published a despatch from its military correspondent, Colonel Repington, which pointed to the shortage of shells as the overriding reason for the failure of the recent operations at Aubers Ridge. 'The infantry did splendidly,' Repington wrote, 'but the conditions were too hard. The want of an unlimited supply of high explosives was a fatal bar to our success.'[128] Twenty-four hours later, Admiral of the Fleet Lord Fisher tendered his resignation as First Sea Lord after a sharp disagreement with Churchill over the use of sea power in the Dardanelles campaign.

The background to the 'Shells Scandal', as the furore following the release of Repington's despatch was to be labelled, has been fully explored by other writers and need not be described in detail in the present context.[129] It now seems clear that the shell shortage in France, if not illusory, was exaggerated by Sir John French, the Commander-in-Chief of the British Expeditionary Force, to shift attention away from his own tactical shortcomings, and was also used by Lloyd George to force a Ministry of Munitions and a co-ordinated munitions policy on the government. Together with Fisher's resignation it certainly provided Asquith with an opportunity to create a coalition government, a step he now regarded as essential in order to preserve national unity. This much he made plain on 17 May when he asked all his Cabinet Ministers to resign:

I have for some time past come, with increasing conviction, to the conclusion that the continued prosecution of the War requires what is called a 'broad-based' government. Under existing conditions, criticism, inspired by party motives and interests, has full reign, and is an asset of much value to the enemy. . . . The resignation of Lord Fisher . . . and the more than plausible Parliamentary case in regard to the alleged deficiency of high-explosive shells, would, if duly exploited (as they would have been) in the House of Commons at this moment, have had the most disastrous effect on the general political and strategic situation. . . .[130]

On 25 May Asquith announced the formation of a coalition Cabinet, which would include several leading Conservatives, and on 26 May the country was told that a new Ministry of Munitions, under Lloyd George, had been created to take over from the Admiralty and War Office the duty of supplying munitions to the Royal Navy and the army. In hastening a Cabinet reshuffle and the establishment of the Ministry of Munitions the combination of Fisher's resignation and the exposure of the shell shortage also heralded the end of the government's haphazard approach to the manpower question.

Notes

1 Monthly recruiting figures, September 1914–February 1915, *Statistics of the Military Effort of the British Empire*, p. 364.
2 Monthly recruiting figures for cities, September 1914–February 1915, NATS 1/85.
3 *The Times*, 10 September 1914.
4 *Parliamentary Debates, House of Commons*, 1914, LXVI, col. 968; *Increased Rates of Separation Allowances for the Wives and Children of Soldiers*, PP, 1914–16, XXXIX, Cd 7623, p. 1.
5 *Soldiers' and Sailors' Families Association, Annual Report, 1914–1915*, pp. 26–32; *Tyneside Scottish Dependants' Aid Committee, Case Register, 1914–1915*, IWM DPB/777894; Arthur Marwick, *Women at War, 1914–1918*, Fontana, London, 1977, p. 37.
6 See J. M. Winter, *The Great War and the British People*, Macmillan, London, 1986, pp. 33–7; P. E. Dewey, 'Military recruiting and the British labour force

during the First World War', *Historical Journal*, XXVII, No. 1, 1984, pp. 199–224; and Ian F. W. Beckett, 'The nation in arms, 1914–18', in Ian F. W. Beckett and Keith Simpson (eds.), *A Nation in Arms: a Social Study of the British Army in the First World War*, Manchester University Press, 1985, pp. 9–10.

7   Board of Trade, *Labour Gazette*, 1914, pp. 321, 348.

8   *Report of the Board of Trade on the State of Employment in the United Kingdom in October 1914*, PP, 1914–16, XXI, Cd 7703, p. 5.

9   *Ibid.*, p. 5.

10 John A. Lee, *Todmorden and the Great War: a Local Record*, Waddington, Todmorden, 1922, pp. 134–5.

11 M. D. Blanch, 'Nation, Empire and the Birmingham Working Class, 1899–1914', Ph.D. thesis, Birmingham, 1975, pp. 341–67.

12 Local Government Board Circular PRD 7, 20 August 1914. A copy can be found in the papers of the War Emergency Workers' National Committee, Transport House, WEWNC C/7–18.

13 *Report of the Board of Trade on the State of Employment in October 1914*, Cd 7703, p. 5.

14 *Labour Gazette*, 1914, pp. 357, 393, 429; 1915, pp. 1–2.

15 *Ibid.*, 1914, p. 367.

16 *Ibid.*, p. 369.

17 *Ibid.*, pp. 371–3.

18 *Bristol Times and Mirror*, 30 September 1914.

19 *Labour Gazette*, 1914, p. 341.

20 *Report of the Board of Trade on the State of Employment in October 1914*, Cd 7703, p. 5; *Labour Gazette*, 1914, pp. 400–15.

21 *Report of the Board of Trade on the State of Employment in February 1915*, PP, 1914–16, XXI, Cd 7850, p. 4.

22 *Labour Gazette*, 1915, p. 273.

23 *Ibid.*, pp. 105, 142.

24 *The Times*, 16 October 1914.

25 Minutes of the Executive Committee of the Bristol Citizens' Recruiting Committee, 31 December 1914; F. P. Armitage, *Leicester, 1914–1918*, Backus, Leicester, 1933, p. 79.

26 Board of Trade, 'Enlistment from the Industrial Classes and the State of Employment on Government and other Work in mid-February 1916', Reconstruction papers, PRO RECON 1/832; see also Winter, *The Great War and the British People*, p. 34.

27 Board of Trade, 'Enlistment from the Industrial Classes', pp. 8–9; Dewey, 'Military recruiting and the British labour force', pp. 210–11.

28 *Report on the State of Employment in February 1915*, p. 11.

29 See *Report of the Departmental Committee appointed to Enquire into Conditions prevailing in the Coal Mining Industry due to the War*, PP, 1914–16, XXVIII, Cd 7939; *Report of the Board of Trade on the State of Employment in October 1914*, pp. 28–39; R. Page Arnot, *The Miners, Years of Struggle: a History of the Miners' Federation of Great Britain from 1910 onwards*, Allen & Unwin, London, 1960, p. 160.

30 *Second General Report of the Departmental Committee appointed to Enquire into Conditions Prevailing in the Coal Mining Industry due to the War*, PP, 1914–16, XXVIII, Cd 8147, p. 307.

31 A. L. Bowley, *Prices and Wages in the United Kingdom, 1914–1920*, Clarendon Press, Oxford, 1921, pp. 113–83; Dewey, *op. cit.*, pp. 208–9.

32 E. A. Pratt, *British Railways and the Great War*, Selwyn & Blount, London,

1921, I, pp. 349–50.

33 *Report on the State of Employment in February 1915*, p. 15.

34 *Report on the State of Employment in July 1915*, pp. 3 *et seq.*

35 Humbert Wolfe, *Labour Supply and Regulation*, Oxford University Press, 1923, pp. 19–27.

36 *Parliamentary Debates, House of Lords, 1915*, XVIII, col. 351.

37 *Parliamentary Debates, House of Commons, 1914*, LXV, cols. 1828–9.

38 *Freeman's Journal*, 2 September 1914.

39 Denis Gwynn, *The Life of John Redmond*, Harrap, London, 1932, p. 366.

40 Percy Illingworth to Kitchener, 7 August 1914, Kitchener papers, PRO 30/57/60.

41 *Freeman's Journal*, 12 September 1914.

42 Note by A. P. Graves of a conversation with Sir Edward Carson, 13 March 1915, C. P. Scott papers, BL Add. Mss 50908.

43 *Freeman's Journal*, 22 September 1914; *Irish Independent*, 23 September 1914.

44 *Freeman's Journal*, 21 September 1914.

45 *The Times*, 26 September 1914.

46 Asquith to Redmond, 30 September 1914, Redmond papers, 15165 (4).

47 Gwynn, *The Life of John Redmond*, pp. 396–411.

48 Trevor Royle, *The Kitchener Enigma*, Joseph, London, 1985, pp. 274–5.

49 Gwynn, *Redmond*, p. 390.

50 *Ibid.*, p. 401; *Freeman's Journal*, 26 October 1914.

51 Patrick Callan, 'British recruitment in Ireland, 1914–1918', *Revue Internationale d'Histoire Militaire*, No. 63, Freiburg, 1985, p. 49.

52 *Parliamentary Debates, House of Commons, 1914–1915*, LXI, cols. 841–2.

53 Callan, 'British recruitment in Ireland, p. 43.

54 *Ibid.*, p. 44.

55 *Irish Independent*, 19 August 1914.

56 Anti-recruiting leaflet circulated in Waterford, October 1914, IWM DPB/K. 33666.

57 Memorandum by Birrell on 'The state of Ireland', 24 November 1914, CAB 37/122.

58 Brendan Mac Giolla Choille (ed.), *Intelligence Notes, 1913–16*, State Paper Office, Dublin, 1966, pp. 119, 166–74.

59 Monthly recruiting figures for Ireland, August 1914–May 1915, Redmond papers, 15259.

60 *Labour Leader*, 6 August 1914.

61 *Ibid.*, 3 September 1914.

62 *Daily Express*, 11 September 1914.

63 A. M. B. Meakin, *Enlistment or Conscription*, Routledge, London, 1915, pp. 10–11.

64 Notes on recruiting kept by the Rev. E. H. L. Reeve, Rector of Stondon Massey, 1914–16, ERO TP 188/3.

65 'Recruiting, transfers and discharges', in *History of the Development and Work of the Directorate of Organisation, August 1914–December 1918*, War Office, London, 1919, p. 84. A copy can be found in WO 162/6 at the Public Record Office.

66 *Locally Raised Units*, War Office, 1916, pp. 1–11. This is a list of units raised by communities and individuals who undertook to clothe, house and feed them at the public expense until such time as the military authorities were prepared to assume these duties. A copy of the list is in the Kitchener papers, PRO 30/57/73.

67 *Ibid.*, pp. 1–11.

68 Minutes of the Recruiting Committee of the Metropolitan Borough of St

Marylebone, 11 May 1915.

69 Figures taken from details given in Becke, *Order of Battle of Divisions*, Parts 1–4, and James, *British Regiments, 1914–1918*.

70 Sidney Allinson, *The Bantams: the Untold Story of World War I*, Baker, London, 1981, pp. 37–9; Arthur Crookenden, *The History of the Cheshire Regiment in the Great War*, Evans, Chester, n.d., pp. 346–7.

71 Lieutenant-Colonel F. E. Whitton, *History of the 40th Division*, Gale & Polden, Aldershot, 1926, pp. 8–9.

72 Minutes of meeting of the Finance Committee of the Parliamentary Recruiting Committee, 28 October 1914, BL Add. Mss 54192.

73 *The Times*, 6 January 1915.

74 Minutes of meeting of the General Purposes Committee of the Parliamentary Recruiting Committee, 21 October 1914, BL Add. Mss 54192.

75 *The Times*, 7 November 1914.

76 Minutes of meetings of the General Purposes Committee, PRC, 21 and 26 October 1914, BL Add. Mss 54192.

77 Roy Douglas, 'Voluntary enlistment in the First World War and the work of the Parliamentary Recruiting Committee', *Journal of Modern History*, Vol. 42, No. 4, 1970, p. 572.

78 *Parliamentary Debates, House of Lords, 1915*, XVIII, col. 225.

79 *Parliamentary Debates, House of Commons, 1914–1915*, LXXIII, col. 146.

80 *The Times*, 30 March 1915.

81 Michael MacDonagh, *In London, during the Great War*, Eyre & Spottiswoode, London, 1935, p. 51.

82 *London Opinion*, 12 September 1914.

83 *Ibid.*, 26 September 1914.

84 Eric Field, *Advertising: the Forgotten Years*, Benn, London, 1959, pp. 28–9.

85 Parliamentary Recruiting Committee poster No. 79, IWM DA/0311; Arthur Marwick, *The Deluge: British Society and the First World War*, Bodley Head, London, 1965, p. 52.

86 PRC poster No. 75, IWM DA/2763; London recruiting poster, 1914–1915, IWM DA/4903.

87 *Punch*, 21 October 1914.

88 *Daily Telegraph*, 9 November 1914.

89 MacDonagh, *In London during the Great War*, p. 44.

90 Central London Recruiting Depot poster, November 1914, IWM DA/0970.

91 MacDonagh, *op. cit.*, p. 79.

92 A. R. Kennewell, letter of 24 May 1964, IWM BBC/GW.

93 Carl Wehner, letter of 23 May 1964, IWM BBC/GW.

94 *Dumfries Standard*, 16 September 1914; *The Times*, 18 September 1914.

95 Robert Graves, *Good-bye to all that*, Cape, London, 1929, pp. 99–100.

96 *Statistics of the Military Effort of the British Empire*, p. 364.

97 *Parliamentary Debates, House of Commons, 1914–1915*, LXVIII, col. 1119.

98 *Debates on Army Affairs, House of Lords, 1914–1916*, col. 293.

99 A. J. Balfour, memorandum on 'Limits of Enlistment', 5 January 1915, CAB 42/1/7.

100 Llewellyn Smith to R. H. Brade, 25 January 1915, PRO BT 13/603/E 271908.

101 Llewellyn Smith, note on 'Limits of Enlistment', 11 January 1915, CAB 42/1/14; Llewellyn Smith, Statistical supplement to note on 'Limits of Enlistment', 23 January 1915, CAB 42/1/21; *History of the Ministry of Munitions*, Vol. I, Part II, pp. 7–9; David French, *British Economic and Strategic Planning, 1905–1915*, Allen & Unwin, London, 1982, p. 157.

102 Minutes of the 131st meeting of the Committee of Imperial Defence, 27 January

1915, CAB 42/1/24.

103 Memorandum by Lord Curzon, undated, *c.* 27–28 January 1915, Balfour papers, BL Add. Mss 49693.

104 *Parliamentary Debates, House of Commons, 1914–1915,* LXIX, col. 330.

105 *Ibid.,* LXX, cols. 595, 1553.

106 *Ibid.,* LXXI, cols. 172–3.

107 *Debates on Army Affairs, House of Lords, 1914–1916,* col. 575.

108 Account by Second Lieutenant T. R. H. Smyth in *The Snapper,* journal of the East Yorkshire Regiment, Vol. X, No. 6, June 1915, pp. 115–16.

109 *Parliamentary Debates, House of Lords, 1914,* XVII, col. 736.

110 Lloyd George, *War Memoirs,* I, p. 120.

111 *History of the Ministry of Munitions,* Vol. I, Part I, pp. 93–112; 'Notes on the Supply of Guns prior to the Formation of the Ministry of Munitions, August 1914–June 1915', PRO MUN 5/6/170/30; French, *British Economic and Strategic Planning,* p. 135; R. J. Q. Adams, *Arms and the Wizard: Lloyd George and the Ministry of Munitions, 1915–1916,* Cassell, London, 1978, p. 20.

112 Adams, *Arms and the Wizard,* p. 20; French, *op. cit.,* pp. 133–4; Duncan Crow, *A Man of Push and Go: the Life of George Macaulay Booth,* Hart-Davis, London, 1965, pp. 75–6, 86–7.

113 Memorandum by Lloyd George, 'Some further Considerations on the Conduct of the War', 22 February 1915, CAB 37/124.

114 Balfour to Lloyd George, 5 March 1915, Balfour papers, BL Add. Mss 49692.

115 Lloyd George to Balfour, 6 March 1915, Balfour papers, BL Add. Mss 49692.

116 *Parliamentary Debates, House of Lords, 1915,* XVIII, cols. 721–4.

117 Crow, *A Man of Push and Go,* pp. 91–109.

118 Asquith to Kitchener, 23 March 1915, Kitchener papers, PRO 30/57/82.

119 Kitchener to Asquith, 25 March 1915, Kitchener papers, PRO 30/57/82.

120 Lloyd George to Kitchener, 25 March 1915, Kitchener papers, PRO 30/57/82.

121 Asquith to Venetia Stanley, 28 March 1915, see Michael and Eleanor Brock (eds.), *H. H. Asquith: Letters to Venetia Stanley,* Oxford University Press, 1982, p. 514.

122 Asquith to Kitchener, 31 March 1915, Kitchener papers, PRO 30/57/82.

123 Minute by Asquith on the Munitions of War Committee, 8 April 1915, Kitchener papers, PRO 30/57/82.

124 Lloyd George to Balfour, 8 April 1915, Lloyd George papers, HLRO C/3/3/4; Cassar, *Kitchener: Architect of Victory,* p. 345; French, *op. cit.,* p. 165; Royle, *The Kitchener Enigma,* p. 288.

125 Minutes of meeting of the Armaments Output Committee, 20 April 1915, MUN 5/7/171/1; *History of the Ministry of Munitions,* Vol. I, Part III, pp. 40–2; Adams, *op. cit.,* p. 58; French, *op. cit.,* p. 165.

126 *History of the Ministry of Munitions,* Vol. I, Part III, pp. 70–1; see also MUN 5/342/170/11 for the paper prepared by Girouard for the meeting of the Munitions of War Committee on 26 April 1915.

127 Notice issued by Kitchener from the War Office, 28 April 1915, MUN 5/342/170/2/11.

128 *The Times,* 14 May 1915.

129 See, for example, Peter Fraser, 'The British "Shells Scandal" of 1915', *Canadian Journal of History,* Vol. XVIII, No. 1, 1983, pp. 69–86; French, *op. cit.,* pp. 138–49, 165–7; Cassar, *op. cit.,* pp. 348–60; Royle, *op. cit.,* pp. 280–99.

130 Asquith to the Cabinet, 17 May 1915, CAB 37/128/19.

5

The coming of conscription

The controversy over the supply of munitions and the formation of the coalition government in May 1915 briefly diverted attention from the manpower question. However, as the summer wore on the debate on compulsory service entered a more intense phase. 'The attempt to stampede the country into conscription is now in full swing', declared the Liberal *Manchester Guardian* on 1 June, less than a fortnight after the establishment of the coalition.[1] The new Cabinet included twelve Liberals, eight Conservatives and the Labour leader, Arthur Henderson, as well as Kitchener, aptly described by Dr John Rae as 'the guest of honour who had become an embarrassment but who could not be asked to leave'.[2] Although Liberals still held most of the key posts, the campaign for compulsion was now greatly strengthened by the presence in the Cabinet of a group of influential politicians whose open support for such a policy was not conditioned by loyalty to Asquith or devotion to Liberal principles.

At this stage the division of opinion on the conscription issue did not necessarily follow rigid party lines. Broadly speaking, Conservatives urged the adoption of compulsory service while the Liberals and organised labour were opposed to it. On the other hand some Liberals, notably Lloyd George and Churchill, favoured conscription and a few Conservatives resisted its introduction. Discussions on compulsion within the Cabinet usually ended in deadlock, but the frequent disagreements served to weaken the already fragile coalition further. Thus, from the start, the reshaped Cabinet was a cumbersome and quarrelsome body, depicted by Leo Amery as 'little more than a debating society in which everybody differed, and in which nothing was ever definitely decided until events forced some sort of decision'.[3] In this situation the positions on conscription taken up by three of the Cabinet's most prominent members – Asquith, Lloyd George and Kitchener – assumed a crucial significance.

The Prime Minister held no doctrinaire attachment to the voluntary principle but was prepared to defend it as long as it fulfilled its purpose. His main concern was to preserve the unity of the Cabinet and country while remaining as true as possible to the tenets of *laissez-faire* Liberalism, and he was loath to back conscription until he was sure that there was a universal demand for the replacement of the voluntary system. Up to July 1915 the monthly recruiting figures, though much lower than in the autumn of 1914, were still sufficiently high to sustain Asquith's view that the nation did not yet want conscription and that the voluntary system would continue to provide the required numbers of men. Nevertheless, any emphatic drop in the enlistment totals would make this position much more difficult to maintain.

While Asquith's reasons for defending the voluntary system are reasonably clear, Lloyd George's motives in advocating conscription have been the subject of considerable argument among historians. Professor Trevor Wilson has accused him of 'blatant disloyalty to his colleagues, open intriguing for office, and a ready acceptance of compulsion and Conservatives allies', adding that he was 'bent on advancing both the war effort and his political career, and mobile in his party allegiance if it meant furthering either'.[4] An alternative view has been put forward by Dr Cameron Hazlehurst, who claims that 'Lloyd George perceived no greater advantage for himself in a coalition than in a party government'.[5] As is so often the case, the truth probably lies somewhere in between. Lloyd George was certainly too much of a political animal to be entirely free from ambition for the highest office and he can hardly have been unaware that the course he was following in mid-1915 would undermine Asquith's authority. All the same, even Professor Wilson has conceded that 'however dubious his methods, he acted from motives of patriotism as well as self-interest'.[6] After his initial wavering on the question of Britain's entry into the conflict, Lloyd George had soon thrown himself behind the recruiting campaign with all the fervour of the recently converted and by mid-October 1914 was second to none in calling for a more vigorous prosecution of the war effort. During the next few months his feeling that not enough was being done to bring the war to a successful conclusion hardened into a firm conviction and inevitably coloured his relationships with his Cabinet colleagues. It was almost certainly this conviction rather than personal antagonism or ambition that led to his confrontations, first with Kitchener over the munitions problem and later with Asquith on the conscription issue.

It will also be recalled that, as late as April 1915, Lloyd George was still following the government line on compulsion, at least in his public pronouncements, and even if he had accepted by then that any failure of voluntary recruiting would necessitate conscription, this did not mean that he hoped the voluntary system would be found wanting. In any event, his attention in the spring of 1915 was largely occupied by the munitions problem and the need for the more efficient mobilisation and control of industrial manpower. Not until after the formation of the coalition government and the creation of the Ministry of Munitions did he come down

ORD KITCHENER SAYS:-

'MEN, MATERIALS & MONEY ARE THE IMMEDIATE NECESSITIES. ......

DOES THE CALL OF DUTY FIND NO RESPONSE IN YOU UNTIL REINFORCED — LET US RATHER SAY SUPERSEDED — BY THE CALL OF COMPULSION?'

Lord Kitchener. Speaking at Guildhall. July 9th 1915.

NLIST TO-DAY.

solidly on the side of conscription. By that time it was, for Lloyd George, but a short step from advocating industrial mobilisation to pressing for compulsory military service.

With the Cabinet thus split over conscription, both sides looked to Kitchener for encouragement. The hold which Kitchener maintained on the national imagination was indicated by the indignant public reaction to the attacks on him during the 'Shells Scandal' campaign in the Northcliffe press, and helped him to survive the political crisis of May 1915. However, the removal from the War Office of control over munitions production revealed how far Kitchener's power in the Cabinet had diminished since the previous autumn. Lacking experience in the cut and thrust of Parliamentary debate, he was particularly ill at ease in the new Cabinet. Herbert Samuel has described the clashes between Lloyd George and Kitchener, for example, as being 'like a fight between the nimble swordfish and the massive whale'.[7] No longer able to command unquestioning support for his decisions, Kitchener was now increasingly liable to criticism and judgement simply as a member of a team. Even so, leading conscriptionists in the Cabinet, such as Lord Curzon and Sir Edward Carson, regarded Kitchener's backing as essential, believing that if he promoted the idea of compulsory service the nation would be more likely to accept it. In fact Kitchener refrained from giving a clear lead during the summer of 1915. He was not opposed to compulsion in principle but felt that it was still too early to adopt such a policy. Quite apart from his loyalty to Asquith, he was also convinced that a massive influx of conscript soldiers in 1916 would exhaust the country's reserves of men before the special problems posed by trench warfare had really been solved, and he was therefore anxious that Britain should keep enough men in hand to deliver the decisive blow at the right moment.

In May and June 1915 the debate centred around the question of national registration. Conscriptionists had recognised for some time that, so long as the government refused to undertake a systematic analysis of its resources, no complete mobilisation of the nation's industrial or military manpower would be possible. In the House of Commons on 19 May, shortly after Asquith had announced the establishment of the coalition, Sir Ivor Herbert rose to suggest that it was now a good moment 'to take stock of what we have got in the way of men in this country, and to take stock also of the manner in which they can be most usefully applied'. He also pointed out the weaknesses of the indiscriminate recruiting policy which had been pursued the previous autumn:

We were transforming our military force from the small professional body, which existed before the war, into a great national Army on the basis of Continental armies. . . . I think it is not unduly critical if I say that, having regard to the immensity of that change and the pressure of other important matters, the whole matter was not thoroughly and adequately considered in relation to the effect which was going to be produced on the industrial population of this country. . . . We have now an Army that we can reckon by millions. That has been produced by patriotic efforts, and not by any elaborate and co-ordinated official effort.

Herbert called for machinery to be set up to regulate the supply of men to industry and the army and proposed that, as a preliminary measure, the government should 'take a census and registration of the whole male population of this country, noting and verifying the capacities of each one'. The proposal was welcomed by Conservative back-benchers and some Liberal MPs, including Ellis Griffith, who claimed, somewhat prematurely, that an immense majority of the House was in favour of compulsory service. Replying for the government, H. J. Tennant made a statement which was not only a classic exposition of Asquith's 'wait and see' approach but also mirrored the divisions within the Cabinet. Compulsion, he said, was 'foreign to the British nation, to the British character, and to the genius of our people. It would be with reluctance that one would have to embark upon a policy which involved coercion. But I do not deny it may be possible that there may arise a time when such a policy may be desirable.'[8]

Herbert's practical suggestion provided the conscriptionists with a new avenue of attack which they were quick to exploit. One of the leaders of the assault was Lord Milner, who had remained relatively silent on the national service issue for some months but now returned to the fray with redoubled energy. A forceful and prophetic letter was published in *The Times* on 27 May, a few weeks before he became chairman of the General Council of the National Service League. 'The State,' he wrote, 'ought not to be obliged to tout for fighting men. It ought to be in a position to call out the number it wants as and when it wants them, and to call them out in the right order.' Milner went on to raise doubts about the wisdom of Kitchener's recent appeal for 300,000 more men:

If it succeeds, it will still be, like previous levies of the same kind, needlessly disorganising and wasteful. Many men will go who would be far more use at home than others who will not go. The unfairness of leaving it to individual intelligence or good will to decide who is to bear the burden will become increasingly evident and disturbing to the public mind. And how about the next 300,000 and the next after that? . . .

Throughout these weeks the demands of the conscriptionists were widely publicised in the Northcliffe newspapers, enabling them to apply a degree of public pressure which could not have been achieved if their campaign had been limited to the Cabinet and the House of Commons. However, much as Asquith may have disliked seeing the debate conducted so extensively in the press, extra-parliamentary pressure by itself was not likely to deflect the Prime Minister from his course. Unfortunately for him, the precarious balance of the Cabinet was seriously threatened by the open defection of Lloyd George. At Manchester on 3 June, in his first public address as Minister of Munitions, Lloyd George declared that conscription was a question not of principle but of necessity and, if the necessity arose, he was certain that no man of any party would protest. He also denied that compulsory service was undemocratic: 'It has been the greatest weapon in the hands of Democracy many a time for the winning and preservation of freedom.'[10] Whatever their merits, such remarks were bound to expose the rifts within the Cabinet and to contribute to Lloyd George's growing estrangement from large sections of the Liberal Party and from organised labour. It is interesting to note that critics of his Manchester speech complained not so much about its content as about the manner in which Lloyd George had aired his views. As the *Nation* commented caustically on 5 June:

Mr George works on the malleable material of a Coalition, but even such a body may call for some method and deliberation of procedure. We are not aware that the Coalition has as yet come to any decision on the policy of putting workmen under martial law, or has even completed an inquiry into it. Why, therefore, does Mr George foreshadow such action or announce his own conversion to it? That is not government by Cabinet. It is *Daily Mail* statesmanship.[11]

Although Asquith could still count on the support of the majority of Liberals, this public revelation of Cabinet differences made it much more difficult for him to resist the introduction of some form of national registration. Answering a parliamentary question from Herbert on 8 June he reported that registration was 'receiving the careful consideration of the Government'.[12] By 21 June he had given further ground. On that day Tennant told the House, 'I would not be one to say a word against any scheme of registration – in fact, I consider it a not undesirable policy at all, as it may perfectly well keep the door of voluntarism open. I have never said a word here or anywhere by which the door of voluntarism would be, I will not say slammed or barred, but even closed at all.'[13] As this statement undoubtedly echoed the Prime Minister's own views, it seems clear that Asquith regarded national registration as the lesser of two evils and even nursed a vague hope that it might offer him some sort of shield against compulsion.

The National Registration Bill, which was drafted by Walter Long, the President of the Local Government Board, was introduced by the government on 29 June. Its principal object was to provide a complete record of the number and distribution of men in the country so that the government could calculate the supply of manpower available for military service and war industry. At its first reading Long summarised it as 'a grand voluntary movement to secure knowledge of the forces which the country possesses'.[14] He reverted to this theme during the second reading on 5 July, after Asquith himself had affirmed that no action on conscription was contemplated. Long strongly denied that the Bill contained 'in some mysterious and concealed fashion the policy of conscription for the Army', adding that 'This Bill leaves the question of compulsory service exactly where it is and where it has been; it does not effect it one way or the other. The only effect that it has on the military question is . . . that it will enable the War Office . . . to avoid taking men who ought not to be taken.'

Very few MPs were deceived by these protestations. Asquith may have intended to keep the door open for the voluntary system but many believed that it was the spectre of conscription that was most likely to enter. This much was evident from the strength of feeling on both sides of the House during the second reading. There was even dissension within the Labour ranks. Philip Snowden alleged that the new coalition government had surrendered to outside agitation and had allowed its policy to be dictated by the Northcliffe press, warning that 'the appetite grows by what it feeds on'. In Snowden's view, this could not be the last demand to be made by the conscriptionists: 'There is no doubt about it that if this Bill becomes an Act, and if this register be compiled, then at once a violent press agitation will be begun for the use of the material of this register for the purpose of enforcing compulsory military service.' Arthur Henderson countered by defending the government which he had recently joined. National registration, he said, would furnish 'that very knowledge and information that we essentially need if we are going to complete the war on the voluntary principle'. However, evidence presented to the House by James Hogge, the anti-conscription Liberal MP for Edinburgh East, suggested that Snowden's prediction might well prove the more accurate. Hogge read out a letter written by a recruiting officer to potential volunteers which made it plain that some recruiting officers were already anticipating compulsion. It began:

Dear Sir, – Unless you have some good and genuine reason for not enlisting, which I am agreeable to investigate, I advise you to offer to join the Army before you are made to. This is an entirely private and friendly piece of advice. Compulsion may not be so far off as you think. I am only waiting the word to call up every man of eligible age, and you see, I have you on my list. It is possible that you may be one of those to whom this advice does not apply . . . but if you are, I can tell you that I have good reason to believe that you will be mightily sorry in the end if you wait until you are fetched . . .[15]

The Bill passed its third reading on 8 July and became law as the National Registration Act a week later. It empowered the Local Government Board to compile a register of all persons between fifteen and sixty-five. Both men and women were required to complete a form giving particulars of their birth, family and occupation, and saying whether they were skilled in, or able to perform, any work other than that in which they were currently employed. 'When this registration is completed,' Kitchener said in a speech at the Guildhall on 9 July, 'we shall, anyhow, be able to note the men between the ages of nineteen and forty not required for munition or other necessary industrial work, and therefore available, if physically fit, for the fighting line. Steps will be taken to approach, with a view to enlistment, all possible candidates for the Army – unmarried men to be preferred before married men, as far as may be.'[16]

Kitchener, meanwhile, had again revised his programme for the expansion of the army in the field. After the creation of the Ministry of Munitions, Sir

John French submitted his demands for future supplies to the War Office on 25 June and 8 July 1915, basing them upon a gradual increase in the strength of the BEF, from its existing total of twenty-two divisions to the accepted target of fifty. According to French's calculations, the desired total of fifty divisions in France would not be reached until March or April 1916. In communicating the first of these letters to the Ministry of Munitions the War Office actually increased the overall demand to a figure which would allow for the equipment of seventy rather than fifty divisions.[17] The higher figure was also tentatively announced by Kitchener at the Anglo-French conference held in Calais during the first week of July. From a purely military point of view there were sound reasons for this revision, but by prescribing a standard of seventy divisions Kitchener was leaving himself less room for manoeuvre on the conscription front.

Attempts by Lloyd George to secure the transfer of the Ordnance Board to the Ministry of Munitions did little to help Kitchener's position or to heal the rifts in the Cabinet during the first half of July. Bitter attacks were launched in Parliament and in the Northcliffe press against General von Donop, who, as Master-General of the Ordnance, was singled out as the person chiefly responsible for the shortages of munitions. By 12 July the *Daily Mail* was calling for his immediate removal.[18] As it happened, Lloyd George's pointed refusal to defend von Donop in the House of Commons the week before aroused equal condemnation. The *Morning Post* accused him of stirring up the campaign against von Donop to further his own ends and Asquith told Lord Crewe that Lloyd George's behaviour was 'quite inexcusable'.[19] Faced with such criticism, Lloyd George shelved his plans to take control of the Ordnance Board until a more favourable moment arose.

There was to be no similar relaxation of the conscription campaign. On 28 July, just before Parliament adjourned for the summer recess, a small but vocal group of Liberal MPs, including Captain F. E. Guest and Josiah Wedgwood, joined conscriptionists like Leo Amery in a plea for the Prime Minister to give the country a more positive lead. 'If we persevere in waiting and seeing,' said Amery, 'if we persevere in half-measures, if we persevere with this dogged irresolution on every question of importance, the only end of our perseverence must be invitable defeat.' Wedgwood claimed that, in times of war, the individual had to be sacrificed to the community: 'You have got to have a dictator, if possible; a man who will direct. I do not care whether he takes risks or makes mistakes, but for God's sake give us a leader who will lead without fear of consequences.'[20] Unhappily for Asquith, these fresh assaults coincided with a noticeable drop in the recruiting figures. The total number of enlistments in July 1915 was 95,413, only the second time the returns had fallen below 100,000 a month since the beginning of the war.[21]

Asquith endeavoured to remove the sting from the controversy during the recess by appointing a Cabinet committee, called the War Policy Committee, to investigate the manpower situation and the financing of the war. With

Lord Crewe as chairman, the committee comprised Lord Curzon, Churchill, Austen Chamberlain, Lord Selborne and Arthur Henderson. The committee held twelve meetings in August and interviewed various Ministers and civil servants. On 16 August Lloyd George told the committee that compulsory service was vital. 'The longer you delay,' he cautioned, 'the nearer you will be to disaster,' adding that if the Germans succeeded in putting the Russians out of action as an offensive force in 1916 it would be suicide for Britain simply to keep seventy divisions at the front. 'Not only that,' Lloyd George insisted, 'it is murder, because to send a number of men who are obviously inadequate is just murdering our own countrymen without attaining any purpose at all.'[22] Walter Runciman, President of the Board of Trade, and Reginald McKenna, Chancellor of the Exchequer, naturally took a different approach as two of the principal anti-conscriptionists in the Cabinet. Runciman argued that on the basis of his own department's statistics the nation could only maintain thirty-five divisions if industry was to remain adequately manned.[23] McKenna also remarked that it was doubtful whether Britain could afford to carry on giving financial aid to her allies and at the same time keep a force of seventy divisions in the field.[24]

Kitchener was asked by Crewe to give his evidence on 22 August concerning the army's manpower requirements. At first Kitchener tried to avoid meeting the committee, informing Crewe that he would prefer to answer questions in writing as presenting evidence 'without reference to records is not easy and generally unsatisfactory'.[25] It is fairly clear that what Kitchener really objected to was the idea of oral interrogation. 'I must leave the matter in your hands but I think I ought to let you know that if this system is adopted during the war I should be forced to resign,' he wrote to Asquith.[26] The Prime Minister persuaded him to change his mind and Kitchener met the committee on 24 August. He conceded that he could not achieve the new seventy-division standard entirely by voluntary means and indicated that he would probably demand a conscription Bill by the end of the year but wished to see the figures produced by the National Register before deciding. He regretted the raising of the question at this juncture as he had wanted to wait for the moment when a conscription Bill could be put before Parliament on a non-party basis.[27]

When Crewe made his report to Asquith early in September he explained that the conflicting evidence of the witnesses had prevented the committee from reaching a firm conclusion. Churchill, Chamberlain, Curzon and Selborne, the conscriptionists on the committee, disagreed and submitted a 'Supplementary Memorandum' arguing that the voluntary system was not producing a military effort compatible with the national resources. After considering the likely cost as well as naval and industrial manpower requirements they insisted that an army of 100 rather than seventy divisions 'would bear a truer relation both to our dangers and to the exertions of our Allies'. Doubting that even a force of seventy divisions could be achieved by voluntary methods, they recommended that conscription should be introduced without delay.[28]

The National Register had been taken on 15 August. It is ironic that this precursor of conscription depended on yet another massive voluntary effort from the civilian population. Not only the delivery and collection of the registration forms but also their subsequent classification and enumeration had to be carried out largely by volunteer helpers. In Preston, for instance, some 225 schoolteachers undertook this work under the supervision of the Town Clerk. In Hyde, Cheshire, 150 enumerators dealt with the forms collected from the 8,395 dwelling houses in the borough. The task of delivering nearly 350,000 forms in Leeds was performed by corporation officials, teachers and members of the Volunteer Training Corps. Some 114,000 houses in Leeds were visited during the second week of August.[29] When the forms were returned to the Local Government Board offices the details of every man between the ages of eighteen and forty-one were transferred to a pink form. The forms of men engaged in essential war industries, such as coal mining, munitions work, railway work and certain branches of agriculture, were then marked with a black star. The register showed that 5,012,146 men of military age were not in the forces. 2,179,231 of these were single and 2,832,210 were married. Of the single men, only 690,138 were in 'starred' occupations. Thus, even without the married men, 1,489,093 single men were theoretically available for military service almost at once.[30]

Kitchener refused to be hurried into siding with the conscriptionists. His evidence to the War Policy Committee had led the Conservatives to believe that he was now leaning towards compulsion and, on 15 September, Lord Selborne renewed the attempt to enlist his support. 'Nobody in his senses will take compulsion because Northcliffe presses it upon him,' he wrote. 'But the Trades Unions and the entire nation will take it from you if you tell them that it is necessary.' He also gave a thinly veiled hint that Kitchener's credibility with the officers and rank and file of the army depended on his coming out strongly in favour of conscription, as 'if they think that you delay too long to ask for it, there will be a serious revulsion in their feelings towards you'.[31] Kitchener stuck to his position, replying, 'I daresay notwithstanding the delay the army will trust me to do my best for them whatever that is worth.'[32]

Selborne was at least partly accurate in his interpretation of the army's mood, for when Kitchener had discussed conscription with Haig in France on 19 August the latter had told him that compulsory service 'would hearten our allies, and show that we were in earnest'.[33] Moreover, when Parliament was recalled on 14 September the National Service League issued a statement in favour of compulsion which bore the signatures of thirty MPs and twenty-two peers, all of whom were on active service.[34] Selborne's assessment of the attitude of the trade unions fell wider of the mark. At the TUC annual conference in Bristol on 7 September there was considerable hostility towards compulsory service of any kind and the TUC Parliamentary Committee submitted a resolution denouncing 'the sinister efforts of a section of the reactionary press . . . to foist on this country conscription, which always proves a burden to the workers, and will divide the nation at a time when absolute unanimity is essential'. The resolution also promised that the unions would give every aid to the government's efforts to bring the war to a successful conclusion through a properly organised system.[35] The Congress represented 3 million members and its opposition to conscription could not easily be overlooked, but in declaring their support for the war itself the unions were following a policy which might one day make it inconsistent for them to continue to oppose compulsory service.

The Independent Labour Party and the allied No Conscription Fellowship, sensing that compulsory service might be imminent, intensified their own propaganda campaign. In September the NCF issued its first manifesto, drawing attention to the outright refusal of its members to take up arms. 'Whatever the purpose to be achieved by the war,' the manifesto stated, 'however high the ideals for which belligerent nations may struggle, for us "Thou shalt not kill" means what it says.'[36] In October the ILP organised 'Stop Conscription' meetings all over the country addressed by Sylvia Pankhurst, George Lansbury and others. These movements took some heart from an assurance given by the militant miners' leader, Robert Smillie, at the Miners' Federation conference on 5 October, that the great Triple Alliance of miners, transport workers and railwaymen would 'fight the right of one class to conscript another class until they have first conscripted the land and capital of the country'.[37] However, in the final analysis, there was little that such pressure groups could do without substantial parliamentary backing or united working-class opposition to the war, for it was in Parliament and the Cabinet that the decisive battle over conscription was being fought.

Fuel was added to the debate by the publication on 13 September of a collection of Lloyd George's war speeches. In his preface Lloyd George alluded as pointedly as he could to his views on conscription. Predictably, he was praised by *The Times* but came under fire from the Liberal *Daily News* and *Westminster Gazette*. 'It is no exaggeration to say that at this moment, the two most unpopular and distrusted men in the party are Lloyd George and Winston Churchill,' Asquith wrote to Balfour on 18 September. The Prime Minister went on to say that even if he were to announce his own reluctant conversion to conscription, it would alienate 'some of the best, and in the country some of the most powerful, elements in the Liberal party', but, in any case, there was 'no evidence that Compulsion in any form would have given, or could now give, more satisfactory results'.[38] Lloyd George was still uncertain about his alignment with the Conservative leaders and so was unwilling to break away totally from Asquith for the moment. He also told Frances Stevenson on 13 October that he had no desire to become Prime Minister yet, as he saw a series of disasters ahead and wanted Asquith to take full responsibility for them.[39]

It was Kitchener who shifted his posture first. Only 71,617 men enlisted in September 1915, the lowest monthly total to date.[40] Concomitant with this disturbing decline in recruiting, the BEF, including some of Kitchener's New Army divisions, suffered heavy casualties in the offensive at Loos towards the end of the month. As a result, on 8 October, Kitchener presented the Cabinet with a memorandum which began with the admission that voluntary recruiting was breaking down. He noted that even to keep existing units at strength would require some 35,000 recruits a week, a figure now well above the actual weekly average. He therefore proposed a scheme which combined voluntary and compulsory service. The War Office would allot to each district a quota of men to be recruited by a certain date. If voluntary enlistments fell short of the quota, the balance would be raised by a ballot of the remaining men of military age.[41]

The proposal was rejected by both sides as unwieldy and impracticable. With the unity of the Cabinet dissolving rapidly, Asquith prevailed upon Kitchener to make one last effort to uphold the voluntary principle by appointing Lord Derby as Director-General of Recruiting on 5 October. Derby was given the task of preparing a scheme which would make the best use of the pink forms compiled under the National Register. The choice of Derby demonstrated Asquith's political adroitness, for Derby was a well known supporter of conscription, and if the scheme failed to produce the necessary number of recruits Asquith could justly claim that voluntary recruiting had failed and thereby provide himself with a safe line of tactical withdrawal.

For a few days Derby was unsure quite what was expected of him. 'I will be perfectly frank with you and I think something has got to be done to counteract one effect of your previous appeals,' he told Kitchener on 8 October. 'You have made appeals for a million men; 500,000 men; and 300,000 men. The people are told that you have as a matter of fact enlisted 3 million men and they urge with a certain amount of truth that if they have raised 75 per cent over and above what you ask for, what is the necessity for trying to get any more.' He also asked for guidance as to the numbers his scheme was expected to raise.[42] According to a note prepared by Asquith on 16 October he and Kitchener were thinking in terms of a minimum of 500,000 men – a figure subject to 'revision and amendment' – by 31 March 1916. The note neatly summarised Asquith's current tactical position on conscription:

Compulsion, to be effective, must be adopted with substantial general assent. If the prescribed minimum is not forthcoming, the Cabinet believe that the objection to compulsion, which now so widely exists, would be largely modified if not entirely removed, and hopes that such general assent would be secured.[43]

Derby announced the outlines of his scheme on 15 October, amplifying some of its details in a letter to *The Times Recruiting Supplement* early in November. The scheme did not apply to Ireland, but elsewhere a personal canvass of every man between the ages of eighteen and forty-one was to be carried out on the basis of the National Register. Each man was to be asked either to join up at once or to attest his willingness to serve when summoned. The attested men would be split into two categories, single and married, each subdivided into twenty-three groups according to age. Groups would be called up in strict order as and when required, beginning with single men of nineteen. The youngest married men would not be summoned until all twenty-three age groups of single men had been called up. Derby clarified his intentions in his letter to *The Times Recruiting Supplement*:

I have always urged that it is the duty of every man in this crisis to offer his services to the State, and for the State definitely to allot him his position, whether it be in some branch of His Majesty's forces or in the munition works, or in one of the indispensable industries of this country, or even as an indispensable person in a private business. But it must be the State and not the individual which decides a man's proper place in the machinery of the country. I hope by the present scheme not only to ascertain what is each man's right position, but to induce him voluntarily to take it. But before this can be done a man must actually enlist, not merely promise to do so. By enlisting men in groups, only to come up when called upon, and allowing them before actually joining to appeal to local tribunals to be put in later groups . . ., we shall be able to allot proper places to all men in the 'unstarred' list. Then we must carefully examine the whole of the 'starred' list, and where we find a man wrongly placed in that list, or a man who, though rightly placed in it, can be spared from his industry, that man must be placed in the 'unstarred' list'.[44]

The responsibility for organising the canvass rested with the Parliamentary Recruiting Committee and the Joint Labour Recruiting Committee. In every area a local committee, whether already in existence or yet to be formed, would undertake the work, utilising the services of the political agents of the three main parties and large bodies of civilian helpers. Under the committee for each parliamentary constituency, branch committees were set up where needed in district boroughs, borough wards and groups of villages. Town halls, municipal offices, schools and other buildings were used as canvassing headquarters. Each 'unstarred' man was to receive a letter from Lord Derby emphasising that if this effort did not succeed the country would know 'that everything possible will have been done to make the voluntary system a success, and will have to decide by what method sufficient recruits can be obtained to maintain our Armies in the field at the required strength'.[45] Details about each man were entered by canvassers on cards which contained spaces for the man's name, address, age and marital status, the number of his children or dependants and his employer's name and address. The Parliamentary Recruiting Committee instructed canvassers to make sure that they saw the man himself and not to be put off by statements or assurances from other people. They were then to 'put before him plainly and politely the need of the country' but were not to 'bully or threaten'. However, they were to try to get as many recruits as possible for the infantry, as 'the issue of the war largely depends on this arm'.[46] Attestation sub-committees were established to assist the canvassers in getting the men attested, and particularly to collect men willing to join on certain future dates. The actual work of attestation was left to the War Office recruiting authorities.

The Local Government Board was handed the task of setting up tribunals to which men could apply for exemption from attestation or, failing that, for the postponement of their call-up on grounds of personal hardship or essential war work. Walter Long, as President of the Local Government Board, ordered every Local Registration Authority to appoint tribunals of not more than five members, preferably men 'of impartial and balanced judgement'.[47] Applications for exemption could be made only by employers on behalf of their employees. The employer had to convince the tribunal that the services of the man in question were vital to him, that the man's work was itself of national importance and that every effort had been made to replace him with another man over enlistment age, or a woman. If a recruiting officer contested an application for exemption or postponement he sent a Military Representative to the tribunal to voice his objections. As a further safeguard to its interests, the War Office appointed an Advisory Committee in each district, consisting of men with knowledge of local industry who could examine the applications and suggest how the Military Representative might best present his case. This was a subtle means of putting pressure on the tribunals, since they were often composed of the same councillors and businessmen who had played the leading role in the various local recruiting drives. Such men, fresh from their patriotic endeavours, were not easily induced to reject the combined views of the recruiting officer and his advisory committee and sometimes even permitted the Military Representative to conduct a hearing. In effect, this meant that, under the Derby Scheme, applications for exemption or postponement were unlikely to succeed without the backing of the military authorities.

For a time Asquith's gamble seemed to be paying off, as the launching of the Derby Scheme gained him a temporary respite from conscriptionist demands. Lloyd George, Curzon, Carson, and other conscriptionists in the Cabinet signed a memorandum on 16 October in which they agreed 'to give the new efforts which are being made to secure the number required by voluntary methods all possible support', although the document ominously stated that they were only willing to give these methods 'a fair trial' up to the end of November. If by that date it was obvious that the voluntary system could not produce the necessary numbers they would expect Asquith to introduce conscription. In the intervening period they would prepare their own draft Bill for compulsory military service.[48]

As if cheated of their prey, the Cabinet dissidents now made Kitchener the chief target of their criticisms. The failure of offensive operations in the Dardanelles and on the western front in the summer and autumn had further reduced his credit with his Cabinet colleagues, and on 17 October Asquith warned him of a plot by Curzon and Lloyd George to drive a wedge between them and oust Kitchener from office. 'So long as you and I stand together,' Asquith wrote, 'we carry the whole country with us. Otherwise, the Deluge!'[49] The crisis was brought to a head by Lloyd George, who, on 31 October, sent a long letter to Asquith, blaming Kitchener for not taking adequate steps to meet the Austro-German invasion of Serbia, and attributing the setbacks in France to Kitchener's mismanagement of the munitions problem. Lloyd George threatened to raise these issues in the Cabinet and forecast that 'the moment these facts are told in the House of Commons I have very little doubt what will be thought and said by all sections'.[50] A major confrontation was narrowly averted by sending Kitchener to the Dardanelles to report on the situation there, with Asquith taking charge of the War Office while he was away. 'We avoid by this method of procedure the immediate supersession of K. as War Minister, while attaining the same result,' Asquith explained to Lloyd George on 3 November.[51]

Even now, Kitchener's popularity with the British people as a whole was still sufficient to deter most of his opponents from publicly calling for his removal. Sir George Riddell, the newspaper proprietor, noted in his diary on 30 November, 'If K. resigns the Government will be much weakened in the country. The people implicitly believe in K. and distrust the politicians.'[52] Nevertheless, advantage was taken of his absence to knock away many of the remaining props of his power and Asquith, fighting a rearguard action on two fronts, was unable to offer him the kind of support which he had enjoyed in the opening months of the war. Having already taken over the Royal Ordnance Factories in August, Lloyd George at last secured the transfer of the Ordnance Board and its entire research and development establishment to the Ministry of Munitions, leaving the War Office with few duties in this sphere save those of fixing the army's requirements in munitions and supervising their distribution. During November the ground was also laid for the appointment of Sir William Robertson as Chief of the Imperial General Staff the following month. As a condition of taking office Robertson insisted that the CIGS should henceforth become the one authoritative channel through which the Cabinet received advice on military operations. Thus although Kitchener retained constitutional authority for the army, he was shorn of responsibility as to how and where it should be employed. By the end of 1915 his real influence was confined solely to matters of War Office administration, recruiting and supply.

Meanwhile, the Derby Scheme had been put into operation. At first it looked like being a success. Attracted by the opportunity the scheme provided to volunteer without an immediate obligation for service, and spurred on by government propaganda and the personal canvass, a flood of men came forward to attest in the early weeks. There was some confusion, however, about the exact position of the married men if the single men failed to respond on an adequate scale. Asquith, therefore, sought to clear up this point in a statement to the House of Commons on 2 November. He stressed that he had no objection to compulsion in principle but would resort to it only when there was general, if not universal, consent, promising a full evaluation of the Derby Scheme as soon as it closed on 30 November. Then, referring to the married men, he said:

I am told by Lord Derby and others that there is some doubt among married men who are now being asked to enlist, whether, having enlisted, or promised to enlist, they may not be called upon to serve while younger and unmarried men are holding back. . . . Let them at once disabuse themselves of that notion. . . . So far as I am concerned, I should certainly say the obligation of the married men to serve ought not to be enforced or held to be binding unless and until – I hope by voluntary effort, if it be needed in the last resort, as I have explained by other means – the unmarried men are dealt with.[53]

Though this was merely a personal pronouncement, Asquith's assurance to the married men was erected into a full government commitment the following week. To remove any remaining doubts, Derby issued a statement, with Asquith's approval, on 11 November, confirming that the Prime Minister had 'pledged not only himself but his Government when he stated that if young men do not, under the stress of national duty, come forward voluntarily, other and compulsory means would be taken before the married men are called upon to fulfil their engagement to serve'.[54] This declaration determined the whole future course of the debate, for it could be used as a weapon by both Asquith and by the convinced proponents of compulsory service. If the conscription of single men had to be enforced in the near future, as now appeared increasingly probable, Asquith could rally the majority of Liberals behind the measure by claiming that it was not only the product of military necessity but also a redemption of his pledge of 2 November. By the same token, the conscriptionists too could insist that Asquith kept his promise to the married men if this last big effort of voluntary recruiting failed. The conscriptionists, in fact, used Asquith's pledge as the main plank of their campaign over the next few weeks. In a speech at Bristol on 13 November, Walter Long proclaimed, 'Single men may be perfectly certain that if they fail today, at this hour of their country's need, they will be called upon compulsorily to take their place in the ranks.'[55] Some recruiting officers adopted a similarly aggressive approach. An advertisement which was published, under cover of the Royal Arms, in the *Glasgow Herald* on 15 November read: 'Enlist before 30 November. If you do not, the Prime Minister has pledged himself and his Government that compulsory means will be taken.'[56]

These latest developments gave a new urgency to the actitivies of the anti-conscription pressure groups. At the first national convention of the No Conscription Fellowship, which was held at the Memorial Hall in London on 27 November, plans were made to meet the threat of compulsory service and possible persecution. The whole organisation was to be built in duplicate, with local branches being advised to appoint shadow officers to replace any who might be arrested. Delegates also passed a resolution moved by the president, Clifford Allen, reaffirming the NCF's intention 'to resist conscription, whatever the penalties may be'.[57] Their resolve was soon tested. Over the next week or two the NCF and other anti-conscription organisations were subjected to considerable harrassment. A meeting of the Union of Democratic Control at the Memorial Hall on 29 November was disrupted by a group of about a hundred people, many of them soldiers in uniform, who got in with what the UDC later alleged to be forged tickets. Waving flags and banners, the protesters, led by the editor of the *Daily Express,* ejected the UDC's platform party, which included Ramsay MacDonald. In Halifax local Territorials paraded outside a hall during an anti-conscription meeting and then broke in, bringing the proceedings to a premature end. A similar incident occurred in Nelson, Lancashire. In Bradford a meeting which was due to be held in the Mechanics' Institute on 2 December was cancelled when the owners of the premises objected, although the NCF asserted that soldiers had prevented the meeting by surrounding the building. There were also complaints about the Glasgow's Corporation's refusal to make public halls available for anti-conscription gatherings.[58]

The basic dilemma of the NCF was that the more successful its members were in persuading men not to attest, the more likely it became that the Derby Scheme would founder and compulsory service would be introduced. In December other events conspired to push the country further along the path to conscription. On 6 December the Inter-Allied Military Conference at Chantilly recommended that in 1916 the Austro-German armies should be attacked with maximum forces in the main theatres of war and that, pending these attacks, powers such as Britain which still possessed reserves of manpower should embark on vigorous action to wear down the enemy. In the same month the government admitted that the Dardanelles campaign had been a failure and agreed to evacuate the forces from Gallipoli. This withdrawal, coupled with the appointment of Robertson as CIGS, swung British strategic counsels firmly towards concentration on the Western Front as the decisive theatre. In the absence of a viable alternative, the government's options on conscription were greatly reduced, since few disputed that huge numbers of men would have to be deployed in France and Belgium to break the trench deadlock.

For the supporters of the voluntary system everything now depended on the outcome of the Derby Scheme. The canvassing campaign was originally scheduled to end on 30 November but, as that day approached, the recruiting offices were overwhelmed by a rush of men wishing to attest. Just as in the boom period of August and September 1914 men were forced to wait for hours before the recruiting staffs could deal with them. The closing date for attestation was therefore extended, first to 4 December, then to 11 December and finally to 15 December. Those who drew some encouragement from the queues at the recruiting offices were shortly to be disappointed. Although the figures were not made public until after Christmas, Derby presented his preliminary findings to the Cabinet on 15 December and Asquith knew at once that all hopes of preserving voluntary recruiting were gone. A Cabinet committee under Walter Long was immediately appointed to draft a Bill for the compulsory enlistment of single men. As was confirmed when Derby submitted his main report on 20 December, the married men, anticipating that they would be called up last of all, had come forward in larger numbers than the single men. Moreover, of the 2,179,231 bachelors whom the National Register had shown to be available, 1,029,231, or nearly half, had not attested. Those unaccounted for included 651,160 single men not in 'starred' occupations. Making allowances for possible exemptions or rejections on medical grounds, Derby estimated that the scheme had produced only 343,386 single men, a total well below the 'prescribed minimum'. He therefore concluded that, in order to redeem Asquith's pledge, 'it will not be possible to hold the married men to their attestation unless and until the services of single men have been obtained by other means'.[59]

This report effectively removed the last major obstacle to compulsory military service. On 28 December the Cabinet accepted the outlines of Long's Bill and agreed to conscript the single men who had declined to attest under the Derby Scheme. The full draft of the Bill was discussed at a Cabinet meeting on 1 January 1916. The leading anti-conscriptionists in the Cabinet – Grey, Runciman, McKenna and Sir John Simon – all expressed dissent, but when it came to the point only Simon, the Home Secretary, actually resigned, for Asquith successfully appealed to Grey's sense of loyalty and persuaded him to use his conciliatory influence on Runciman and McKenna.[60]

The first Military Service Bill, which established the principle of conscription, was placed before Parliament on 5 January 1916. It was to apply only to unmarried men, and widowers without children or dependants, between the ages of eighteen and forty-one, exempting those who were engaged on important war work, the sole supporters of dependants, the unfit and approved conscientious objectors. The tribunals constituted under the Derby Scheme to consider applications for exemption were to be given statutory authority, with local Appeal Tribunals and also a Central Appeal Tribunal being set up to review special cases. When the vote on the first reading was taken in the House of Commons on 6 January, 403 voted for the Bill and 105 against, the opponents including sixty Irish Nationalists, thirty-four Liberals and eleven Labour MPs.[61] By the second reading on 11 and 12 January the opposition had dwindled. On this occasion the Irish Nationalists, having made their protest, abstained from voting on an issue which they now regarded as a purely British concern, Ireland being excluded from the provisions of the Bill on the grounds that the Derby Scheme had not applied there. Most Labour MPs were mollified in turn by an assurance from Asquith that the Bill would not be extended to embrace industrial conscription. Consequently, the second reading was carried by 431 votes to thirty-nine. Only thirty-six members voted against the measure at its third reading on 24 January.[62] When the Labour Party conference opened at Bristol on 26 January a motion opposing the Bill was carried on a card vote by 1,716,000 votes to 360,000, but an ensuing motion calling for the Labour movement to agitate for the Bill's repeal if it became law was narrowly defeated.[63] As before, the Labour leaders and the unions were not inclined to carry their hostility to conscription to a point where they would be compelled to come out in opposition to the war itself. In any case, the battle had already been lost in Parliament. On 27 January the Bill received the Royal Assent and was now the law of the land.

The introduction of the first Military Service Act did not bring the conflict over compulsory service to end. As early as the first week in January the Liberal anti-conscriptionists in the Cabinet changed their tactics and began to contend that the size of the army should be fixed at fifty-seven divisions to avoid placing an unbearable strain on vital industries and on the nation's financial resources. Such arguments were curtly refuted by Kitchener, who exclaimed to Haig, 'When one looks at the streets full of loafers, and sees the extravagance going on in all Departments of Government, their statements are given the lie.'[64] Runciman and McKenna were partly appeased by the creation of a Cabinet committee to analyse the competing economic and military factors surrounding compulsory service. This body reported at the beginning of February that Britain should aim to have sixty-two divisions in the field by the end of June, with three months' reserve, and that the requirements of home defence could be met by five divisions without reserves. It was believed that these targets could be attained without disaster, 'though not without grave dislocation of industry, and even some risk'.[65] These recommendations were basically in accord with current War Office thinking and were subsequently approved by the Cabinet.[66]

Others, like Lloyd George, felt that the first Act had not gone far enough, and the recruiting returns were certainly still insufficient to maintain the army at the newly agreed size or to provide replacements for the casualties expected in the summer offensive. Only 65,965 men joined the army in January 1916 and 98,629 the following month.[67] The local tribunals were, if anything, too liberal in granting exemptions. Between 1 March 1916 and 31 March 1917, 779,936 men were exempted from military service while only 371,500 were compulsorily enlisted.[68] This was, as Denis Hayes has said, 'compulsion with the velvet glove'.[69] In March 1916 the War Office was forced to call up the younger married men who had attested under the Derby Scheme, thus provoking a storm of protest in the press that these men should not be sent to the front when the nation's resources in single men had not been fully exploited. The cry was now for total conscription and equality of sacrifice.

As a new Cabinet crisis loomed, the War Office once more came to occupy an important position in the debate. Sir William Robertson supported the call for universal conscription but Kitchener, for a while, stuck by his own belief that the unattested married men should be held back until 1917. He perceptively remarked to Lord Esher that 'if Robertson and Haig feel unduly strong they may embark upon enterprises that will eat up all our available reserves, and . . . next year when the French are exhausted we shall find ourselves in a similar dilemma'.[70] Much to his credit, Robertson did not permit the conscriptionists to exploit these differences of opinion to force Kitchener out of office, but he continued to put forward his own views. He reminded the Cabinet on 21 March of the critical manpower situation, observing that the recruiting returns were barely adequate to meet normal wastage on the Western Front and would not offer any reserve capacity for major offensives or operations in other theatres. He reported that of 193,891 men called up under the Military Service Act 57,416 had failed to appear. 'We cannot expect to secure a favourable peace without hard fighting,' Robertson insisted, 'and that means heavy losses which we must be prepared to suffer and replace.'[71]

Kitchener now knew that his influence in the country and with the army would fade completely if he withheld his backing any longer, and he consented to a proposal that the Army Council should draw up a paper confirming Robertson's arguments. In this memorandum, which was circulated to the Cabinet on 6 April, the Army Council warned of disaster unless every fit man who was not needed for industry could be made available to the army.[72] With Kitchener and Robertson presenting a united front on the question of universal compulsory service, albeit for different reasons, Asquith was squeezed into a corner and could do nothing to dilute their demands. His last-ditch efforts to stave off general compulsion were wrecked by another Army Council memorandum on 15 April in which the military leaders stressed that there were still only fifty-two divisions overseas instead of sixty-two, and even these were some 60,000 men below strength. Since the full effects of any legislation would not be felt for some months, particularly on the fighting fronts, they took the view that to delay general conscription any longer would be to invite calamity.[73] To prevent the break-up of his Cabinet, Asquith therefore introduced a second Military Service Bill on 3 May, extending liability for military service to all men, single and married, between the age of eighteen and forty-one, although as far as possible men were not to be sent abroad until they were nineteen. Provision was also made for an amendment to the Territorial and Reserve Forces Act to enable men whose time for discharge occurred before the end of the war to be retained for a period not exceeding the duration of the conflict. Voluntary recruiting was to remain in operation only in Ireland, where, in the aftermath of the Easter Rising, any attempt to impose conscription would be likely to prove a perilous course. The new Bill passed quickly through both Houses and received the Royal Assent on 25 May 1916. Britain had finally acknowledged that her long tradition of voluntary recruiting for the army was no answer to the demands of modern war.

Notes

1 *Manchester Guardian*, 1 June 1915.
2 John Rae, *Conscience and Politics*, Oxford University Press, 1970, p. 5.
3 Amery, *My Political Life*, II, p. 67.
4 Trevor Wilson, *The Downfall of the Liberal Party*, *1914–1935*, Collins, London, 1966, pp. 41, 52.
5 Cameron Hazlehurst, *Politicians at War, July 1914 to May 1915*, Cape, London, 1971, p. 301.
6 Wilson, *op. cit.*, p. 45.
7 Viscount Samuel, *Memoirs*, Cresset, London, 19145, p. 118.
8 *Parliamentary Debates, House of Commons, 1914–15*, LXXI, cols. 2395–7, 2416, 2420–1.
9 Letter from Lord Milner to *The Times*, 27 May 1915.
10 *The Times*, 4 June 1915.
11 *Nation*, 5 June 1915.
12 *Parliamentary Debates, House of Commons, 1914–15*, LXXII, col. 179.
13 *Ibid.*, LXXII, col. 1016.
14 *Ibid.*, LXXII, col. 1655.
15 *Ibid.*, LXXIII, cols. 59, 106–13, 145, 426.
16 *The Times*, 10 July 1915; *Spectator*, 17 July 1915.
17 *History of the Ministry of Munitions*, Vol. I, Part I, HMSO, London, 1922, pp. 11–12.
18 *Daily Mail*, 12 July 1915.
19 Asquith to Crewe, 4 July 1915, Asquith papers, Vol. 46; *Morning Post*, 16 July 1915.
20 *Parliamentary Debates, House of Commons, 1914–15*, LXXIII, cols. 2408, 2421–2.
21 *Statistics of the Military Effort of the British Empire*, p. 364.
22 Lloyd George to War Policy Committee, 16 August 1915, CAB 37/132/21.
23 Runciman to War Policy Committee, 19 August 1915, CAB 37/133/1.
24 McKenna to War Policy Committee, 23 August 1915, CAB 37/133/5.
25 Kitchener to Crewe, 21 August 1915, Kitchener papers, PRO 30/57/76.
26 Kitchener to Asquith, 22 August 1915, Kitchener papers, PRO 30/57/76.
27 Kitchener to War Policy Committee, 24 August 1915, CAB 37/133/10.
28 Supplementary Report by the Cabinet Committee on Manpower, 2 September 1915, CAB 37/134/3; Revised Supplementary Report, 7 September 1915, CAB 37/134/7; Report of War Policy Committee, 8 September 1915, CAB 37/134/9.
29 H. Cartmell, *For Remembrance*, Toulmin, Preston, 1919, p. 43; Randal Sidebotham, *Hyde in Wartime*, p. 25; W. H. Scott, *Leeds in the Great War*, p. 29.
30 Figures given in the *Report on Recruiting by the Earl of Derby, Director-General of Recruiting*, Parliamentary Papers, 1914–16, XXXIX, Cd 8149.
31 Selborne to Kitchener, 15 September 1915, Selborne papers, 80.
32 Kitchener to Selborne, 17 September 1915, Selborne papers, 80.
33 Robert Blake (ed.), *The Private Papers of Douglas Haig, 1914–1919*, Eyre & Spottiswoode, London, 1952, p. 101.
34 *The Times*, 14 September 1915.
35 *Annual Register*, 1915, p. 154.
36 *Labour Leader*, 9 September 1915.
37 *The Times*, 6 October 1915.

38 Asquith to Balfour, 18 September 1915, Balfour papers, BL Add. Mss 49692.
39 A. J. P. Taylor (ed.), *Lloyd George: a Diary by Frances Stevenson,* Hutchinson, London, 1971, p. 69.
40 *Statistics of the Military Effort of the British Empire,* p. 364.
41 Memorandum by Kitchener on 'Recruiting for the Army', 8 October 1915, WO 159–4.
42 Derby to Kitchener, 8 October 1915, Kitchener papers, PRO 30/57/73.
43 Note by the Prime Minister, 16 October 1915, Kitchener papers, PRO 30/57/73.
44 *The Times,* 16 October 1915; Lord Derby, letter to *The Times Recruiting Supplement,* 3 November 1915. The idea of the canvass appears to have been borrowed from a proposal made by Derby's predecessor as Director of Recruiting, Major-General R. A. Montgomery, see Minutes of the General Purposes Committee of the Parliamentary Recruiting Committee, 5 October 1915, BL Add. Mss 54192.
45 Circular from Lord Derby, dated 'October 1915'. A copy can be found in the Kitchener papers, PRO 30/57/73.
46 Minutes of meeting of the General Purposes Committee of the Parliamentary Recruiting Committee, 5 October 1915, BL Add. Mss 54192; *The Times History of the War,* Vol. VI, *The Times,* 1916, p. 310.
47 Local Government Board to Local Registration Authorities, 26 October 1915, PRO MH 10/79/84.
48 Memorandum signed by Lansdowne, Curzon, Selborne, Chamberlain, Carson, Long, Bonar Law, Lloyd George and Churchill, 16 October 1915, Kitchener papers, PRO 30/57/73; a copy of the draft Bill for 'Universal Military Service', prepared by Curzon and Amery, can be found in the Asquith papers, Vol. 82.
49 Asquith to Kitchener, 17 October 1915, Kitchener papers, PRO 30/57/76.
50 Lloyd George, *War Memoirs,* pp. 514–18.
51 Asquith to Lloyd George, 3 November 1915, Lloyd George papers, HLRO Ll.G. D/18/2/12.
52 Lord Riddell, *War Diary,* Nicholson & Watson, London, 1933, p. 140.
53 *Parliamentary Debates, House of Commons, 1914–15,* LXXV, col. 524.
54 *The Times,* 12 November 1915.
55 *Ibid.,* 15 November 1915.
56 *Glasgow Herald,* 15 November 1915.
57 John W. Graham, *Conscription and Conscience,* Allen & Unwin, London, 1922, pp. 176–82.
58 *Parliamentary Debates, House of Commons, 1914–15,* LXXVI, cols. 871, 1007–8, 1157, 1161, 1406, 1593, 2053–4.
59 Lord Derby, *Report on Recruiting,* PP, 1916, XXXIX, Cd 8149, pp. 5–7.
60 Report to the King on the Cabinet meeting of 28 December 1915, CAB 41/36/56, and 1 January 1916, CAB 41/37/1.
61 *Parliamentary Debates, House of Commons, 1914–15,* LXXVII, cols. 1251–5.
62 *Ibid.,* LXXVIII, cols., 1038–42.
63 *The Times,* 28 January 1916.
64 Kitchener to Haig, 14 January 1916, Kitchener papers, PRO 30/57/53.
65 Report of the Cabinet Committee on the Co-orindation of Military and Financial Effort, 4 February 1916, CAB 37/142/11.
66 Note by Kitchener on the report of the Cabinet Committee, 7 February 1916, CAB 37/142/17.
67 *Statistics of the Military Effort of the British Empire,* p. 364.
68 *Ibid.,* p. 367.
69 Denis Hayes, *Conscription Conflict,* Sheppard, London, 1949, p. 201.
70 Brett and Esher (eds.), *Journals and Letters,* IV, p. 17.

71 Memorandum by Robertson, 21 March 1916, Robertson papers, KCL 1/11.
72 Army Council memorandum, 6 April 1916, Chamberlain papers, AC 19/1/36.
73 Army Council memorandum, 15 April 1916, Asquith papers, Vol. 126.

Part II

Enlistment, equipment and training

6

Taking the King's shilling:
experiences of enlistment

I

Until recently many writers on the First World War were content to view the recruiting flood of 1914 simply as the product of patriotism and idealism, even if some were at pains to point out that the patriotism was misguided and the ideals were illusory. The impression most frequently conveyed was that of crowds of cheerful volunteers flocking to the recruiting offices, all imbued with a strong sense of duty to King and Country and an unquestioning faith in the rightness of Britain's cause. 'Youth flew to the shambles without once asking why,' one observer has claimed. 'Not the faintest suspicion is betrayed that any other course could be conceivable.'[1] Another has written:

Each of them quite seriously thought of himself as a molecule in the body of a nation that was really, and not just figuratively, 'straining every nerve' to discharge an obligation of honour. . . . All the air was ringing with rousing assurances. France to be saved, Belgium righted, freedom and civilisation re-won, a sour, soiled, crooked old world to be rid of bullies and crooks and reclaimed for straightness, decency, good-nature, the ways of common men dealing with common men.[2]

Sir Philip Magnus, one of Kitchener's principal biographers, offers no explanation for the voluntary enlistment of nearly two and a half million men other than that they sprang forward 'in the mood to which Rupert Brooke gave touching expression':[3]

Now, God be thanked Who has matched us with His hour
And caught our youth, and wakened us from sleeping . . .[4]

The image of a tragic 'lost generation' of young men rushing headlong into something which they did not fully comprehend has been planted deep in the national consciousness and persists to this day. However, the social, political and economic forces which drove men to enlist were far more varied and complex than these writers have implied. Patriotism in 1914 encompassed many subtle shades and nuances.

It must be said, of course, that large numbers of the men who joined the army in the early months of the war *were* motivated by straightforward

patriotic ideals. In a letter to the *Nation* in December 1919 'A Soldier of the War' stated that 'our patriotism was inspired by an exalted pride in our country. What we knew, in fact, was the ideal, and it was more than the real to us. . . . We really believed that we were going to fight for freedom, as the Press and Government told us.'[5] For such men, conditioned as they were by the values of Edwardian society, the way ahead was clearly defined. Ulric Nisbet, who had left Marlborough at the end of the summer term in July 1914, later summed up how he felt at the outbreak of war:

It wasn't a matter of 'our Country, right or wrong'. Our country was 100 per cent right and Germany 100 per cent wrong. We were fighting for King and Country and Empire, and 'gallant little Belgium'. We were fighting to uphold the principles of justice and freedom, and international morality and to smash Kaiserism and German militarism. . . . We had been taught to worship God one day a week but to worship Country and Empire seven days a week. The British Empire was the greatest empire the world had ever known, and its greatness was due to the superior qualities of the British. Foreigners weren't cast in the same mould.[6]

Arthur Bliss, who subsequently became Master of the Queen's Musick, described his decision to enlist as 'purely automatic, sparked off by a feeling of outrage at the cause of the war, of a debt owed'.[7] W. T. Colyer, a former pupil of Merchant Taylors', remembered sitting at his office desk in London on the first morning of the war, full of angry thoughts about the Germans. 'I wished to goodness I were in the army. I felt restless, excited, eager to do something for the cause of England. And then the impulse came, sending the blood tingling all over my body: why not join the army now?'[8] These sentiments were not confined solely to ex-public school boys. George Morgan joined the 1st Bradford Pals convinced that Britain was the best country in the world and that he should play his part in defending her. 'The history taught us at school showed that we were better than other people . . . and now all the news was that Germany was the aggressor and we wanted to show the Germans what we could do.'[9]

Widespread indignation at Germany's actions was now added to this long-held belief in the natural superiority of the British people. As Colin Nicolson has remarked, the invasion of Belgium 'proved to be a *Leitmotiv* which fused the moralistic and the custodial streams of British patriotism into a powerful crusading torrent'.[10] W. R. Owen, a civil servant from Cardiff, volunteered with five office colleagues 'to fight for freedom. This was not a sentimental whim; we were genuinely moved by the raping of Belgium by the Hun.'[11] Owen's motives were shared by Thomas Bickerton, a recruit of the 3rd Hertfordshire Regiment. 'I felt that what we were going to do was something that had just got to be done; had not the Kaiser invaded little Belgium, and were not the Germans a bad crowd? And our intention was to defeat them and put them back in their proper place.'[12] A few, like G. W. Evans of the 2/4th Cheshire Regiment, were more concerned with the threat from German industry than with the plight of Belgium. To Evans the war was 'the only effective course to protect the trade interests of the nation and counteract the unemployment caused by the dumping of cheap German manufactured goods'.[13]

A fair proportion of the men who led the rush to the colours were spurred on by a conviction that the war would last no more than a few months and by the thought that any delay in enlisting might rob them of the chance to become personally involved in the greatest event of the epoch. 'Our major anxiety was by hook or by crook not to miss it,' wrote Harold Macmillan.[14] W. C. D. Maile, a young doctor, was another who was frightened that he would 'miss all the fun'. He made five separate visits to the War Office in an attempt to offer his services to the Royal Army Medical Corps, but was told that he was not required as yet and must go home and carry on with his practice until further notice. Undeterred, though by now 'feeling desperate', Maile took the advice of a friend and enlisted in the ranks of the 2/3rd Home Counties Field Ambulance, a newly formed second-line Territorial unit. Here he was greeted with open arms and was soon granted a commission. 'I could not resist going to see the Director-General again to tell him I had jumped the gun and was in the army. He was extremely angry and sent me off with a flea in my ear! However, I had won!'[15]

The prevailing opinion that the war would be short had precisely the opposite effect on some men. Barclay Buxton, a member of the Cambridge Inter-collegiate Christian Union, had gone with a party of undergraduates to the Isle of Wight to preach at various seaside resorts during the summer vacation. Buxton did not object to enlistment on religious grounds, believing that 'if death was abroad, if wrong was to be resisted, a Christian should be right in amongst it'. On the other hand, he saw no reason to abandon his seaside mission. 'We were quite clear that Germany would be defeated by the 7th October when we would go back to Cambridge,' he explained. Several weeks elapsed before he joined the 1st East Anglian Field Ambulance in response to an appeal from his cousin, Patrick Buxton, who was already serving in that unit.[16]

The daily recruiting returns for the first four months of the war suggest that, for the majority, the decision to volunteer was not automatic. The number of recruits attested daily rose gradually to 7,020 on 11 August and 9,699 a week later, falling away to 5,922 on 22 August. The figures did not top 10,000 a day until 25 August, then climbed steeply to a peak of 33,204 on 3 September. By 18 September they had dropped to under 5,000 and, from 1 October to 23 December, hovered between 1,500 and 4,600 apart from a brief flurry during the second week of November, when they exceeded 6,000 on three successive days.[17] It seems, therefore, that even many of the most ardent patriots hesitated for at least three or four weeks before joining up.

For some, the problem was an intellectual or moral one. A man who served in the East Surrey Regiment remembered, over half a century later, 'the agony of mind' he had suffered in the six weeks before he enlisted. 'As a convinced

Christian it gave me time to consider Christ's attitude to war. However, like many other young men, I decided there was nothing for it but to fight to keep the enemy away from our shores.'[18] Llewellyn Woodward, having recently graduated from Oxford, was beset by a mixture of doubts:

Could I be satisfied that, behind the appeals to patriotism and duty, the background of the war was not just another squabble over markets? Was not England enmeshed in the same political selfishness as Germany, less crudely and boastfully, but caught up in the same predatory social system? Anyhow, why should we interfere in what was primarily an Austro-Russian dispute over areas of political influence in south-eastern Europe? What claim had society upon me to help in getting it out of the political impasse into which it had blundered? Above all, would I be justified in killing Germans? Killing was murder, whatever the recruiting slogans might say about my King and Country needing me.

Woodward volunteered eventually because he could find 'no answer to the argument of Socrates', namely that 'if you have enjoyed the benefit of the laws of your country, you must not refuse obedience to them even when you think they are mistaken'.[19]

Other men, although anxious to join the Army, were restrained by family and business commitments. Andrew Buxton held a senior position in the Westminster branch of Barclay's Bank at the outbreak of the war. On 7 August he wrote, 'How dearly I should like to enlist at this moment, but it is impossible to leave the bank at so critical a time . . . I am bound to drag on, anyhow for a few days, and see how the bank will be able to manage with a smaller staff.'[20] Similar responsibilities affected A. A. Bardo, the assistant accountant to the Cardiff Board of Guardians. Bardo had to complete the half-yearly accounts before seeking the board's permission to enlist.[21] Civil servants who wished to volunteer were expected to refrain from undertaking any form of military liability until they had obtained the consent of the head of their particular department.[22] Employers did not always grant such permission at once. E. J. Robinson, a Post Office worker, was obliged to wait for a month before being released by the East Central District Office to join the 1/8th London Regiment (Post Office Rifles).[23] W. R. Owen had 'three weeks of wrangling' with his government department in Cardiff prior to enlisting.[24] Many tired of waiting. Bertram Glover was one of a dozen clerks who downed pens and walked out of a City office on 9 September to join the 1/6th London Regiment (City of London Rifles). 'This movement,' Glover admitted, 'was very much resented by the office manager who could foresee that nothing but chaos would follow such a depletion of his staff.'[25] These men were less patient than Emlyn Davies, who, between 5 August 1914 and 27 July 1915, made several applications to be released from the Post Office at Oswestry. On the latter date, his nineteenth birthday, his patience finally ran out and he joined the 17th Royal Welsh Fusiliers. According to Davis, his Head Postmaster was 'very angry, not to say nasty'.[26] Percy Croney's employer used a variety of arguments to dissuade him from volunteering.

First, Croney was told that, because the war would soon be over, enlistment would be a waste of time. When this approach failed, it was suggested that Croney owed it to his parents to finish his apprenticeship. At last his employer agreed that, if the war was still in progress at the end of November 1914, Croney would be released, provided he promised not to enlist until after Christmas.[27]

There is ample evidence to indicate that events in France and Belgium had a considerable influence on recruiting in the opening months of the war. It has already been noted that recruiting returns rose sharply in the fortnight after the battles of Mons and Le Cateau, dropped after the Allied success on the Marne in September, and then improved again for a short period during the first battle of Ypres in November. News of British reverses swept away the doubts and reservations of many. Alexander Thompson, an articled clerk in a Newcastle solicitors' office, warned his mother on 28 August that 'unless the Allied forces' prospects are better on Monday than they are at present, . . . I will join Kitchener's Army . . . There are thousands and thousands of people in this country who do not realise the position.'[28] Two days later Thompson joined the Quayside Company of the 9th Northumberland Fusiliers. The retreat of the British Expeditionary Force from Mons also served to persuade Andrew Buxton that he could no longer postpone the decision to leave his bank. 'I know you don't want me to enlist,' he told his sister on 31 August, 'but I cannot help thinking it my duty from every point of view (including example) to do so soon – say next week or the week following. I am not a born soldier, but I am a bachelor and I have an idea of rifle shooting, and with every available man being required I cannot stand out.'[29]

The autobiographical account written by John F. Tucker offers a typical example of a young man who had every reason to be among the first to enlist but held back until he was sure he was needed. At the outbreak of war Tucker, aged seventeen and a half, was a junior clerk with a firm of export agents in the Strand, London, and found office life repugnant. From childhood he had been obsessed with military matters, devoting much of his spare time to reading about British battles of the past. His cousin was a sergeant in the Grenadier Guards and his uncle an officer in a Territorial battalion of the Suffolk Regiment. Tucker himself had gained some knowledge of drill in the Church Lads' Brigade and was attracted by the strict discipline of army life. Thus, although he was under age and had a slight disability in his rib cage, the army exerted a strong pull on him. Nevertheless, it was not until mid-November that Tucker enlisted in the 13th London Regiment. 'We all thought it would be a short and sharp war,' he recalled, 'but after about two months it was obvious that it was going to be a long-drawn-out affair.' He then felt that 'it was up to me to take my place beside those who were sacrificing life and limb to protect our homes, families and country from the enemy'.[30]

Ernest and Elliott Sheard, two brothers from Pudsey in Yorkshire, joined the Leeds Bantams in December for similar reasons. As Ernest Sheard commented:

Every day one read in the papers about the small Army of the British being rapidly pushed back by the great masses of troops which Germany was able to place in the field. They were sorely in need of support, and their only hope was the men who were casting aside their civilian attire and donning khaki.[31]

A special kind of pressure was felt by men with close relatives in the BEF. 'My eldest brother was in the retreat from Mons,' wrote E. C. Haddrell, 'and in his letters home to his family he pleaded that his brothers should join up and do their share. Consequently, I decided to enlist in the 5th Wiltshire Regiment.'[32] Others awoke to the seriousness of the situation when the first hospital trains began to arrive at London stations. Passing Charing Cross station on his way home from work on 9 September, E. J. O. Bird saw ambulances filled with wounded being driven away to the hospitals. 'I was so outraged by the sight that I determined to join up that same evening. I went home, had a hasty meal, smartened up and duly presented myself at the HQ of the 24th London Regiment.'[33]

While most of the men quoted so far were driven into the army by patriotic ideals or a sense of obligation, thousands simply appear to have succumbed to the heady atmosphere which enveloped them in the early months of the war, particularly as the national and local recruiting campaigns got into their stride. One was Alfred Allen, a sixteen-year-old Brighton lad, who became 'infatuated with the marching brass bands which patrolled the streets of Brighton urging all likely males to join the ranks of Kitchener's Army. It did not take many days for me to present myself at the local Church Street drill hall.'[34] Another sixteen-year-old, George Coppard, was also caught up in the general excitement. 'News placards screamed out at every street corner, and military bands blared out their martial music in the main streets of Croydon. This was too much for me to resist and, as if drawn by a magnet, I knew I had to enlist straight away.'[35] An account by F. L. Goldthorpe, who joined the 1/5th Duke of Wellington's Regiment, illustrates just how difficult it was for a young man to ignore the call. Goldthorpe was in Lancaster on 5 August and witnessed the mobilisation of the local Territorials:

I remember marching alongside them, stirred like most of the onlookers by the noise of the bugles, and the electric atmosphere of that August day. Possibly I got bitten with the fever germ then. Our folks always said so, and although I know there were strong reasons why I should not leave business, I was pretty restless for the next few weeks. During this time I was subjected to a continual bombardment of skilled propaganda from the War office, newspapers, friends who had joined up, recruiting meetings, and even the pulpits . . . The accusing finger of Kitchener stabbed me at every bill-posting, and tales of German atrocities and stricken Belgium dinned into my ears daily. I suppose it was a combination of these many urgings which sent me to the local drill hall on November 15th. My age then was 17½.[36]

In the case of many lower middle-class and working-class recruits, the chance of escaping from an arduous or depressing job far outweighed patriotism as a motive for enlistment. This was undoubtedly one of the main reasons why the major industrial and mining areas produced such large numbers of volunteers, sometimes out of all proportion to their actual population. Not surprisingly, men who worked long hours in dismal conditions for low wages, and who rarely left their own immediate neighbourhood except for an occasional visit to the seaside, saw the war as a unique opportunity for travel and excitement. William Fraser, an Aberdeen man, was oppressed by the 'closed in' environment of his factory and joined the 2nd Highland Field Company of the Royal Engineers partly for the 'open air and the exercise' which the army offered.[37] A farm worker's son from Yorkshire confessed, 'My patriotism wasn't very deep, and Belgian atrocities didn't cut much ice, but I was fearfully sick of a humdrum life that led nowhere and promised nothing.'[38] Normal Ellison, bored with the dull routine of an office, seized the chance of 'getting out of a rut.' In his own words, 'It was most certainly not to guarantee the integrity of Belgium, nor ultra-patriotic motives that impelled me, on 10 August, to go to the barracks of Liverpool's crack Territorial Regiment, the Liverpool Rifles, to enlist.'[39] A Rochdale man, J. Norman Dykes, went into the University and Public Schools Brigade, thinking 'it would be a pleasant and welcome change from the uneventful existence of a junior library assistant, – a holiday in fact.'[40]

As in the past, sheer economic necessity forced a substantial number of men to enter the army. Wilfred Cook estimated that in Leeds, apart from those who enlisted 'just to break away from the monotony of civilian life as it then was', many young men volunteered because they had 'little hope of securing a permanent job with a reasonable wage'. Cook himself was paid only 12*s* a week as an apprentice printer, deciding that he had already waited 'quite long enough' when he joined the 3rd West Yorkshire Regiment in March 1915.[41] James Ellis also earned only 12*s* for working more than sixty-five hours a week in a London flour mill before he enlisted at Camberwell Town Hall in September 1914.[42] Even so, Cook and Ellis were in a happier position than Thomas Peers. He recalled that in August 1914:

when I was a raw lad of eighteen, times were hard in my home town of Bradford and I, in common with many others, was working only three days a week and drawing three days' dole money. Idling the time away one day, my friends and I were discussing the dreariness of unemployment, when someone suggested we should enlist and the Hussars were mentioned. This sounded to me a glorious adventure.[43]

Hardship and unemployment were not the only circumstances from which men wished to escape. Robert Graves applied for a commission within a week of the declaration of war, believing that hostilities might last just long enough to delay his going up to Oxford in October, a prospect which he dreaded. In his anxiety to join the army he scarcely stopped to consider the possibility that he might be called upon to serve at the front.[44] Others joined to avoid the clutches of the police. Denis Winter cites the case of Bert Warrant, who enlisted in the 10th London Regiment after stealing £300 from the Hackney

Empire.[45] One platoon of the 10th Essex Regiment contained three professional burglars.[46] T. A. Silver became a private in the East Surrey Regiment after deserting from the Royal Navy.[47] In Ireland, the commanding officer of the 5th Connaught Rangers was willing to take back several old soldiers who had deserted from the regiment some years earlier.[48]

Some men volunteered as a result of pressure from their employers or social superiors. Colonel F. C. Romer, the honorary secretary of Boodle's, took two waiters from the club with him when he was appointed CO of the 8th East Kent Regiment (the Buffs) in September 1914.[49] Landowners frequently selected likely men from among their servants and farm labourers and transported them to the nearest recruiting office. Lieutenant-Colonel A. C. Borton, who owned an estate at Cheveney in Kent and was a local Justice of the Peace, drove his butler, footman and cowman to Maidstone Barracks to enlist.[50] Alfred Mansfield travelled to the depot of the Northumberland Fusiliers in company with eight servants of a peer who had suggested that younger members of his staff should join the forces. The 5th Royal Berkshire Regiment included one platoon of butlers and footmen and another composed almost exclusively of gardeners and workers from a peer's estate.[51]

Yet another class of recruits was made up of men whose chief reason for joining the army was that all their friends were going. There were thousands like Eric Wainwright, an apprentice pharmacist who enlisted in the 2/4th King's Own Yorkshire Light Infantry because 'it was the done thing'.[52] Those who hesitated, if only for a week or two, quickly began to sense that they were no longer in step with the majority of young men of their own generation. This feeling of being 'left out' lay behind J. W. Stephenson's decision to volunteer. He wrote, 'Before the end of August, all the young fellows I knew had gone to the drill hall and enlisted in the Skipton Company of the Duke of Wellington's Regiment, and many of the boys of my age had enlisted by giving their wrong ages to the Recruiting Officer . . . causing much envy among those of us still at home.'[53] Shortly after going up to Oriel College, Oxford, in October 1914, Andrew McGregor, a Rhodes Scholar from South Africa, informed his father that he intended to apply for a commission:

There are very few chaps at College now; nearly all have taken commissions or are in some regiment. Last year our numbers were 133, this year they are only thirty-four, twenty of whom are freshers. . . . Our numbers, being so depleted, makes everything rather slow, and there can by no possibility be any such thing as Varsity sport this year. . . . I have joined the OTC – Officers Training Corps – with the object of preparing myself for a commission. It appears the only necessary and right thing to do and is what most of the chaps here are doing.[54]

Perry Webb carried on working in his family's food business in Dorset until late in 1915. In the end he enlisted because 'there was hardly anybody about, everybody seemed to be joining up . . . and I just got fed up'.[55]

The receipt of a white feather shamed some into enlisting, even when they had valid reasons for staying out of the army. A poignant story is told by Mrs

J. Upjohn, who remembered her father, Robert Smith, being given a white feather while working in Westminster, 'That night he come home and cried his heart out. My father was no coward, but he had been reluctant to leave his family.' Smith, who was then aged thirty-four, was married with two small children, and his wife, having recently recovered from a serious illness, was expecting another baby. Nevertheless, Smith volunteered soon after this incident.[56] A similar case was that of George Taylor, who was presented with a white feather in Euston Square early in 1915. Taylor's first child was not yet two, and his wife was now pregnant again, but he enlisted in the East Surrey Regiment almost immediately. 'Notwithstanding my home ties I must confess that I felt terribly guilty and made up my mind to join up,' he later acknowledged.[57] For single men who were eager to serve but considered themselves too young, a white feather often provided the final push. One such youth was Gunner H. Symonds of the 182nd Brigade, Royal Field Artillery:

I was listening to a ginger-haired girl giving a recruiting speech at Hyde Park Corner on 24 July 1915. I was seventeen at that time, but eager to go. So when 'Ginger' gently tucked a white feather into my buttonhole, I went off to the recruiting office. . . . When, some three or four days later in uniform I again stood in Hyde Park and listened to 'Ginger' she recognised me and, in front of the crowd round her stand, she came up to me and asked for the return of her feather. Amidst mixed cheering and booing I handed it to her. She had tears in her eyes as she kissed me and said 'God Bless'.[58]

There remained a large body of recruits whose motives for enlistment fitted none of the above categories. Sidney Rogerson has related how his servant Bob Parkin, a 'steel worker and public house bookie' from Rotherham, joined the West Yorkshire Regiment in a moment of alcoholic exuberance after seeing a friend off to the front: 'He never remembered taking the shilling, and "when the sergeant come and claimed" him next morning he was as surprised as his wife was annoyed.'[59]

One old soldier re-enlisted in the Leinster Regiment firmly believing that he was going to fight the French.[60] Some men avoided the normal recruiting process altogether and simply attached themselves to a column on the march. The officers of the 8th Norfolk Regiment noticed that a company would start a route march 300 strong and return with 310, 'and no one knew or could find out who were the new men'.[61] When recruits of the 11th Lancashire Fusiliers left the depot at Bury for Codford in Wiltshire, 'a great number of friends who had come to see them off thought they would like a holiday in the south and went too'.[62] Even as late as mid-1915, men were still volunteering on the spur of the moment. Few can have acted more impulsively than Private H. Sullivan, a sixteen-year-old from Mile End in east London, who joined the Shoreditch Battalion (20th Middlesex Regiment) in June 1915:

I was looking at some Army posters in the Commercial Road. A recruiting sergeant tapped me on the shoulder – 'What about it, mate? Like to join?' – I was about to say 'I'm only sixteen,' changed my mind, and being a cute Cockney thought 'Here's a lark!' I said, 'Yes mate, if I'm big enough!' . . . What a blinking lark it turned out to be!'[63]

II

Whatever his motives and expectations were, the mere fact that a man had resolved to volunteer did not, of course, guarantee that he would be taken by the army. He had first to offer himself for enlistment at a recruiting office, where, after answering the eleven questions on the official attestation form, he underwent a medical examination. If he was passed fit and accepted the conditions of service, he then took the oath of allegiance and was given the King's shilling – one day's basic pay for a private – as confirmation that he had formally enlisted. Bound by the oath and his acceptance of the King's shilling, he was now a soldier.

In theory, a volunteer could choose for himself the unit in which he was to serve. This applied not only to men enlisting directly into specific Pals battalions or Territorial formations but also to those who passed through the traditional War Office recruiting channels. To some extent, recruiting officers were allowed to use their discretion concerning the branch of the army to which a man enlisting for general service should be posted.[64] However, instructions issued by the Adjutant-General's Department on 21 August 1914 contained a clear reminder that if a recruit on enlistment stated a preference for any particular corps or regiment the recruiting officer 'should as far as possible accede to his wishes, provided he is not obviously unsuitable'.[65] If the formation in question was closed for recruiting, having reached full strength, or if the volunteer was patently unfitted for such a unit, it was then up to the recruiting officer to explain the problem and suggest an alternative.[66] Given a choice, most men opted to serve with their friends in a battalion of their local county regiment, although a few preferred to go elsewhere, sometimes for quite trivial reasons. Martin Middlebrook quotes the case of Lance-Corporal H. Fellows, who had lost both his parents, was very poor and had never had a holiday in his life. When he enlisted in Nottingham, Fellows turned down the opportunity to join a local unit and, of the battalions open to him, picked the 12th Northumberland Fusiliers because that gave him the longest train ride.[67]

In practice, many men discovered that joining the unit of their choice was a far more complicated business than they had imagined. The enlistement process itself presented a number of obstacles for the would-be recruit. For example, those who had volunteered during the peak period in August and September 1914 often found it almost impossible to get inside a recruiting office. In order to enlist in the Queen's Westminster Rifles (16th London Regiment) on 31 August Sidney Burridge had to join a queue which stretched from Buckingham Palace Gate and down Victoria Street to Westminster Abbey.[68] J. G. Gordon has recorded that in Middlesbrough mounted police were brought in to help control hundreds of men who were hoping to enlist in the Green Howards: 'I got near to the door and was amused by the remarks of one of these stalwarts. He yelled, "If you don't stop this bloody shoving not one of you will get into the Army." '[69] Mounted police were also needed to marshal the crowds outside the Central London Recruiting Depot in Great Scotland Yard early in August. Leonard Preuss waited there for three days with his brother and friends before deciding to move on.[70]

Although, in most places, the crowds were orderly and patient, some volunteers plainly felt that they had a greater right to enlist than others in the queue. William Linton Andrews, a journalist, incurred the hostility of a mob of unemployed men at a recruiting office in Dundee:

A gaunt man in a muffler towered over me. He looked down, and said, not without sympathy: 'Out o' work, chum?' I was a trifle huffy. Out of work, indeed. I was the News Editor . . . of an important morning paper, the *Dundee Advertiser*. But I could not go into that. I told the big man I had a goodish job. 'Then you make way for us lads wi'out jobs,' he said. And forthwith I was hustled back to the edge of the crowd. Funny (I thought to myself), I never knew it was so hard to become a soldier. I waited an hour or two. Still no good. I went back sorrowfully to my desk, and tried again the next day, and the next . . .[71]

Conversely, men who knew someone in authority were able to jump the queue. When Norman Ellison went to enlist in the Liverpool Rifles he found that the sentry on guard was an old school friend, and he was smuggled in through the door without further ado.[72] Lionel Ferguson received similar help at the headquarters of the Liverpool Scottish:

What sights I saw on my way to Fraser Street; a queue of men over two miles long in the Haymarket; the recruiting office took over a week to pass in all these thousands. At Fraser Street HQ things seemed hopeless; in fact I was giving up hope of ever getting in, when I saw Rennison, an officer of the battalion, and he invited me into the mess, getting me in front of hundreds of others.[73]

Because crowds on this scale were so common in the opening months of the war, the unit which a man joined was frequently determined by chance rather than design. Having abandoned the attempt to enlist at Great Scotland Yard, Leonard Preuss next went to the headquarters of the Surrey Rifles (21st London Regiment) in Camberwell, only to be told that there were no more vacancies for the time being. He finished up by enlisting in the 24th London Regiment at New Street in Kennington.[74] H. Sargent, a Manchester printer, tried to join the Royal Artillery, thinking that his knowledge of machinery might be useful. 'The queue was terrific,' he wrote, 'so being eager to "get at 'em", my friend and I went over to the 2/6th Manchesters.'[75]

With such an abundance of volunteers in the early weeks, some units could afford to be highly selective. E. Robinson, the Yorkshire farm workers' son mentioned above, was turned down when he tried to enlist in the Leeds Pals on 3 September:

I was asked what my father did for a living, much to my surprise, and I suggested I wanted to join and not my father. I said I was a clerk, but they insisted I should say what my father did. It was curiouser and curiouser, but eventually I said he was a farm worker. Very politely, very firmly, it was told to me that only professional men's sons, or men whose fathers had businesses, could join for a day or two – it was exclusive.[76]

Rejected by the Leeds Pals, Robinson presented himself at another recruiting office and became a gunner in the Royal Artillery. A friend who had gone with him to the Leeds Town Hall, and who had also been unsuccessful, returned to his job in disgust and never again attempted to enlist.

Similar elitism was revealed by a handful of Territorial units at this time. Norman Ellison was soon made aware of the qualifications needed to join the Liverpool Rifles. 'The whole of Europe might be in flames,' he commented, 'but the Rifles still had a reputation to maintain; only men of good standing were enrolled in their ranks. Major T. told us this and made no bones about it. My job? Where educated? What games did I play? My answers evidently were satisfactory, so I passed the doctor, took the oath . . . and was told to report next morning.'[77] Some battalions actually charged an entrance fee. Roy Besch had to part with £5 to join the Artists' Rifles; Sidney Burridge was charged 25s to enlist in the Queen's Westminster Rifles; and Edmund Herd paid 10s 6d to enrol as a private in the Liverpool Scottish.[78] The recruiting boom also gave long-serving Territorials an opportunity to gain some revenge for the scorn heaped upon the Territorial Force by the public before the war. Charles Taylor was one of many recruits who were forced to listen to an impassioned address from a sergeant-major of the 5th London Regiment:

'Feather bed soldiers you called us, and the Saturday afternoon army, and now you are clamouring to join. We don't want all of you and you'll get no uniforms for a long time.' Thus, Sergeant Major Hawkey, from a soap box, harangued the thousands of volunteers lining the streets from the London Rifle Brigade drill hall in Bunhill Row right out to Finsbury . . . He succeeded in turning away the lukewarm and, with the assistance of the Medical Officer, in recruiting only those who were really keen on joining the regiment.[79]

To men with physical shortcomings the medical examination was the biggest hurdle of all. The standards of medical inspections varied widely according to time, place and circumstance. In the early autumn of 1914, when thousands were pouring into the recruiting offices daily, it was difficult for doctors to perform anything but the most cursory examinations. One doctor was known to have examined 400 men a day over a ten-day period.[80] As a result, hard-pressed medical officers and civilian doctors passed many recruits who should have been failed outright. Reginald Cockburn claimed that a man with a wooden foot managed to get into the 10th King's Royal Rifle Corps. 'The foot would possibly not have been discovered, had he not been marched into the Orderly Room one day. The Orderly Room, unfortumately, had a wooden floor.'[81]

Standards could vary even among a team of doctors working simultaneously at a single recruiting centre. Dr H. de Carle Woodcock recorded the following impressions of one recruiting office in Leeds at the beginning of the war:

Any medical man who could spare the time to examine recruits was welcomed. These boys lined up naked against the walls of the Tram Offices . . . How anxious they were to join up! A whole bunch of them swerved over to the group of medical men because we were rejecting few and passing recruits in quickly. One drunken volunteer was turned out by an austere doctor who said that the army must not be degraded by drink. However, the recruit came up again. I saw him enter the room, and in a few minutes he was in the army. One old man who had been at Tel el Kebir came before me. When he was rejected as far too old he said, 'You'll want me before you've finished.' The examination was a strange one. Men who could jump and hop and shout 'Who goes there?' were thought by some examiners to be strong in wind and limb, strong enough to fight, whilst men with the classical faults of the recruiting tests, variocele, flat foot, varicose veins, and the like, were rejected in large numbers.[82]

Many recruits who feared they would be turned down on account of poor eyesight, or because they were too short, were astonished by the superficial nature of the examination. Private T. H. Merrifield of the 10th Royal Welsh Fusiliers enlisted at Swansea on 5 September 1914: 'The Medical Officer, after the usual tests, put me to sight testing and when he found my left eye very weak, he said 'Ah well, you always shut that when you are firing your rifle, so that won't matter as your right eye is 100 per cent.'[83] John Tucker was struck by the casual attitude of the medical officer at the Kensington drill hall of the 13th London Regiment: 'I answered the various questions, giving a fictitious age of nineteen, and was sent up to the gallery to await the Medical Officer, who eventually turned up, evidently from his enjoyable lunch. I took off my jacket and was told to hold out my arms, open and close my fingers; the MO said OK and turning on his heel walked off. No stethoscope was used and no pulse rate taken.'[84] When Wilfred Cook enlisted at Leeds in 1915 he was unhappy about the poor standard of hygiene shown by a doctor whose only instruments were a stethoscope and a flashlight 'which probed one's mouth and then other parts of the anatomy of each man. I never saw any attempt at sterilisation of these instruments and there were some queer-looking individuals just before me.'[85]

Even where the medical examinations were more stringent, men could sometimes bluff their way into the army. Early in September 1914 J. Beeken, a schoolteacher, went with a group of friends to Wenlock Barracks to join the Hull Commercials (10th East Yorkshire Regiment). Beeken had no trouble passing but knew that one of his friends was blind in one eye:

I watched him anxiously as his sight test came along. He was told to cover up one eye and read the letters on a test card. He covered up the left eye and easily read the letters. When told to cover up the other eye, he calmly covered up the left eye and so passed the sight test. He was declared to be physically fit.[86]

Morris Bickersteth was granted a commission in the Leeds Pals although he too suffered from bad eyesight. He succeeded in passing the sight test because he had memorised the letters and numerals on identical cards at Aitchison's, the opticians, before proceeding to the town hall.[87] At Salisbury, George Eyston (later holder of the world land speed record) had to face the same problem when he took his medical for the University and Public Schools

Brigade of the Royal Fusiliers. Eyston was taken to a local doctor's consulting room with several other volunteers and was made to stand some feet away from the test cards. The doctor was called out of the room in the middle of the examination and Eyston did his best to learn the cards by heart. 'When it came to my turn,' he wrote, 'I could read the small ones and the big fellows but not the intermediate kind. I had forgotten the darned things. However, as the doctor was busy he gave it up as a bad job – and signed me up, fit for service.'[88]

Not everyone passed at the first attempt. To begin with, Eric Wainwright, the trainee pharmacist, had tried to join the Royal Army Medical Corps but, being only 5ft 2in. in height, was rejected as too short by an officer who was barely an inch taller. He then proceeded to the drill hall of the 4th King's Own Yorkshire Light Infantry at Wakefield, where the doctor took a more lenient view of his stature. 'I was tall enough to stick Germans with a bayonet but not to dispense medicines in a hospital,' Wainwright remarked.[89] W. S. Tremain, who was the same height as Wainwright, applied at thirteen different recruiting offices before he was accepted by the 19th London Regiment in March 1915.[90]

Since so many men went to enlist with their friends or workmates in the hope that they would be permitted to serve together, the rejection of one on medical grounds often influenced the fate of the entire group. The length of the queues at recruiting offices in Cardiff prompted W. R. Owen and his five colleagues to go by train to Penarth, where they hoped they would encounter fewer problems:

We had already decided we should like to join the 21st Lancers. It sounded grandiloquent and presented to us a picture of well-upholstered recruits in the resplendent uniform of a Lancer charging, in due course, like the German Uhlans of whom we had read and whom we cursed for their inhumanity . . . The sergeant fumbled away among the heaps of dirty paper on his table and asked if we had ever ridden a horse. No, we hadn't, but this was apparently not an impediment. According to his schedule we had to be at least 5 feet 6 inches tall. This sounded reasonable enough, but even in that melée of disorganisation it was worth his checking that we did conform with his initial requirement. We all did except our spokesman who was 5 feet 4 inches. We retired to the landing and were persuaded by our spokesman that we should join the Rifle Brigade.[91]

It is impossible to establish how many volunteers were below the stipulated minimum age of nineteen. As the true age of such recruits would not have been entered on the attestation forms, the official records of enlistment cannot be expected to provide a reliable figure. However, judging by the frequent references to boy soldiers in the surviving diaries and personal accounts of the period, it seems safe to assume that the number of under-age recruits ran into tens of thousands. Some of them were very young indeed. For instance, Private Harry Whittaker from Hyde in Cheshire was just thirteen years and eight months old when he volunteered for service in the 2/6th Cheshire Regiment in November 1914.[92] Private E. Lugg of the 13th Royal

Sussex Regiment was one month older than Whittaker.[93] Perhaps the youngest of all was Private S. Lewis, who joined the East Surreys in August 1915 at the age of twelve and served for six weeks on the Somme.[94]

In the nineteenth century recruiting parties had received a 'bringing in' fee of 15s for every man produced and generally did not trouble themselves about anything other than the physique of the individual concerned.[95] The system of recruiting rewards still existed in 1914 although the bonuses were much lower, 5s being paid for each man obtained for the Foot Guards, the Royal Artillery, the Royal Engineers and the Mechanical Transport Section of the Army Service Corps, and 2s 6d in the case of recruits for cavalry units, line infantry regiments, the Royal Army Medical Corps, the Army Ordnance Corps and branches of the Army Service Corps other than the MT Section. The enlistment boom of August and September 1914 made it not only too costly but also unnecessary to maintain payments at these levels and the rewards were reduced to a standard sum of 1s by a Royal Warrant on 20 October that year.[96] Nevertheless, with volunteers coming forward in such profusion, a recruiting sergeant could amass a substantial sum from rewards, particularly if he was prepared to bend the regulations a little. This may help to explain why the majority of under-age recruits appear to have joined with comparative ease. The benevolence shown to George Coppard was typical: 'The sergeant asked my age, and when told replied "Clear off, son. Come back tomorrow and see if you're nineteen, eh?" So I turned up again the next day and gave my age as nineteen. I attested in a batch of a dozen others and, holding up my right hand, swore to fight for King and Country. The sergeant winked as he gave me the King's shilling . . .'[97] Others did not even have to wait this long to be attested. On stating that his age was sixteen, E. J. O. Bird was told to go outside, turn round three times, then come back and say he was nineteen: 'Disappointed, but not dismayed, I returned, having "lived" another three years in the space of about ten minutes.'[98] At a recruiting office in Llandudno in October 1914, sixteen-year-old Lewis Roberts enlisted in the 10th Royal Welsh Fusiliers having followed the sergeant's suggestion that he should 'walk round the table twice' before giving a false age.[99]

Some had to seek alternative means of hiding their youth. Charles Cameron, who was fifteen at the outbreak of war, became a private in the 7th Seaforth Highlanders by wearing his brother's long trousers when he went to enlist.[100] Thomas McIndoe of the 12th Middlesex Regiment had displayed equal resourcefulness after being turned away from a recruiting office in Harlesden:

I never said anything to my parents, and I picked up the bowler hat which my mother had bought me and which was only taken into wear on Sundays. I donned that, thinking it would make me look older, and I presented myself to the recruiting officer again . . . This time there were no queries, and I was accepted.[101]

Whenever the age regulations were strictly enforced youthful volunteers could find it very hard to get into the army. For J. W. Stephenson, from Skipton in Yorkshire, the path which led to enlistment in the 3/7th Duke of Wellington's Regiment proved long and tortuous:

Along I went with a few pals to enlist in the Ordnance Corps. However, the recruiting officer and his staff knew me, and that I was under age, so he sent me straight back home. Some weeks after . . . again with some pals, off we went to the recruiting office to join the Royal Horse Artillery. What a reception we got! We were packed off almost before we got in the drill hall, and told not to come again until we were nineteen. We were getting somewhat disheartened when we heard that, at a nearby town called Otley, a battery of howitzers was being formed. What a howitzer was I had not the slightest idea, only the name seemed to mean something, so off we went to join them. However, the CO there had heard of us. He telephoned my father to verify our story, and that was the end of our journey, back home we had to go. The year 1915 came and, to us, time was slipping by very fast, so we decided to go to Keighley, ten miles away, where no one knew anything about us, and join something, we had no idea what. . . . We were unknown there, were all passed fit, and accepted.[102]

Unlike Stephenson, Arthur Wadsworth quickly realised that he must travel outside his own district to enlist. Wadsworth, aged sixteen, was so annoyed at being rejected by the Bradford Pals because of his youth – in contrast to George Morgan, who was accepted at the same age – that he walked to Leeds and joined the Leeds Pals, remembering, on this occasion, to give a false date of birth.[103]

Unless they were orphans or had run away from home, most under-age recruits were obliged, sooner or later, to break the news to their parents. Many of those who elected to reveal their intentions before going to enlist found that their parents, if not wildly enthusiastic, would at least refrain from standing in their way. To H. E. L. Mellersh, who described himself as 'an unquestioningly dutiful son', the moment when he announced his desire to join up came as something of an anti-climax: 'They had obviously been more than half expecting me to do just that; my father may even have been hoping so, though if so he had been concealing the fact pretty successfully.'[104] Some parents gave their consent only because they were convinced that their son would be rejected by the army. T. H. Barnes, whose family owned a colliery near Chesterfield, had left Eton in the summer of 1914 and was due to go up to Cambridge that autumn. He has described how, after seeing Kitchener's initial appeal in a morning newspaper, he took the first steps towards a commission in the 9th Sherwood Foresters (Notts and Derby Regiment):

. . . I got on my bicycle and rode the five miles to our colliery and asked my father for the car to go to Derby. He asked me the reason and I said 'to join the army' and showed him the paper. I was 17½. He said 'You can have the car, but I am sure they will not accept you.' When we arrived at Normanton Barracks in Derby, the sergeant of the guard said to me, 'You will have to see the medical officer first' and directed me to his office. . . . I was told to strip to the waist. After examining me he said 'You are a bit thin, what is your age?' I told him. He replied 'You will grow to it, you are in!' I went back home and not surprisingly my father was very shocked.[105]

The blow was much greater for parents who had no knowledge of a son's enlistment until after the event. It took Emlyn Davies two days to pluck up the courage to tell his mother that he had joined the 17th Royal Welsh Fusiliers: 'She suspected there was something out of the ordinary. She thought I had been sacked. It was a terrible shock to her . . . Until my departure, and probably long afterwards, she was in a state of near collapse!'[106] George Morgan recalled, 'When I told my mother that I had joined up she said that I was a fool and she'd give me a good hiding, but I said "I'm a man now, and you can't hit a man." '[107] A boy soldier could be discharged, however, if his parents chose to inform the authorities of his true date of birth, as in the case of Alfred Allen from Brighton:

. . . my mother, a widow, soon sickened at the sight of her only son, under age for authentic enlistment, dashing out of the house at the sound of a bugle call and lining up in the roadway for roll call in the early mornings . . . My worried mother divulged my real age to the officer in charge of my detachment. At heart dismayed, but not daring to do otherwise. I packed my so-called uniform up in a brown paper parcel and an evening or two later I crept into the drill hall to deposit the parcel on one of the forms which lined the hall. I then crept out again, ashamed, dishonoured and unsung!'[108]

Understandably, men who feared rejection because they were too young, too short or medically unsound were, in the end, happy to settle for any unit that would take them, but it was not unusual for a recruit who met all the required standards to be persuaded to join the regiment of a county far removed from the place where he lived and worked. This was happening very early in the war as regiments from the sparsely populated rural areas began to encounter difficulties in bringing their New Army battalions up to strength and so were forced to turn to the cities and industrial centres for help. Thus when George Butterworth and his friends went to enlist at Great Scotland Yard towards the end of August 1914 they were advised by the authorities there to join the Duke of Cornwall's Light Infantry, 'as it had been decided to recruit for that regiment in large numbers, and this would give a better chance for parties of friends to join *en bloc*'.[109] Some men, however, had only a vague idea what they were joining. Andrews, the journalist who enlisted in the 1/4th Black Watch at Dundee, continued to write articles to stimulate recruiting and signed several of them as 'One of Kitchener's Hundred Thousand' before he realised that he was in a Territorial battalion.[110] While Andrews conceded that the mistake was his own, other volunteers felt either that their choice of unit had been totally ignored or, worse still, that they had been deceived. For instance, G. T. Walton enlisted at Deaf Hill, Co. Durham, on Friday 4 September 1914 and was accepted for the Durham Light Infantry. The next day he was sent to Sunderland, where 'hundreds of us were put on a train and arrived at Carlisle late on Saturday night. On Sunday we had a surprise when they told us we were in the Border Regiment.'[111] In November 1914 Eric Scullin, who had already decided against joining the infantry because he thought 'marching would be a rather tiring game', saw a notice outside Fenton Street Barracks in Leeds which called for volunteers for an anti-aircraft gun section. This appealed to him, so he presented himself the following day and, though under age, was accepted without trouble. 'I found out later I was in the Field Artillery,' he wrote. 'Whether the notice that had enticed me was a "blind" or not, I never knew.'[112]

A few men even succeeded in joining more than one unit. The experiences of Private Charles Cain were characteristic of the confusion and irregularities which attended the birth of the New Armies. At the outbreak of war Cain, who was under eighteen and only 4ft 11in. tall, was working in a Manchester office. He had no father and his mother was employed as a barmaid in the Isle of Man. When he enlisted in September 1914 the recruiting staff at the Ardwick drill hall gave him a box to stand on so that he could make the required height of 5ft 3in. Cain enrolled as a boy bugler in the 19th Manchester Regiment (4th City Battalion) and was instructed to return to his job until the battalion was called for training. After waiting for over a fortnight, he felt impatient and therefore switched battalions on his own initiative, attaching himself to the 17th Manchester (2nd City Battalion) when the latter moved off to camp at Heaton Park on 19 September. He stayed with this unit until the last week of October, but was then arrested for 'desertion' from the 19th Battalion and discharged from the army because the War Office, now aware of his real age, decreed that he was not old enough for military service. Unperturbed, Cain went to Wigan three days later and enlisted as a bandsman in the 2/5th Manchesters, a Territorial battalion. This time he had no problems about his height and age, although in order to pass the eyesight test he had to ask a fellow recruit to read the cards out to him before he reached the doctor.[113] Considering the immense difficulties which it faced in the autumn of 1914, it is small wonder that the War Office was unable to keep track of men possessing this degree of enthusiasm and determination.

Whereas Cain's movements were dictated by a genuine desire to serve, other volunteers had more sinister motives. These men, known in official parlance as 'absconded recruits' would go through the attestation process to secure their first day's pay – and a uniform if it was available – and would then disappear. With luck they might repeat this trick several times at different recruiting offices, no doubt giving a false name on each occasion. The 12th (Bermondsey) Battalion of the East Surrey Regiment, which was raised in mid-1915, had to contend with a large number of absconded recruits. Eventually it transpired that a recruiting sergeant was the source of the trouble. According to the battalion historians, his *modus operandi* consisted of 'encouraging youngsters to enlist, get a free kit, and sell that same kit to the aforesaid sergeant in the evening, who in turn disposed of it to a notorious "old clothes man". A bit of detective work by RSM Solomon resulted in the bemedalled hero getting three months' hard labour at Tower Bridge Police

Court.'[114] In all, one officer and 456 men were court-martialled for fraudulent enlistment between 4 August 1914 and 30 September 1915.[115]

Such cases, though comparatively rare, offer further proof that not all Kitchener's volunteers came forward in a spirit of romantic idealism. The prospect of adventure and the opportunity to escape from poverty, dreary surroundings or a tedious job played their part in drawing men to the recruiting offices. Indeed, the factors which impelled so many to enlist were as diverse as the recruits themselves. Probably only a small number had a single overriding motive for enlistment, most recruits being driven to join by a combination of external pressures and personal desires and loyalties.

This is not to deny the presence of a powerful stream of moralistic patriotism in 1914. The men of Kitchener's army had been brought up to believe that Britain occupied a unique position on the world stage and that her historic mission was to act as a force for good in international affairs. The related codes of duty, discipline and self-sacrifice which had permeated to every level of late Victorian and Edwardian society did much to shape the attitudes and aspirations of Kitchener's volunteers. Yet, prior to August 1914, neither patriotism on the one hand nor hardship and unemployment on the other had provided a solution to the army's recruiting problems. Why, then, was Kitchener able to call upon the services of men for whom the army had earlier held little or no attraction?

One answer is that the declaration of war pulled together the various strands of patriotic sentiment and welded them into a coherent whole. What for most people had been a series of abstract concepts and ideals suddenly took on a definite form and meaning. The issues now appeared to be clear-cut and there was a real enemy to be fought. Men were far more willing to commit themselves to the nation's cause when the threat from outside was positive and recognisable instead of being just a vague shadow on the horizon.

The declaration of hostilities therefore gave Britain a renewed feeling of national unity and purpose, symbolised by the appointment of Kitchener as Secretary of State for War. While many people had anticipated that there would be a general European conflict one day, few had envisaged it as an immediate possibility. As Professor Marwick has pointed out, when war came it 'brought both a sense of long-sought release and an atmosphere of panic and untempered emergency'.[116] A country beset by political, social and economic problems greeted this greater, all-embracing crisis almost with relief and, for several weeks after the outbreak of war, abandoned itself to a mood of excitement and exhilaration in which extraordinary acts of individual and collective patriotism became commonplace.

In this situation the army, buttressed by the weight of Kitchener's personal prestige, acquired a new status in the eyes of the people. Before the war, all attempts to increase the yearly intake and to attract a better class of recruit had failed, largely because of the social stigma attached to service in the ranks. Now that the soldier was a popular hero and was treated with respect rather than contempt, the army seemed infinitely more alluring, particularly to men whose lives were otherwise drab and anonymous. Since enlistment in the ranks was no longer seen as the last resort of the unskilled and unemployed but as a noble thing to do for one's country, Kitchener's call struck a responsive chord among men of all classes, enabling him, virtually overnight, to widen the base of the army's social composition.

The special character of this expanded army, with its large number of Pals and Territorial formations, must also be taken into account in any analysis of enlistment patterns in 1914 and 1915. No British army in history has contained such a high proportion of units directly linked to individual communities. The idea of serving with one's friends in a battalion which was closely identified with one's own town, district or workplace appealed strongly to many thousands of men and often proved the decisive factor in persuading them to enlist. Certainly, the importance of local pride as a stimulus to recruiting should not be underestimated. Some areas were still capable of producing locally raised units in mid-1915 when the national recruiting figures were in decline.

The private citizen, moreover, was subjected to an unrelenting barrage of recruiting propaganda in the opening months of the war. By mobilising voluntary civilian help to an unprecedented degree, and by making full use of local government machinery and the constituency organisations of the major political parties, the War Office and the Parliamentary Recruiting Committee found it possible to mount sustained recruiting campaigns in every corner of the land. In relatively small communities the social and psychological pressures on individuals were intensified, and it became progressively harder for a man to stand back when more and more of his friends and neighbours were seen to be joining up.

However, it would be inaccurate to say that the flower of British manhood was merely swept into the army on a tide of national hysteria. It may be true that the majority had a tragically unrealistic conception of war and misplaced confidence in their own ability to bring the conflict to a speedy and successful conclusion, yet a significant proportion of them waited until they were sure that they were required. Less than one-third of all volunteers were involved in the first rush to the colours in August and September 1914. The remainder hesitated for two months or longer, by which time the exhilaration and partial panic of the early weeks had begun to evaporate.

In fact the records left by many of those who enlisted reflect a more restrained and objective attitude to the war than is usually ascribed to the recruits of 1914 and 1915. Soon after applying for a commission in August 1914 the poet Charles Sorley observed, 'I could wager that out of twelve million eventual combatants there aren't twelve who really want it. And serving one's country is so unpicturesque and unheroic when it comes to the point.'[117] Stanley Casson also felt that he ought to seek a commission even though he was under no illusions about the nature of war. 'Heaven knows,' he wrote, 'I was filled with mortal and deadly fear when I signed the fatal document that promised me unlimited hopes of slaughter for King and Country. I knew exactly what I was in for, and I decided then and there that no false heroics would ever persuade me to throw my life away except for some most urgent and compelling reason.'[118]

The evidence suggests, therefore, that the bulk of Kitchener's volunteers were motivated by a sense of duty and obligation rather than missionary zeal. In this respect Charles Douie, who served as an officer in the 7th Dorset Regiment, has perhaps come as close as anyone to capturing the spirit of Kitchener's army:

Few of them professed any real pleasure in the life of a soldier. They took soldiering intensely seriously, as a means to an end, in their hope of a rapid end . . . The war was not a crusade in their eyes; it was a disagreeable job which had to be seen though, however long it took and whatever sacrifice it entailed . . . If any soldier had delivered a speech on love of country, or the justice of our cause, consternation would have reigned among his comrades. These were matters which were taken for granted.[119]

Notes

1   Caroline E. Playne, *Society at War, 1914–1916,* Allen & Unwin, London, 1931, p. 26.

2   C. E. Montague, *Disenchantment,* Chatto & Windus, London, 1922, pp. 2–3.

3   Sir Philip Magnus, *Kitchener: Portrait of an Imperialist,* Murray, London, 1958, p. 289.

4   Rupert Brooke, *Peace (1914): the Collected Poems of Rupert Brooke,* Sidgwick & Jackson, London, 1918, p. 5.

5   'A Soldier of the War', letter to the *Nation,* 27 December 1919.

6   H. U. S. Nisbet, *Diaries and Memories of the Great War,* unpublished account, 1974, IWM 78/3/1.

7   Sir Arthur Bliss, *As I Remember,* Faber, London, 1970, p. 30.

8   W. T. Colyer, unpublished account, n.d., IWM 76/51/1.

9   George Morgan, interview with Malcolm Brown, 13 February 1976. Transcript supplied to the author.

10   Colin Nicolson, *Edwardian England and the Coming of the First World War,* in Alan O'Day (ed.), *The Edwardian Age: Conflict and Stability, 1900–1914,* Macmillan, London, 1979, p. 166.

11   W. R. Owen, letter of 16 July 1963, IWM BBC/GW.

12   Thomas Bickerton, *The Wartime Experiences of an Ordinary Tommy,* unpublished account, 1964, IWM 80/43/1.

13   G. W. Evans, letter of 24 September 1963, IWM BBC/GW.

14   Harold Macmillan, *Winds of Change, 1914–1939,* Macmillan, London, 1966, p. 59.

15   W. C. D. Maile, *Recollections of the First World War,* unpublished account, 1974, IWM 76/65/1.

16   Interview with B. G. Buxton, IWM Department of Sound Records, 000299/05.

17   Daily recruiting returns submitted to the Adjutant-General, 4 August–27 December 1914, Adjutant-General's papers, WO 162/3.

18   L. Howell, letter to Malcom Brown, n.d., *c.* March 1976.

19   Sir Llewellyn Woodward, *Great Britain and the War of 1914–1918,* Methuen,

London, 1967, pp. xiv–xvi.

20 Edward S. Woods (ed.), *Andrew R. Buxton: a memoir,* Scott, London, 1918, p. 38.

21 A. A. Bardo, letter to Malcolm Brown, 9 April 1976.

22 *Parliamentary Debates, House of Commons, 1914–15,* LXX, col. 1428; Army Order I of 29 August 1914 (AO 338 of 1914).

23 Note from the introduction to the First World War diary of E. J. Robinson, IWM 77/131/1.

24 W. R. Owen, letter of 16 July 1963, IWM BBC/GW.

25 Bertram Glover, undated letter, *c.* July 1963, IWM BBC/GW.

26 Emlyn Davies, *Taffy went to War,* privately published, *c.* 1968.

27 Percy Croney, *Soldier's Luck: Memoirs of a Soldier of the Great War,* Stockwell, Ilfracombe, 1965, pp. 9–10.

28 Alexander Thompson to his mother, 28 August 1914, IWM 79/55/1.

29 Woods, *Andrew R. Buxton,* p. 39.

30 John F. Tucker, *Johnny got you Gun: a Personal Narrative of the Somme, Ypres and Arras,* Kimber, London, 1978, pp. 11–12.

31 Ernest Sheard, *My Great Adventure: the Great War, 1914–1918,* unpublished account, n.d., IWM P. 285.

32 E. C. Haddrell, undated letter, *c.* July 1963, IWM BBC/GW.

33 E. J. O Bird, undated letter, *c.* July 1963, IWM BBC/GW.

34 Alfred G. Allen, letter of 31 May 1964, IWM BBC/GW.

35 George Coppard, *With a Machine Gun to Cambrai,* Imperial War Museum (HMSO), London, 1969, p. 1.

36 F. L. Goldthorpe, *Memoirs of my War Service, 1914–1919,* unpublished account, *c.* 1934, IWM P. 113.

37 William Fraser, letter of 8 July 1963, IWM BBC/GW.

38 E. Robinson, undated letter, *c.* July 1963, IWM BBC/GW.

39 Norman F. Ellison, *War Diary, 1914–1919,* unpublished account, *c.* 1958, IWM DS/MISC/49.

40 J. Norman Dykes, *You are in the Army now,* unpublished account, 1969, IWM PP/MCR/60.

41 Wilfred Cook, *The Lengthened Shadow,* unpublished account, 1968, IWM P. 101.

42 James H. Ellis, letter of 3 July 1963, IWM BBC/GW.

43 Thomas Peers, letter of 14 July 1963, IWM BBC/GW.

44 Robert Graves, *Good-bye to all that,* Cape, London, 1929, p. 99.

45 Denis Winter, *Death's Men: Soldiers of the Great War,* Allen Lane, London, 1978, p. 35.

46 Lieutenant-Colonel T. M. Banks and Captain R. A. Chell, *With the 10th Essex in France,* Gay & Hancock, London, 1921, p. 18.

47 T. A. Silver, unpublished account, *c.* 1970, IWM 74/108/1.

48 Lieutenant-Colonel H. F. N. Jourdain, *Ranging Memories,* Oxford University Press, 1934, p. 163.

49 Colonel R. S. H. Moody, *Historical Records of the Buffs (East Kent Regiment), 1914–1919,* Medici Society, London, 1922, p. 75.

50 G. Slater (ed.), *My Warrior Sons: the Borton Family Diary, 1914–1918,* Peter Davies, London, 1973, pp. 11–12.

51 Alfred Mansfield, *Looking Back,* unpublished account, *c.* 1983, IWM 86/30/1; F. Loraine Petre, *The Royal Berkshire Regiment,* Vol. II, *1914–1918,* The Barracks, Reading, 1925, p. 206.

52 J. Eric Wainwright, undated letter, *c.* July 1963, IWM BBC/GW.

53 J. W. Stephenson, *With the Dukes in Flanders,* unpublished account, 1976,

IWM 78/36/1.

54 A. W. McGregor to his father, 16 October 1914, from *A. W. McGregor: a Memoir by his Father,* Cape Times, Cape Town, 1917, pp. 63–4.

55 Interview with Perry Webb, IWM Department of Sound Records, 000578/08.

56 Mrs J. Upjohn, letter of 15 May 1964, IWM BBC/GW.

57 G. F. Taylor, letter of 17 May 1964, IWM BBC/GW.

58 H. Symonds, letter of 18 May 1964, IWM BBC/GW.

59 Sidney Rogerson, *Twelve Days,* Barker, London, 1933, p. 40.

60 Lieutenant-Colonel F. E. Whitton (ed.), *The History of the Prince of Wales's Leinster Regiment (Royal Canadians),* Part II, *The Great War and the Disbandment of the Regiment,* Gale & Polden, Aldershot, 1924, p. 87.

61 F. Loraine Petre, *The History of the Norfolk Regiment, 1685–1918,* Vol. II, *4 August 1914 to 31 December 1918,* Jarrold, Norwich, n.d., p. 209.

62 Major-General J. C. Latter, *The History of the Lancashire Fusiliers, 1914–1918,* Gale & Polden, Aldershot, 1949, I, p. 93.

63 H. Sullivan, letter of 10 September 1963, IWM BBC/GW.

64 Telegram from Adjutant-General's Department to Officers Commanding. Districts, 17 August 1914, WO 159/18.

65 *Recruiting Memorandum: General Instructions,* issued by the Adjutant-General's Department, 21 August 1914, WO 159/18.

66 Coulson Kernahan, *The Experiences of a Recruiting Officer,* Hodder & Stoughton, London, 1915, p. 85.

67 Martin Middlebrook, *The First Day on the Somme,* Allen Lane, London, 1971, p. 9.

68 Sidney W. Burridge, letter to Malcolm Brown, 7 April 1976.

69 J. G. Gordon, letter of 22 July 1963, IWM BBC/GW.

70 Leonard Preuss, letter of 3 December 1963, IWM BBC/GW.

71 William Linton Andrews, *Haunting Years: the Commentaries of a War Territorial,* Hutchinson, London, n.d., p. 11.

72 Norman F. Ellison, *War Diary, 1914–1919,* IWM DS/MISC/49.

73 Lionel I. L. Ferguson, *War Diary, 1914–1919,* unpublished diary and account, 1921, IWM 77/66/1.

74 Leonard Preuss, letter of 3 December 1963, IWM BBC/GW.

75 H. Sargent, letter of 4 October 1963, IWM BBC/GW.

76 E. Robinson, undated letter, *c.* July 1963, IWM BBC/GW.

77 Ellison, *War Diary,* IWM DS/MISC/49.

78 R. C. F. Besch, *Some Personal Memories of the First World War,* unpublished account, 1972, IWM PP/MCR/61; Sidney W. Burridge, letter to Malcolm Brown, 7 April 1976; Edmund Herd, *War Diary,* entry of 9 December 1914, IWM DS/MISC/48.

79 C. W. G. Taylor, undated letter, *c.* July 1963, IWM BBC/GW.

80 Evidence of Lieutenant-Colonel H. Clay, Chief Recruiting Staff Officer, London District, *Report of the War Office Committee of Enquiry into Shellshock,* HMSO, London, 1922, p. 175.

81 R. S. Cockburn, *First World War Diary and Recollections,* unpublished account, 1965, IWM P. 258.

82 Account by Dr H. de Carle Woodcock, in W. H. Scott, *Leeds in the Great War, 1914–1918,* p. 18.

83 T. H. Merrifield, letter of 16 July 1963, IWM BBC/GW.

84 John F. Tucker, *op. cit.,* p. 13.

85 Wilfred Cook, *The Lengthened Shadow,* IWM P. 101.

86 J. Beeken, unpublished account, 1973, IWM 74/129/1.

87 The Rev. Samuel Bickersteth, *Morris Bickersteth, 1891–1916,* Cambridge

University Press, 1931, p. 68.
88 George Eyston, *Safety Last,* Vincent, London, 1975, p. 25.
89 J. Eric Wainwright, undated letter, *c.* July 1963, IWM BBC/GW.
90 W. S. Tremain, letter of 8 October 1963, IWM BBC/GW.
91 W. R. Owen, letter of 16 July 1963, IWM BBC/GW.
92 Randal Sidebotham (ed.), *Hyde in Wartime,* p. 127.
93 E. Lugg, undated letter, *c.* July 1963, IWM BBC/GW.
94 *Daily Mirror,* 18 September 1916.
95 Edward M. Spiers, *The Army and Society, 1815–1914,* Longman, London, 1980, p. 41.
96 *Royal Warrant for Pay, Appointment and non-effective Pay of the Army, 1914,* p. 303, paras. 1259–61; *Royal Warrant of 20 October 1914*; Army Order X of 22 October 1914 (AO 433 of 1914).
97 Coppard, *op. cit.,* p. 1.
98 E. J. O. Bird, undated letter, *c.* July 1963, IWM BBC/GW.
99 The Rev. Lewis E. Roberts, letter of 21 September 1963, IWM BBC/GW.
100 Charles Cameron, letter of 15 July 1963, IWM BBC/GW.
101 Interview with Thomas McIndoe, IWM Department of Sound Records, 000568/08.
102 J. W. Stephenson, *With the Dukes in Flanders,* IWM 78/36/1.
103 R. N. Hudson, *The Bradford Pals: a Short History of the 16th and 18th (Service) Battalions of the Prince of Wales's Own West Yorkshire Regiment,* privately published, Bradford, 1977, p. 8.
104 H. E. L. Mellersh, *Schoolboy into War,* Kimber, London, 1978, p. 31.
105 T. H. Barnes, *Learning to be a Soldier,* privately published, 1969, p. 1.
106 Emlyn Davies, *op. cit.,* p. 2.
107 George Morgan, quoted in R. N. Hudson, *op. cit.,* pp. 7–8.
108 Alfred G. Allen, letter of 31 May 1964, IWM BBC/GW.
109 George Butterworth, *Extracts from Diary and Letters,* Delittle & Fenwick, London, 1918, p. 17.
110 Andrews, *Haunting Years,* pp. 12–13.
111 G. T. Walton, undated letter, *c.* July 1963, IWM BBC/GW.
112 Eric Scullin, *The War Experiences of a Driver in the R.F.A.,* unpublished account, 1926, IWM PP/MCR/137.
113 C. A. Cain, *The Footsloggers,* unpublished account, 1967–73, IWM PP/MCR/48.
114 J. Ashton and L. M. Duggan, *The History of the 12th (Bermondsey) Battalion,' East Surrey Regiment,* Union Press, London, 1936, pp. 4–5.
115 *Statistics of the Military Effort of the British Empire,* pp. 651–4.
116 Arthur Marwick, *The Deluge,* p. 29.
117 Charles Sorley to A. E. Hutchinson, 10(?) August 1914, *The Letters of Charles Sorley,* Cambridge University Press, 1919, p. 211.
118 Stanley Casson, *Steady Drummer,* Bell, London, 1935, p. 23.
119 Charles Douie, *The Weary Road: Recollections of a Subaltern of Infantry,* Murray, London, 1929, pp. 30–3.

7

Adjusting to life in the army

Once attested, most Kitchener recruits were issued with a railway warrant and ordered to report for duty the next day, or soon afterwards, at the permanent depot of the regiment or corps which they had joined. The general system adopted for the first three New Armies was to collect the men at the depots before dispatching them in groups to the training centres where the task of organising them into battalions and other units was largely carried out. Recruits remained at the depots for anything from one day to a fortnight or more, receiving preliminary instruction in the rudiments of squad drill and, if they were lucky, being provided with such items of clothing and equipment as might still be available from pre-war stocks. Here too they began to assume a new identity. Alfred Henderson of the 68th Field Company, Royal Engineers, wrote of his arrival at Chatham, 'I was given an official number, 59652, never to be forgotten, in fact, more important than one's name, which was often false.'[1]

It was at the regimental depots, therefore, that the majority of Kitchener men had their real introduction to the army and its methods. Many found this period of initiation a disappointing and distressing experience which served only to emphasise the sudden and profound upheaval that had occurred in their personal lives. Ironically, the volunteers whose enthusiasm and patriotism had placed them in the forefront of the rush to the colours suffered most from the confusion which prevailed at the depots at the height of the recruiting boom in August and September of 1914. For the men of the first three New Armies conditions were particularly bad at the very time when they were struggling to come to terms with the army. In their case the process of transition from civilian to military life was all the more abrupt and painful.

To some recruits the journey to the regimental depot was itself a major event. Private Arthur Gaunt spent nearly two days travelling from Rochdale to the depot of the Devonshire Regiment at Exeter. As he recorded a few months later, it was his 'first time away from home, rather strange but not bad'.[2] Frank Longson, who enlisted as a private in the 1/6th Sherwood

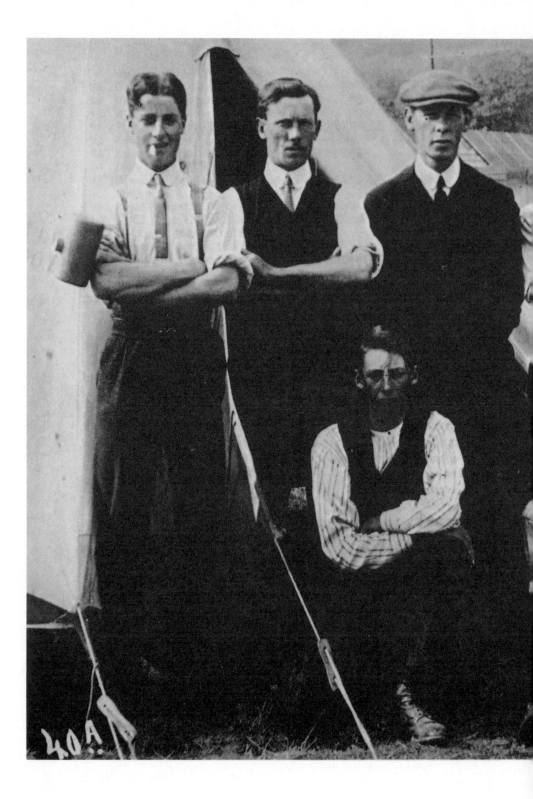

Foresters, had a memorable send-off from his home town of Chapel en le
Frith in Derbyshire at the end of August 1914. 'A band was hastily called
together from the various factories to head our contingent to the railway
station. During the march friends and acquaintances pressed cigarettes and
tobacco upon us, waved us goodbye and we were on our way.'[3] George
Butterworth, a former music master at Radley, was one of a batch of recruits
for the 6th Duke of Cornwall's Light Infantry who left Horse Guards Parade
for Bodmin with similar ceremony on 2 September, being escorted to
Charing Cross Underground station by a brass band amid cheering crowds.
He was less impressed by the arrangements at Paddington. 'The train was an
ordinary one, and the amount of space reserved quite insufficient, many
having standing room only. Notwithstanding, the journey down was a hila-
rious one – beer and singing *ad lib* – it was many days before we were so
cheerful again.'[4]

The chaos which men encountered on arrival at their destination
dampened the spirits of all but the most ardent patriots. Since, at the outbreak of war, there was only enough accommodation in barracks for
174,800 single men, the resources of the regimental depots were rapidly
overwhelmed by the massive influx of recruits in the first two months. The
depot of the South Wales Borderers at Brecon, which normally housed 300
men, soon had to cater for five times that number.[5] At Shrewsbury the depot
of the King's Shropshire Light Infantry could accommodate about 250 men
in peacetime, but in September 1914 as many as 1,500 were sleeping there
each night.[6] The situation at Chichester in the latter half of August, described
graphically by an officer of the Royal Sussex Regiment, was typical of almost
every depot in England, Scotland and Wales at this time:

A depot filled beyond capacity with recruits and more arriving every few hours, most
of them with nothing more than the clothes they stood in, and without documents to
show to what regiment, or even corps, they had been posted; all joyfully expecting to
be immediately issued with rifle and bayonet and sent to France. Stereotyped regulations, hopelessly inelastic to deal with such abnormal problems; undisciplined
humanity, drilled for ten hours daily, many unaccustomed to hardship and lacking
even toilet essentials.[7]

One recruit for whom the first night in barracks proved to be something of an
ordeal was Private Charles Jones of the 8th Royal Sussex Regiment. Jones,
who had worked in a solicitor's office in London before the war, reached the
Chichester depot on 7 September 1914 and, after three days, recorded his
experience in a long letter to his wife:

. . . we naturally expected to be met at the station by an NCO but none did so and we
wandered up to the barracks some mile and quarter in small groups. The barracks are
old fashioned, consisting of a large enclosed space with numerous erections built bun-
galow style sufficient for the comfortable accommodation of 500 men. In all there
were about 1,200 in the barracks on the day of our arrival, all raw recruits. There
were only about six NCOs to take charge of the whole lot . . . Having formally
reported, everyone enquired about food and we were then informed that none could

be given us. The language used by the majority of the recruits, consisting mainly of London roughs and country yokels of the worst description, I cannot repeat here but Damns and Bloodys etc etc were introduced into every sentence. Some had extremely good grounds of complaint. One poor fellow had come from Warwick. He said he had been paid nothing on enlistment and unable to get any food all day. In his own words: 'I've had no grub, no money and have got nowt' . . . The authorities being bankrupt of food and drink we made our way to the canteen and an institution called the Army Temperance Association. At neither could we obtain either food or drink. We then made for a pub outside, where one or two corporals were drinking, stood them beers and had one or two ourselves. My portion consisted of two glasses of 'old six' and a hunk of bread and cheese.

On his return to the barracks Jones was handed a blanket, which was stolen when he left it unattended during the evening. He was told he was to sleep in the depot's library:

It sounded alright and we all marched along with light hearts anticipating a refreshing night's sleep after a tiring day. We were quickly undeceived. The library we found to be quite a small room covered with dirty lino on which we had to sleep packed like sardines and with one of the noisiest and obscene collections of human beings it has ever been my misfortune to meet, and the smell of them packed into a small building after a hot day was truly sickening . . . The bed itself was enough to make sleep impossible but add to the discomfort of this a din which beggars description from 10 p.m. to 1.30 a.m. with an occasional boot travelling across the room and language which would have disgraced Billingsgate porters and you will not need to be told that we all turned out quite early in the morning (about 4.30) feeling far from refreshed.[8]

Jones, who at least spent the night with a roof over his head, was more fortunate than many recruits. Thousands slept in the open on the parade grounds of the respective depots. Basil Chase, a private in the Norfolk Regiment, passed his first night in the army on an officers' tennis court at Norwich.[9] Another Norfolk Regiment recruit, Private C. J. Butler, sought cover in a carriage in some neighbouring railway sidings.[10] Private O. I. Dickson, of the 3rd Essex Regiment, bedded down under a hedge in a field near Warley Barracks.[11] Arriving at Bodmin after dark, George Butterworth was informed that the sleeping accommodation was already full, so, with about twenty others, he selected a suitable-looking spot under a clump of trees:

Few made any attempts to sleep and those who tried were not given much chance . . . At 2 a.m. we were joined by several unfortunates who had found their tents already occupied (by lice) and preferred the open air and the wet grass. Altogether it was a remarkable experience, the most surprising thing about it being the complete absence of any attempt at discipline.[12]

With every inch of space in the barracks taken up, the hard-pressed depot staffs were forced to call upon the help of local authorities, church organisations and private citizens to house the overflow of recruits. Fulwood Barracks at Preston served as a depot for both the East Lancashire and the Loyal North Lancashire Regiments and had accommodation for about 1,000 men. During August 1914, however, almost double that number assembled there every day. Alderman H. Cartmell, Mayor of Preston from 1913 to 1919, noted that men asked for permission to sleep in suburban gardens, 'declining the offer of a bed, but not too proud to accept a certain breakfast there rather than an uncertain one at the Barracks'. When the weather broke after some three weeks the people of Preston rose to the occasion, welcoming soldiers as guests in their houses, transforming schools, clubs and other institutions into dormitories, and providing entertainments and hot-pot suppers for the men:

The Tramway power station opened its doors nightly for the reception of five hundred soldiers. With a plentiful supply of hay the lofts were regarded as luxurious sleeping quarters. What happened at the power station was rather typical than exceptional. At a moderate computation, some three thousand men must in this way have enjoyed the hospitality of our townsmen during this trying period of congestion at the Barracks.[13]

The measures taken to alleviate the strain on accommodation at Preston were repeated in towns and cities throughout the country. Before entraining for Tidworth on 20 August, recruits of the 8th Cheshire Regiment were housed in the grandstand of the racecourse at Chester,[14] while at Pontefract a skating rink afforded shelter for men of the 9th York and Lancaster Regiment.[15] Householders in Inverness allowed newly enlisted men of the Cameron Highlanders to use their sitting rooms for the writing of letters and the airing of clothes. This latter arrangement was greatly appreciated, as a large number of these men were obliged to sleep on the draughty and rat-infested stone floor of a local distillery where there were no heating or drying facilities for the troops.[16] In some areas, however, even considerable help from the civilian population failed to relieve the difficulties. For example, at one stage as many as 5,000 recruits for the Service battalions of the Green Howards were housed in barracks and billets at Richmond in Yorkshire. The local gentry, farmers and townspeople furnished blankets, rugs and straw, opened recreation rooms, and supplied free suppers for the men. Nevertheless, the town became so congested that the commanding officer of the depot had to send 500 men from Middlesbrough and Sunderland home on extended leave. An officer travelled from Richmond every week to pay the men at their nearest town hall.[17]

Under such circumstances it was not unusual for recruits to be left to their own devices. W. R. Owen, of the 13th Rifle Brigade, arrived at Winchester from Wales with his five friends early in September 1914. The Rifle Brigade depot was so full that they quickly realised they would have to find a resting place outside:

We returned to the cafe where, at 6 a.m. we had had breakfast – of bacon and eggs; the last meal of bacon and eggs for a long time. Yes, said Mr Sharp the owner, we could sleep in empty rooms above the shop for 1/- a head per night. We stretched ourselves, on the floor and on a mahogany table among empty glass cake covers. The remainder of the homeless thousands paraded the streets all night. We vacated the rooms after three nights and found an empty room above a greengrocer's at 3*d* a night with ample straw floor-covering with its accompanying fleas and spiders – presaging a lice-life at the Front. We later slept on and under the pews, floor and gallery of the Congregational Church, free of charge, and later still on the floor of the already chock-full YMCA . . . We never slept in the barracks; we became super-tramps in crumpled mackintoshes with shaving kit in our pockets because we came full of hope that we should be in uniform in a day or two.[18]

The relative freedom enjoyed by Owen was by no means universal, for the restrictions imposed on recruits varied from depot to depot. Private Harold Aylott, a seventeen-year-old from Manchester who joined the 6th Border Regiment, was one of many locked inside the Carlisle depot at night.[19] Men of the 8th Royal West Kent Regiment at Maidstone were also confined to barracks, although a few slept in the town, as 'the military police on duty let it be known that it was possible to get through the railings without being seen'.[20]

   Apart from the problem of sleeping accommodation, food was the other main preoccupation of depot staffs and recruits alike. Those who were provided with a meal on their arrival at the depot were fortunate indeed. Francis Cowing, a trooper in the 18th Hussars, had enlisted in Islington, London, on 23 August 1914 while on his way to work. He managed to secure something to eat and drink on his first evening at Horfield Barracks, Bristol, but it required some effort on his part:

Blankets were issued one a man and sleep where you are. I soon found out to move from that spot and leave my blanket was fatal. It got swiped and someone else moved in, so I chummed up and asked if they would look after my place and blanket while I scouted round . . . A field kitchen had been set up and a queue a mile long was filing past, some with jam tins others with tin basins . . . Tea and bread and jam that night, but before I could get any I had first to scrounge a jam tin, swipe a spoon and borrow a knife.[21]

At Beverley, Private Ernest Goulden of the 6th East Yorkshire Regiment had to queue up for bully beef sandwiches in the mess hall, entering by the door and leaving through the window.[22] William Day's only meal on joining the Middlesex Regiment at Mill Hill was a German sausage with dry bread. As he wryly recalled, 'I had started to eat 'em before I could kill 'em.'[23] Men swiftly grasped that they would have to abandon the manners and conventions of civilian life if they were to survive in this new environment. Private R. F. E. Evans of the 7th Duke of Cornwall's Light Infantry wrote that, in the early days, an orderly entering a hut with a pan of roast beef 'might find himself rushed off his feet, the food ending up on the floor, where the men would be fighting for chunks of meat'.[24] George Coppard awoke after his first night at Stoughton Barracks, Guildford, to hear that 'gunfire' (tea) was available at the cookhouse:

A scramble followed, but there were few mugs to drink from. I drank mine from a soup plate, not an easy task at the first attempt. After a day or two of this kind of thing, I realised the simple decencies of the table I had left at home. One had to hog it or else run the risk of not getting anything at all. I learned this lesson quicker than anything else.[25]

Initially the more fastidious recruits could not overcome their qualms at having to share eating or drinking utensils with a crowd of strangers. Having reported to his depot at Hounslow, Private Charles Quinnell of the 9th Royal Fusiliers was placed in a barrack room with twenty-seven others, including several Reservists:

Two of these reservists went down the stairs and about five minutes later they arrived back with a dixie full of stew and one pint mug. This pint mug was handed round between the reservists . . . each taking a sup out of it, but another young chap and I decided we didn't want any of that so we went to the canteen and had a plate of rice.[26]

Thomas Sloan, who joined the 9th Border Regiment as a private, sat down to his first breakfast at Carlisle only to observe that one basin had to meet the needs of twelve men. 'There was an old tramp at our table who got it first. We simply could not drink after him, but I must say it wasn't long before we made sure the tramp was last.'[27] Often the way in which the food was served caused more dissatisfaction than the content of the meal itself. Charles Jones, following his traumatic reception at Chichester, was pleasantly surprised by the dinner of stewed beef and potatoes the next day. His portion was dished up on a chipped enamel plate which had been used previously and merely dipped in a bucket of cold water to remove the worst of the grease. 'I just cut the meat and potatoes with a penknife and put the pieces in my mouth with my fingers. The liquor I drank from the plate. The food was really quite good . . . Served decently there would have been nothing whatever to complain about.'[28] If they had enough money, and were allowed out of the depot, men could normally supplement their scanty army rations by purchasing food from local shops. On the other hand, supply did not always match demand. Private T. H. Merrifield of the 10th Royal Welsh Fusiliers had to walk miles to get bread 'because Wrexham was so crowded that we found all the shops sold out of everything edible'.[29]

The primitive sanitary arrangements at most depots came as a severe shock to men from comfortable middle-class homes. A surveyor from Newport, A. E. Perriman, who had enlisted as a private in the 11th South Wales Borderers, was disgusted by the toilet facilities at Brecon. 'On each floor landing was a two-handled tank of considerable proportions which was filled, or thereabouts, during the night by barrack-room occupants.'[30] Private H. F. Hooton of the 8th Northamptonshire Regiment recalled that at Northampton Barracks there were 'overflowing buckets all along the passages . . . really filthy!'[31]

Dirt and discomfort were not exclusive to the men of the first three New Armies. For a few days after the outbreak of war, the existing first-line Territorial battalions stayed in their home areas while mobilising and recruiting to bring themselves up to war strength. Like the depots of the regular army, the Territorial headquarters and drill halls had not been built to provide sleeping quarters for full-strength units. Schools and other large buildings were therefore commandeered for the purpose. Lionel Ferguson, who joined the Liverpool Scottish as a private on 5 August, marched off with the battalion to the stadium in Pudsey Street, Liverpool, three days later:

We made the best of very bad and dirty accommodation and our only leave was for ¾ of an hour during that evening, then only within a half mile radius, as orders were then expected for a move at the shortest notice. We lay down to rest at 11 p.m. all tired and cross. During the night we were aroused by one of the men in his dreams, giving the alarm and we seized our rifles in the most soldier-like manner, but before we all had time to find them all was quiet once again.[32]

The following day Ferguson was able to leave the stadium for half an hour before dinner and had a hot bath at the London & North Western Railway hotel:

. . . not before it was needed, as the dirt and dust was awful, also our company had only one tap to wash under, situated about 2 feet from the floor in a very dirty urinal. Hot pot and bread for dinner and our last meal that day; however, we thought it excellent after eternal Bully and Biscuits. An hour's leave in the evening and Oh how bored I was with life for we had nothing to do but sit on a hard and dirty floor.[33]

The experiences of London Territorials in the early weeks of the war mirrored those of Ferguson. Ralph Thompson of the Civil Service Rifles (15th London) described his battalion's mobilisation at Somerset House:

The men were not allowed to go to their homes even though these, in many cases, were but a few miles from Headquarters. For several nights we slept out in the open on the parade ground; luckily the weather was warm and we suffered no material discomfort. Then a government building in the neighbourhood was placed at our disposal each night. We slept in the corridors, on tables, under tables, in fact *anywhere* after all available floor space had been filled. Arrangments for our morning ablutions were quite inadequate as there were only a dozen wash bowls to be shared by about 800 men, consequently not a few unshaven chins appeared on morning parade.[34]

Given that the social composition of the army had changed so radically within such a short time, with large numbers of well educated and questioning men now serving in the ranks, it is perhaps surprising that organised protests at depots and drill halls during the opening months of the war were relatively uncommon. Certainly, most protests in this period appear to have been in the nature of spontaneous individual responses to what was considered unfair treatment rather than the product of concerted action by recruits. Butterworth believed that, at Bodmin, 'not a few actually deserted on their second day of service'.[35] George Escritt, a private in the 9th King's Own Yorkshire Light Infantry, simply strolled out of the depot at Pontefract, having had little food and being desperately short of money. He walked home to Leeds with a friend who had enlisted at the same time as himself:

We had to take the chaff that we had come home for our Sunday dinner. Our mothers said we would get shot for desertion. Well, we went back by train the following

Wednesday and in the field before you came to the Barracks there were crowds of volunteers so we mingled amongst them and then ambled down to the railway station and were taken to Tring in Hertfordshire.[36]

Because so many recruits were swarming in and around the depots, it was no easy matter for the overworked military authorities to keep a daily check on the movements of individuals. It was doubly difficult to do so in the case of men who had not yet been given a regimental number and thus had not been enrolled formally on the strength of any particular unit. Moreover, as there was a seemingly endless supply of recruits in August and September 1914, the disappearance of one or two hardly constituted a crisis of discipline in the eyes of the depot staffs. Absence without leave and sporadic instances of desertion were the least of their problems. However, it was impossible for them to turn a blind eye to incidents involving scores of men. Private E. W. Prosser was one of 120 recruits of the Middlesex Regiment who were transferred from Mill Hill to a depot at Gravesend towards the end of August. The group, which included a lawyer and a boxer, reached Gravesend at 6.30 p.m. and the men were locked immediately inside a gymnasium:

By now we were in a very rebellious mood, we'd had no food since 6.30 a.m. and were now locked up like a lot of convicts. Some were for breaking down the doors and windows to get out. The lawyer bloke and a few more managed to persuade the rest of us to make the best of it but we all decided that we would obey no orders from anyone until we'd been fed . . . About 7 a.m. the next morning the doors were unlocked and a loud voice yelled, 'Turn out you lot.' They'd evidently found out that we were here. With one accord we yelled back, 'we are taking no orders until we've been fed.' 'Fall in' yelled the loud voice. We just took no notice. He then really got going. I expect in pre-war times such a barrage of words was meant to terrify half-witted recruits. They left us unmoved. We even had a good laugh out of it.[37]

Ultimately Prosser and his comrades were placated by an understanding officer and a scratch meal of 'bully beef and salmon sandwiches and several gallons of tea'. Protests of this type could be handled by the depot staffs themselves without recourse to mass punishment, provided that they dealt quickly with the original grievance and reimposed discipline before the trouble could escalate. Sometimes, however, the dispute was sufficiently serious to require intervention from the civil authorities. Despite all the efforts of the inhabitants of Preston to relieve pressure on the local depot, some 250 Welsh recruits left Fulwood Barracks on 11 September carrying a banner which bore the words 'No Food, No Shelter, No Money'. Heading for the railway station, they were intercepted by a police inspector who persuaded them to accompany him to the courtyard of the police headquarters after giving assurances that their complaints would be investigated. There they were met by Sir George Toulmin, MP for Bury and Managing Director of the *Lancashire Daily Post* and *Preston Guardian*. Toulmin invited the men to be his guests at the Public Hall, an exhibition centre, where a meal was served, but the ringleader was still not satisfied and demanded an interview with the

Mayor. When Alderman Cartmell duly arrived at the Public Hall, this man recited the grievances of the recruits 'with a very aggressive air':

They were all from South Wales, he explained. They had been in the town a fortnight but had not yet received their papers. They had nothing to do but walk about the streets in the rainy weather in old boots, down at the heel, and with no money in their pockets. That was their main trouble – lack of money. They were mostly miners, their wages, when at work, never being less than £2 a week. They had given up everything to serve their country. They had left their wives at home and had no money to send them. They would not go back to the Barracks unless their pay was secured.

Cartmell undertook to see what could be done and, together with Toulmin and the Town Clerk, went to Fulwood Barracks to speak to the commanding officer and his staff:

The Adjutant said that on the previous night he had remained at his desk until 3 o'clock and would have gone on longer if one of his clerks had not fallen off his stool in a swoon. He explained that in the case of the men sent over from South Wales the records ought to follow them almost immediately but it appeared there were centres even more congested than Preston and there was often a delay of many days before recruits could receive their numbers and be put on the establishment for pay. Eventually an arrangement was made that, notwithstanding the regulations, the men from South Wales should on the following morning receive a payment on account. I suppose that according to all the rules there had been a very serious infraction of military law and I am afraid that technically someone had been aiding and abetting a mutiny. At first the officers seemed disposed to take that view, but they were sensible men and in the end they must have been very pleased to see the incident closed without a scandal. The Welshmen . . . returned to the Barracks the following day and received their money.[38]

There were several reasons why incidents of this type were isolated rather than widespread. Undoubtedly the most significant factor was the tremendous surge of popular support for the war, never again so intense as it was in these early months, when Kitchener's New Armies were forming. The patriotism and enthusiasm which had led men to enlist also helped to carry them through their period of adjustment to army life. Officers and NCOs at the depots, though few in number, were thus able to tap a vast reservoir of goodwill as they strove to produce order out of the chaos. Regular officers were not slow to recognise what splendid material they now had at their disposal. Colonel A. H. Doyle, who was in command of the depot at Shrewsbury in August 1914, remarked, 'The keenness of the men to learn was wonderful. At the end of the first week an experienced drill instructor said to me that in peacetime he should have thought the squads had been a month or six weeks on the square.'[39] An officer of the 9th East Lancashire Regiment wrote that the recruits of his battalion 'were all animated with a desire to come to grips as quickly as possible with the enemy and were prepared to put up with any discomfort in the way of accommodation and to use every endeavour to train themselves as quickly as possible for their self-imposed task.'[40] Major H. P. Berney-Ficklin of the 8th Norfolk Regiment noted that deputations for longer and even additional parades were frequent. 'Of crime there was practically none, and such as there was received such severe (and unauthorised) punishment at the hands of the men, long before the instigator was hauled before the commanding officer, that few strayed from the paths of righteousness.'[41]

The almost embarrassing kindness shown to recruits by the public at large was another factor which did much to stifle latent discontent. Recalling his battalion's daily marches to Hampstead Heath for training, John Nettleton of the Artists' Rifles (28th London) observed that 'troops of any sort, even the Artists, were potential heroes. We nearly always halted for a breather half way up Haverstock Hill and people used to come out of their houses and present us with chocolate and cigarettes.'[42] Reginald Cockburn, who joined the Inns of Court OTC on 5 August 1914, recorded that, whenever his unit marched back, singing, to Lincoln's Inn after night training in Regent's Park, 'heads would appear at windows, and handkerchiefs were waved to us from top storeys. People did not seem to mind being woken up.'[43] A distinct change in public attitudes towards young people and towards soldiers was discerned by Private Harold Hunt of the 1/7th City of London Battalion. 'Up to the war,' he wrote, 'we youths had counted but little in the scheme of things. We were regarded as decadent by our elders but now we had become knights in shining armour and I must confess I for one revelled in it all.'[43] Arthur MacGregor, a private in the London Scottish (14th London), was puzzled by the scale of the response. Writing to a friend on 22 September 1914, after training on Wimbledon Common, he commented:

Why on earth all the girls in Putney High Street still rush to the doors and windows and all the old women wave handkerchiefs – I don't know. I should have thought they would have been sick of the sight of us. One old woman in Fulham always gets a cheer from every company in the battalion. She stands outside her window on a little balcony, whenever we pass both going out and coming back, and all the time the regiment is passing she holds her feeble old right hand at the salute and with her left she swings over the balcony railing a large piece of cardboard with a black cat pasted on it – murmuring all the time 'Good luck, good luck'.[45]

More practical demonstrations of public enthusiasm were particularly appreciated by soldiers. Rifleman Percy Jones of the 1st Queen's Westminster Rifles (16th London) described the reception accorded to the battalion when they moved to St Albans in August 1914:

The people along the line of route showered things on us and refused to take any money. A gentleman in Watford bought out a whole fruit stall as it stood, and told the lucky coster to give us the lot. When we halted people rushed out of their houses to distribute food and drink. A little boy in Kilburn had a huge quantity of gassy ginger beer to give us and was broken-hearted when the officers refused to let us drink it. We stopped in a little back street in Edgware near a tiny shop where someone was trying to make a living as a greengrocer . . . We asked a poor-looking woman the price of her apples, on which she gave us every apple and tomato in the shop and would not take a penny for them. We passed the hat round and as she still protested she wouldn't take any money, we gave it to her baby.[46]

In many cities and towns, soldiers were permitted to travel free on buses and trams, Cockburn regarding this as 'a novel and exhilarating experience'.[47] Nettleton, however, discovered that, by 1915, patriotic gestures were being tempered by other considerations, the travel concessions being withdrawn 'as there was no room left for civilians'. Similarly, the cheap lunches provided for soldiers at the Imperial Hotel in Russell Square were also discontinued as the dining rooms were too often filled to overflowing by the hungry military.[48] Nevertheless, while they lasted, such gestures made the process of becoming a soldier more tolerable.

For the majority of working-class recruits, accustomed to long hours and poor conditions, being in the army simply substituted one set of hardships for another, and even offered certain compensations. The historian of the Green Howards quotes an officer of the 6th Battalion who observed that the men under his command, mostly miners, 'look upon this as the finest holiday they have ever had, in spite of the seven and a half hours – at one time eight hours – of work that they now put in daily'.[49] Freed from the drudgery of factory and mine, or from the demands of a professional career, the average recruit found that, in many ways, life was now a much simpler affair. In the words of C. E. Montague, all his worries 'seemed, by some magical change, to have dropped from him . . . All was fixed from above, down to the time of his going to bed and the way he must lace up his boots.'[50] William Linton Andrews felt that, after the bustle of a newspaper office, his early training in the 1/4th Black Watch was 'a great lark'. He added:

It was just like being back at school. Responsibilities had been lifted off our shoulders. We did not worry about money, for gifts of chocolates, delicacies, cigarettes, socks, theatre tickets, magazines, books and invitations to tea poured in upon us. Learning how to march was kindergarten stuff after my nightly anxiety of getting a paper to press to catch trains.[51]

The realisation that other people were worse off than themselves played a part in persuading some recruits to accept their lot. Richard Patston, an assistant storeman with a motor accessories firm, enlisted in the 1st City of London Rifles (6th London) on 7 August 1914 at the age of fifteen. Billeted in a school near the battalion's drill hall in Farringdon Road, he was reminded constantly of the plight of the London poor. 'After meal times, a crowd of hungry children would gather outside the school with bowls and dishes and line up for left-overs dispensed by the cooks. They had a grand treat when the meal had been stew.'[52] George Butterworth felt a twinge of guilt when he and his friends left the Bodmin depot to have a wash and a meal in the town's best hotel, confessing that 'in normal circumstances I should be against using our comparative wealth for acquiring luxuries which are denied our comrades, but considering the shortage of supplies of all kinds, there is no alternative'.[53]

Men joining the Pals battalions or second-line Territorial units generally fared much better than those who enlisted in the first three New Armies, as, in many cases, they were allowed to live at home on a subsistence allowance and ordered to report daily while their training camps were being prepared. Thus a significant proportion of the recruits attested after the beginning of September 1914 had a relatively comfortable introduction to army life. For instance, men of the Sheffield City Battalion (12th York and Lancaster Regiment) and the 1st Bradford Pals (16th West Yorkshire Regiment) were billeted at home for some three months after formation. The Hull Commercials (10th East Yorkshire Regiment), raised in the first week of September, did not move out to Hornsea until 17 November, and the 1st Salford Battalion (15th Lancashire Fusiliers), formed only a few days after the Hull Commercials, remained in and around Salford until the end of December. The Accrington Pals (11th East Lancashire Regiment) spent an even longer period at home. Having reached full strength on 24 September, they departed for billets in Wales as late as 23 February 1915.

The extent to which local support eased the problems of the Pals battalions in the early weeks of their existence can be illustrated with reference to the story of the Salford Brigade. The Corporation Tramways Committee laid on free transport for men living some distance away from the centre of Salford. The Baths Committee provided free baths for the recruits, and training grounds were made available by the Parks and Cleansing Department. Officers of the National Reserve opened their premises in Astley Street for use as a company headquarters, while further space for drill was furnished by the Broadway Mission, the Charleston Congregational School, the trustees of Teneriffe Street Schools and the governing authorities of a nearby racecourse. In addition, Messrs J. Mandleberg & Co. Ltd allowed the raising committee to take over part of the firm's premises in Cobden Street for the depot and offices of the brigade. A fine new warehouse owned by the same firm became the brigade's store, being offered complete with the services of an expert storekeeper.[54] The help and generosity extended to the Salford battalions was typical of what was going on in cities and towns all over Britain, especially in the industrial north. This massive outpouring of goodwill and voluntary effort was perhaps the finest reflection of the mood of the nation in the autumn of 1914.

The advantages enjoyed by a recruit living at home during his first weeks in the army are summed up by the following extract from an account by John Ramsden, who enlisted as a gunner in the 2/IInd West Riding Brigade, Royal Field Artillery, a Territorial unit, in 1915:

There were about twenty of us. We used to catch the 6 a.m. tram at the bottom of Hick Lane, Batley, and had to be on parade at Bradford at 8 a.m. You can guess we were always there in time, because if we had been one minute late, we should sharply have been told to sleep at the Barracks, and this meant on the concrete floor and either two or three blankets allowed . . . You can be sure a bed at home was to be preferred. One or two unlucky ones had to stay there, being too far from home to get there in time. I tried it out of curiosity once, but I did not care for it, and the blankets gave you the creeps.[55]

Whatever conditions recruits met on enlistment, all had to adjust to army discipline. According to C. Midwinter, then a private in the 32nd Field Ambulance, civilian likes and dislikes clashed one after another with the restraints imposed by the army. 'We acknowledged silently the genius of those gentlemen who devised the King's Regulations. That formidable volume had a remedy for every civilian frailty and commanded our profound respect.'[56] John Nettleton recalled how lessons were frequently learned the hard way:

Our first introduction to Army *mores* was when a man was slaughtered for blowing his nose while standing at attention. It happened that the C.O. himself was taking the parade and he made an example of this unfortunate man by ordering him to report at Duke's Road at 6 a.m. every morning for a month. We thought this very harsh. But the 'let it drip' order was just another peculiar rule of this new school . . . A dripping nose might be ungentlemanly but it was obviously better than having to be on parade every morning at six, so we dripped.[57]

Reginald Lester also began his military service in the ranks of the Artists' Rifles. Like Nettleton, he long remembered his 'breaking in' period as a recruit in 1915 and the emphasis which the army placed on punctuality and cleanliness:

We may have felt that the last named was carried to an extreme degree, when we found ourselves given two hours of extra evening drill for coming on parade with one button less bright than the rest, for having a speck of dust or mud on a boot, or for the freshness of the morning shave having slightly worn off to reveal a somewhat darker tinge on the chin which could not escape the sergeant-major's eagle eye. We were also made to realise at the outset of our military career how vital is perfect punctuality. One evening when coming on parade after the tea break my watch let me down by being a few minutes slow, with the result that I arrived exactly half a minute late. The half-minute let me in for two hours' stiff extra drill at the end of the day.[58]

Some young officers, themselves new to the army, felt a great deal of sympathy for their men in these circumstances. Writing from Inkerman Barracks, Woking, on 12 October 1914, Second Lieutenant I. V. B. Melhuish of the 7th Somerset Light Infantry told his mother:

. . . several of our Company were put in prison merely for smoking cigarettes after they had been ordered not to. Of course most of the worst offences are punishable with penal servitude and death. This comes particularly hard on many of these men, who have not grasped what discipline means. Now that the first rush of excitement is over lots of these people are beginning to find that life is not all music, their sense of personal comfort is greater than their patriotism, they are anxious to get away. They are not allowed to do this unless medically or physically unfit for service. They become sulky and insubordinate, and then there is trouble. It is extremely disagreeable work, cutting their pay short, and sending them to prison. I only hope none of my men do anything worthy of death.[59]

Sheer ignorance of King's Regulations and army customs was the basic cause of transgression on the part of many raw recruits. Alfred Henderson relates that, on his first parade at Chatham, an officer asked him a number of personal questions. 'Almost immediately I was reprimanded for not answering every question with "Sir". Later I was to learn that one could be "crimed" for even not looking appropriately servile. Dumb insolence it was called.'[60] Others deliberately resisted authority for as long as they could. G. T. Walton of the 7th Border Regiment admitted that during his preliminary training at Carlisle:

> . . . there was some attempt to discipline us but it was of no avail. I remember one day a man came to me and told me to go and clean the toilets out, and then make up some beds in the barracks. We were gambling at the time. I took no notice of him . . . He went away and came back with a much smaller man who had proper soldier's clothes on. I knew later he was an officer. I told him, 'I don't do it for him who is bigger than you' and that was the end. Most of us had a stock answer to anything they asked us to do and that was 'we have come to fight the Germans, not to wash up'.[61]

'Jankers' was the most common form of punishment for defaulters. Normally this meant that the sinner would be confined to barracks for two or three days, sometimes longer, and ordered to perform unpleasant and onerous fatigues, such as emptying urinal tubs, peeling potatoes or washing hundreds of plates. George Coppard claimed that he enjoyed 'jankers', as it gave him an excuse to grouse, the soldier's traditional privilege. He also states that, in one sense, 'it was an important part of my army training learning how to be sly and cunning'.[62] Most men restricted themselves to grousing and made little positive attempt to challenge the authority of officers and NCOs. Even the most intractable of recruits could be moulded into efficient soldiers in the end. A. E. Perriman relates how, at the Brecon depot of the South Wales Borderers, one man was so incensed about the poor food and conditions that he picked up a basin of tea and threw it into the face of a sergeant. The man in question was Ivor Rees, who later became a sergeant himself and went on to win the Victoria Cross at Ypres in 1917.[63]

Inevitably, individual reactions to the army ranged from outright hostility to unqualified acceptance. Charles Sorley, then a subaltern in the 7th Suffolk Regiment, informed a friend on 20 September 1914 that he now regarded himself as 'a decimal' who had resigned all claims to his own person. 'I am not a living creature,' he explained, 'but a temporary second lieutenant.'[64] J. H. Allen, a former president of the Cambridge Union, had given up a promising career as a barrister to become a subaltern in the 13th Worcestershire Regiment, and viewed the war and the army as 'hateful' because of the changes they had wrought in his life. In a letter to his sister he observed that, although some welcomed the war as an opportunity to make a career in the army, it had for him 'put out of reach all the things about which I cared most and for which I had worked hardest'.[65] Brian Lawrence, who also served briefly in the ranks of the Artists' Rifles before gaining a commission in the 9th North Staffordshire Regiment, remarked to C. K. Ogden, editor of *The Cambridge Magazine,* 'I have no use for the military system; it seems to aim at accomplishing a minimum with a maximum of energy, most of which is wasted on mere red tape and vulgar pageantry.'[66] In contrast, Gordon Bartlett, following two months' service as an officer in the 1/5th King's Liverpool Regiment, believed that he would find it difficult to revert to being an undergraduate at the end of the war. 'It will certainly be a job to settle down to books after this,' he wrote to his mother; 'it is a glorious life indeed this, and suits me down to the ground.'[67]

Besides adjusting to army life, recruits also had to come to terms with each other. As has been shown in previous chapters, the rapid expansion of the army in 1914 had thrown together men from all social classes and occupational backgrounds. Stockbrokers, engineers, lawyers, and teachers and students now rubbed shoulders in the ranks with miners, fishermen, clerks, shop assistants and farm labourers, particularly in the units of the first three New Armies, which were recruited on a more random basis than later formations. This type of social mix was often at its most pronounced in units from rural counties which had found it necessary to take recruits from industrial centres in order to bring themselves up to strength. A description by R. F. E. Evans of his fellow recruits in the 7th Duke of Cornwall's Light Infantry gives some idea of their diverse backgrounds and of their mutual curiosity:

The Sixth Battalion of our Regiment having become greatly over strength, it had hived off many of the roughest and toughest of its recruits to form the nucleus of the Seventh Battalion . . . Though my own draft happened to include a professional burglar, we were a mild enough lot; indeed one of us was a somewhat elderly butler with flat feet who must have lied desperately about his age. When we got talking on the way to the depot, a Cockney barrow-boy earnestly enquired of a young waiter from the Royal Automobile Club, 'Does gents eat whelks?'[68]

It had been one thing to put up with men from different classes in the course of intermittent contacts at work and play, but living in close proximity to them in a barrack room or tent was quite another problem for some. Shortly after joining the 8th Norfolk Regiment, Private A. K. Aston wrote, 'This Regiment seems to be composed of the riff-raff of England, mind you keen men as they show by their drilling but they smell horribly some of them. Of course they are all sorts and I should think [there are] about 200 gentlemen amongst us.'[69] Private Wilfred Cook, who began his military service in the 3rd West Yorkshire Regiment, declared that the language of the barrack room struck him like a thunderclap. 'Never had I expected to hear such utterly coarse and meaningless words from men. Coming from the shelter of a religious family made it more painful.'[70] William Linton Andrews was shocked by the rowdiness of the men in the 1/4th Black Watch, recording how they played football up and down the centre of the drill hall. When his boots were stolen after a couple of days, he asked a sergeant what he should do, only to receive the answer, 'Watch yourself, laddie. They'll steal the milk from your tea in this mob.'[71] As a Yorkshireman in a Highland unit, and a vegetarian and a teetotaller, Andrews was conscious of being an outsider and only started to enjoy the army when several of his colleagues from the *Dundee Advertiser* enlisted in the battalion. At that point, he remembered, 'it seemed to me that this intolerably filthy and brainless life would now be mitigated by true comradeship'.[71]

The friendships which men formed during their first days in the army were unquestionably a sustaining influence. Shared tribulations were easier to endure. Wilfred Cook struck up a close relationship with a soldier named Pratt, who had once been an apprentice steward at sea:

He was of my own age, tall and well-built, a useful man if trouble arose and it looked likely as we had one or two of the quarrelsome kind who would have to be dealt with some time. The grouser was present, of course, whose grub was always lousy according to him yet he had to be held back when the distribution of it was going on. It would be someone like Pratt who usually flattened these individuals for good and we heard no more from them . . . Every soldier needs a particular chum. The lone wolf is really lonely and I was always fortunate in having one, and often more, really good friends to whom I could talk sensibly and who would share with me the bitter and the sweet of what any situation held for us.[73]

Since they were largely recruited from a particular town or county, or composed of men from the same social or working environment, the majority of Pals battalions and many Territorial units suffered comparatively little from the sudden mixture of widely disparate elements in their ranks. However, even minute regional differences could make it difficult for a battalion to establish a corporate identity. On transferring from a Manchester Pals battalion to the 2/5th Manchesters at Wigan, Private Charles Cain might almost have been a foreigner. He noted that 'whereas the men I had left at Heaton Park were drawn from offices, warehouses, shops, even the legal profession, the battalion I had now joined consisted of miners, mill hands, labourers, who spoke in a very broad Lancashire accent. At times I could not understand them myself, although I had met some broad accents at Besses o' the Barn two miles from where I lived.'[74] Second Lieutenant Arthur Behrend from Liverpool was made to feel he was an 'outlander' when he joined the 1/4th East Lancashire Regiment at Blackburn in August 1914. As he later remarked, regionalism could be carried to excess:

Blackburn, Accrington, Clitheroe, Darwen, these towns were close enough to one another in distance, but in cousinly spirit they were far apart. Our D Company from Clitheroe – countrymen mostly – was the most exclusive. And, for all the friends and acquaintances we had among them, our 5th Battalion from ten miles away over at Burnley – and with whom we were brigaded – might have belonged to a hostile army.[75]

These examples from the accounts by Cain and Behrend stand as a reminder of the underlying parochialism and immobility of a substantial proportion of the population in 1914. Although workers continued to move from the country to the great cities and towns in the decades before the First World War, the rate of migration was much slower than it had been in the middle years of the nineteenth century. When they had settled down in their new surroundings, working-class families rarely strayed across the boundaries of the central urban districts to which they were confined by their income. The husband's job was, of course, the principal factor in determining a family's place of residence, but other considerations, such as the ability to obtain credit at a corner shop or a man's social standing at a local pub or working men's club, might also help to fix them in one area. Moving would only mean that the family would have to face a fresh battle to re-establish such relationships in another district. In his study of working-class life in Salford in the first quarter of the twentieth century Robert Roberts has pointed out that all these factors, together with fear of change, combined to keep poor families, if not in the same street, at least in the same neighbourhood for generations.[76] This tendency to stay put was certainly diminishing by 1914 as, with the increasing availability of cheap public transport, particularly motor buses and electric trams, entire working-class suburbs were springing up outside the older urban centres to house the workers who were willing and able to travel in to their jobs each day. Moreover, recent advances in education, and the dissemination of national and international news through the growing popular press, gave people a new interest in, and curiosity about, the world which lay beyond the end of their street. Yet, while the ingrained parochialism of the industrial centres was breaking down by 1914, it had by no means disappeared. Deep-rooted local loyalties contributed greatly to the success of the Pals movement in the first year of the war, even if they, in their turn, were further undermined by the war itself and by the general mixing of social classes in Kitchener's New Armies.

Notes

1   Alfred E. Henderson, *Your Country Needs You: a Sapper's Story of Experiences in the Trenches of Flanders and Picardy during the Great War*, unpublished account, 1978, IWM PP/MCR/190.

2   Arthur Gaunt, *Diary of Life as a Soldier*, unpublished account, July–September 1915, IWM 81/23/1.

3   Frank Longson, *As We Saw It*, unpublished account, n.d., IWM DPB/K. 51452.

4   George Butterworth, 1885–1916, *Extracts from Diary and Letters*, Delittle, Fenwick, London, 1919, p. 19.

5   C. T. Atkinson, *The History of the South Wales Borderers, 1914–1918*, Medici Society, London, 1931, p. 3.

6   Account by Colonel A. H. Doyle, in Major W. de B. Wood (ed.), *The History of the King's Shropshire Light Infantry in the Great War, 1914–1918*, Medici Society, London, 1925, p. 302.

7   Colonel J. L. Sleeman, quoted in Owen Rutter (ed.), *The History of the Seventh (Service) Battalion, the Royal Sussex Regiment*, Times Publishing Company, London, 1934, pp. 1–2.

8   Charles Jones to his wife, 10 September 1914, IWM CON/CJ.

9   Basil H. Chase, letter of 3 July 1963, IWM BBC/GW.

10   C. J. Butler, letter of 10 July 1963, IWM BBC/GW.

11   O. I. Dickson, transcript of interview by D. L. Jones of the Chelmsford and Essex

Museum, 10 December 1974, p. 1.
12 George Butterworth, *op. cit.*, p. 20.
13 H. Cartmell, *For Remembrance*, p. 32.
14 Arthur Crookenden, *The History of the Cheshire Regiment in the Great War*, p. 343.
15 J. B. Montague, *A History of the 9th (Service) Battalion, the York and Lancaster Regiment, 1914–1919*, privately published, n.d., p. 1.
16 *Historical Records of the Queen's Own Cameron Highlanders*, Vol. IV, Blackwood, Edinburgh, 1931, p. 273.
17 Colonel H. C. Wylly, *The Green Howards in the Great War*, privately published, Richmond, 1926, p. 384.
18 W. R. Owen, letter of 16 July 1963, IWM BBC/GW.
19 Harold Aylott, undated letter, *c.* July 1963, IWM BBC/GW.
20 Lieutenant-Colonel H. J. Wenyon and Major H. S. Brown, *The History of the Eighth Battalion the Queen's Own Royal West Kent Regiment, 1914–1919*, Hazell Watson & Viney, London, 1921, p. 2.
21 Francis T. Cowing, letter of 4 July 1963, IWM BBC/GW.
22 Ernest Goulden, letter of 22 September 1963, IWM BBC/GW.
23 William Day, letter of 10 July 1963, IWM BBC/GW.
24 R. F. E. Evans, *Some Wartime Experiences*, unpublished account, n.d., IWM PP/MCR/75.
25 George Coppard, *With a Machine Gun to Cambrai*, p. 2.
26 Interview with Charles R. Quinnell, IWM Department of Sound Records, 000554/18.
27 Thomas Sloan, undated letter, *c.* July 1963, IWM BBC/GW.
28 Charles Jones to his wife, 11 September 1914, IWM CON/CJ.
29 T. H. Merrifield, letter of 16 July 1963, IWM BBC/GW.
30 A. E. Perriman, unpublished account, 1976, IWM 80/43/1.
31 H. F. Hooton, *Salient Extracts from my Daily Diary*, unpublished account, 1971, IWM PP/MCR/50.
32 Lionel I. L. Ferguson, *War Diary, 1914–1919*, IWM 77/166/1.
33 *Ibid.*, IWM 77/166/1.
34 Ralph J. Thompson, *Adventure Glorious*, IWM 78/58/1.
35 Butterworth, *op. cit.*, p. 21.
36 George Escritt, letter to L. D. Spicer, 20 March 1979, Spicer papers, KCL.
37 E. W. Prosser, *Never Again: a Soldier's Impressions of the Great War, 1914–1918*, unpublished account, n.d., IWM PBS/MCR/128.
38 Cartmell, *op. cit.*, pp. 34–5.
39 Account of Colonel A. H. Doyle, in Major W. de B. Wood, *op. cit.*, p. 302.
40 Account by Lieutenant-Colonel S. A. Pearse, in Major-General Sir C. Lothian Nicholson and Major H. T. MacMullen, *History of the East Lancashire Regiment in the Great War*, p. 451.
41 Major H. P. Berney-Ficklin, unpublished account, n.d., IWM 75/30/1.
42 John Nettleton, *The Anger of the Guns*, Kimber, London, 1979, p. 17.
43 Major R. S. Cockburn, *First World War Dairy and Recollections*, unpublished account, 1965, IWM P. 258.
44 H. E. Hunt, *The Saga of a Citizen Soldier*, unpublished account, 1973, IWM P. 268.
45 Arthur MacGregor to Dulcie Newling, 22 September 1914, IWM CON/AEM.
46 P. H. Jones, unpublished account, 1919, IWM P. 246.
47 Cockburn, *op. cit.*, IWM P. 258.
48 John Nettleton, *Journal*, 1964, IWM P. 194. The bulk of this account was later published under the title *The Anger of the Guns*, although this quote does not

appear in the published version.
49 Colonel C. H. Wylly, *op. cit.*, p. 170.
50 C. E. Montague, *Disenchantment*, p. 6.
51 William Linton Andrews, *Haunting Years*, p. 21.
52 R. S. Patston, unpublished account, 1977, IWM 78/4/1.
53 Butterworth, *op. cit.*, p. 22.
54 Sir C. A. Montague Barlow (ed.), *The Lancashire Fusiliers: the Roll of Honour of the Salford Brigade*, pp. 41–4.
55 John Ramsden, *A Common Soldier's 1914–1918 War Diary*, unpublished account, *c.* 1928, IWM PBS/MCR/73.
56 C. Midwinter, *Memories of the 32nd Field Ambulance, 10th (Irish) Division*, Foulger, Bexleyheath, 1933, p. 1.
57 Nettleton, *The Anger of the Guns*, p. 17.
58 Lieutenant-Colonel R. M. Lester, *The Years that Changed the World*, unpublished account, *c.* 1970, IWM P. 271
59 I. V. B. Melhuish to his mother, 12 October 1914, IWM PP/MCR/69.
60 Alfred E. Henderson, *op. cit.*, IWM PP/MCR/190.
61 G. T. Walton, undated letter, *c.* July 1963, IWM BBC/GW.
62 Coppard, *op. cit.*, p. 7.
63 A. E. Perriman, *op. cit.*, IWM 80/43/1.
64 Charles Sorley to A. E. Hutchinson, 20 September 1914, see *The Letters of Charles Sorley*, Cambridge University Press, 1919, p. 226.
65 Ina Montgomery, *John Hugh Allen of the Gallant Company: a Memoir*, Arnold, London, 1919, p. 145.
66 B. L. Lawrence to C. K. Ogden, 16 September 1914, IWM 81/28/1.
67 A. G. Bartlett to his mother, 14 November 1914, IWM 68/9/1.
68 R. F. E. Evans, *op. cit.*, IWM PP/MCR/75.
69 A. Kyme Aston to his mother, undated letter, *c.* early September 1914, IWM CON/CCA.
70 Wilfred Cook, *The Lengthened Shadow*, IWM P. 101.
71 Andrews, *op. cit.*, p. 15.
72 *Ibid.*, p. 19.
73 Cook, *op. cit.*, IWM P. 101.
74 Charles Cain, *The Footsloggers*, IWM PP/MCR/48.
75 Arghur Behrend, *Make me a Soldier*, Eyre & Spottiswoode, London, 1961, p. 26.
76 Robert Roberts, *The Classic Slum*, Pelican edition, London, 1973, pp. 29–30.

8

Officers and NCOs

I

In deciding to create the New Armies, Kitchener was keenly aware of the lack of instructors, officers and non commissioned officers, a shortage which was accentuated by the mobilisation of the British Expeditionary Force and the departure for France of the majority of Regular officers and NCOs with experience of training recruits. At the outbreak of war there were 28,060 officers available, including 12,738 Regulars, 9,563 Territorials, 3,202 in the Reserve of Officers and 2,557 in the Special Reserve Units.[1] To provide for the New Army and Territorial infantry battalions raised during his term as Secretary of State for War, Kitchener had to find 30,000 additional officers at the very least, without taking into account the demands of all other branches of the army or the need to replace officer casualties in the field. Like so many of the difficulties which he faced at the beginning of the war, it was not a problem that could be solved with a mere wave of a magic wand, but within a week of entering the War Office Kitchener had already taken several steps to rectify the situation.

One of his first acts was to order each infantry battalion of the BEF to leave behind three officers and a number of NCOs to form a framework for the new battalions at the depots. Proportionate cadres from other units of the BEF were also to be retained at home. This caused some resentment, as the officers and NCOs selected to remain behind found themselves relegated to what they regarded as an inglorious role at the depots. It was, nevertheless, a measure which Kitchener had to adopt if his plans for the rapid expansion of the army were to stand any chance of success. The same was true of his decision to detain some 500 officers who were at home on leave from the Indian Army when war was declared. 'We are in a tight place and I am sure you will give me every possible assistance,' Kitchener explained in a telegram to General Sir Beauchamp Duff, the Commander-in-Chief, India, on 6 August. 'We want officers badly. Let me know privately if you can spare any from British battalions.'[2] Four days later an appeal was published for two thousand junior officers to serve with the Regular army until the war was concluded.

Unmarried men, aged between seventeen and thirty, who were cadets or ex-cadets of a university Officers' Training Corps, or members of a university, were invited to apply to the commanding officer of their particular OTC or to the university authorities. Other young men 'of good education' were requested to apply to the CO of their nearest depot.[3]

The appeal for junior officers produced an immediate rush of applications for temporary commissions, the numbers far exceeding those for which Kitchener had asked. However, it was recognised that it would take months to turn these eager young men into efficient officers and, until this could be achieved, Kitchener was compelled to cut down replacements for the BEF to the absolute minimum. The conflicting needs of the BEF and the New Armies were a constant source of anxiety to him during the opening months of the war, as was revealed by his wire to Sir John French on 16 September 1914:

We have sent you, since the war began, 593 officers to fill vacancies, and at rate demands are coming in from the front we shall soon be unable to supply well-trained officers. Units will then have to work with reduced numbers and staffs, which in some cases are apparently redundant and will have to be cut down . . . I am trying to get well-trained officers everywhere, and hope to get a few more from India. Many of the officers sent home are only slightly wounded and sick, and will rejoin their units in a short time. I hope to be able to continue to send drafts with a due proportion of officers, but it seems to me that, unless we stop all preparations of larger forces to continue the war, forces which are now being trained with the smallest number possible of Regular, Reserve, and dug-out officers . . . we shall be forced to take steps I have indicated.[4]

The pressure on Kitchener to give the BEF priority in the supply of officers did not come only from General Headquarters in France. On 17 September Lord Roberts urged Kitchener to raise only such new divisions as could be provided with officers after the demands of the BEF had been met:

. . . In other words, it would be better to keep up the present eight Regular divisions in a thoroughly fighting condition, than to let them run short of officers by raising too many new divisions. Another advantage of limiting the number of new divisions would be that these could be better officered and staffed than it is possible for the larger number to be, and as a result recruits would be made efficient in a shorter time. The same argument holds good as regards Non-Commissioned Officers, of whom we are lamentably short.[5]

By this time, of course, it was too late for Kitchener to change his policy, even if he had been open to persuasion, for the first three New Armies were now in being and the recruiting of the Pals formations and second-line Territorial units was forging ahead at a pace which surpassed all expectations. All the same, Roberts had identified some key issues, one of which was the scarcity of Regular or ex-Regular officers capable of handling a formation the size of a brigade or division in the field. Once the BEF had crossed to France there were very few officers left for the New Armies who possessed such experience, and those who did have it were often too old or in other ways unfit for strenuous service. Moreover, despite the limited choice, Kitchener had pushed on with

the raising of the New Armies so fast that he did not allow himself enough time always to make the most careful selections from the senior officers available.

In some cases the divisional commands were filled by promoting brigadier-generals taken directly from the BEF. An outstanding example was Major-General Ivor Maxse, one of the ablest officers of his generation, who was transferred from the command of the 1st (Guards) Brigade in France to that of the 18th (Eastern) Division in the Second New Army. Major-General R. H. Davies, a New Zealander, came from the 6th Infantry Brigade to the command of the 20th (Light) Division, while Major-General E. C. Ingouville-Williams was subsequently taken from the 16th Infantry Brigade to command the 34th Division. However, the original BEF had only eighteen infantry brigades and clearly could not be denuded of all its best commanders at this level, so Kitchener had to look elsewhere for the remainder of his divisional commanders. Most of those he picked were retired officers whose personal character, previous experience and physical fitness seemed likely to make them suitable all-round candidates for the new appointments. For instance, the command of the 23rd Division was given to Major-General J. M. Babington, an officer with varied experience and a creditable record who had spent some time in command of the New Zealand Defence Force. He was sixty-one when appointed to the 23rd Division but was one of the most successful of all Kitchener's selections. The officer chosen to lead the 10th (Irish) Division was Lieutenant-General Sir Bryan Mahon, a fifty-two year-old cavalryman who had seen service in Egypt and South Africa and who had commanded the Lucknow Division in India from 1909 until early in 1914. Mahon, described by an officer of the 10th Division as 'a bronzed slim figure who sat his horse like a subaltern', had a number of mild eccentricities which won him the affection of his troops. He smoked incessantly, spoke to almost everyone he met, and as a general officer he still wore his old soft cavalry regimental cap, the red band nearly hidden by a large chin strap.[6]

Similar candidates were found for the commands of brigades. One who carried out his new task with great distinction was Trevor Ternan. Having retired as a brigadier-general in 1907, he remained in the Reserve of Officers and on the outbreak of war was appointed Assistant Adjutant and Quartermaster-General on the staff of the Northumbrian Territorial Division. As he put it, 'In short, I was a dug-out.' Ternan took over as the commanding officer of the 102nd Brigade (Tyneside Scottish) in the 34th Division just after Christmas 1914.[7] The first CO of the 103rd Brigade (Tyneside Irish), also in the 34th Division, was Brigadier-General W. A. Collings, who had retired in 1908 after a career spanning thirty-eight years, including service in the Sudan in 1884–85. Portrayed by one writer as 'a robust, breezy Brigadier', Collings was not Irish but quickly earned the respect of the men under his command.[8]

Some elderly officers, on the other hand, were incapable of rising to the challenge. A former Volunteer officer who became the acting commander of a Territorial brigade in the 55th (West Lancashire) Division in the autumn of 1914 turned out to be a disastrous choice, as Lord Derby complained to General Sir Henry Mackinnon, the GOC Western Command, on 30 November:

. . . he has managed to get the whole Brigade by the ear and has been most insulting to the Commanding Officers and to their methods of training. I want to stop it coming formally before you and so I am going up there this week to see him and I shall tell him for his own sake that he had much better resign his command. He has effectually stopped recruiting in Lancaster by his conduct and he really has produced something very nearly approaching a mutiny amongst the officers. I suppose we can always remove him, can't we, if he won't go on his own acount? . . .[9]

Apart from their inexperience in handling large formations, many retired officers who were suddenly handed senior commands found that they could not adapt to the changes wrought in drill, tactics and equipment in the decade before the war, and particularly since the introduction of the new Field Service Regulations in 1909. For talented brigade commanders and serving Regulars like Ivor Maxse it was still a big step to move from the command of some 4,000 men in a brigade to that of some 20,000 in a division. It was yet more daunting for officers who were out of touch with current weapons, equipment and tactical thought.

Another massive problem for Kitchener was that of providing the New Armies with good battalion and company commanders. To achieve this he was prepared to employ methods which, at times, bordered on the unethical. At the begining of September 1914 he instructed the Adjutant-General to 'get from Post Offices names and addresses of every officer to whom letters are arriving addressed Colonel, Major, Captain and Lieutenant; and write a civil letter to each of them, if he has not already sent in his name, inviting him to do so in such a manner that he can hardly refuse'.[10]

The First New Army, which was formed in August 1914, at least enjoyed the advantage of starting with a number of Regular or recently retired officers at battalion and company command levels, thanks to Kitchener's prompt action in transferring some trained officers from the BEF. For example, the 8th Black Watch, which formed part of the 9th (Scottish) Division at Aldershot, had seven Regular or ex-Regular officers, including the battalion commander, Lieutenant-Colonel Lord Sempill. In the 12th (Eastern) Division, the 5th Royal Berkshire Regiment had four serving Regular officers, the battalion commander himself having been in charge of the depot at Reading when war was declared. In addition there were two officers who had retired only a short time before. The 6th South Lancashire Regiment in the 13th (Western) Division contained as many as seven serving Regular officers by November 1914, including the CO, an adjutant from the Indian Army, a major and a captain from the 1st Battalion, two majors from the 2nd Battalion and the Lieutenant and Quartermaster. Another major came from the Reserve of Officers.[11]

The reservoir of serving Regular officers was running dry when the Second New Army came into being on 11 September 1914, and so the Second, Third and subsequent New Armies had to rely much more heavily on retired officers or 'dug-outs' who, fortunately for the War Office, were offering their services in considerable numbers. Whereas the 6th Battalion of the Border Regiment, part of the 11th (Northern) Division in the First New Army, started life with one Regular major, three Regular lieutenants and three second lieutenants from the 3rd (Special Reserve) Battalion, the 7th Battalion, a unit of the 17th (Northern) Division in the Second New Army, was formed around a nucleus of one captain from the 3rd Battalion and one NCO.[12] Scarcely any of the battalions of the 15th (Scottish) Division possessed more than four officers on formation. The 7th Royal Scots initially had just one officer and he had only recently received a commission after serving as a quartermaster-sergeant in the Royal Garrison Artillery. For a brief period he was in sole command of 900 men. The number of Regular officers with the division averaged out at less than one per battalion. In no brigade were there more than five Regular officers, including those on the brigade staffs. The senior officers of the battalions were therefore mainly retired Regulars or former Militia and Territorial officers.[13]

Some battalions in the Second New Army eventually managed to stitch together a patchwork of trained officers for their senior ranks. The command of the 9th Black Watch in the 15th Division was filled by promoting a major from the Reserve of Officers. There was also a Regular quartermaster, and Lord Sempill transferred one of the three serving Regular officers in the 8th Battalion to act as the 9th Battalion's adjutant. A captain from the Reserve of Officers became a company commander and later the battalion's second-in-command. The other company officers were at first all newly commissioned second lieutenants.[14] By comparison, several other Second New Army units even had trouble finding enough 'dug-outs' in the early weeks. Viscount Buckmaster recalled the odd assortment of officers in the 7th Duke of Cornwall's Light Infantry when he joined the battalion as a young subaltern in the autumn of 1914:

Our Adjutant, a Regular of the DCLI, who had been wounded, was the only officer competent to lead men in the field. Of the others, one was a middle-aged war correspondent; one a Boer War cavalry officer; the Colonel was a dug-out, fond of the bottle; the rest, like myself, utterly ignorant of all military matters.[15]

It was a greater struggle still to produce officers from the active list for the Third New Army. In the 21st Division every one of the battalion commanders had been in retirement on the outbreak of war and, besides these, only fourteen officers in the entire division had any previous experience in the Regular army. The remainder, over 400 in number, had all been granted commissions since the war began and were mostly without officer training.

As more and more battalions were raised the total of experienced officers in each was progressively reduced, and within a short time men who had been the adjutant or second-in-command of a battalion in the First or Second New Army were themselves appointed to the command of later formations.

Just how thinly the serving Regular officers and 'dug-outs' were spread in the Third New Army may be illustrated by looking at two of its battalions. In the 7th King's Shropshire Light Infantry, a battalion of the 25th Division, the first commanding officer and adjutant had both served in the old Militia. The Lieutenant and Quartermaster was a former regimental sergeant-major. None of the other officers had more than three weeks' service when they joined the unit. The only serving Regular officer the battalion ever had before going overseas was its third commanding officer, Major Weir, who came from the 1st Royal Irish Rifles to take over the battalion in January 1915. When the battalion went to France in September 1915 it was under its fourth commanding officer, Weir having returned to the BEF in April that year.[16] The 8th Royal Berkshire Regiment in the 26th Division was commanded by an officer from the Indian Army but again, apart from the adjutant, not one of the remaining officers had any previous Regular service. However, the battalion did benefit from having the same commanding officer throughout its ten months of training.[17]

In the Pals battalions, command was generally given to an elderly retired officer on the recommendation of the Mayor or head of the raising committee. While open to abuse, this method of selection also had some virtues, as such officers often lived in the town or city concerned and were known to the raisers as a result of their connections with a local Volunteer, Militia or Territorial unit. The raisers thus had more control over the choice of senior officers and were able to take more care during the selection process than would have been the case if they were required simply to accept unknown candidates supplied by the War Office. Personal influence, however, clearly played a part in such appointments, as when Lord Derby wrote to General Mackinnon proposing that his own brother should receive the command of the 89th Brigade, which contained the four Liverpool City Battalions;

I do hope that Ferdy may be given it. He is not of course the senior but . . . Ferdy has practically for two months done Brigadier's work. The whole of the selection of officers not only for his own but for the other battalions has practically [to] be done by him and if it had not been for his assistance when I was taken ill the battalions could never have been raised at all . . . I do hope therefore if you can you will press his appointment. If you agree with this and will allow me to do so I will press privately in London for it.[18]

The following month Derby's brother was duly elevated to the command of the brigade with the rank of temporary brigadier-general, although it must be added that the appointment was highly successful and Stanley stayed in the post until April 1918.

It should also be pointed out that, in many instances, the 'dug-out' battalion and company commanders did a great deal to increase the efficiency of the new formations. A Pals unit which was extremely fortunate in this respect was the 11th Battalion of the Border Regiment, raised by Lord Lonsdale in September 1914. The battalion's first commander was Lieutenant-Colonel Percy Machell, a retired officer of the Essex Regiment who had served mainly in Egypt and the Sudan during the 1880s and 1890s and had been Military Adviser to the Egyptian Ministry of the Interior for ten years until 1908. With no serving Regulars and only a handful of ex-Volunteer or Territorial officers to call upon, Machell had to perform the work of several men in the unit's early days. The battalion's adjutant, who did not arrive himself until 3 December, later wrote of Machell:

Every detail had to be taught by him, for the officers, with very few exceptions, knew no more than the men, and had to be taught themselves before they could teach. The simplest orderly-room work, such as making out 'crimes' 'guard reports', and 'details' etc, were done by him . . . and he always checked each of the returns personally. All attestations were made out, and recruits personally approved by him, while the separation allowances claimed his particular attention. He organised the feeding of the men . . . he arranged for the hutting, the clothing, the water supply, the lighting and conservancy of the camp, and he it was who averted a strike that threatened over the wages question among the men engaged to build the huts. These things alone would have occupied the activities of six ordinary men, but in addition to all this the CO was constantly on parade, training and smartening up both officers and men, drawing up the programmes of work and seeing that they were carried out.[19]

Despite this immense work load, Machell was still in command when the battalion left for France and he was subsequently awarded the Distinguished Service Order. He was killed in action on the Somme on 1 July 1916.

Machell obviously represented the best type of 'dug-out' officer and but for men like him the New Armies would never have been organised and trained in so short a time. Conversely, many 'dug-outs' were unable to meet the heavy demands placed upon them. A large proportion of these were medically unfit. A captain in the 9th Essex Regiment was found to be suffering from heart trouble and severe gout and on one occasion had to be prevented from taking a company parade in a bath chair.[20] In the 10th Royal Welsh Fusiliers an officer who had re-enlisted at the age of sixty-five dropped dead from a heart attack while on parade.[21]. E. W. Prosser recalled that the commanding officer of a Reserve battalion of the Middlesex Regiment was seriously overweight: 'On route marches his groom had to take a spare horse, one for the outward trip and one home. One horse would never have stood up to that 18 to 20 stones. He also had to have a loading platform, almost like the Knights of old.'[22] Others, while in reasonably good health, were regarded as too old for active service. Of the four original battalion commanders in the Salford Brigade, for example, three had to relinquish their appointments on age grounds before their respective units went overseas.[23] Buckmaster's company commander in the 7th Duke of Cornwall's Light Infantry had been a cavalry officer in the South African War: 'A middle-aged man, he could not master infantry drill, and though he did not actually order us to trot instead of march, he gave commands in terms of cavalry troops or squadrons.'[24]

Because good battalion and company officers were in short supply to begin with, it was not at all easy to replace those who were found wanting. The scale of the problem may be best appreciated if one bears in mind that many Territorial units faced precisely the same difficulties as the New Armies in this direction. Even those who commanded existing first-line Territorial units at the outbreak of the war were sometimes cruelly exposed by the rigours of full-time training. One officer, who had commanded the 1/4th Battalion of the Loyal North Lancashire Regiment since 1911, was described by Lord Derby in February 1915 as 'absolutely useless'. Derby told Mackinnon, 'He does not know his work and he is a first class shirker. He has at last resigned and to show you what sort of man he is he says he cannot go out now to the Front but he would be ready to go out later when the weather gets warmer.'[25]

In marked contrast, once war was declared there was no shortage of applicants for temporary commissions at a more junior level. The main source of supply was the Officers' Training Corps. Between August 1914 and March 1915, 20,577 members or former members of the OTC were commissioned. These came from the twenty-four units of the OTC's Senior Division at the universities and the Inns of Court, and from 166 units of the Junior Division at public schools and grammar schools. Of the major public schools, Marlborough alone contributed 506, Charterhouse 411, Wellington 403 and Eton 350.[26] The scale of the OTC's contribution meant that there was no sudden and radical change in the social composition of the officer corps during the first year of the war, unlike that of the rank and file. Indeed, in the early months it was often difficult for a man without OTC training or a public school background to become an officer. R. C. Sherriff's account of his first attempt to obtain a commission in August 1914 is reasonably familiar but worth repeating in this context:

'School?' enquired the adjutant. I told him and his face fell. He took up a printed list and searched through it. 'I'm sorry,' he said, 'but I'm afraid it isn't a public school.' I was mystified. I told him that my school, though small, was a very old and good one – founded, I said by Queen Elizabeth in 1567. The adjutant was not impressed. He had lost all interest in me. 'I'm sorry,' he repeated. 'But our instructions are that all applicants for commissions must be selected from the recognised public schools and yours is not among them.' And that was that. It was a long, hard pull before I was at last accepted as an officer.[27]

The proportion of men with a public school education who entered the army as officers was certainly greater in 1914 than it had been towards the end of the nineteenth century. A. H. H. MacLean has calculated that the only schools from which more than one-fifth of their former pupils served in the South African War were Eton, Harrow and Wellington.[28] At the beginning of the First World War it seems to have been almost instinctive for young men from public schools to apply for a commission. It is interesting to compare the numbers of men from public school OTC contingents who became officers between August 1914 and March 1915 against those from the same schools who enlisted in the ranks during this period. From Marlborough, for example, 506 were granted a commission and eighty-nine joined the ranks; Charterhouse contributed 411 officers and seventy-nine other ranks; and from Eton 350 were gazetted whereas only thirteen joined as privates or NCOs. In the case of the Wellington and Rugby contingents, which provided 403 and 291 officers respectively, no one appears to have enlisted in the ranks up to March 1915. The figures from the smaller public schools and grammar schools tell a different story. Sixty-two from the Mill Hill School OTC became officers in this period, whereas 350 served first as other ranks; from St Dunstan's College, Catford, the totals were thirty-nine officers and 450 other ranks; and from Queen Mary's Grammar School, Walsall, six were commissioned and 130 enlisted in the ranks.[29]

Both the raisers and the commanders of the New Army and Territorial formations did their best to preserve the gentleman officer tradition. By the beginning of September 1914 Kitchener had decided to allow the commanding officers of the New Army battalions 'to select names of candidates for commissions in their units, the names being forwarded to the War Office for approval'.[30] The presidents of the Territorial Force County Associations were already empowered to submit recommendations for the appointment of junior officers and, from September 1914 onwards, raisers of Pals battalions were also given considerable latitude in this matter. In the Sheffield City Battalion (12th York and Lancaster Regiment) a preliminary list of proposed officers was compiled by the battalion commander, then submitted to the Lord Mayor and the Pro-Chancellor of the university for approval before being sent to the War Office.[31] Applications for commissions in each of the four Salford battalions were reviewed by the chairman and secretary of the raising committee and the commanding officer and adjutant of the battalion concerned. The names of candidates who were found suitable were then forwarded to the War Office through the GOC Western Command at Chester. The recommendations of the raising committee were accepted by the War Office in every case.[32] Yet, despite this widespread devolution of responsibility, most of those involved in the selection of junior officers continued to follow pre-war criteria and to recruit subalterns from a fairly restricted social stratum. Brigadier-General Ternan of the Tyneside Scottish Brigade refused to consider any application unless the candidate possessed previous military experience or had served in the OTC.[33] The officers of the 2/7th West Yorkshire Regiment, a Leeds Territorial unit whose CO was an Old Harrovian, also came largely from Eton, Harrow and other leading public schools.[34] Similar preferences were displayed in some Special Reserve battalions. When Ulric Nisbet left Marlborough and joined the 3rd Queen's Own Royal West Kent Regiment in 1914, the battalion commander was

Lieutenant-Colonel Sir Arthur Griffith-Boscawen, MP for Dudley and an old Rugbeian. 'He asked me,' wrote Nisbet, 'to try to get other Old Marlburians to apply for commissions in it. The result was that sometime during that first winter Old Rugbeians and Old Marlburians were numerous enough to field a rugger side against officers in the battalion from other public schools.'[35]

As the army went on expanding the OTC contingents could not supply all the junior officers needed and many temporary commissions were granted to school leavers, undergraduates and men with responsible positions in civil life who did not posses the Certificate A or B of an OTC unit but who otherwise seemed capable of excercising command. Large numbers of young men who returned from jobs abroad also obtained commissions. Of the twenty-nine officers in the 7th Oxfordshire and Buckinghamshire Light Infantry in mid-1915, three had come from Australia, two from South Africa, one from Canada and one from Ceylon. Practically all the battalion's officers, however, had served in the OTC or the Territorial Force before the war.[36] The sons of local businessmen or substantial tradesmen began to feature more prominently among the officers of the Pals units as well as the Territorial battalions, though a university, public school or grammar school education was still a standard qualification for entry. Sixteen of the thirty-seven officers who served in the 3rd Tyneside Irish (26th Northumberland Fusiliers) during 1914 and 1915 were born in or near Newcastle and all but four of these had been to a grammar school or university. Of the remaining twenty-one officers only four had not attended a grammar school or public school, and one of these had received a private education.[37] Even so, in a few locally raised battalions the officers were drawn almost entirely from outside the unit's place of origin. Such was the case with the 15th Royal Irish Rifles in the 36th (Ulster) Division. This battalion came from north Belfast, a predominantly working-class area with a low proportion of men of the accepted officer type. Consequently the battalion had to take suitable candidates from all quarters of the United Kingdom.[38]

Those seeking commissions frequently found that knowing someone in a position of influence helped to expedite their application. R. D. Oliver, a civil servant and former Territorial sergeant, was personally acquainted with the Lord Mayor of Newcastle and, chiefly on the strength of the latter's recommendation, was granted a commission in the 4th Tyneside Irish (27th Northumberland Fusiliers). A month later Oliver was a company commander.[39] For David Kelly the chance came through a fellow private in the University and Public Schools' Brigade at Epsom:

A platoon friend, George Gillett, told me that a friend with whom he used to play cricket and who was now Colonel of a Kitchener battalion – the 6th Leicestershires, at Aldershot – had offered him a commission, and one for any friend he liked to bring. Together we drove over on a Saturday afternoon to Aldershot and had tea with the Colonel . . . A week later a commission in the Leicesters reached me . . .[40]

Percival Sharp became an officer in the Stockbrokers' Battalion (10th Royal

Fusiliers) without applying personally for a commission. In September 1914 he was serving as a private in a Territorial battalion, the 1/15th London Regiment, and one morning, after a route march, his was one of four names called out by the sergeant-major:

'I could not recall any misdemeanour so I wondered! We were fallen in together . . . and marched into the Orderly Room in front of the Adjutant who told us to stand at ease and then said 'Gentlemen, I have the honour to inform you that each one of you has been granted a commission in His Majesty's forces, and you A, B, and C, will report to so and so, and you Lieutenant Sharp to the Officer Commanding 10th Royal Fusiliers at Colchester . . . I may add I had made no application for a commission but my old school had been approached by the War Office and asked to recommend suitable candidates. As I held Certificate A and had been Colour Sergeant in the Cadet Corps, my name was sent in.[41]

When using their discretionary powers in the selection of candidates for commissions, commanding officers inevitably left themselves open to criticism, particularly if it was felt that their choice had been dictated by personal prejudice. By the end of October 1914 John Redmond, the Irish Nationalist leader, found that virtually every man whom he put forward for a commission was being rejected by Lieutenant-General Sir Lawrence Parsons, the commander of the 16th (Irish) Division. On 29 October Parsons wrote to Redmond to say that, as a special concession, he would give commissions to two National Volunteer leaders who called on him, but only on condition that they succeeded in bringing in recruits with them. Not one colonel in the whole division was a Catholic and even six months later there were no more than half a dozen Catholic field officers. Redmond's own son was refused a commission at first and joined the division as a private.[42] Other commanding officers, like Lieutenant-Colonel A. J. Richardson of the Hull Commercials (10th East Yorkshire Regiment) remained steadfastly impartial. Richardson told applicants he would not recommend anyone who lacked the character and determination needed to ensure discipline or the mental capacity required to assimilate the army's regulations and instructions, 'no matter how many employers, fathers, or grandmothers try to pull the strings'.[43]

Complaints were also made that Kitchener's indiscriminate recruiting policy at the beginning of the war had allowed too many potential officers to slip through the net. A brigadier-general, writing of the 15th (Scottish) Division, described one company of the 6th Cameron Highlanders, composed largely of men from Glasgow University and Glasgow high schools, as 'the finest material I ever saw . . . a shocking waste of good officer material'.[44] In fact, in several New Army battalions almost all the original members applied successfully for commissions. The four battalions of the University and Public Schools' Brigade had together yielded up some 1,700 men for commissions by January 1915, causing the raisers such concern that Kitchener had to reassure them that 'the Brigade is not to be utilised as an OTC'. The need for officers was so great, however, that the promise could not be kept and the raising committee was soon forced to agree to more men being taken. In April 1915 the total of other ranks who had received commissions reached 3,000 and eventually rose to over 7,000. Because of the continuing drain on the brigade's manpower, three of its four battalions were disbanded in April 1916.[45] The 16th (Public Schools) Battalion of the Middlesex Regiment narrowly escaped the same fate. Three hundred and fifty of its NCOs and men were gazetted before the end of 1914 and the battalion was called upon to supply another 150 in January 1915. In all, 1,400 other ranks of the battalion were commisssioned.[46]

This process was not restricted to units recruited primarily from public schools. The 1st Birmingham Battalion (14th Royal Warwickshire Regiment) lost 302 other ranks in this way up to the end of 1915, while between 400 and 500 men of the Leeds Pals (15th West Yorkshire Regiment) became officers before the unit left England.[47] The loss of other ranks was sufficiently alarming to persuade some commanding officers to try to stem the tide. In December 1914 the CO of the 9th Northumberland Fusiliers actually issued an order that no one would be allowed to apply for a commission, and in both the 16th Battalion of the Middlesex Regiment and the 23rd (Sportsman's) Battalion of the Royal Fusiliers it was insisted that any applicants should first provide one or more recruits as substitutes.[48] The fact that these measures had to be taken at all suggests that it was not difficult for a man to obtain promotion from the ranks in 1914 and 1915, given enough determination on his part. As the Directorate of Military Training reminded commanding officers in December 1914, lack of experience in handling troops in the field should not be a bar to promotion provided that promising men were 'otherwise suitable in all respects to hold temporary commissions'.[49] Whatever individual commanding officers might feel about the constant drain on their units, the casualty rates on the Western Front alone kept the demand for fresh officers at a high level and the War Office was driven to turn time and time again to the ranks of the New Armies in its quest for replacements.

II

The methods employed to ensure an adequate supply of NCOs were much more varied, and in many cases far more rudimentary, than those adopted for the selection of officers. For his NCOs and drill instructors Kitchener looked first to the large numbers of old soldiers who applied to rejoin their regiments at the outbreak of war. As early as 11 August 1914 the War Office laid down that NCOs for the new formations should be selected initially from re-enlisted ex-Regular NCOs and men 'who may be promoted from the rank they formerly held'. Commanding officers were also told that 'one ex-soldier may be selected and promoted to sergeant for every twenty-five recruits and one corporal for every 20 recruits enlisted for the new Army. Paid lance-corporals, selected from ex-soldiers and suitable recruits, may be appointed in the proportion of three lance-corporals to every 50 recruits.'[50] Six days later it was announced that any re-enlisted ex-Regular NCO up to the age of forty-five would be 'posted whenever possible to a unit of his former corps in the new six divisions and army troops and promoted forthwith to the rank he held on discharge'.[51] The upper age limit for re-enlisted NCOs was extended to fifty before the end of the month.

The huge increase in the size of the army at the beginning of September made it necessary for the War Office to step up its search for trained NCOs. A request was submitted to the India Office on 1 September for one quartermaster-sergeant or battery sergeant-major to be sent from the Indian Army for each new Royal Horse Artillery or Royal Field Artillery brigade in the United Kingdom. In addition, the War Office asked for two colour-sergeants and eight sergeants from each Regular infantry battalion stationed in India.[52] At home, the commanders of Special Reserve battalions were ordered to select twenty Regular privates or old soldiers from their ranks to serve as instructors for units in the Second New Army.[53] Arrangements were also made with the Home Office for the loan of policemen and prison warders to help drill the raw recruits at the depots, and the Board of Education co-operated by providing qualified teachers to act as physical training instructors.[54]

As with the 'dug-out' officers, the best of the re-enlisted NCOs proved invaluable to the New Armies, especially during the difficult early days when newly commissioned subalterns and recruits alike started on a common level of more or less complete military ignorance. Regimental Sergeant-Major Harry Cave of the 15th Highland Light Infantry (Glasgow Tramways Battalion) was just such a man. An employee of the Glasgow Corporation, he had seen service as a Regular with the Cameronians and was also a former drill instructor to the 1st Lanark Rifle Volunteers. Though too old to go overseas, Cave was largely instrumental in transforming the 15th Highland Light Infantry into a well organised and disciplined battalion. According to the unit's historian:

He knew everything of soldiering in precise detail from the orderly room to the cookhouse. For his assistance in arranging the company formations, selecting the non commissioned ranks and drawing up the details of drilling and training, the commanding officer and the adjutant were deeply indebted. His enthusiasm was no less than his skill. None of those young officers and soldiers who spanked along the roads of Ayrshire with him on those bright early mornings . . . or heard that high-pitched, long-carrying voice which rang for half a mile over the golf courses and beaches, will ever forget Cave, kindly efficient Cave, one of the type of men who made Kitchener's Army a living reality.[55]

Not all old soldiers came up to this standard. An officer of the 7th King's Shropshire Light Infantry wrote, 'Many of the latter were elderly men who had been out of the service anything from ten to twenty years, activated by the highest motives but with a scanty knowledge of the new drill. The word "platoon", for example was a novelty, and was variously rendered "pathoon", "pontoon" and even "spitoon" . . .'[56] Another difficulty was that the recruits of the New Armies were, on the whole, much better educated than their pre-war counterparts and therefore less inclined to tolerate the shortcomings of re-enlisted NCOs. Private Charles Jones of the 8th Royal Sussex Regiment was particularly critical of the ex-Regulars at Colchester:

One of the most pitiful things here is the incompetence of our instructors. They are nearly all illiterates and most have been out of the Army some 10 years. One slouches about in a bowler hat just like an East End pub lounger, candidly confesses he does not understand some of the drills and on occasions gets quarrelsome and threatens to fight some of the recruits in the evening if any are disposed to take him on . . . The Company Sergeant-Major is a weak, stupid fellow, looks 55 or 60, doesn't know his business but fusses about like a fish out of water.[57]

Very few New Army units ever had enough competent re-enlisted soldiers to fill all their non commissioned officer ranks and, consequently, the majority of battalion commanders had to make up the required number simply by choosing promising recruits. In the 5th Cameron Highlanders the problem was dealt with by promoting forty men from a company composed mainly of men from the Glasgow Stock Exchange.[58] In the 15th and 16th Battalions of the Cheshire Regiment (1st and 2nd Birkenhead Bantams), any man who had been a Boy Scout was made an NCO on the spot.[59] The commanding officer of the 6th Northamptonshire Regiment also gave preference to former Boy Scouts or members of the Boys' Brigade and Church Lads' Brigade.[60] Many COs selected those who seemed the most intelligent and who picked up the drill with the greatest ease, while others, like the commander of the 10th Essex Regiment, opted for the smartly dressed: 'A straw hat or a bowler determined the choice of the lance-corporal, while a really clean white collar in addition to a decent hat was the sure passport to the rank of corporal.'[61] An equally unorthodox system was adopted by Second Lieutenant Harold Hemming when he was helping to select NCOs from the recruits of the 12th West Yorkshire Regiment:

There was no use picking out a few bright-looking chaps and telling them that they were corporals, for there was no way of indicating their rank. We did not even have brassards with stripes on them that they could wear over their coat sleeves. So I counted the men who had moustaches and found that I had just enough, so I made them all lance-corporals there and then . . . Actually I did not realise it at first, but I had hit upon a wizard idea. Nearly all the men were coal miners and coal miners do not have moustaches because of the coal dust. At any rate not those who gc underground. So the chaps at the pit heads and in the mine offices sported moustaches – I suppose to show off that they were superior beings; so I had automatically selected the brain-workers to be my lance-corporals.[62]

Such methods sometimes led to awkward social situations within the ranks. Soon after the formation of the 1st Manchester City Battalion (16th Manchester Regiment) an elderly private protested to his company commander, 'If you please, sir, you've placed us in a bit of a predicament. It's this way, you see, we all come from the same warehouse, and him as has been made the head of the tent is the office boy, sir, and I'm the head of the department!' One sergeant of the battalion humorously complained to his officer that he was in an inferior social position to every man in his platoon.[63] Lieutenant I. L. Read of the 8th Leicestershire Regiment remarked, 'Where friends enlisted in groups, generally speaking none would take stripes – in the event an unwritten law which took months to break down.'[64] Raymond Turner of the 7th East Kent Regiment was one of countless soldiers for whom comradeship was more important than promotion. 'No doubt you want to know why I am a private again,' he wrote to his sister in the spring of 1915. 'Well, I had had enough of a stripe and they wanted to shift me from my pals. I did not care for that so I asked to be put back in the ranks.'[65]

More often than not, however, the system of picking NCOs almost at random worked surprisingly well. A real strength of Kitchener's Army was its ample supply of earnest, intelligent men with the personality and determination necessary to make them good squad and section leaders, like the young soldier described by H. V. Drinkwater of the 2nd Birmingham Battalion (15th Royal Warwickshire Regiment):

We were told on parade . . . that any fellow who liked to volunteer for a stripe, his application would be considered, but we thought this is going to be a short sharp war, quick training, over to France and back again, and finished . . . With the foregoing in our minds and the fact that for the most part we were fellows with something in common, we decided in the main that as we had joined as privates we would remain privates. Therefore when shortly afterwards our platoon officer, Lt. Rubery, asked any fellow desiring a stripe to step forward, we remained in the ranks. It was some moments before there stepped forward a pale, anaemic, undersized little fellow who might have been eighteen for Army purposes, but actually looked barely sixteen. We looked aghast at this boy when we thought he might be made an NCO. We were staggered a few days later when we found he had been made a lance-corporal and, still worse, in charge of the section we were in, but we agreed that we had had an equal chance and it was therefore up to us now to play the game. In a month we liked him, in six months we said he was as good as any other NCO in the battalion, in twelve months time we were glad to help him carry out any difficult command he had to obey, in eighteen months we would have cleaned his boots. He had a great hold on us, this little fellow. He seemed to have made up his mind at an early date that he would do his job . . . and he always got it done, first by showing the way himself.[66]

Notes

1 *Statistics of the Military Effort of the British Empire*, p. 234.
2 Kitchener to Duff, 6 August 1914, Creedy papers, IWM 72/22/1.
3 *The Times*, 10 August 1914
4 Kitchener to French, 16 September 1914, quoted in Arthur, *Life of Lord Kitchener*, III, p. 45.
5. Roberts to Kitchener, 17 September 1914, Creedy papers, IWM 72/22/1.
6 Major Bryan Cooper, *The Tenth (Irish) Division in Gallipoli*, Herbert Jenkins, London, 1918, pp. 3–5.
7 Brigadier-General Trevor Ternan, *The Story of the Tyneside Scottish*, p. 9.
8 Felix Lavery (ed.), *Irish Heroes in the War*, Part II, p. 135.
9 Derby to Mackinnon, 30 November 1914, Derby papers, LRO 920 DER (17) 33.

10 Notes on 'Supply of Officers: Instructions of Secretary of State', 6 September 1914, Adjutant-General's papers, WO 162/2.
11 Major-General A. G. Wauchope (ed.), *A History of The Black Watch (Royal Highlanders) in the Great War, 1914–1918*, III, p. 3; F. Loraine Petre, *The Royal Berkshire Regiment (Princess Charlotte of Wales's)*, II, p. 208; Captain H. Whalley-Kelly, *Ich Dien: the Prince of Wales's Volunteers (South Lancashire) 1914–1934*, Gale & Polden, Aldershot, 1935, p. 148.
12 Colonel H. C. Wylly, *The Border Regiment in the Great War*, Gale & Polden, Aldershot, 1924, pp. 22–7.
13 John Buchan and Lieutenant-Colonel J. Stewart, *The Fifteenth (Scottish) Division, 1914–1919*, Blackwood, Edinburgh, 1926, pp. 3–4.
14 Wauchope (ed.), *op. cit.*, p. 107.
15 Viscount Buckmaster, *Roundabout*, Witherby, London, 1969, p. 120.
16 Major W. de B. Wood (ed.), *The History of the King's Shropshire Light Infantry in the Great War, 1914–1918*, pp. 204–14.
17 F. Loraine Petre, *op. cit.*, pp. 318–20.
18 Derby to Mackinnon, 4 November 1914, Derby papers, LRO 920 DER (17) 33.
19 Captain P. G. W. Diggle in 'V.M.' (ed.), *Record of the XIth (Service) Battalion Border Regiment (Lonsdale) from September 1914 to July 1st 1916*, pp. 7–8.
20 J. W. Burrows, *Essex Units in the War, 1914–1919*, Vol. 6; *Service Batalions*, Burrows, Southend, 1935, p. 8.
21 Lieutenant-Colonel F. N. Burton (ed.), *The War Diary of the 10th (Service) Battalion Royal Welsh Fusiliers*, Brendon, Plymouth, 1926, p. 5.
22 E. W. Prosser, *Never Again: a Soldier's Impressions of the Great War, 1914–1919*, unpublished account, post–1945, IWM PBS/MCR/128.
23 Sir C. A. Montague Barlow (ed.), *The Lancashire Fusiliers: the Roll of Honour of the Salford Brigade*, pp. 36–7.
24 Buckmaster, *op. cit.*, p. 122.
25 Derby to Mackinnon, 13 February 1915, Derby papers, LRO 920 DER(17)33.
26 Captain A. R. Haig-Brown, *The O.T.C. and the Great War*, Country Life, London, 1915, pp. 99–106.
27 R. C. Sherriff, 'The English public schools in the war', in George A. Panichas (ed.), *Promise of Greatness*, Cassell, London, 1968, pp. 134–54.
28 A. H. H. MacLean, *Public Schools and the War in South Africa*, Simpson & Marshall, London, 1902, p. 19.
29 Haig-Brown, *op. cit.*, pp. 99–106
30 Minutes of meetings of the Military Members of the Army Council, 4 September 1914, WO 163/44
31 Richard A. Sparling, *History of the 12th (Service) Battalion York and Lancaster Regiment*, Northend, Sheffield, 1920, p. 4.
32 Barlow (ed.), *op. cit.*, p. 27.
33 Ternan, *op. cit.*, p. 29.
34 Patricia M. Morris, *The Leeds Rifles and the First World War*; paper given at the conference on 'The British Army in the Great War', RMA Sandhurst, November 1978.
35 H. U. S. Nisbet, *Diaries and Memories of the Great War*, unpublished account, 1974, IWM 78/3/1.
36 Major C. Wheeler, in *The Oxfordshire and Buckinghamshire Light Infantry Chronicle*, Vol. XXIV, 1914–15, p. 422.
37 Lavery, *op. cit.*, pp. 157–63.
38 J. L. Stewart-Moore, *Random Recollections*, Part II *The Great War, 1914–1918*, unpublished account, 1976, IWM 77/39/1.
39 Major R. D. Oliver, *The First World War: Personal Reminiscences*, unpublished

account, 1971, IWM DS/MISC/51.

40   Sir David Kelly, *The Ruling Few*, Hollis & Carter, London, 1952, pp. 89–90.
41   Captain P. M. Sharp, *Two World Wars*, unpublished account, n.d., IWM 78/69/1.
42   Denis Gwynn, *The Life of John Redmond*, pp. 399–400, 410–11.
43   Captain C. I. Hadrill (ed.), *A History of the 10th (Service) Battalion the East Yorkshire Regiment (Hull Commercials) 1914–1919*, p. 11.
44   Buchan and Stewart, *op. cit.*, p. 5.
45   Anon., *The History of the Royal Fusiliers 'U.P.S.': University and Public Schools Brigade (Formation and Training)*, pp. 60–3.
46   H. W. Wallis Grain, *The 16th (Public Schools) Service Battalion (the Duke of Cambridge's Own) Middlesex Regiment and the Great War, 1914–1918*, pp. 31–2.
47   Sir William H. Bowater (ed.), *Birmingham City Battalions: Book of Honour*, pp. 23–9; W. H. Scott, *Leeds in the Great War*, p. 113.
48   Captain C. H. Cooke, *Historical Records of the 9th (Service) Battalion Northumberland Fusiliers*, p. 7; H. W. Wallis Grain, *op. cit.*, p. 32; F. W. Ward, *The 23rd (Service) Battalion Royal Fusiliers (First Sportsman's): a record of its Services in the Great War, 1914–1919*, p. 19; *Sportsman's Gazette*, Vol. 2, No. 22, 25 June 1915.
49   Circular from Directorate of Military Training to GOCs-in-C. of Commands, 16 December 1914, WO162/2.
50   Letter from Adjutant-General's Department to GOCs-in-C of Commands, 11 August 1914, WO 162/3.
51   Recruiting memorandum issued by Adjutant-General's Department, 17 August 1914, WO 159/18: Army Order I of 17 August 1914 (AO 315 of 1914).
52   Adjutant-General to Under-Secretary of State for India, 1 September 1914, WO 162/3.
53   Letter from Adjutant-General's Department to GOCs-in-C of Commands, 4 September 1914, WO 162/3.
54   Letter from Adjutant-General's Department to GOC's-in-C of Commands, 12 September 1914; copy of circular from Board of Education to Local Education Authorities, 19 October 1914, WO 162/3.
55   Thomas Chalmers (ed.), *An Epic of Glasgow: History of the 15th Battalion the Highland Light Infantry*, p. 5.
56   Major W. de B. Wood (ed.), *op. cit.*, p. 204.
57   Charles Jones to his wife, 15 September 1914, IWM CON/CJ.
58   *Historical Records of the Queen's Own Cameron Highlanders*, Vol. IV, Blackwood, Edinburgh, 1931, p. 51.
59   Arthur Crookenden, *The History of the Cheshire Regiment in the Great War*, p. 347.
60   Peter Jackson, *The Glorious Sixth*, privately published, 1975, p. 4.
61   Lieutenant-Colonel T. M. Banks and Captain R. A. Chell, *With the 10th Essex in France*, p. 16.
62   Lieutenant-Colonel H. H. Hemming, *Preparing for War*, unpublished account, 1976, IWM PP/MCR/155.
63   Lieutenant-Colonel H. L. James (ed.), *Sixteenth, Seventeenth, Eighteenth, Nineteenth Battalions, the Manchester Regiment (First City Brigade): a Record, 1914–1918*, pp. 5–6.
64   Lieutenant I. L. Read, *A Narrative, 1914–1919*, unpublished account, 1968, IWM DS/MISC/68.
65   Raymond Turner to his sister, undated letter, *c*. March 1915, IWM CON/RHT.
66   H. V. Drinkwater, *Diary of the War*, unpublished account, *c*. 1920, IWM DS/MISC/54.

9

Training camps and billets

At the outset, one of the most urgent tasks confronting the War Office was the provision of suitable accommodation and training grounds for the New Armies. Prior to August 1914 the allocation of troops to any quarters, new or old, was co-ordinated by a body known as the Peace Distribution Committee, on which every branch of the Army Council was represented. In 1913 Major-General G. K. Scott-Moncrieff, the Director of Fortifications and Works in the Department of the Master-General of the Ordnance, had succeeded Sir Archibald Murray as president of this committee. While no one knew exactly how much extra accommodation might be required in the event of war, the committee had been able to lay down general criteria governing the selection of sites for new barracks and hutted camps, stressing the importance of good terrain for training purposes, the availability of water and electricity and ease of access for supply and movement. Thus it was to the Peace Distribution Committee that the Army Council turned for guidance on accommodation questions as soon as Kitchener's initial appeal for volunteers had been published.

On 9 August 1914 the Military Members of the Army Council decided that the Peace Distribution Committee should meet at once to prepare a scheme for the quartering of the New Expeditionary Force, as the First New Army was then called. They also recommended that recruits should remain at the depots for about a week before being posted to training centres, where the barracks vacated by the units of the original BEF could be used to house the new formations.[1] Barely forty-eight hours later, a start had been made in the choice of training centres for the six divisions of the First New Army, the Army Council proposing that the Scottish and Light Infantry Divisions should be concentrated in and around Aldershot, the Irish Division at Dublin and the Curragh, and the Eastern Division at Colchester. At this point the precise destinations of the Western and Northern Divisions were left unresolved, though it was indicated that the latter would be quartered somewhere on Salisbury Plain.[2]

The Army Council realised almost immediately that it would be difficult to find accommodation in existing barracks for the whole of Kitchener's 'first hundred thousand' and that 'an alternative scheme for quartering units of the New Expeditionary Force may have to be drawn up.[3] The choice of training centres was re-examined and, on 12 August, it was decided to switch the Western Division to Salisbury Plain and to look for another site for the Northern Division, this problem being referred to the Peace Distribution Committee for further consideration. In addition, some units of the Eastern Division were to be sent to Shorncliffe in Kent and to the Rainham–Purfleet area in Essex in order to avoid overcrowding at Colchester. The troops at Rainham and Purfleet would be housed in tents pending the construction of hutments, as would the overflow from barracks at other centres.[4]

Since there was already a clear need for some extra accommodation, the Peace Distribution Committee was directed to submit plans for a standard hutted camp to house one battalion at war strength. If they proved acceptable, the plans could then serve as a model for any future construction programme. Having done a great deal of the necessary groundwork before the war, the design branch of the Directorate of Fortifications and Works, under Major B. H. O. Armstrong, produced a complete set of drawings for a typical battalion hutment within two days. Armstrong proposed that the huts to be built as sleeping quarters should each be 60 ft long by 20 ft wide, with an average height of 10 ft. Allowing for space down the centre for tables and benches, a single hut could house thirty men. Forty such huts would be provided for each battalion. The plans also catered for other essential buildings, including officers' and sergeants' messes, a recreation hut and a large central cookhouse with a dining hall for a half-battalion on either side. The huts were to be constructed on a wooden framework, with corrugated iron on the roof and external surfaces, and an asbestos lining inside. By 17 August Armstrong's designs had been approved by the Army Council. They were subsequently copied in large numbers and sent to the regional commands, followed by similar plans for the housing of artillery, engineer and Army Service Corps units, for hospitals, and for remount depots containing 1,000 horses each.[5]

In the meantime, representatives of the Peace Distribution Committee were busy investigating sites for the Western and Northern Divisions. After an area near Liverpool had been rejected, the Army Council agreed to the committee's suggestion that the Northern Division should be quartered at Belton Park, near Grantham, on land which Lord Brownlow had generously agreed to place at the disposal of the War Office.[6] The divisional artillery, however, was to remain temporarily in Leeds and Sheffield.[7] Tidworth was selected as the training centre for the Western Division despite the fact that at least one of its three infantry brigades would have to go under canvas until huts had been erected at Chiseldon near Swindon.[8] Contracts for a divisional hutment at Grantham and a brigade hutment at Chiseldon were issued as early as

23 August.

General Scott-Moncrieff doubted whether these camps could be completed before the onset of winter and felt that, in the first instance, only the central facilities, such as the messes and cookhouses, should be constructed. In his opinion the officers and men should live in tents while the larger buildings were being put up and should then move into the sleeping huts as the latter became available during the second phase of construction. He believed it would be preferable for the men to sleep under canvas and have a warm recreation room to sit in rather than run the risk of having neither huts nor recreation rooms ready in time. These ideas were opposed by the Quartermaster-General, Sir John Cowans, who was convinced that every effort should be made to complete the sleeping quarters and central facilities simultaneously.[9] In mid-August, when it was still possible to think in terms of controlled expansion of the army, the course proposed by Cowans appeared the more sensible of the two and it was his view which prevailed.

The War Office had certainly tackled the accommodation problem with commendable speed. Nonetheless, in the last week of August, as the recruiting figures continued to climb, it became obvious that the scale of the problem had been underestimated. An attempt was therefore made to streamline the machinery for the quartering of troops. On 26 August the old Directorate of Supplies and Quartering in the Quartermaster-General's Department was split into two distinct branches. Major-General C. E. Heath was appointed Director of Quartering and given a strengthened staff with an experienced engineer officer from the retired list as Assistant Director. Scott-Moncrieff was informed that responsibility for the selection of sites had now been transferred to the Department of the Quartermaster-General. As he later recounted:

I was bidden to attend a Council Meeting, and found all the four military members there under the chairmanship of the Chief of the Imperial General Staff, Sir Charles Douglas. He told me with some asperity that we were at war, and that peace procedure, including the Peace Distribution Committee, was now past, that in future all sites for hutments would be selected by the Quartermaster-General, and that I was to build where he wished. When I asked that I might have some opportunity, on engineering grounds, to co-operate in the selection. I was refused with, I think, gratuitous rudeness. I therefore bowed and left the room.[10]

Major-General Heath was not permitted the luxury of settling gradually into his post, for the creation of the Second and Third New Armies threw an immediate strain upon the resources and imagination of the Quartering Directorate. Yet, on 2 September, less than twenty-four hours after the Army Council had recorded that the formation of the Second New Army would now begin, training centres had been earmarked for its six divisions.[11] The scheme was refined over the next few days and on 11 September, when the Second New Army officially came into existence, the destinations of the 15th to 20th Divisions were confirmed. The 15th (Scottish) Division and one brigade of the 20th (Light) Division would camp in the vicinity of barracks at Aldershot, with the other two brigades of the 20th Division at Blackdown and Bordon. The 16th (Irish) Division was to go to Tipperary and Fermoy, the 17th (Northern) Division to Wool, Wareham and Lulworth in Dorset, the 18th (Eastern) Division to Shorncliffe and Purfleet, and the 19th (Western) Division to Tidworth, Bulford and Swindon.[12]

Even when the married quarters had been taken over and the allowance of space per man had been reduced from 600 to 400 cubic feet, accommodation in barracks could still only be provided for a maximum of 262,000 recruits, so more than two-thirds of the Second New Army had to be placed under canvas at the start.[13] Moreover, the total space available at the existing training centres was now running out. As a result, a whole series of previously unexploited sites had to be found for the Third New Army. Heath, working in close co-operation with Brigadier-General L. E. Kiggell, the Director of Military Training, and Brigadier-General H. G. Fitton, the Director of Organisation in the Adjutant-General's Department, began considering the possibilities on 3 September, submitting outline proposals to the Army Council a week later.[14] These were embodied in the Army Order under which the Third New Army was created on 13 September. The 21st Division was to be stationed at Halton Park, between Tring and Wendover, the 22nd Division on the South Downs at Seaford in Sussex, and the 23rd at Frensham in Surrey. Another site in Sussex, this time at Shoreham, was picked for the 24th Division. The 25th and 26th Divisions were to go into camps west of Salisbury, the former around Codford St Mary and Codford St Peter and the latter at Sherrington, Stockton and Wylye. The men of the 21st and 22nd Divisions, however, would have to be housed in billets at Tring and Lewes while their respective training areas were being prepared for occupation.[15]

The formation of the Second and Third New Armies caused the hutting programme to be revised and greatly enlarged, but again there was very little delay in issuing the necessary contracts. On 17 September H. J. Tennant, the Under-Secretary of State for War, was able to state in the House of Commons that ten large new training camps had been opened and that hutting for some 490,000 men had been ordered. He reminded the House that as the work of constructing these huts was 'of enormous magnitude' it was impossible to say when they would be ready, but thought it unlikely that all would be completed before the end of November.[16]

The programme announced by Tennant offered only a partial solution to the accommodation problem in the autumn of 1914. Quarters also had to be provided for the growing numbers of men in the Special Reserve battalions at their coast defence stations; for the reserve battalions of the first three New Armies; for the first-line Territorial units remaining at home as part of the Central Force; for the new second-line Territorial units; and for the battalions being raised by local authorities. The billeting of many Territorial units in private houses and hired buildings from August onwards eased the pressure to some extent, as did Kitchener's decision that the raisers of Pals battalions should make their own arrangements for housing their recruits during the winter months.[17] These palliative measures notwithstanding, the overall task was still huge. As the autumn wore on, the War Office was compelled to expand the hutting programme once more and to plan sufficient camps to meet the requirements of some 850,000 men.[18] The sites chosen for these additional camps included Larkhill, Perham Down and Fovant, near Salisbury; Witley Common and Bramshott, near Aldershot; Kinmel Park, in North Wales; Prees Heath and Oswestry, in Shropshire; Clipstone, in Nottinghamshire; and Ripon and Richmond, in Yorkshire.[19]

Powers for the compulsory acquisition of land and property had been conferred on the War Office by the Defence of the Realm (No. 2) Act of 28 August 1914. Before that date the Director of Military Training had informed the regional commands that the normal procedure to be followed in the case of land wanted for camps and training grounds 'will be for the Command Land Agent to obtain the required facilities by mutual agreement with the owner or occupier.[20] In fact the War Office continued to display care and tact in the acquisition of land, using the compulsory powers only in the last resort. The regional commands were told on 26 September that, when taking possession of land, they were to interfere as little as possible with 'the amenities of the civilian population' and should take every precaution 'to avoid unnecessary damage to private property or complaints of discourtesy to local inhabitants'.[21] These warnings were reinforced on 2 October, when it was emphasised that there was a danger 'not only of considerable friction with local owners and occupiers which may react unfavourably upon manoeuvring and training facilities in the future, but also of serious loss in the crops and beasts which form an important element in the national food supply at the present moment.' A detailed list of suggestions as to how to avoid damage then followed: troops were not to frighten sheep during the lambing season; fields containing herds of cattle were to be out of bounds; gates were to be closed after the passage of troops; no fires were to be lit near buildings and haystacks; golf greens were not to be crossed by mounted units; and no gaps were to be made in hedges or fences except by order of an officer.[22] Praiseworthy as these precautions were, the restrictions which they imposed on training hardly encouraged proper preparation for total war.

As it happened, the men of the first three New Armies had far more to worry about than shutting gates. If anything, the conditions they encountered at the training centres in the early weeks were worse than those which they had endured at the depots. Severe overcrowding was the main problem for the units which were housed in barracks. At Aldershot buildings intended for a single battalion now had to accommodate two. For example, Salamanca Barracks, considered full in peacetime with 800 men, housed 2,000 in September 1914. Both there and at Maida Barracks, where the 5th Cameron Highlanders shared quarters with the 8th Black Watch, beds and furniture had to be removed so that the men could be packed in side by side on the floor.[23] Somehow, space was found at Tipperary Barracks for all four battalions of the 49th Infantry Brigade.[24] Second Lieutenant I. V. B. Melhuish told his mother about conditions facing the 7th Somerset Light Infantry at Inkerman Barracks, Woking, admitting that the men were going through 'a pretty rough time'. He explained that 'there have been very few beds and a great lack of blankets, most of the men having to sleep on the floor. Also the rooms are overcrowded, a room for 22 is made to hold 60 and over.'[25]

Such men at least gained some benefits, being posted to established military centres. Those sent to the new training camps had greater cause for complaint. Seven hundred men of the 8th Royal West Kents, a battalion of the 24th Division, reached Shoreham in teeming rain on Saturday 12 September to discover that no arrangements had been made to receive them. They were marched from the station to an empty field and told to stay under some trees to keep dry. By this time every man was wet through and, as there appeared to be no one present without overall authority and little prospect of an improvement, many simply went home by train, returning the following Monday when things were rather better. For the men who remained, bell tents were eventually pitched and some damp blankets and equally wet loaves of bread were issued. No eating utensils were available for a few days, and pieces of wood were used as plates.[26] Private William Day of the 13th Middlesex Regiment was another who arrived at Shoreham about this time. 'For our first meal,' he wrote, 'they brought round a galvanised bath full of kippers. We had no plates, so we ate them off our ½*d* daily paper.'[27] At Shorncliffe men of the 6th Northamptonshire Regiment ransacked the camp dustbins to obtain empty condensed milk tins which could be used as cups, while two enterprising recruits found a chamber pot in which they were able to get rations of stew or tea for their tent-mates when the food was served out. Private F. B. Howe recalled that it was 'two weeks before we were issued with eating utensils, by which time I was able to eat anything'.[28]

The camping ground allotted to the 7th Green Howards at Wareham consisted of two fields by the side of a road. At first there were only enough tents to house half the battalion, the unlucky ones being compelled to wander into the town each night to seek shelter. The commanding officer, Lieutenant-Colonel Fife, purchased a large supply of straw from a farmer to provide bedding for the men and also procured as many knives, forks, plates and mugs as he could from the neighbouring town of Poole. In order to pay the battalion he cashed a cheque at a local bank, using up all the money in his personal account.[29] Territorials of the Liverpool Scottish, who were under canvas at Edinburgh in August and September 1914, managed to augment their meagre rations by buying bowls of porridge from women who appeared outside the walls surrounding the camp at 7 a.m. every morning.[30]

As at the depots, tempers quickly frayed under these conditions. A harrassed officer of the 10th Essex Regiment at Shorncliffe quelled an incipient strike over lack of food only by throwing off his tunic and offering to fight the hungry men one by one, beginning with the ringleader.[31] Bovington, near Wool, in Dorset, was yet another camp where arrangements for receiving the recruits left a great deal to be desired. An account by M. J. H. Drummond, who as a subaltern in the 10th Lancashire Fusiliers was stationed there in the autumn of 1914, shows how easily trouble could flare up.

One night we had a young mutiny. The men were mostly in rags, they were too many in a tent, they had very few blankets, and after two solid days of rain the mud was appalling and the tents flooded out ... They threatened to pull the officers' tents down. The RSM ... being the worse for drink, called them 'Northern Cowards' which did not improve matters. However, my company commander, Major Scott, a dear old man, appeased them and promised improvements.[32]

Private Alexander Thompson of the 9th Northumberland Fusiliers, writing from the same camp on 14 September, described how the miners in his battalion were taking the law into their own hands:

The pitmen here have been looting for all they were worth. They met a cart filled with apples. They took every apple and sold what they did not eat to others. They have also been stealing cups etc. from pubs! They cannot be blamed really because we all came unprepared for what awaited us and the pitmen have very little cash to buy food.[33]

Living under canvas presented its own special difficulties. Although the number of men allocated to each tent varied from camp to camp, overcrowding was common. When the 6th Cameron Highlanders moved out of Maida Barracks, Aldershot, into a camp at Rushmoor Bottom, the tents were so full that the men had to undress in relays. Those who returned to the tent first slipped into their places and the latecomers stood on top of them to disrobe. According to one writer. 'When we were all firmly wedged into position moving was out of the question till the next morning.'[34] George Coppard had never been under canvas before the 7th East Surreys went to Purfleet. He swiftly grasped the importance of securing a good place in a tent:

The flap was the point of entry and, with twenty-two men stampeding to get in, somebody had to get the flap division as his portion of territory. I got it. This meant that I couldn't lie down until everyone was in the tent. There were forty-four feet built up in tangled layers converging in the general direction of the centre pole. Nights were a nightmare to me and I dreaded them. Outside the tent flap within a yard of my head stood a urinal tub, and throughout the night boozy types would stagger and lunge towards the tent flap in order to urinate, I got showered every time and worst of all, it became a joke. At last revulsion overcame me, and one night I suddenly went berserk and lashed out violently at someone. There followed a riotous eruption and the tent collapsed.[35]

Many soldiers discovered that, in a tented camp, it was an unending struggle to protect one's individual possessions. Private H. F. Hooton of the 6th Northamptonshire Regiment recalled:

With fifteen or more in a tent one can imagine the conditions for sleeping. We at first had ground-sheets – later on we had floor boards. In the morning the sides of the tents were rolled up from the bottoms and personal things could be tucked inside. These personal items soon began to disappear, and although lines-men were appointed to patrol each line of tents, the thieving continued and it became impossible to leave spare articles in the tents.[36]

The majority of recruits accepted these hardships as a basic and unavoidable aspect of army life. W. R. Owen of the 13th Rifle Brigade was sent from Winchester to Halton Park, where the camp was sited on land belonging to Lord Rothschild:

We were the first to set foot in a somnolent countryside among a sparse womanhood which had so far retained its purity. We were placed in tents – fifteen to twenty men to each tent – which in the dryness of a dying summer was bearable and because it was our first experience of tent life and we were prepared to put up with anything which paved the way to make soldiers of us.[37]

Kitchener himself was not as sympathetic as he might have been concerning the problems of the recruits. As Asquith noted on 8 September 1914, 'I told him that the new recruits were badly overcrowded. He did not deny it, but smiled grimly and said the damned fools of doctors were always insisting on ridiculous allowances of cubic space . . . He added that there was an ample supply of tents, which in this weather one would think preferable to barracks.'[38] So long as the fine weather lasted, there was some truth in Kitchener's claim. To men from the big industrial centres, camp life in the late summer and early autumn of 1914 represented a marked change for the better compared with the conditions they had known at home and at work. The historian of the 11th Sherwood Foresters (Notts and Derby Regiment) observed that the countryside around Frensham in Surrey was 'an unmixed delight' to the miners in his battalion: 'Almost immediately an improvement came over the appearance of the men; the exercise in the fresh air did wonders for them in the physical sense.'[39]

Unfortunately for the men in the tented camps, the weather broke in mid-October and a period of almost incessant rain began. Under this down-pour the conditions in most camps rapidly deteriorated. Alexander Thompson wrote from Bovington on 4 November:

We have had continuous rain for over a fortnight and the last week has been far beyond a joke. Our tents will not stop the rain coming in and many nights were spent, with candles lit, in trying to stop the rain from soaking us . . . All our blankets have been quite damp for several days and the tent generally has been like a pigsty.[40]

R. W. Murphy, an officer of the 41st Field Ambulance, remembered November 1914 as 'one of the worst months'. At Tidworth, he recalled:

The parade ground was usually about a foot deep in sticky, chalky mud, while round the tents slush was knee-deep. Icy mud flowed over the floor boards, sometimes up to a height of 2 inches. Tent pegs lost their hold, with the inevitable result that each increase in mud and rain was marked by the wholesale collapse of tents. Blankets, bedding, clothes and men became plastered with mud and conditions began to have an effect on health. Numbers dwindled through sickness and parades became impossible.[41]

The bad weather also revealed that insufficient care had been taken in selecting the sites for many of the new training centres. Codford, Sherrington and Chiseldon were three of the worst in this respect. At Codford the site originally chosen for the camp of the 11th Cameronians (Scottish Rifles) was in a field bounded by a stream on three sides. Warnings from a local resident that the field was often flooded and used for skating in winter appear to have been ignored. The heavy November rains turned the camp into a quagmire.[42] Similar predictions from farmers failed to prevent the War Office from siting Sherrington Camp on gently sloping land close to the river Wylye, with equally dire results.[43] The low-lying fields in which the 4th South Wales Borderers were encamped at Chiseldon actually contained the source of a stream. When this overflowed the site was transformed into a lake, making the tents uninhabitable.[44]

The appalling state of these and other camps was soon reflected in an increase in cases of sickness among the men of the New Armies. F. T. Mullins, who was stationed at Codford as a private in the 10th Devonshire Regiment, noted that 'We country lads could stick it much better than the town boys. Scores of them fell sick and soon our numbers went down.'[45] Private G. F. Cribley, training with the 8th Gloucestershire Regiment at Tidworth, was one of many soldiers taken ill during this period: 'I myself went home with pneumonia. The doctor said I had come home just in time.'[46] Some units survived the ordeal with only minor reductions in their parade strength. In the 7th East Lancashire Regiment at Tidworth, for instance, the average number of men reporting sick each morning represented only 2 per cent of the battalion.[47] Indeed, H. J. Tennant, replying to a question in the House of Commons on 20 November, denied that the number of cases of pneumonia in the camps was abnormal.[48] Nevertheless, only three months later he was obliged to admit that, up to 31 January 1915, 1,508 cases of pneumonia had been recorded among British troops in training in the United Kingdom. Of these, 301 had died.[49]

Things might not have been so bad for the troops had the War Office been able to adhere to its hutting programme, but by mid-November serious delays had arisen at several of the key sites. The poor weather, of course, played a major part in causing such hold-ups. The mud and rain frequently prevented the contractors from doing any work at all for days on end, and country roads, churned up by vehicles bringing materials to the sites, soon became impassable. However, the delays were not wholly attributable to the weather. Unrestricted enlistment in the opening weeks of the war had already resulted in a shortage of skilled building workers. A thousand members of the Amalgamated Society of Carpenters and Joiners joined the army in August 1914 alone and by September 1915 over 4,000 had volunteered. This union had approached the War Office in the first month of the war, offering to supply enough skilled labour for hut building, provided that its working rules were observed. Although the offer was accepted, the subsequent demand for huts had become so urgent and extensive that the union was unable to supply all the men required from within its membership. Understandably the War Office then applied to the labour exchanges for help and, in consequence, all sorts of men who said they could use a hammer and chisel were drafted to hut-building. It is, in fact, doubtful whether the enlargement of the pool of labour produced any real benefits. On the contrary, the widespread employment of unskilled labourers brought about a disturbing increase in examples of poor workmanship. Furthermore, the policy also led to a worsening of relations between the War Office and the Amalgamated Society of Carpenters and Joiners at a crucial stage in the hutting programme. Before the end of November the union had presented to the National Workers' War Emergency Committee detailed evidence from various camps of the violation of its rules, of the extensive use of inferior materials and of the prevalence of scamped work.[50]

Shortages of materials, particularly of seasoned timber, also slowed down the rate of construction in the winter of 1914–15. Galvanised sheets became almost unobtainable, since practically the whole of the zinc trade of the world was under German control and with the cessation of German overseas trade the supply ceased. Unseasoned wood therefore had to be used as an alternative building material in many camps, though some unscrupulous contractors did this all along in an attempt to improve their profit margins. Kitchener himself added to the problems by insisting on economies in the hutting programme. The estimated cost of a battalion hutment, as designed by Armstrong, was £15,000, or £15 per man, and at the time the programme was submitted to the Army Council the anticipated increase in costs over the next six months was worked out at a possible £5 per man extra. This £20 was intended to cover all external and accessory services. In fact the cost eventually came to about £23 per man on the average, and it included not only water supply, drainage, roads and railways, lighting and power, but also rifle ranges and hospitals. However, Kitchener considered even the first estimate of £15 per man as too high and ordered every possible reduction. Thus a large number of camps had no central dining halls, which Kitchener regarded as 'luxuries', and the men's meals had to be conveyed, in some cases, considerable distances to the sleeping huts.[51]

To be fair to Kitchener, he gave a good deal of personal attention to the matter of accommodation and, while he was anxious to cut expenditure, he also put pressure on his subordinates to ensure that the hut-building was pushed on with all speed. For instance, early in November, he sent for Lieutenant-General W. Pitcairn Campbell, the GOC Southern Command, and told him that he was not satisfied with the progress to date. 'Unless it improves, you go,' he pointedly remarked. Pitcairn Campbell replied that the huts in his command were being built under contracts given out by the Quartermaster-General, that the civilian labourers would not come out in the wet and that there were not enough tools and mackintoshes for the workmen.

'You must do what you can,' said Kitchener. 'I give you a free hand to buy what is required.'[52]

For all these efforts, very few of the hutments constructed in the autumn of 1914 were anywhere near completion by the end of November but, because of the dreadful conditions in many of the tented camps, it was essential to move as many troops as possible into the available huts, even where they were only half finished. To the soldiers who were rehoused in this way, the defects of the new huts were all too apparent. At Sandling Camp, near Shorncliffe, men of the 6th Buffs (East Kent Regiment) had to put up tents inside the huts to keep dry.[53] The situation at Bramshott, as described by a member of the 6th Cameron Highlanders, was no better:

Very cosy and homely did these huts look – at a distance. It was only on a closer inspection that we found they were mere shells – half-inch boarding for walls, and brown paper for roofs, no cookhouses, no washing accommodation ... That first night was for most of us the coldest we had ever spent. In vain did we roll ourselves more closely in the suit lengths which did duty for blankets. There was absolutely no heating system whatever, so we just lay and waited painfully for morning ... It was weeks before the place became habitable, and when it rained the walls and roofs leaked like sieves.[54]

At the depots and during their early days at the training centres, most recruits had accepted discomfort, believing that conditions would soon get better. Now that they had been in the army for some three months they were less tolerant of poor treatment. The month of November 1914 was marked by a wave of unrest among battalions of the first three New Armies, Codford and Seaford being the training centres most seriously affected. Mass meetings were held in the 25th Divison at Codford and whole companies refused to go on parade.[55] Trouble in the 11th Cheshire Regiment was narrowly averted by an issue of extra beer.[56] The 26th Division too had its share of protests. There were demonstrations in the camp of the 7th Oxfordshire and Buckinghamshire Light Infantry, while F. T. Mullins mentions a riot in B Company of the 10th Devonshire Regiment.[57] Strikes were also recorded at Seaford, particularly in a brigade of the 22nd Division which was composed largely of Welsh miners. Here, according to Private I. P. James of the 11th Welsh Regiment, the men lived under canvas by day but had to sleep in some unfinished huts which did little to keep out the rain:

To get to and from the huts we had to walk somewhere about one and a half miles over fields which soon became a thick and sticky quagmire with the numbers of us who travelled daily through the mess. We were by now really browned off and while we expected these conditions in France we did not see why someone else's mistakes should cause us to be treated simply as a lot of numbers.

Complaints were made to the commanding officer, who listened sympathetically and instructed the quartermaster to give the men extra blankets, but, as James goes on to relate:

Our company commander seemed to think we were being spoiled and gave orders for us to fall in for a march to the huts . . . However, instead of turning to the direction of the huts, he started leading us towards the town. This was too much. We fell out on to the side of the road and the company commander immediately swung his horse around and came back to us. He then began telling us that this was mutiny, that we could be shot and that he was entitled to call on one of the other battalions to fire on us. We explained that, if he thought it the right thing, to call them. We could only die once and had been prepared to do so in France but still did not see why he should issue such orders whilst the Colonel had sympathy for our case. The result of this adventure was that we returned to camp and after another night in the huts were told by our CO next day that billets were being prepared for us in Hastings.[58]

The protest in the Welsh Regiment appears to have been confined to the company in which James was serving. Oswald Sturdy, a sergeant in the same battalion, has described how the battalion as a whole rejected an appeal from a neighbouring battalion of the South Wales Borderers to join them in a strike:

We said no. We had joined the army to rough it and must put up with it. Their reply was 'There's plenty of time to rough it when you get overseas. No need to rough it in England. Other troops are in billets – we ought to be in billets.' We still refused so they called us a lot of chocolate soldiers. But the strike was effective. Two days later we entrained for Hastings.[59]

This evidence of a strike at Seaford is supported by Sir Charles Woolley, who joined the 8th South Wales Borderers as a subaltern in December 1914. He recalled that, after taking strike action, the men of his battalion were granted a fortnight's leave on full pay, 'on the expiry of which they returned to a man and there was no more trouble of any kind'.[60]

II

By the beginning of December the wet weather and the rising level of discontent in the training camps had forced the War Office to seek an alternative short-term solution to the accommodation problem. Many Territorial units and Special Reserve battalions had been billeted in private houses and other buildings since August and it was now decided to extend this policy to include the bulk of the New Armies. As a result, some 800,000 troops were billeted on the civilian population during the winter of 1914–15. The nation therefore came face to face with its army on an unprecedented scale.

Having considered the best methods of selecting suitable billets, Sir John Cowans, the Quartermaster-General, recognised that this task would have to be carried out at a local level. In each of the home commands he set up an Area Quartering Committee under a Permanent President to supervise and co-ordinate all arrangements for housing troops other than in barracks or hutments. These committees were in turn subdivided into smaller bodies so that billeting in every district could be controlled and preparations made for quartering troops in any given area. The Permanent Presidents, who had War Office valuers attached to them, were responsible for the assessment of rent and damage and for the periodic inspection of the premises involved.[61]

The billets occupied by troops varied according to local conditions and circumstances. Billeting was an expensive process and, with the need to save public money firmly in mind, the Permanent Presidents saw to it that, wherever possible, public buildings or empty houses were used. Thus when the 10th Black Watch moved from Codford to Bristol, two companies were quartered in the Colston Hall, another at the Victoria Gallery and the fourth at a large skating rink.[62] Most soldiers, however, had to be billeted in occupied private dwellings.

Once an area had been allocated to a particular unit, a small party would be sent on ahead to find billets for the main body. This was usually done by knocking on the door of each house and asking the occupants how many soldiers they were prepared to take in, if any. Depending on the reply, the number of men to be accommodated in that house would then be marked in chalk on the wall or door. This could be an exhausting business for the billeting parties. Arthur MacGregor, now a sergeant in the 2nd London Scottish, wrote from Watford in 1915:

It ain't quite a picnic. I was given a list of about 250 billets – and today I visited 100 of them. Just think of that. 100 frowsy women in the slummiest part of Watford – 100 stairs to climb, steep and dark – 100 times to say the same thing and answer the same questions. By gum, I *was* fed up by the time 6 o'clock came round.[63]

The reception given to billeting parties was not always friendly. Rifleman Norman Ellison of the 1/6th King's (Liverpool) Regiment commented, 'Patriotism undergoes an acid test when there comes a knock at your door and, without warning, you are asked to provide a billet for the strange soldiers.'[64] Lieutenant C. D. Jay of the 7th Royal Sussex Regiment remembered how a brother officer informed the landlady of a boarding house in Folkestone that he was going to billet men in her establishment. In Jay's words, 'She looked at him scornfully, snapped, "Young man, you will do nothing of the sort!" and banged the door in his face.'[65] Such reactions demonstrated that traditional attitudes towards the 'brutal and licentious soldiery' had not yet totally disappeared. On their arrival in Epsom, David Kelly and a fellow recruit of the University and Public Schools' Brigade experienced at first hand what Kelly described as 'the complete aloofness mingled with fear which the old middle class felt for our professional army':

I was told off with a Vickers engineer to a billet in a small street, where the landlady with folded arms greeted us with 'Go away – I don't want you!' Being hungry and disgruntled we forced our way in, and installed ourselves in the kitchen, where the hostess reluctantly produced bread and onions. My companion and I, ignoring her, talked together for five minutes, when the lady, who had been regarding us with suspicion and hostility changing to bewilderment, suddenly broke in with 'Are you volunteers?' We agreed. 'Oh' (with intense relief), 'I thought you were common soldiers!'[66]

Ellison discovered that even those who had once served in the army did not fully understand that its social composition had now significantly changed. In Whitstable a retired army surgeon told a billeting officer that he would be pleased to have soldiers in his house, 'provided they are clean men who will not spit upon the wallpaper'. As Ellison noted, 'The war was still young and the idea of educated civilian soldiers unknown to him.'[67]

Some communities displayed considerable anxiety about the possible effects of having soldiers billeted on them. Private John Tucker of the 2/13th London Regiment wrote that, at Saffron Walden, the inhabitants 'were mostly Quakers, who kept their daughters out of sight. We hardly saw a young girl all the time we were there.'[68] When the Leeds Bantams (17th West Yorkshire Regiment) moved into billets a few miles away at Ilkley in February 1915, Lance-Corporal Earnest Sheard observed, with some amusement, that 'the Ilkley people, especially the mothers, had formed a League, its object being to keep the girls away from the soldiers'.[69]

Distrust of soldiers was not the only prejudice which the billeting system brought to the surface. The men of Scottish battalions were viewed with particular suspicion by the inhabitants of places like Basingstoke, where the 6th Cameron Highlanders were billeted, or Bedford, where the Territorials of the 51st (Highland) Division were stationed. Alex Runcie, then a private in the 1/6th Gordon Highlanders, wrote of his battalion's stay in Bedford:

When we got to know the folks well, they told us they were a bit alarmed when they heard that a kilted army was to be quartered on them. They had visions of all kinds of savages armed with claymores descending on them. One girl of my acquaintance, who worked as a manageress in a laundry, told me her boss had called together all the employees, and painted a truly bloodthirsty picture of us, and a warning not to mix with us. We hadn't been there long before they realised we were quiet law-abiding people like themselves. One girl asked me if I didn't feel the cold at night, on the hills with only my plaid to cover me while sleeping. Another, knowing the house we were quartered in, remarked that the bath in it would be a great surprise for us never having seen one before. As the said bath had no water laid on and was upstairs, so that hot water had to be carried from the basement to the bath, this was quite a laugh.[70]

Money helped to overcome prejudices, an allowance of up to 3s 4½d per day per man being paid to householders by the army. This included a basic sum of 9d a night for lodging, 7½d for breakfast, 1s 7½d for dinner and 4½d for supper. The rate for officers was set at 3s per night, although they were required to pay separately for their own food.[71] In some cases only a room and bed were required, with the troops being fed on army rations in centralised messes, while in others the landlady was expected to feed the men out of the billeting allowance. A third method was to distribute army rations to the billets, leaving the landlady to do the best she could with them. Ellison had painted a vivid picture of the difficulties which this presented:

Any fine day, the same scene was enacted in a dozen streets; a handcart laden with rations and on the pavement a worried corporal and two men subdividing the meat, the butter, the bread, and even the pepper and salt, into a number of small heaps, each for a particular house. To apportion one tin of jam between five men living in three houses was a puzzle usually solved by the spinning of a coin.[72]

Geoffry Christie-Miller, who was a captain in the 2/1st Buckinghamshire Battalion at this time, called such methods 'tedious and wasteful', believing that it was beneath the dignity of soldiers to go round working-class streets for a whole afternoon dispensing slices of bacon and slabs of meat. He considered that the more general system of billeting with subsistence was preferable, but conceded that, if rations were pooled in a house, all could benefit: 'Army rations, when administered by a working class housewife, contained more bread and meat than was required by the men alone. In exchange for bread and meat, "Ma" did a lot for them in the way of extras – pies and puddings, apple tarts and cakes etc.'[73]

There was no lack of people willing to take advantage of the billeting system. The 3rd (Special Reserve) Battalion of the East Lancashire Regiment encountered initial hostility from the inhabitants of Plymouth, although as soon as details of the billeting allowance became known 'there was no more grumbling'.[74] Stanley Casson, an officer in this battalion, recorded that some houses took in as many as ten men, the soldiers often having to sleep on the floor:

For these slight services the official recompense to the landladies for each man was 24s. a week! What they [the soldiers] got was worth about five shillings, so the eagerness and patriotic fervour of the citizens of Plymouth knew no bounds ... Imagine the wealth they must have pocketed! We were besieged by prospective landladies who begged us to let them take the 'dear boys' in and cherish them. Cherishing was a popular entertainment in those days.[75]

Private W. J. Wood of the 1/5th Gloucestershire Regiment was billeted on a landlady 'of the shark type' at Chelmsford. 'Every weekend we were "bled" for extras, imaginary and otherwise,' he complained.[76] At Dunmow in Essex, where men of the 1/5th Sherwood Foresters were quartered, one woman admitted that the billeting allowance would be used for her daughter's dowry.[77] The soldiers who were unfortunate enough to meet with unfriendly or unscrupulous householders did not hesitate to express their feelings. Second Lieutenant P. H. Pilditch of the 7th London Brigade, Royal Field Artillery, was highly critical of the people of Boxmoor in Hertfordshire, noting in his diary that not many had been prepared to welcome his men: 'It made me absolutely wild. I wished a few of them could experience the hardships of an invasion, and go through what these poor fellows will have, before long, to go through for them.'[78] Alexander Thompson wrote of his 'hosts' at Wimborne in Dorset, 'This species of animal rather makes one feel as though one wished one hadn't joined the army, for all they are fit for is to be shot. They are of no use to the nation as far as I can see. Dirty, lazy and caring for no one but themselves.'[79] A novel form of direct action was taken by a woman in Canterbury to get rid of Normal Ellison and one of his comrades: 'She did not want anybody billeted on her and we were not welcome. A series of incidents brought matters to a head, when we found the bolts of our rifles full of jam. She said her child had done it. We wondered, but were moved to another house.'[80]

Criticism was not the prerogative of the soldiers alone, for the behaviour of a minority of recruits appeared to justify the worst fears of the civilian population. Pilditch wrote in February 1915 that men of his unit had been stealing coal from a house: 'It's this sort of thing that makes it so hard to answer those people who won't put themselves out to billet men and horses.'[81] The chance to indulge in petty theft was not the only temptation to which soldiers succumbed. The billeting system threw together large numbers of men and women under circumstances which greatly increased the opportunities for sexual adventure. Men living away from home, many for the first time in their lives, felt themselves liberated from at least some of the social and moral conventions imposed by their family, neighbourhood and class. At the same time, women whose own husbands and fathers had left home to join the army could not always resist the charms of the young soldiers billeted on them. Charles Cain confessed that he learned much about 'the wine, women and song bit' when the 2/5th Manchester Regiment was billeted at Southport in the winter of 1914–15:

The men I was with were rough with women, boasted of their conquests, many of whom were actually raped, but there were no prosecutions to my knowledge. Suffice it to say that ten soldiers were billeted on one woman who had three teenage daughters, and the mother and all the daughters finished up in the family way.[82]

Cases of this sort were plentiful enough to provoke widespread discussion in the press. In April 1915 Ronald McNeill, Conservative MP for the St Augustine Division of Kent, wrote to the *Morning Post* claiming that, in districts where many troops had been quartered, 'a great number of girls' were about to become unmarried mothers.[83] The fact that the illegitimate birth rate in 1915 was exceptionally low suggests that McNeill was exaggerating the true situation.[84] Women were constrained by more than the risk of incurring social opprobrium. The wives of soldiers, for example, faced the possibility that all allowances and pensions would be withdrawn as a result of any 'gross misconduct' on their part.[85] Soldier husbands too were quick to warn their womenfolk of the dangers which billeting presented. Private Gilbert Nash of the 1/1st Buckinghamshire Battalion, writing from his own billet in Chelmsford, told his wife not to accept any men at their home in High Wycombe:

You have not got anywhere for them to sleep and they want a good place for that money. I know that it would come in handy for you but I don't think that you could do it with your handful you have got at home and I myself think that it would be best if you did not have any, for you never know what you are going to get . . . It is all chance work for there is a lot of rough ones about just now, so if you can do without I would sooner you did not have any.[86]

That not all sexual adventures ended in conquest is shown in the account by

Charles Cain. He tells of a muscular ex-miner in his billet who was in the habit of walking around the house stark naked. 'He called this advertising, but as far as I know it had the opposite effect to what he wanted, for she [the landlady] locked herself and her family in the kitchen, and her complaints landed Charlie in the guard room.'[87] Nonetheless, the illegitimate birth rate did rise in 1916, one reason being, as the Registrar-General remarked, 'the freedom from home restraints of large numbers of young persons of both sexes'.[88]

Drunkenness was perhaps the most common cause of complaint. Perry Webb relates that, before he left to enlist, eleven men of the 12th Manchester Regiment were billeted at his home in Ferndown, Dorset. Webb remembered them as 'rather a beery lot' who could be extremely unpleasant. 'I had a sister there, you see, and she used to bring in the coffee and that at night for them and if they were partly drunk they'd throw a cup of coffee at her … My mother didn't think a great deal of it because of the destruction that they caused.'[89] Trouble could also start if units from different parts of the country were quartered in the same town. Richard Patston wrote that when his battalion, the 1st City of London Rifles, moved to the Braintree area they found the 1/5th Sherwood Foresters had already occupied the best billets: 'We had street fights with them and went about with entrenching-tool handles tucked down our trousers. We always went in pairs, but luckily I never got hurt.'[90]

Quite apart from causing social problems, billeting also hindered training, for it took time to assemble the men each morning before marching them off to a suitable open space for drill or field exercises, and the day would also be cut short so that they could get back to their billets for the evening meal. Moreover, with men scattered through a town, it became correspondingly difficult to establish any real *esprit de corps* above platoon or company level. However, there were some advantages. Since companies were often billeted by themselves in adjoining streets, company and platoon officers had a chance to supervise and take a personal interest in the welfare of their men to a degree which was not always possible in barracks or hutted camps. This fostered a spirit of camaraderie between platoon commanders and their men which was to prove immensely valuable on active service.

It must be added that many soldiers later looked back on their stay in billets as the happiest part of their military service, a period when they were at least able to enjoy the relative luxury of a soft bed and regular home-cooked meals. The 15th Royal Welsh Fusiliers, for instance, were billeted in hotels and boarding houses at Llandudno in the winter of 1914–15. 'The troops were received almost as holiday visitors,' recalled Private W. A. Tucker. 'They occupied ordinary bedrooms and were catered for by the hotel waitresses and general staff.'[91] Private Arthur Winstanley of the 2/5th Manchesters had similarly fond memories of his hosts at Colchester: 'This family did all in their power to make us happy and comfortable … We lads never went out at night; after a day's work under the NCOs and officers of various types, we thought of nothing, only getting into a light pair of slippers, and gathering together with the family in the drawing room.'[92]

III

The majority of the Pals battalions were spared the worst of the conditions suffered by units of the first three New Armies, since they were either billeted at home or housed in buildings and tented camps in or near their place of origin while their own hutments were being made ready. During this period they trained on any open spaces or in any large halls which were available. The Sheffield City Battalion, for instance, began squad drill at Sheffield United's football ground at Bramall Lane and received its first instruction in extended order drill and attack among the trees of Norfolk Park.[93] The Bradford Pals established their headquarters at a skating rink, drilling in nearby Manningham Park.[94] In Newcastle the 16th Northumberland Fusiliers (Newcastle Commercials) trained in the spacious grounds of the Royal Grammar School, while in the Hull the three battalions raised by Lord Nunburnholme in September used the Hull Fairground, West Park, the Anlaby Road cricket ground and the playing fields belonging to Hull Grammar School.[95]

Other Pals units moved into camps and improvised barracks almost at once. By the end of September the whole of the North Eastern Railway Battalion (17th Northumberland Fusiliers) had taken up residence in two large warehouses owned by the NER at the recently opened King George Dock in Hull. The conversion of the warehouses into barracks was supervised by the company's Deputy Architect and Clerk of Works, and the accommodation included two massive dormitories and a recreation room which alone measured 200 ft by 70 ft. Some recruits, however, complained that the warehouses were very draughty, or found it a trying experience sharing a dormitory with 500 men.[96]

The 1st Liverpool City Battalion was housed in a watch factory at Prescot and the 2nd City Battalion at Hooton Park racecourse. The 3rd Liverpool Pals trained in Sefton Park until they moved into a hutted camp on Lord Derby's estate at Knowsley Park, where they were later joined by the 2nd City Battalion.[97] Both the 1st and 2nd Manchester City Battalions went to Heaton Park before the end of September, living under canvas until their huts were completed. At first the 3rd City Battalion was stationed at the White City, Manchester. Parades were held daily in the City Hall, varied by marches to Alexandra Park, the battalion transferring to Heaton Park in February 1915. The 4th Manchester Pals carried out their preliminary training at the City Exhibition Hall and then shifted to Belle Vue Gardens, using the animal houses of the local zoo for drill in wet weather before occupying huts at Heaton Park on 30 November. There were, of course, some drawbacks in having units quartered close to their home city, for men were frequently tempted to overstay their weekend leave. Another distraction during training was the constant presence of onlookers, many of them friends and relatives of the recruits. As an officer of the 4th Manchester Pals wrote, 'Their criticisms, which were sometimes overheard, were kindly meant but hard to bear.'[98]

On the whole, the hutted camps built for Pals battalions were finished much earlier, and were of a considerably higher standard, than those provided for the first three New Armies under direct War Office contracts. This was largely because the raisers of Pals units could make extensive use of local government machinery to expedite matters. Unlike the War Office, they knew local conditions and contractors well and could more easily regulate the progress of the work. The superior quality of some of the camps constructed for locally raised units is indicated by the following description of the hutments at Farnley Hall, near Otley, which were ready for the Miners' Battalion (12th King's Own Yorkshire Light Infantry) by the beginning of November 1914:

Each hut housed 30 men . . . They were raised from the ground on concrete piles, had a double thickness in walls and floors, were covered . . . with stout felting, and were absolutely weatherproof . . . Other buildings in the camp included a cookhouse fitted with the best-known pattern cooking range and boiler for 1,000 men, a library, recreation room, gymnasium, store rooms, canteens, regimental offices and guard rooms, and a well-appointed rifle range. The camp was lit with electricity transmitted through overhead wires, and water was laid on from the Farnley Hall mains. For training purposes the camp was most excellently situated, for we had on the one side arable land and undulating pasture, and on the other the hilly country and the moors . . . Another advantage was the absence of any very large town close at hand, so that the counter-attractions to military discipline were not too powerful.[99]

Considering that the local raisers were allowed a great deal of latitude in the field of camp construction, there were astonishingly few cases of corruption. Nevertheless, some did exploit the loopholes in the system. In 1915 a court of enquiry set up by the Army Council concluded that two of the original members of the raising committee of the Empire Battalion (17th Royal Fusiliers) were guilty of misconduct in persuading their colleagues on the committee to issue the hutting contract for the battalion's camp at Warlingham to a firm which these two men had established only a short time before. The fact that they had resigned forty-eight hours prior to receiving the contract 'did not, in the Court's opinion, affect the unfair advantage which they had enjoyed.'[100]

In spite of all the delays caused by bad weather, labour disputes and shortages of building materials, most New Army units were able to move out of billets into huts in the spring of 1915, although the soldiers were often called upon to help complete the construction of their own quarters. By the autumn there were sufficient huts for 850,000 men, and several of the camps had assumed immense proportions. One of the biggest complexes was at Catterick in Yorkshire, conceived by Kitchener as a future 'Aldershot of the

North'. Here the two camps at Hipswell and Scotton could together hold 40,000 men, or the equivalent of two divisions, the huts being built of light steel and concrete instead of the usual timber and corrugated iron.[101] Inevitably, the growth of such camps transformed the appearance of the countryside and had far-reaching social effects. The Rev. L. L. Jeeves, chaplain to the 55th Infantry Brigade in the 18th Division, commented upon the scene at Codford in the summer of 1915:

The two villages, Codford St Mary and St Peter, which joined together could scarcely muster 700 souls, find themselves changed at last . . . The old sleepy village is half filled with horrid booths and shanties, where tobacco, hosiery, and a thousand odds and ends can be bought at an increased cost, for the owner of the property has asked £1 a week in rent for a glorified cupboard which now constitutes a shop. A cottage lets its front parlour to a bank, and the wax fruit with the Family Bible have gone, and money bags replace the old institutions . . .[102]

The accommodation problem became much less severe in the latter half of 1915, as, by that time, many of the earliest New Army units had gone overseas, enabling the War Office to move the later formations into the camps and training centres they had vacated. Even so, the housing of the New Armies remains as one of the great unrecognised achievements of the First World War. Within two years, at a cost of approximately £24,500,000, accommodation had been provided for a military community which was larger in size than the civilian population of Bristol, Cardiff and Newcastle combined.[103]

Notes

1   Minutes of meeting of the Military Members of the Army Council, 9 August 1914, WO 163/44.
2   Minutes of Proceedings of the Army Council, 1914, 11 August 1914, WO 163/21.
3   Minutes of meeting of the Military Members of the Army Council, 10 August 1914, WO 163/44.
4   *Ibid.*, 12 August 1914, WO 163/44.
5   Major-General H. L. Pritchard (ed.), *History of the Corps of Royal Engineers*, Vol. V, Institution of Royal Engineers, Chatham, 1952, pp. 69–70; Major D. Chapman-Huston and Major Owen Rutter, *General Sir John Cowans: the Quartermaster General of the Great War*, II, p. 21.
6   Minutes of meeting of the Military Members of the Army Council, 17 August 1914, WO 163/44.
7   *Ibid.*, 18 August 1914, WO 163/44
8   *Ibid.*, 20 August 1914, WO 163/44.
9   Chapman-Huston and Rutter, *op. cit.*, p. 21.
10 Account by Major-General Sir George Scott-Moncrieff, quoted in Chapman-Huston and Rutter, *op. cit.*, p. 22.
11 Minutes of meeting of the Military Members of the Army Council, 1 September 1914, WO 163/44; Circular from Adjutant-General's Department to GOCs-in-C of Commands, 2 September 1914, WO 32/11341.
12 Army Order XII of 11 September 1914 (AO 382 of 1914).
13 General Sir John Cowans, *Supply Services during the war, Part 1, Quartering,*

published in *Statistics of the Military Effort of the British Empire*, p. 833.

14 Minutes of meetings of the Military Members of the Army Council, 3 and 10 September 1914, WO 163/44.

15 Army Order XVIII of 13 September 1914 (AO 388 of 1914), Appendix B.

16 *Parliamentary Debates, House of Commons 1914*, LXVI, col. 983.

17 Minutes of meetings of the Military Members of the Army Council, 12 September 1914, WO 163/44.

18 Cowans, op. cit., p. 834.

19 Chapman-Huston and Rutter, *op. cit*, pp. 28–9

20 Directorate of Military Training to GOCs-in-C of Commands, 25 August 1914, WO 162/3.

21 Directorate of Fortifications and Works to GOCs-in-C of Commands, 26 September 1914, WO 162/3.

22 Directorate of Military Training to GOCs-in-C of Commands, 2 October 1914, WO 162/3.

23 *Historical Records of the Queen's Own Cameron Highlanders*, Vol. IV, p. 274; Lieutenant-Colonel Norman MacLeod, *War History of the 6th (Service) Battalion Queen's Own Cameron Highlanders*, p. 2.

24 G. A. Cooper-Walker, *The Book of the Seventh Service Battalion the Royal Inniskilling Fusiliers: from Tipperary to Ypres*, p. 3.

25 I. V. B. Melhuish to his mother, 4 October 1914, IWM PP/MCR/69.

26 Lieutenant-Colonel H. J. Wenyon and Major H. S. Brown (eds.), *The History of the Eighth Battalion the Queen's Own Royal West Kent Regiment*, Hazell Watson & Viney, London, 1921, p. 2.

27 William Day, letter of 10 July 1963, IWM BBC/GW.

28 F. B. Howe, quoted in Peter Jackson, *The Glorious Sixth: a day to day history recording the movements of the 6th Battalion Northamptonshire Regiment in the Great War*, privately printed, 1975, p. 3.

29 Lieutenant-Colonel Ronald Fife, *Mosaic of Memories*, Heath Cranton, London, 1943, pp. 61–2.

30 Lionel I. L. Ferguson, *War Diary, 1914–1919*, IWM 77/166/1.; G. Eric Rutherford, letter of 8 July 1963, IWM BBC/GW.

31 Lieutenant-Colonel T. M. Banks and Captain R. A. Chell, *With the 10th Essex in France*, pp. 13–14.

32 M. J. H. Drummond, unpublished account, *c.* 1963, IWM DS/MISC/29.

33 Alexander Thompson to his mother, 14 September 1914, IWM 79/55/1.

34 MacLeod, *op. cit.*, p. 3.

35 George Coppard, *With a Machine Gun to Cambrai*, p. 3.

36 H. F. Hooton, *Salient Extracts from my Daily Diary*, unpublished account, 1971, PP/MCR/50.

37 W. R. Owen, letter of 16 July 1963, IWM BBC/GW.

38 Asquith, *Memories and Reflections*, II, p. 32.

39 Percy Fryer, *The Men from the Greenwood: the War History of the 11th (Service) Battalion, Sherwood Foresters*, Cresswell & Oaksford, Nottingham, 1920, p. 13.

40 Alexander Thompson to his mother, 4 November 1914, IWM 79/55/1.

41 R. W. Murphy, *Some Experiences of a Field Ambulance*, unpublished account, *c.* 1916–18, IWM 78/57/1.

42 Colonel H. H. Story, *History of the Cameronians (Scottish Rifles) 1910–1933*, Hazell Watson & Viney, Aylesbury, 1961, p. 241.

43 Lieutenant-Colonel C. Wheeler, (ed.), *Memorial Record of the Seventh (Service) Battalion, the Oxfordshire and Buckinghamshire Light Infantry*, Blackwell, Oxford, 1921, p. 3.

44   C. T. Atkinson, *The History of the South Wales Borderers, 1914–1918*, p. 61.
45   F. T. Mullins, *What it was like to Serve, 1914–1918*, unpublished account, 1973, IWM P. 101.
46   G. F. Cribley, letter to Malcolm Brown, 16 March 1976.
47   Major-General Sir C. Lothian Nicholson and Major H. T. MacMullen, *History of the East Lancashire Regiment in the Great War*, p. 358.
48   *Parliamentary Debates, House of Commons, 1914–15*, LXVIII, col. 555.
49   *Parliamentary Debates, House of Commons, 1914–15*, LXIX, cols. 901–2.
50   S. Higenbottam, *Our Society's History*, Amalgamated Society of Woodworkers, Manchester, 1939, pp. 191–2.
51   Major-General Sir George Scott-Moncrieff, 'The hutting problem in the war', *Royal Engineers Journal*, XXXVIII, 1924, p. 368.
52   General Sir W. Pitcairn Campbell, quoted in Chapman-Huston and Rutter, *op. cit.*, p. 29.
53   Colonel R. S. H. Moody, *Historical Records of the Buffs (East Kent Regiment), 1914–1919*, Medici Society, London, 1922, p. 70.
54   'W.D.R.' (ed.), *Souvenir Booklet of the Sixth Cameron Highlanders*, Glasgow Herald, 1916, p. 14.
55   Major W. de B. Wood (ed.), *The History of the King's Shropshire Light Infantry in the Great War*, pp. 207–8.
56   Arthur Crookenden, *The History of the Cheshire Regiment in the Great War*, p. 345.
57   Wheeler (ed.), *op. cit.*, p. 5; F. T. Mullins, *op. cit.*, IWM P. 101.
58   I. P. James, undated latter, *c.* July 1963, IWM BBC/GW.
59   Oswald Sturdy, undated letter, *c.* July 1963, IWM BBC/GW.
60   Sir Charles Woolley, letter to the author, 17 November 1978.
61   Cowans, *op. cit.*, pp. 833–4.
62   Major-General A. G. Wauchope (ed.), *A History of the Black Watch (Royal Highlanders) in the Great War*, III, p. 205.
63   Arthur MacGregor to Dulcie Newling, 17 March 1915, IWM CON/AEM.
64   Norman Ellison, *War Diary, 1914–1919*, IWM DS/MISC/49.
65   Account by Lieutenant C. D. Jay, quoted in Major Owen Rutter (ed.), *The History of the Seventh (Service) Battalion, the Royal Sussex Regiment*, p. 8.
66   Sir David Kelly, *The Ruling Few*, Hollis & Carter, London, 1952, p. 89.
67   Ellison, *op. cit.*, IWM DS/MISC/49.
68   John F. Tucker, *Johnny get your gun: a personal narrative of the Somme, Ypres and Arras*, Kimber, London, 1978, p. 17.
69   Ernest Sheard, *My Great Adventure: the Great War, 1914–1918*, unpublished account, n.d., IWM PP/MCR/133.
70   Alex Runcie, *Territorial Mob*, unpublished account, *c.* 1960, IWM P. 185.
71   Army Order 289 of 4 August 1914; Army Order VII of 23 April 1915 (AO 164 of 1915).
72   Ellison, *op. cit.*, IWM DS/MISC/49.
73   Colonel Sir Geoffry Christie-Miller, *Memoirs*, unpublished account, 1919, IWM 80/32/1.
74   Nicholson and MacMullen, *op. cit.*, p. 198.
75   Stanley Casson, *Steady Drummer*, p. 36.
76   W. J. Wood, 'With the 5th Gloucesters at Home and Overseas', *The Back Badge*, journal of the Gloucestershire Regiment, 1936, p. 105.
77   L. W. de Grave, *The War History of the Fifth Battalion the Sherwood Foresters: Notts and Derby Regiment, 1914–1918*, Bemrose, Derby, 1930, p. 6.
78   P. H. Pilditch, *The War Diary of an Artillery Officer, 1914–1919*, entry for 14 December 1914, IWM CON/PHP.

79 Alexander Thompson to his mother, 15 April, IWM 79/55/1.
80 Ellison, *op. cit.*, IWM DS/MISC/49.
81 P. H. Pilditch, *War Diary*, entry of 6 February 1915, IWM CON/PHP.
82 Charles Cain, *The Footsloggers*, IWM PP/MCR/48.
83 *Morning Post*, 17 April 1915; *Daily Mail*, 17 April 1915; *Observer*, 18 and 25 April 1915; *Sunday Pictorial*, 18 April 1915.
84 *Annual Report of the Registrar-General for 1915*, Parliamentary Papers, 1917–18, V, Cd 8484, p. vii.
85 *Parliamentary Debates, House of Commons, 1914–15*, LXX, col. 268.
86 Gilbert Nash to his wife, 12 October 1914, IWM P. 329.
87 Cain, *op. cit.*, IWM PP/MCR/48.
88 *Annual Report of the Registrar-General for 1916*, PP, 1917–18, VI, Cd 8869, p. xix.
89 Interview with Perry Webb, IWM Department of Sound Records, 000578/08.
90 R. S. Patston, unpublished account, 1977, IWM 78/4/1.
91 W. A. Tucker, *The Lousier War*, New English Library, London, 1974, p. 13.
92 Arthur Winstanley, *My Recollections of the War*, unpublished account, 1928, IWM P. 157.
93 Richard A. Sparling, *History of the 12th (Service) Battalion, York and Lancaster Regiment*, pp. 4–5.
94 R. N. Hudson, *The Bradford Pals*, p. 8.
95 Captain C. H. Cooke, *Historical Records of the 16th (Service) Battalion, Northumberland Fusiliers*, p. 4; Peter N. Farrar, 'Hull's New Army 1914', *Journal of Local Studies*, spring 1971, Vol. I, No. 2, p. 35.
96 Lieutenant-Colonel J. Shakespear, *A Record of the 17th and 32nd (Service) Battalions, Northumberland Fusiliers (NER) Pioneers*, pp. 3–4.
97 Brigadier-General F. C. Stanley, *The History of the 89th Brigade 1914–1918*, pp. 23–5.
98 Lieutenant-Colonel H. L. James (Ed.), *Sixteenth, Seventeenth, Eighteenth, Nineteenth Battalions, the Manchester Regiment*, pp. 5, 107, 185, 281–4.
99 Captain R. Ede England, *A Brief History of the 12th Bn. King's Own Yorkshire Light Infantry (Pioneers): the Miners' Battalion*, p. 22.
100 *Report of the Military Court of Enquiry, constituted by the Army Council for the purpose of investigating certain matters connected with the British Empire Committee*, 1914–16, XXXIX, Cd 7681, p. 7.
101 Lieutenant-Colonel Howard N. Cole, *The Story of Catterick Camp, 1915–1972*, Forces Press, Aldershot, 1972, pp. 13–15.
102 The Rev. L. L. Jeeves, 'East and West', article in the parish magazine of St Mary's, Whitechapel, June 1915.
103 *Return showing the approximate cost of the Hutting provided for the accommodation of Troops and Horses in the United Kingdom in the years 1914 to 1916*, PP, 1916, XVII, Cd 8193, pp. 1–2.

10

Uniforms and equipment

I

In addition to food and accommodation, recruits also had to be provided with clothing and personal equipment. Because of the manner in which the army was expanded, responsibility for the procurement and supply of these items was divided three ways during the first ten months of the war. The Quartermaster-General's Department automatically shouldered the burden of clothing and equipping those units of the New Armies which were raised through the normal recruiting channels and which came under the direct control of the War Office from the start. The need of the Pals battalions and other local formations were met by their respective municipal authorities and raising committees until the War Office was ready to take over their administration. In the case of the Territorial Force it had been envisaged that, after embodiment, the County Associations would confine themselves to clothing the men who were recruited either to bring units up to war establishment or to replace casualties and wastage. When such recruits were completely clothed and equipped, all future renewals of their uniforms and accoutrements were to be handled by the Army Ordnance Department and the duties of the Associations in this respect would cease until demobilisation. However, the extra strain on resources imposed by the creation of the New Armies made this plan impracticable and the Army Council had to ask the County Associations not only to continue clothing and equipping Territorial recruits on enlistment but also to deal with all renewals for the units under their charge.[1] This system of divided responsibility had the unfortunate effect of placing many different purchasing bodies in the field, all trying to secure the same articles, but, on the other hand, competition helped to extend the possibilities and sources of supply.

As far as clothing was concerned, each recruit required not only two khaki service dress jackets, and two pairs of service dress trousers, so that he could change his uniform when it became damp or dirty, but also a cap, a greatcoat, boots, puttees, shirts, socks and underclothes – in short, everything he wore. In August 1914 the reserves of clothing served for little more than the fitting-out and upkeep for a few weeks of the original Expeditionary Force and the first-line units of the Territorial Force, and were quite inadequate even for the First New Army, quite apart from the many other formations which were created in the following months. In peacetime the manufacture of uniforms had been confined to a small number of firms, the overall needs of the army being insufficient to attract a wide range of suppliers. Some twenty-five firms in Northamptonshire produced the 245,000 pairs of boots required annually for the peace-time establishment. Thus large-scale expansion could not be achieved at once. Before new firms could begin production, the materials themselves had first to be acquired in large quantities. 'Trivial as this item may appear,' wrote Cowans, 'it is an example of the difficulties obtaining that the trade was wholly unable to meet the sudden call for buttons.'[2]

To achieve the new targets, the leading clothing manufacturers, under War Office contracts, farmed out work to a host of smaller firms throughout the country. The task of mobilising the resources of the boot and shoe industry and of inducing fresh manufacturers to turn out boots of the regulation pattern was also entrusted to civilian experts. These methods eventually achieved the desired results but months passed before the New Armies reaped the full benefits of the vastly increased output. In the meantime the War Office was obliged to resort to various expedients in order to clothe the men who volunteered in the opening weeks. Five hundred thousand suits of blue serge uniform were obtained, partly from Post Office stocks, and between 400,000 and 500,000 greatcoats of civilian patterns were purchased, ready-made, from the clothing trade. Moreover, 1,300,000 jackets and pairs of trousers and 900,000 greatcoats were ordered from Canada and the United States. Although Cowans expressed the view that 'nothing out of the way should be permitted', Kitchener himself was not too concerned about the unorthodox nature of these temporary outfits, deciding that, so long as the men of individual units were clothed alike, it was not essential to stick to standard patterns.[3] For all these efforts, the lack of uniforms in the first two months caused the recruits real hardship. The majority of them, expecting to be issued with a complete uniform on arrival at the depot, had joined up in their oldest civilian clothes, though some had been anxious to create a good impression and wore their best suit when they enlisted. A handful of battalions in the First New Army were lucky enough to be clothed fairly quickly from pre-war reserves. In Ireland, where there was less pressure on existing stores, the 5th Connaught Rangers received service dress within a few days of the battalion's formation in August 1914.[4] The 6th East Lancashire Regiment in the 13th Division was supplied with khaki and almost fully equipped by mid-September.[5] Nevertheless, the available clothing did not stretch very far. The 9th East Lancashires, part of the 22nd Division in the Third New Army, were still without uniforms of any kind at the beginning of November, despite having been raised only a week or so after the 6th Battalion.[6] George Butterworth, of

the 6th Duke of Cornwall's Light Infantry, noted in his diary on 13 September:

This is the chief grievance; every recruit on enlisting was told that he would be provided with full kit immediately, and was consquently advised to bring next to nothing with him. As a fact, for many days nothing at all was supplied; underclothing and boots are now being gradually doled out, but no khaki or overcoats; hence the men have no protection from wet and no proper change of clothes, and every shower of rain means so many more on the sick list.[7]

With recruits being drawn from every corner of society, most Kitchener units inevitably presented a somewhat bizarre image at first. Describing the early parades of the 8th Norfolk Regiment, an officer wrote, 'Costumes were of the weirdest. A gigantic sailor in blue sweater and trousers jostled a companion in a grey suit round which were the colours of a well-known Cambridge college. A swallow-tailed coat, striped trousers and spats concealed a future signal sergeant.'[8] John Hargrave joined the 32nd Field Ambulance in his Boy Scout uniform and was promptly nicknamed 'Kitchener's Cowboy'. His fellow recruits included:

... clerks in bowler hats; 'knuts' in brown suits, brown ties, brown shoes and a horse-shoe tie-pin; tramp-like looking men in rags and tatters and smelling of dirt and beer and rank twist ... shop assistants with polished boots, and some even with kid gloves ... here and there was a farm-hand in corduroys and hob-nailed cowdung-bespattered boots.

The second-line Territorial battalions also lacked uniforms in the early days. Captain C. E. Wurtzburg of the 2/6th King's (Liverpool) Regiment recalled that, although the wearing of bowler hats was discouraged in his battalion, there were few restrictions concerning dress: 'We came daily to the drill-shed for training in every form of costume that can be imagined – some men in everyday clothes of a clerk, some in shooting coats and grey trousers, others in khaki bought at their own expense, and so on.'[10] Clogs were the favourite footwear in several Lancashire battalions. Charles Cain remembered the loud noise they made when the 2/5th Manchesters went for a training run through the streets of Wigan at 5.30 one morning.[11] In the 2/6th Lancashire Fusiliers at Rochdale 'the command "Pick up those feet" could not ... be uttered without a risk that half the force would simultaneously lose its clogs'.[12]

As military tailors tried to keep pace with the ever-growing demand, even officers sometimes experienced delays in obtaining uniforms. One officer of the 7th King's Own Yorkshire Light Infantry drilled his company for several weeks dressed in a Norfolk jacket and a straw hat, 'until the latter collapsed after repeated rainstorms and had to be replaced by the jauntier Homburg'.[13] Many units devised their own means of distinguishing officers and NCOs from the rank and file. For instance, in the 7th Northamptonshire Regiment corporals were given a white armband and sergeants a red one, while sergeant-majors wore a red sash.[14] NCOs of the 10th Cheshire Regiment were asked to provide themselves with ribbons which could be tied round their arm to denote their rank.[15] Similar methods were employed to distinguish one unit from another, particularly among the Pals battalions. The raising committee of the University and Public Schools' Brigade decided to furnish each recruit with a cardboard disc which bore the letters 'UPS' and was worn in the buttonhole, attached by a red cord.[16] The 1st Birmingham Pals were also issued with buttonhole badges bearing the legend 'Birmingham Battalion 1914' beneath the royal cypher.[17] Men of the 11th East Yorkshire Regiment wore blue armbands adorned with the title '2nd Hull' and other ranks of the Newcastle Commercials each sported a piece of red cord round the right shoulder as 'an honourable badge to signify that the wearer had answered the call of his country'.[18]

The civilian clothes in which men had enlisted were soon reduced to rags by the rigours of training. In the 18th Division at Colchester, route marches began with the order: 'Men without boots to the right, men with worn-out trousers to the left.'[19] Officers of the 10th Cameronians at Bordon found it necessary 'when the troops had to appear on the public road, to arrange the numbering in such wise that those men whose garments were still comparatively complete should screen those who were quite unpresentable.'[20] Sergeant C. Midwinter recorded that recruits of the 32nd Field Ambulance remained in 'civvies' for a considerable portion of the unit's stay in Limerick:

More 'seats' were lost during that period than in many a General Election. On this account many of us asked to be excused from parade, but were always told by Sergeant-Major Hinton to put on overcoats. Although the sun might be shining and the day warm, we chose the lesser evil. Promenading through the main streets without our overcoats was far too embarrassing. The protrusive shirt-tail was no badge for a warrior.[21]

In this situation, and with rumblings of discontent over the treatment of recruits beginning to be heard in the House of Commons, the War Office was compelled to adopt a number of stop-gap schemes to alleviate the clothing problems faced by the New Armies. On 8 September Kitchener agreed that an allowance of 8s 6d should be paid to each recruit who provided himself with a serviceable suit, a pair of boots and an overcoat, the army also meeting the cost of carriage if these articles had to be sent from home. The sum was raised to 10s only two days later.[22] While the allowance gave the recruit some compensation for wear and tear to his own clothes, it did not alter the fact that civilian garments were likely to deteriorate more rapidly with the onset of bad weather and might have to be replaced two or three times. 'I have sent for my other pair of grey flannel trousers as those Mother sent me are completely worn out,' Private Alexander Thompson told his father in a letter from Bovington on 13 October.[23]

Another step taken by the War Office was to supply the New Armies with the old scarlet tunics worn by the line regiments in the late nineteenth century, and with items of ceremonial uniform which had been withdrawn and returned to store, the wearing of full dress, except by the Household Cavalry and Foot Guards, having been discontinued on 5 August.[24] Unfortunately for the recruits, the resultant mixture of civilian clothes and full dress merely made them look more comical than ever and did nothing to build up their sense of *esprit de corps*. As one former member of the 6th Cameron Highlanders said of the battalion's first motley uniforms:

Who can recall them without a shudder? The startling reds of the tunics, the postmen's trousers with the thin red stripes, and the crowning absurdity – the cap comforter which we wore in lieu of better headgear. Those men who could made the best of a bad job by purchasing Glengarrys and badges just to show that we were a Highland regiment and not a Red Alsatian Band.[25]

A third, and far more successful, short-term solution was achieved by directing commanding officers to use their own initiative in finding local sources of supply for clothing and equipment as well as making provisions for the housing and feeding of the troops. A telegram sent to the staffs of the regional commands and depots on 9 September clearly indicated what Kitchener expected of them:

From numerous complaints which are being received at the War Office, it would appear that all officers in charge of Depots do not realise that they have full powers to make all arrangements for the comfort of recruits by billeting, local purchase of necessaries, arrangements for cooking etc, etc. Understand that you have full powers and will be held responsible for exercising them so as to prevent continuance of these complaints.[26]

Granted the unaccustomed luxury of being able to buy articles that were urgently required without any fear of the Finance Department quibbling over details or disallowing any of the expenditure, each of the regional commands soon began to assume the character of a big business organisation in the width and variety of its purchasing activities. Under the supervision of the command staffs, the commanding officers of individual units were encouraged to take advantage of this novel freedom from bureaucratic constraints. One CO who demonstrated what could be done was Lieutenant-Colonel W. L. Osborn of the 7th Royal Sussex Regiment in the 13th Division. In September, while the battalion was still at Chichester, Osborn sought and received permission to purchase much-needed items for his men at 20 per cent over standard army rates and despatched Captain J. L. Sleeman to London to negotiate with various civilian suppliers. As it turned out, Sleeman managed to buy the many thousand articles required – including shirts, socks, braces, towels and razors – for much less than the normal contract rates, but had it not been for Osborn's initial determination to press the matter, the battalion would probably have gone without for several more weeks.[27] A few battalion commanders were able to secure Kitchener's personal backing for their requests. When the Secretary of State inspected the 8th Norfolks at Shorncliffe towards the end of September, he 'tore away the bindings of red tape and authorised by word of mouth the private purchase of boots, forks, spoons and basins out of public funds'. The battalion bought 1,000 pairs of boots that afternoon.[28] Occasionally the purchases were made at divisional level, as when Major-General J. M Babington, commanding the 23rd Division at Frensham, obtained approval to spend £17,000 on clothing and sent two officers to the north of England with powers to buy 20,000 sets of underclothes and boots.[29]

The enterprise displayed by Osborn and Babington was not matched on all sides. On 17 September the War Office had to remind commanding officers of the directive issued earlier that month, and reinforced the message with a stronger warning. 'It should now be clearly understood,' this latest telegram read, 'that serious action will be taken in cases where it is found that these orders have not been fully complied with.'[30] In some instances, however, the continuing shortages stemmed more from poor supervision than anything else. Viscount Buckmaster has related how, when he was serving as a junior officer with the 7th Duke of Cornwall's Light Infantry at Woking in the autumn of 1914, one man's greed caused the whole battalion to suffer:

We had no Quartermaster at the time, and the Regimental Quartermaster-Sergeant was told at all costs at least to get some boots. He said that he had indented for these again and again but that none ever came; certainly there were never any in his store. Then one day the truth came out. He was an ex-regular with a bad record and had hit on a simple plan. As boots came in he put them into sacks, took them into Woking in his car, and sold them in the town. Those men who could afford it then bought them back from the boot-shops. He deserted just as we were going to arrest him; and in spite of all we did to catch him, he was never traced.[31]

This sort of problem was exacerbated by petty theft in the ranks, as illustrated by a letter which Private J. H. M. Staniforth of the 6th Connaught Rangers wrote from Fermoy on 18 October:

. . . I have got the two biggest villians of the lot in with me. We have to leave a man in the room all day, but lots of things have been stolen already. (These two jewels lost their kits as soon as they got them, got drunk on the proceeds, and reported the kits as 'missing, probably stolen, sir!') . . . The thieving is simply incredible. Pat Cavanagh left his shirt on his bed to run into the next room for a light. He was back in thirty seconds, but the shirt was 'whipped on him' as someone said.[32]

During the latter half of September the first deliveries of the makeshift blue serge outfits procured by the Quartermaster-General's Department were made to units at the New Armies.[33] Over the next three months these uniforms, which became known to all as 'Kitchener blue', were issued in increasing numbers, ultimately at the rate of 10,000 suits a day.[34] In the absence of proper khaki service dress, Kitchener blue did much to ease the clothing problems of the New Armies and represented a marked improvement on the motley apparel which had preceded it. With their men dressed identically, most units at last took on a more military appearance. All the same, Kitchener blue was widely unpopular with the recruits themselves, who felt that they resembled postmen or convicts rather than soldiers. The men of the 19th Manchesters (4th City Battalion) were subjected to taunts that they looked like 'tram guards'.[35] Arthur Taylor, a leading member of the raising committee of the Manchester Pals, believed that 'clothing recruits like Barnardo Boys' had contributed to the decline in enlistments by November.[36] Even the Welsh Methodist weekly *Y Goleuad* criticised the use of Kitchener blue, claiming that 'it would be difficult for the most unimaginative and unsympathetic officer to devise anything uglier than that uniform'.[37] In the 10th Essex Regiment, recruits were ashamed to be seen in this emergency clothing by their families and friends, the battalion historians noting that 'a section would club together to buy a suit of khaki and each man took his turn to wear it as his time for leave came round'.[38]

The speed with which the Pals battalions were clothed, and the type of uniforms they received, depended largely on the energy and efficiency of their raisers. Some units were extremely fortunate in this respect and were supplied with khaki long before their brethren in the Second and Third New Armies. The 36th (Ulster) Division was one of the first formations to be issued with service dress, a considerable proportion of the Ulster Volunteer Force having been supplied with khaki prior to the war. In August, immediately after Kitchener had given authority for the recruiting of the division to proceed, Captain James Craig went straight to a firm in London with whom he had dealt previously on behalf of the UVF and ordered another 10,000 complete outfits. On returning to the House of Commons he began to worry where the money would come from to pay for them, and discussed his dilemma with Oliver Locker-Lampson, the Conservative MP for North Huntingdonshire and a staunch friend of Ulster. Locker-Lampson pulled out a cheque book and exclaimed, 'Don't say another word! There's a thousand pounds to go on with, and nine more will follow in a day or two. This is out of a special fund just available for your purpose.' The benefits of Craig's initiative were felt as soon as enlistment got under way early in September. In Belfast a building near the Old Town Hall was taken over as a recruiting station and as each volunteer came out after attestation, he entered the Old Town Hall and passed from department to department, emerging as a recruit in uniform and leaving his civilian clothing to be packed up and sent home.[39]

Other locally raised units were not far behind. Private C. B. Arnold of the 1st Liverpool Pals was measured for his uniform on 24 September, recording in his diary that 'we are very relieved to know we are to get khaki and not blue as we had been told'. A week later he wrote:

We received our uniform (but are not to wear it, till all are served). We have got a very complete outfit. Khaki trousers, puttees, jacket, two shirts . . . two (winter weight) underpants, two towels, two white hankies, toothbrush, knife, fork, shaving brush, comb, good hollow-ground razor, flax, holdall, housewife, jolly fine brown boots, two pr. good heavy sox, navy blue knitted jersey. We have not yet got our webbing bandoliers, rifle, bayonet, hats or greatcoats. For the rest . . . we have had good treatment.[40]

The Hull Commercials and Hull Tradesmen (10th and 11th East Yorkshire) were issued with service dress in November 1914 and the North Eastern Railway Battalion (17th Northumberland Fusiliers) had received theirs by 2 December.[41] The Mayor of Kensington was able to clothe the 22nd Royal Fusiliers by mid-December with the help of the big London stores. Through Sir Richard Burbidge, the Managing Director of Harrods, he purchased some of the last spare khaki in the capital, while Messrs Derry & Toms supplied high-quality shirts and razors to the battalion at reasonable prices.[42]

Though formed later than many similar bodies, the Tyneside Scottish Brigade Committee showed just how efficient local raisers could be at their best. The committee's aim was to supply all essential clothing and personal equipment to the recruits by Christmas 1914. Apart from the infantry equipment, such as belts, ammunition pouches and packs, thirty-eight items of clothing and necessaries were required for each soldier. To cater for the four battalions and their depot companies, the committee placed 136 separate contracts for an overall supply of 205,200 articles involving a total expenditure of some £40,000. Stores were opened at a building in Thornton Street, Newcastle, and, to ensure prompt deliveries, the chief storekeeper went to the committee's office every evening to make a written report. This enabled the committee to keep a daily check on progress and to identify defaulting contractors. Happily there were few of these, and by the end of December, only ten weeks after the first recruit had enrolled, virtually the whole brigade was supplied with regulation clothing and necessaries.[43]

However, the fact remained that, until the clothing industry as a whole had geared itself to cope with the demands of a mass army, there was precious little khaki to be had anywhere. Thus, despite their freedom of action in matters of procurement and supply, many raising committees found it impossible to obtain standard service dress in the autumn of 1914. Since the Pals battalions needed uniforms no less urgently than the first three New Armies, most raisers decided early on to settle for Kitchener blue, though it was mid-December before some units, like the 1st and 2nd Birmingham Pals, received even this emergency clothing.[44] A few battalions accepted other substitutes for regulation service dress. In the 1st Bradford Pals each man was supplied with two blue uniforms of the best worsted that local mills could weave.[45] For the Cardiff Commercial Battalion (11th Welsh Regiment), Messrs Jotham of Cardiff produced brown uniforms which were of a slightly darker shade than the normal khaki. 'The rest of the Brigade, who did not get khaki for nearly a year, retaliated by calling us "Chocolate Soldiers",' wrote Lieutenant E. I. G. Richards.[46] Nationalistic sentiment contributed to the Welsh National Executive Committee's decision to adopt grey Welsh homespun, or 'Brethyn Llwyd', for the units of the 38th Division, but while local manufacturers were stimulated to produce the cloth at an unprecedented rate, no more than 8,440 complete uniforms were ever delivered, this quantity meeting the needs of only two-thirds of the division's infantry battalions. Recourse therefore had to be made to Kitchener blue to supplement the native homespun.[47] In the north of England the Lonsdale Battalion (11th Border Regiment) at first wore dark grey uniforms similar to those of the old Cumberland Volunteers, and outfits of a dull bluish-grey colour were procured for the Newcastle Commercials, yet these alternatives proved almost as unpopular as Kitchener blue. As an officer of the Newcastle Commercials declared, 'No one liked the grey uniform. The material was very serviceable and stood much hard wear. But it seemed as though a substitute for khaki meant a relegation to a backwater of military activity.'[48]

Officers were expected to purchase their own uniform and camp kit from a military outfitter. Besides a service dress jacket, breeches, boots, greatcoat, cap and other articles of clothing, a newly commissioned subaltern had to provide himself with a sword, scabbard, revolver, Sam Browne belt, clasp knife, haversack, compass, wrist watch, whistle, field glasses and a water bottle. Optional extras included such items as a camp bed, camp kettle, lantern, canvas bucket and wash stand, and a valise, although an officer had to ensure that the total weight of his personal equipment to be carried in the unit's transport train did not exceed 35 lb.[49] In August 1914 each officer was paid an allowance of £20 towards the cost of his outfit and camp kit, this grant being raised to £30 on 14 September and to £50 on 4 December.[50] These increases became necessary as competition for limited stocks tended to force the prices of some articles up. Arthur Behrend of the 1/4th East Lancashires obtained most of what he needed for £14 7s 6d before the battalion left Blackburn in August 1914, yet only two months later another territorial officer, Second Lieutenant Graham Greenwell of the 1/4th Oxfordshire and Buckinghamshire Light Infantry, had to accept second-hand items in order to make ends meet:

My second tunic arrived from Harrods this morning: luckily I hadn't got very wet yet and so had managed to do with one up to the present. My bill, £35, is horrifying, especially as I have got to get a sword and revolver as well. But I think I can get the sword Rosa gave me adapted, and buy a leather scabbard for it. It caused tremendous amusement in the Mess on its arrival as it is an ancient pattern and dented in several places. But it is the only one that has seen service and it is a very good blade they tell me . . . I am negotiating a deal for a service revolver from an officer here for £2 10s which, of course, is very cheap as they are seven or eight pounds anywhere else.[51]

Costs were higher for officers in Highland regiments, for they also had to buy a kilt with a khaki apron, tartan trews, garters and hose tops, a dirk and a *skean dhu* amongst other items. When W. Norman Collins was gazetted as a second lieutenant in the 3/4th Seaforth Highlanders in the summer of 1916 he estimated that the total cost of his uniform and accoutrements would be about £75. A letter he wrote a few months earlier, just before he applied for a commission, reveals how prices varied between different outfitters, making it essential for a young officer to exercise care in his purchases:

The Newcastle firms are all very dear. I have price lists from Glasgow, Dundee and London firms and Hobson's (London) is easily the best. The majority of our officers go there and the material and prices are very good. The price of a pair of tartan trousers is £2 5s, kilt £5 5s. The Newcastle firms charge £4 4s for a tunic without badges or buttons.[52]

In spite of the general shortages in the autumn of 1914, many military outfitters were still able to lay their hands on sufficient khaki material to meet orders from newly commissioned officers within a week or two at most. Some officers who were gazetted in August and September had to wait a little longer as firms strove to adjust to the increased demand, but even during this period it was possible for a young subaltern to secure all he required in a few days. Such was the experience of Second Lieutenant P. M. Sharp on joining the 10th Royal Fusiliers in September 1914:

... clothed in a crumpled pair of grey flannel trousers etc, I set off for Colchester. There I reported to a very military officer, Major The Hon Robert White, of the Jameson raid fame. He took one look at me and said 'Go away, and don't come back until you are properly dressed.' I returned weary and rather depressed to London, getting there about 5.30 p.m. The Regimental Tailors could not kit me out before Christmas so I went to Moss Brothers near Covent Garden. I was told I could have a fitting in three days and delivery in a week or so ... When I reported to Colchester again, I got a good mark for being the first of the 'young officers' to turn up in uniform and ready for duty.[53]

Other ranks did not enjoy these advantages, and men who were lucky enough to be issued with service dress shortly after enlistment quickly aroused the envy of their less fortunate comrades. 'We were the first draft to arrive fully fitted out in khaki,' observed Private R. F. E. Evans of the 7th Duke of Cornwall's Light Infantry,' and for some time found it advisable to move around after dark in pairs to avoid being violently robbed of bits of uniform.'[54] However, as the autumn wore on, and the various schemes fostered by the War Office began to take effect, there were signs that the worst of the clothing crisis would soon be over. Most units of the First New Army had been issued with service dress by the end of October, and deliveries of khaki were gradually accelerated in the following months. The Second New Army received theirs in stages between December 1914 and the end of March 1915, while the bulk of the Third New Army were clothed in khaki by April. Moreover, of the locally raised battalions in the Fourth and Fifth New Armies, very few were still wearing emergency clothing after the end of July 1915, and these were nearly all units which had only recently been raised. Whatever the date of issue, the delivery of khaki invariably gave an enormous boost to morale, particularly if it coincided with the acquisition of rifles. In the words of an officer of the 12th King's Own Yorkshire Light Infantry, 'with the arrival of our actual uniforms and rifles we were at last able to regard ourselves with pardonable pride as fully-fledged soldiers.'[55]

Some idea of the huge effort which lay behind these deliveries may be gained by looking at the activities of just one distribution centre – the Northern Area Army Clothing Department, based in Leeds. Early in the war the tramway shed in Swinegate was taken over as the department's first store, but as local mills, tanneries and boot factories raised their output to fulfil government contracts it was deemed necessary to requisition the adjacent King's Mills to house the overflow. In May 1915 the Cattle Market buildings in Gelderd Road also came into use as a store and were soon filled from end to end with 9 million yards of cloth. Subsequently other premises were made available, including a great warehouse belonging to the Aire & Calder Navigation, where over 3 million garments could be stored in bales; the North Eastern Railway station; and part of Gibraltar Barracks in Claypit Lane. At a building in Park Row some 80,000 shirts were inspected every week. The woollen and cotton materials received at these depots in 1915 amounted to nearly 30 million yards, of which 20 million yards were issued to clothing contractors in the district.[56]

II

The clothing question taxed the War Office heavily enough, but the supply of accoutrements and personal equipment for the expanded army was an even more complex task. Although vast quantities of uniforms had to be produced, the range of specific articles of clothing involved was fairly limited. In contrast, over 30,000 separate items of equipment were listed in the official 'Vocabulary of Stores', including such varied articles as groundsheets, blankets, water bottles, mess tins, entrenching tools, clothes pegs and drawing pins. Because there was a constant public demand for less specialised items like plates, drinking mugs and cooking utensils, some of the more pressing personal needs of the men could be met almost immediately from commercial stocks, particularly when commanding officers and raisers of units were given a free hand to make local purchases. In many places, too, the civilian population came forward with gifts of blankets or subscribed to funds to provide comforts for the troops. These expedients, however, could not answer all the army's requirements. On 22 November 1914, in a letter to Lieutenant-General R. C. Maxwell of the Quartermaster-General's Branch at GHQ in France, Cowans indicated how the emphasis of the supply problem had altered since August. 'You will be glad to hear,' he wrote, 'that our troubles are about to come to an end, I trust, or be lessened, in regard to clothing, as we are getting about 800,000 suits from Canada and America, to be completed by the middle of January; and the state of the cloth market here has improved immensely. Our main difficulties are in equipment and leather things; also web equipment.'[57]

The provision of infantry equipment for the New Armies was one of the Quartermaster-General's principals anxieties. The standard pattern in use at the beginning of the war was the 1908 Web Equipment, which owed its origins to an American officer, Captain Anson Mills. In the late nineteenth century Mills had patented a method of carrying ammunition in a canvas webbing belt, thereby avoiding the drawbacks of leather, which tended to 'sweat' and corrode brass cartridge cases. The idea was adopted by the British army, and by 1914 the web equipment carried by an infantryman comprised a waist belt, braces with ammunition pouches, a large pack and haversack, a bayonet frog and carriers for his water bottle and entrenching tool. However, as with clothing, the reserves available in August 1914 were designed merely to sustain the six Regular infantry divisions and the first-line Territorials in a war lasting no more than a few months. Prior to mobilisation the army's annual needs totalled only 10,000 sets, and there were just two firms in the country which possessed machinery capable of making the webbing material. Shortly after the declaration of war Cowans arranged for a number of other firms to learn the process of manufacturing webbing, but it rapidly became obvious that attempts to increase production in that way would be hampered by the continuing lack of specialised machinery required for certain parts of the equipment, notably the belt and braces. Until this problem was solved the manufacture of complete sets would still be governed by the capacity of the two original firms.[58]

To overcome these production difficulties a modified version, known as 1914 Pattern Infantry Equipment, was devised and approved within a month of the outbreak of war. In the new equipment only the pack and haversack were made of webbing, leather taking the place of the remainder.[59] Large orders for its manufacture were placed both in the United Kingdom and in America, and it was this equipment, rather than the 1908 pattern, which was later issued to the majority of the New Army and second-line Territorial battalions. Meanwhile, the formation of the 7th Division from Regular units withdrawn from overseas garrisons put extra pressure on existing resources, inducing the Army Council to establish the principle that new divisions should be equipped in the order in which they were expected to proceed abroad.[60] In the circumstances there was really no other course open to the Army Council, but the decision meant that the later Kitchener divisions came relatively low in the scale of priorities.

For three or four months the only items of infantry equipment obtainable by many New Army and second-line Territorial battalions were old tin water bottles which had to be slung from the shoulder or waist by a length of string.[61] In one unit, the 7th Oxfordshire and Buckinghamshire Light Infantry, the men used cords from window blinds for the purpose and carried their greatcoats *en banderole*, tied up with bootlaces.[62] The 2/12th London Regiment (the Rangers) could not even get water bottles and used beer bottles instead. School satchels served as their haversacks.[63] When additional supplies did start to trickle through in small quantities they were usually of obsolete design. For example, the buff leather equipment issued to the 23rd Division in November 1914 was of a pattern dating from 1888, and barely 400 sets were available for each battalion. Old pattern water bottles and white haversacks arrived for the division the following month.[64]

On average, the battalions of the first three New Armies received their 1914 leather equipment about four months after they had been issued with khaki service dress, a delay which was a genuine hindrance to training. It was not until February and March 1915 that the new infantry equipment reached the divisions of the First New Army in any quantity. Although Colonel E. H. Seymour, the Deputy Director of Equipment and Ordnance Stores, reported on 2 April that the fitting out of the First New Army was 'practically complete', just five weeks then remained before some of its formations were due to depart for the fighting fronts.[65] To make matters worse, much of the leather equipment made in America was of poor quality and quickly deteriorated. The bad sets would therefore be used solely for training and 'would have to be replaced by better stuff', Seymour informed Cowans on 11 March.[66] Cowans tried to relieve the situation by asking General Maxwell how much web equipment could be sent back from France. 'There must be a tremendous lot of this returned after all the recent casualties, and we should be extremely glad of it at home – particularly the packs,' he wrote on 22 March.[67] Maxwell admitted that there was 'a large stock of web equipment at Base' and promised that he would order 'all that has been cleaned and repaired to be sent home at once'.[68] Nevertheless, the returned webbing represented no more than a drop in the ocean when viewed against the overall needs of the New Armies and, as production at home gathered momentum, it was British-made 1914 equipment that was substituted for the American leather in the majority of cases. 'The change was a very welcome one,' commented Captain J. C. Morgan of the 6th Green Howards.[69] It was also timely, for this battalion, like others in the 10th (Irish) and 11th (Northern) Divisions, only acquired the superior British leather equipment late in June, little over a fortnight before they sailed for the Dardanelles.

In a review of priorities on 6 May, Cowans stated that, as soon as the First New Army had all it required, every effort should be made to complete the equipment of the Second New Army and give as much as possible to the Third. The same day Kitchener himself confirmed that the Third New Army was to take precedence over the second-line Territorial divisions.[70] In fact the fitting out of the Second and Third New Armies was already well in hand by that date, some battalions of the 24th and 25th Divisions having received their new leather equipment the previous month, though the 9th and 10th King's Own Yorkshire Light Infantry in the 21st Division had to wait until June.[71]

The large measure of independence allowed to the raisers of Pals formations in matters of supply enabled many of them to procure leather equipment for their units at a much earlier stage of training than the War Office itself had done for the first three New Armies. 'We are almost all in uniform and have our equipment, Pack, Haversack, Water-bottle, Entrenching tool etc all scattered round you in wonderful leather harness,' Private Charles Carrington of the 1st Birmingham Pals told his family on 21 January

1915.[72] The Tees-side Pioneers (12th Green Howards), raised in Middles-brough in December, obtained good-quality equipment from local firms by February 1915, whereas the 6th Green Howards, formed the previous August, were then only just receiving sub-standard American leather through War Office contracts.[73] Pals battalions sometimes acquired equipment from unexpected quarters. The resourceful Mayor of Kensington, Alderman W. H. Davison, having secured the necessary patterns from Woolwich, persuaded Lillywhite's, the London sports outfitters, to make equipment for the 22nd Royal Fusiliers out of leather which had been intended for cricket bags. On completion the equipment was pronounced by the War Office to be first-class, and government orders for thousands of sets were subsequently placed with the firm.[74] The leather equipment of the Salford battalions was also found to be above average in quality when the War Office took over the units in the summer of 1915.[75] For the 38th Division the WNEC Clothing and Equipment Committee eventually ordered 18,500 sets of 1914 equipment, largely from firms in London, Liverpool, Glasgow and Manchester, insisting on a standard superior to the official sealed patterns, although, curiously, they also decreed that the leather was to be stained a greenish colour to give the illusion of webbing.[76] Yet, even if some of their decisions or sources of supply were strange, there was no disguising the fact that the raisers of Pals formations frequently obtained equipment of much better quality than was available to units supplied directly by the War Office.

What made their performance all the more creditable was that they generally managed to clothe and equip their units within the financial limits laid down by the War Office. On 31 August 1914 it had been decided that, in the case of formations raised by cities, the municipal authorities would be allowed £7 for the clothing of each recruit, the money to be paid to the raisers when the unit was taken over by the War Office.[77] As prices went up, the overall sum allowed for the clothing and personal kit of other ranks was increased, first to £8 5s 3d, then, in mid-November, to £8 15s per man, or £8 16s 3½d if a recruit was issued with a clasp knife. Many raisers kept well below this upper limit. The Salford Brigade Committee procured uniforms and kit for its four battalions at a cost of only £7 7s 7d per man, thereby effecting a total saving to army funds of over £4,000. The raising committee of the 1st and 2nd South East Lancashire Battalions (17th and 18th Lanca-shire Fusiliers) also clothed their recruits for under £8 per man.[78] The Welsh National Executive Committee spent £313,600 on uniforms and £59,065 on equipment for the 38th Division and claimed to have saved over £37,000 on the War Office grant for these items. This assertion has to be regarded with some caution, however, for the equipment fund administered by the com-mittee was found to be short by some £4,000 when the time came for the War Office to assume responsibility for the division. An appeal was launched to make up the deficiency but it was not until October 1915 that the target was reached. The mysterious shortage was reported in the press, but no mention of it was made in the committee's official report published after the war.[79]

Kitchener has often been accused of favouring the New Armies in questions of clothing and equipment, to the detriment of the second-line Territorials. According to the historians of the 2/6th Lancashire Fusiliers, the battalion was handicapped in its efforts to acquire uniforms and accoutrements because Kitchener battalions 'had a preferential call on the available resources of the country and army contracts were unable and in some cases forbidden to proceed with the equipment of Territorial units until the prior claims of the New Armies had been satisfied.[80] More recently the novelist Dennis Wheatley, a former officer of the 2/1st City of London Brigade, Royal Field Artillery, has argued that 'when equipment started to come through, it was Kitchener's ill-sorted and untrained rabble that got the rifles, boots, uniforms, horses and guns; whereas the unfortunate Territorials were denied everything but the barest necessities'.[81]

Like most generalisations about Kitchener's attitude to the Territorial Force, these statements contain an element of truth but are not entirely supported by the evidence. Up to 20 May 1915 the responsibility for clothing and equipping Territorial units continued to rest with the County Associations, not with the War Office, and on the whole the Associations carried out this work with conspicuous success. The 2/6th Lancashire Fusiliers, for instance, were clothed in khaki by the end of 1914, at least two months in advance of the 11th Lancashire Fusiliers in the Third New Army.[82] Other second-line battalions, such as the 2/4th East Lancashires, the 2/5th Sherwood Foresters and the 2/6th Royal Warwickshire Regiment also had service dress by Christmas.[83] The Somerset County Association was even able to supply 2,000 khaki uniforms to a Kitchener battalion of the North Staffordshire Regiment at Okehampton without harming the interests of its own units.[84] Similar progress was made in the provision of infantry equipment. The Buckinghamshire County Association prided itself on the unequal comparison between the uniforms and equipment possessed by the 2/1st Buckinghamshire Battalion and the civilian clothes worn by Kitchener recruits in the vicinity. In this connection, Colonel Sir Geoffry Christie-Miller, who served as a captain in the battalion, has paid tribute to the accomplishments of a sub-committee appointed by the Association:

Their activity extended to every commercial house available to supply the goods, and they were unhampered by the strangling red tape of a Government department . . . I remember well being sent to London with two blank orders, each for 500 sets of leather equipment, with instructions to place the order with anyone who would deliver the good, how civilly one was treated, and how one came home with a promise of complete delivery by December 1st – a promise which was satisfactorily fulfilled. Not only did this sub-committee fully clothe and equip the battalion, without reference to the Ordnance Department, but they completed the 1st Bucks before we were supplied with an article.[85]

It should be borne in mind that these successes were achieved by County Associations from both rural and industrial areas and with vastly different resources in terms of finance and access to local manufacturers. Thus the shortages suffered by other second-line Territorial units are more likely to have resulted from the inefficiency of their County Associations than from any hostility on Kitchener's part. Since the second-line Territorials were not originally intended for overseas service, it would be unfair to blame Kitchener for giving priority to the New Armies, whose active service role was never in question. In fact, as the War Office admitted in March 1915, Territorial Force recruits had in many cases 'received their clothing in a much shorter time after enlistment than recruits for the New Armies'.[86]

Most County Associations, indeed, appear to have been reasonably satisfied with the system of independent purchase. The advantages and shortcomings of independent purchasing were discussed at a War Office conference on 21 December 1914, when it was decided to ask the County Associations for their comments on the workings of the system, as well as for information about their current stocks and requirements. Thirty-two Associations merely supplied the figures which had been requested and did not bother to comment at all, while a further fifteen Associations maintained a neutral stance, judging that there were both benefits and disadvantages in decentralisation. Of those with more positive views, twenty nine wished to persevere with the existing arrangements, and only seven associations urged that purchasing should be concentrated in the hands of the War Office.[87]

These replies were considered at a second conference which was held at the War Office on 25 March 1915 and attended by the Under-Secretary of State for War, the Director-General of the Territorial Force and representatives of the Finance and Quartermaster-General's Departments. Here it was agreed that independent purchasing offered the best means of exploiting local sources of supply and that recruits could be clothed faster under this system. On the debit side, however, it was felt the competition between many purchasing bodies caused a general inflation of prices and made it doubly difficult to regulate supplies according to needs, the highest bidder usually getting the goods regardless of genuine priorities. Moreover, because relatively few County Associations had adequate machinery for inspection, much of the clothing and equipment they obtained was of indifferent quality. Therefore, although the Associations had not collectively advocated such a course, those present at the conference concluded that, on balance, it would be better to adopt a system of centralised purchase, inspection and distribution for the Territorial Force so that greater control could be exercised over prices, standards and deliveries. The decisions taken at the conference were subsequently embodied in a directive sent to the County Associations on 20 May. Henceforth no purchases of clothing and equipment were to be made without War Office sanction and, once the stocks currently held by the associations were exhausted, all issues to Territorial recruits and all renewals of uniforms and accoutrements were to be provided by the Army Ordnance Department.[88]

In essence, this directive marked the end of independent purchasing, for in the summer of 1915 the War Office also began to assume full responsibility for the Pals battalions, as promised to their raisers at the outset. It had taken the War Office nearly a year to establish a unified system for the supply of clothing and personal equipment, yet, in view of the lack of preparation before the war and the enormous requirements of a mass army, it is doubtful whether centralisation could have been imposed much earlier with any real hope of success. The War Office needed time to adjust to the new situation and could gain the necessary breathing space only by calling upon the County Associations and local raisers for help. As it was, the system of independent purchase proved remarkably effective while it lasted, in spite of all its obvious drawbacks. By sharing the burden of procurement and supply with a multitude of local bodies during the critical phase of expansion the War Office substantially reduced the risk of any single part of the improvised structure collapsing under the unprecedented weight of demand.

Notes

1 General Sir John Cowans, *Supply Services during the War: Part VII, Equipment and Ordnance*, see *Statistics of the Military Effort of the British Empire*, pp. 868–9; letter from War Office to Territorial Force County Associations, 12 September 1914, WO 32/11238; War Office to County Associations, 3 October 1914, WO 32/11238.

2 Cowans, *op. cit.*, p. 868.

3 Minutes of Directors' meeting, Quartermaster-General's Department, 29 August 1914, WO 107/21.

4 Lieutenant-Colonel H. F. N. Jourdain, *Ranging Memories*, Oxford University Press, 1934, p. 162.

5 Major-General Sir C. Lothian Nicholson and Major H. T. MacMullen, *History of the East Lancashire Regiment in the Great War, 1914–1918*, Littlebury, Liverpool, 1936, p. 314.

6 *Ibid.* p. 453.

7 *George Butterworth, 1885–1916: Extracts from Diary and Letters*, Delittle Brown & Fenwick, London, 1918, p. 29.

8 Major H. P. Berney-Ficklin, in F. Loraine Petre, *The History of the Norfolk Regiment, 1685–1918*, Vol. II, 4 August 1914 to 31 December 1918, Jarrold, Norwich, n.d., p. 209.

9 John Hargrave, *At Suvla Bay*, Constable, London, 1916, p. 5.

10 Captain C. E. Wurtzburg, *The History of the 2/6th (Rifle) Battalion, the King's (Liverpool) Regiment, 1914–1919*, Gale & Polden, Aldershot, 1920, p. 3.

11 Charles Cain, *The Footsloggers*, IWM PP/MCR/48.

12 Captain C. H. Potter and Captain A. S. C. Fothergill, *The History of the 2/6th Lancashire Fusiliers*, privately published, Rochdale, 1927, p. 3.

13 Lieutenant-Colonel R. C. Bond, *History of the King's Own Yorkshire Light Infantry in the Great War, 1914–1918*, Lund Humphries, London, 1929, III, p. 781.

14 H. B. King, *The 7th (Service) Battalion, Northamptonshire Regiment*,

1914–1919, Gale & Polden, Aldershot, 1919, p. 2.

15 Arthur Crookenden, *The History of the Cheshire Regiment in the Great War*, p. 344.

16 *The History of the Royal Fusiliers 'U.P.S.': University and Public Schools Brigade (Formation and Training)*, p. 30.

17 J. E. B. Fairclough, *The First Birmingham Battalion in the Great War, 1914–19*, p. 4.

18 The Snapper, journal of the East Yorkshire Regiment, Vol. XI, No. 1, January 1915, p. 20; Captain C. H. Cooke, *Historical Records of the 16th (Service) Battalion, Northumberland Fusiliers*, p. 6.

19 Captain G. H. F. Nichols, *The 18th Division in the Great War*, Blackwood, London, 1922, p. 4.

20 Anon., *The Tenth Battalion the Cameronians (Scottish Rifles): a Record and Memorial, 1914–1918*, privately published, Edinburgh, 1923, p. 7.

21 C. Midwinter, *Memories of the 32nd Field Ambulance, 10th (Irish) Division, 1914–1919*, Foulger, Bexleyheath, 1933, p. 5.

22 Minutes of meeting of the Military Members of the Army Council, 8 September 1914, WO 163/44; Minutes of Directors' meetings, Quartermaster-General's Department, 8 and 10 September 1914, WO 107/21.

23 Alexander Thompson to his father, 13 October 1914, IWM 79/55/1.

24 Army Order III of 5 August 1914 (AO 292 of 1914).

25 Lieutenant-Colonel Norman MacLeod, *War History of the 6th (Service) Battalion, Queen's Own Cameron Highlanders*, Blackwood, Edinburgh, 1934, p. 4.

26 Telegram from War Office to GOCs-in-C of Commands, OCs Districts and OCs Depots, 9 September 1914, WO 159/18.

27 Owen Rutter (ed.), *The History of the Seventh (Service) Battalion, the Royal Sussex Regiment, 1914–1919*, p. 5.

28 Major H. P. Berney-Ficklin, in F. Loraine Petre, *The History of the Norfolk Regiment, 1685–1918*, II, p. 210.

29 Lieutenant-Colonel H. R. Sandilands, *The Twenty-third Division, 1914–1919*, Blackwood, London, 1925, pp. 7–8.

30 Telegram from War Office to GOCs-in-C of Commands, OCs Districts and OCs Depots, 17 September 1914, WO 159/18.

31 Viscount Buckmaster, *Roundabout*, Witherby, London, 1969, p. 122.

32 J. H. M. Staniforth to his family, 18 October 1914, IWM CON/JHS.

33 Minutes of Directors' meeting, Quartermaster-General's Department, 21 September 1914, WO 107/21.

34 Cowans, *op. cit.*, p. 868.

35 Lieutenant-Colonel H. L. James (ed.), *Sixteenth, Seventeenth, Eighteenth, Nineteenth Battalions, the Manchester Regiment (First City Brigade)*, p. 287.

36 Arthur Taylor to Lord Derby, 2 November 1914, Derby papers, LRO 920 DER(17) 14/12.

37 *Y. Goleuad*, 13 November 1914.

38 Lieutenant-Colonel T. M. Banks and Captain R. A. Chell, *With the 10th Essex in France*, p. 19.

39 Cyril Falls, *The History of the 36th (Ulster) Divison*, pp. 4–6; J. L. Stewart-Moore, *Random Recollections, Part II, The Great War, 1914–1918*, unpublished account, 1976, IWM 77/39/1; *The Times*, 11 September 1914.

40 C. B. Arnold, *Diary of One of the Liverpool Pals, 1914–1915*, entries of 24 September and 1 October 1914, IWM 81/30/1.

41 J. Beeken, unpublished account, 1975, IWM 74/129/1; Anon., *A Short Diary of the 11th (Service) Battalion, East Yorkshire Regiment, 1914–1919*, Goddard Walker & Brown, Hull, 1921, p. 2; Lieutenant-Colonel J. Shakespear, *A Record*

of the 17th and 32nd (Service) Battalions, Northumberland Fusiliers (NER)
Pioneers, 1914–1919, pp. 5–6.

42   Major Christopher Stone (ed.), *A History of the 22nd (Service) Battalion Royal
Fusiliers (Kensington)*, privately published, London, 1923, pp. 11–12.

43   *Tyneside Scottish Brigade Committee: First Report of the Honorary Secretaries,
September 1914 – December 1915*, Newcastle, December 1915, pp. 12–13.

44   Fairclough, *op. cit.*, p. 15; H. V. Drinkwater, *Diary of the War*, IWM DS/MISC/
54.

45   R. N. Hudson, *The Bradford Pals*, p. 8.

46   Lieutenant E. I. G. Richards, quoted in Major-General Sir Thomas Marden, *The
History of the Welsh Regiment, Part II 1914–1918*, Western Mail and Echo,
Cardiff, 1932, p. 284.

47   *Welsh Army Corps: Report of the Executive Committee*, Cardiff, 1921, pp. 18,
47.

48   'V.M.', *Record of the XIth (Service) Battalion, Border Regiment (Lonsdale),
from September 1914 to 1st July 1916*, p. 9; Captain C. H. Cooke, *op. cit.*, p. 6.

49   *Field Service Pocket Book*, 1914, pp. 182–8

50   Army Order II of 20 August 1914 (AO 322 of 1914); Army Order XX of 14
September 1914 (AO 390 of 1914); Army Order II of 4 December 1914 (AO 2 of
1915).

51   Arthur Behrend, *Make me a Soldier*, p. 25; Graham Greenwell to his mother, 20
October 1914, IWM P. 272.

52   W. Norman Collins to his family, 15 February and 18 July 1916, IWM CON/
WNC.

53   P. M. Sharp, *Two World Wars*, unpublished account, *c*. 1945, IWM 78/69/1.

54   R. F. E. Evans, *Some Wartime Experiences*, unpublished account, post-1945,
IWM PP/MCR/75.

55   Captain R. Ede England, *A Brief History of the 12th Battalion King's Own
Yorkshire Light Infantry: the Miners' Battalion*, p. 24.

56   W. H. Scott, *Leeds in the Great War*, pp. 190–1.

57   Cowans to Maxwell, 22 November 1914, WO 107/13.

58   Cowans, *op. cit.*, p. 870.

59   *War Office List of Changes in War Matériel and of Patterns of Military Stores*,
No. 16977, 1 December 1914.

60   Minutes of meeting of the Military Members of the Army Council, 20 August
1914, WO 163/44.

61   D. C. Burn, *Peregrinations Pro Patria*, unpublished account, 1919, IWM
PP/MCR/173.

62   Captain C. A. Salvesen, in Lieutenant-Colonel C. Wheeler (ed., *Memorial
Record of the Seventh (Service) Battalion, the Oxfordshire and Buckinghamshire
Light Infantry*, Blackwell, Oxford, 1921, p. 9.

63   Captain A. V. Wheeler-Holohan and Captain G. M. G. Wyatt (eds.), *The
Rangers' Historical Records: from 1859 to the Conclusion of the Great War*,
Harrison, London, 1921, p. 169.

64   Sandilands, *op. cit.*, p. 9.

65   Minutes of Directors' meeting, Quartermaster-General's Department, 2 April
1915, WO 107/21.

66   *Ibid.*, 11 March 1915, WO 107/25.

68   Maxwell to Cowans, 26 March 1915, WO 107/13.

69   Captain J. C. Morgan, in *The Green Howards Gazette*, Vol. XXIII, No. 269,
August 1915, p. 93.

70   Minutes of Directors' meeting, Quartermaster-General's Department, 6 May
1915, WO 107/21.

71 R. C. Bond, *op. cit.*, p. 785.
72 Charles Carrington to his family, 21 January 1915, IWM 75/61/3.
73 *The Green Howards Gazette*, Vol. XXII, No. 264, March 1915, p. 235.
74 Stone, *op. cit.*, p. 11.
75 Barlow (ed.), *The Lancashire Fusiliers: Roll of Honour of the Salford Brigade*, p. 27.
76 Meeting of WNEC Clothing and Equipment Committee, 23 December 1914, NLW/WAC 60; Summary of Activities for the period ending 31 December 1914, 'Discharge Clothing' file, NLW/WAC; W. R. Thomas, *Notes on the 1914–18 War*, unpublished account, n.d., IWM 77/121/1; 'Equipment Stores, Woolwich' file, NLW/WAC C. 54; *Western Mail*, 6 November 1916.
77 Minutes of meeting of the Military Members of the Army Council, 31 August 1914, WO 163/44.
78 Note on War Office Allowances, undated, July 1915, 'Memoranda' file, NLW/WAC; Accounts of the Salford Brigade Committee, Comparative Statement of Expenditure on Kit, 18 December 1916, published in Barlow (ed.), *op. cit.*, pp. 48–50; Major-General J. C. Latter, *The History of the Lancashire Fusiliers, 1914–1918*, Vol. I, Gale & Polden, Aldershot, 1949, p. 98.
79 *Welsh Army Corps, Report of the Executive Committee*, Cardiff, 1921, pp. 40, 46–51; *Liverpool Daily Courier*, 19 August 1915; *Manchester Guardian*, 24 August 1915; *South Wales Daily News*, 1 October 1915.
80 Potter and Fothergill, *op. cit.*, p. 4.
81 Dennis Wheatley, *Officer and Temporary Gentleman, 1914–1919*, Hutchinson, London 1978, p. 44.
82 Potter and Fothergill, *op. cit.*, p. 5; Latter, *op. cit.*, p. 94.
83 Nicholson and MacMullen, *op. cit.*, p. 278; W. G. Hall, *The Green Triangle: the History of the 2/5th Battalion the Sherwood Foresters in the Great European War, 1914–1918*, Garden City Press, Letchworth, 1920, p. 8; various authors, *the History of the 2/6th Battalion the Royal Warwickshire Regiment, 1914–1919*, Cornish, Birmingham, 1929, p. 5.
84 W. G. Fisher, *The History of Somerset Yeomanry, Volunteer and Territorial Units*, Goodman, Taunton, 1924, p. 155.
85 Major-General J. C. Swann, *The 2nd Bucks Battalion, 1914–1918*, Aylesbury, 1926, p. 4; Colonel Sir Geoffry Christie-Miller, *Memoirs*, unpublished account, 1919, IWM 80/32/1.
86 Memorandum on 'The Mode of Provision of Clothing and Personal Equipment for the Territorial Force, 20 March 1915', WO 32/11238.
87 Minutes of Conference on the Supply of Clothing and Equipment for the Territorial Force, 21 December 1914, WO 32/11238; War Office to Territorial Force County Associations, 24 January 1915, WO 32/11238; Précis of Remarks by County Associations on the working of the system of supply of Clothing and Personal Equipment to the Territorial Force, prepared *c.* 20 March 1915, WO 32/11238.
88 Minutes of Conference on the Supply of Clothing and Personal Equipment for the Territorial Force, 25 March 1915, WO 32/11238; War Office to Territorial Force County Associations, 20 May 1915, WO 32/11238.

11

Arms and ammunition

Nowhere was the inadequacy of pre-war calculations more evident than in the sphere of munitions. In August 1914 the output of the Royal Ordnance Factories, and of the small number of private firms which received government contracts, was tailored to the concept of a short war. Scant provision had been made to meet demands other than those arising from the need to sustain the British Expeditionary Force in a campaign expected to last a few months at most. Moreover, there was no immediate way in which the supply could be greatly augmented. The private armament firms were chiefly engaged in the manufacture of munitions for the Royal Navy and could not easily redeploy skilled labour or convert their machinery to handle huge orders for the army. Even those capable of producing rifles and small arms ammunition were in a similar position. For example, the Birmingham Small Arms Company was manufacturing just 700 rifles a week for the War Office and for some time had been forced, through lack of orders, to devote much of its attention to the production of bicycles and sporting guns.[1]

The standard infantry weapon of the British Army in 1914 was the ·303 in. Short Magazine Lee-Enfield (SMLE) Mark III rifle, sighted for use with Mark VII ammunition. The Mark III pattern had been introduced in 1907, but the high-velocity Mark VII ammunition did not appear until 1911. Consequently, although the work of resighting rifles made to take the earlier Mark VI ammunition was being done gradually, there were still large numbers of service rifles which had not been adapted. Other patterns in use were the original short rifle, first issued in 1904 and known as the Mark I, and conversions from 'long' non-charger loading rifles which had been the standard weapon at the time of the South African War and which were now designated Mark II or Mark IV according to whether the conversion had been made to approximate to the Mark I or the Mark III type. In addition, there were old long rifles, known as CLLE rifles Mark I or Mark I*, which had been modified to permit charger loading of magazines, while some unmodified long rifles were in store. Not all these older patterns had been resighted for

Mark VII ammunition.[2]

The average pre-war output of rifles sighted for Mark VII ammunition was 47,280 a year. Of these, the Royal Small Arms Factory at Enfield Lock produced 25,279 for current equipment and the private firms manufactured 10,400, a further 11,601 being made for the replenishment of stocks. By August 1914 166,847 had been delivered. If one includes rifles produced between 1907 and 1911 which had since been resighted, there were 475,000 rifles of the newest pattern available when war was declared, of which 335,000 were actually in service and 140,000 in store. The stock of older long rifles, used mainly by the Territorial Force, amounted to 320,000, with 220,000 in the hands of the troops and 100,000 in store. In short, the country possessed 795,000 serviceable rifles to equip an army which, on mobilisation, numbered approximately 725,000 men. This left a reserve of only 70,000 modern rifles with which to meet wastage and to arm the new formations.[3] As 17,000 rifles were required for each infantry division, the reserve stocks were insufficient even for the First New Army, let alone any subsequent formations.

Machine guns, which soon came to dominate the battlefields of the Western Front, were also in extremely short supply at the beginning of the war, having previously been regarded by the British more as a weapon of opportunity than as an essential requirement for the infantry. Only two machine guns were allotted to each infantry battalion in August 1914. By then the ·303 in. belt-fed water-cooled Vickers gun was superseding the obsolescent Maxim pattern, and 106 of them had been delivered to the War Office. The pre-war stock of the two guns was 1,955. Vickers had a monopoly of their type of gun, which could be made only at their Erith works. The lighter, magazine-fed ·303 in. Lewis gun was still in the process of development. The European patents for this weapon, which was the invention of Colonel I. N. Lewis of the United States Army, were acquired in 1912 by the company Armes Automatiques Lewis. That year the War Office had rejected the gun for land service because it was then thought undesirable to multiply types, but ten Lewis guns were purchased by the Admiralty and War Office in July 1914 for trials as aircraft armament. Experimental guns were also being made for Armes Automatiques Lewis by the Birmingham Small Arms Company and the latter was contemplating putting the weapon into large-scale production.[4]

Specialised weapons for trench warfare were virtually non-existent. Reports on trench warfare conditions which prevailed at the siege of Port Arthur in 1904 led to the introduction of a single British service type of percussion grenade, the No. 1, RL. This was made in tiny quantities by the Ordnance Factories and was neither efficient nor entirely safe. Only about a dozen had been produced just before the outbreak of war. There were also some patent grenades, invented principally by Mr Marten Hale and the monopoly of one firm, the Cotton Powder Company. One form of the Hale rifle grenade had been under consideration by the Ordnance Board for several

months as an aircraft weapon. Output of the RL percussion grenade and the Hale grenade was stricly limited by their detonators, which could not be manufactured rapidly on the plant available, only two British firms possessing the machinery and labour needed for detonator production.[5] The army had no trench mortars in August 1914, nor even an experimental pattern on which future productions might be based. Thus relatively few soldiers had been trained to throw grenades and none at all to use trench mortars. In contrast, grenades as well as trench mortars, or *Minenwerfer*, were standard issue in the Germany army and discussion as to methods of making these weapons was commonplace in German military and engineering journals.

In terms of reserve stocks of weapons, the situation confronting the artillery was almost equally depressing. The rearming of the artillery had begun in 1904 and 1905 when orders were placed for four new types of gun, namely the thirteen-pounder, eighteen-pounder and sixty-pounder and the 4·5 in. howitzer. The re-equipment of the Royal Horse Artillery with thirteen-pounders, and of the Royal Field Artillery with sixty-pounders, was achieved by 1907, while deliveries of eighteen-pounders to the Royal Field Artillery were completed in 1909. The provision of the new 4·5 in. field howitzer began in 1908 and the bulk of the deliveries were made two years later, though production continued until the war. The 4·5 in. howitzer was therefore the only type to be manufactured in any numbers in the five years before 1914. One heavy 9·2 in. howitzer, made by Vickers, was in service, having been approved by the War Office in June 1914. Apart from the Royal Gun Factory at Woolwich Arsenal, production of field guns and howitzers had been confined to five firms, Armstrong, Vickers, Cammell Laird, Beardmore and the Coventry Ordnance Works. Cammell Laird's last deliveries had been made in 1909 and those of Armstrong and the Coventry Ordnance Works in 1911.[6]

The artillery component of the standard infantry division, as laid down for the pre-war Regular army, consisted of four three-battery brigades, three brigades being equipped with eighteen-pdrs and one with 4·5 in. howitzers. In 1914 each battery had six field guns or howitzers, giving a total for the division of fifty-four eighteen-pounders and eighteen 4·5 in. howitzers. Four sixty-pounders were also allocated to each division of the BEF. The artillery of the Territorial Force was largely equipped with obsolescent types, such as the fifteen-pounder and 4·7 in. field guns and the 5 in. howitzer. A Territorial division in 1914 normally had thirty-six fifteen-pounders, eight 5 in. howitzers and four 4·7 in. guns.

On 4 August 1914 906 guns of the new types were available in Britain, including 624 eighteen-pounders, 128 4·5 in howitzers, 126 thirteen-pounders, and twenty-eight sixty-pounder guns. More than half these were earmarked for the original Expeditionary Force of six divisions. As in the case of rifles, this meant that the immediate reserves of field guns and howitzers would barely suffice to equip five new divisions, without taking into account the need to replace battle losses.[7]

Before the war was a week old, the War Office gave instructions to the private armament firms to work up to maximum output as quickly as possible in anticipation of formal orders and contracts were placed for arms and equipment for the six divisions of the First New Army, supplementary to the requirements of the BEF. On 9 August both the Birmingham and the London Small Arms Companies were invited to submit tenders for rifles. The number to be ordered at this point was fixed at 150,000, of which 40,000 were allocated to the Royal Small Arms Factory.[8] Initially the Birmingham Small Arms Company undertook to deliver 35,000 rifles within three months, and the balance up to a total of 72,800 within six months at a rate of 2,700 per week. The London Small Arms Company offered to produce 700 per week, increasing to 1,000 per week early in 1915. However, the progressive enlargement of the New Armies during September compelled the War Office to revise these preliminary targets. By the end of September the Birmingham Small Arms Company had agreed to expand their plant and introduce a system of night shifts to meet an increased order for 300,000 rifles, which would be delivered at a rate of 8,000 per week by July 1915. The London Small Arms Company also promised to raise production to 1,500 a week by January 1915. Meanwhile, the Royal Small Arms Factory at Enfield had doubled its output and by 14 November 3,000 rifles per week were being delivered, while bayonet production reached 2,000 per week in December.[9]

At the same time, arrangements were made to step up the manufacture of field guns, howitzers and machine guns. During the first two months of the war, contracts were issued for a total of 878 eighteen-pounders, of which the Royal Gun Factory was to produce sixty-eight, Vickers 360, and Armstrong's 450. The Coventry Ordnance Works received orders for 120 4·5 in. howitzers, and another thirty were to be made at Woolwich.[10] Contracts were placed with Vickers for 1,792 machine guns to be delivered at a rate of fifty per week by June 1915. Two hundred and forty-five Lewis guns were ordered from the Birmingham Small Arms Company before mid-September, and an additional 400 by the end of the year.[11] Orders for small arms ammunition in the same period totalled more than 327 million rounds.

Although the War Office had acted swiftly, the heavy consumption of munitions on the western front and the massive growth of the army at home raised grave doubts about the adequacy of these preliminary orders and thus prompted the formation of the Cabinet Committee on Munitions on 12 October. At its first meetings the committee considered the provision of artillery for the New Armies, and the members were told by von Donop that 892 guns of the eighteen-pounder type had been ordered, of which 864 would be ready by mid-June. These would equip twenty-four new divisions with four-gun batteries. At the suggestion of Lloyd George and Churchill, the committee decided that deliveries of eighteen-pounder guns should be increased, if possible, to 3,000 by 1 May. Vickers subsequently agreed to do their best to provide 1,000 by 1 July 1915, and Armstrong's promised 850 by that date, with a further 150 a month later. The Coventry Ordnance Works were induced to increase their output of 4·5 in. howitzers to 450, but they refused to guarantee more than 300 by the end of June.[12]

The question of rifles was discussed at the committee's fourth meeting, on 21 October. On this occasion von Donop stated that, on the orders already placed, 781,000 rifles were promised by 1 July 1915. The committee resolved that steps should be taken to raise this total by 400,000. To carry out these instructions, extensions of plant were arranged at Enfield to expand the weekly output to 5,750; the London Small Arms Company undertook to increase production yet again, this time to 2,000 rifles a week by the end of June 1915; Vickers were persuaded to begin rifle production, promising 2,000 per week in July; and a new firm, the Standard Small Arms Company, was given financial aid to enable it to start rifle manufacture, aiming at 1,250 weapons per week within eight months.

The largest orders, however, were placed in North America. One contract had already been issued, in September, to the Ross Rifle Company of Canada for 100,000 rifles. In November agreements were concluded with the Winchester Arms Company and the Remington Arms Union Metallic Cartridge Company for 200,000 rifles each, the first deliveries of 1,000 a day being promised for July 1915. Further contracts followed early in 1915, the Remington company receiving a second order for 200,000 in February, with deliveries at 500 a day due to commence in November that year.[13] Besides these American orders, the War Office augmented supplies by making various purchases abroad. The Indian government, for instance, was able to provide 50,000 rifles, and a consignment of 130,000 Japanese rifles was also obtained in this way.

Perhaps the most important result of the Cabinet committee's deliberations was the progress made in decentralising munition production. The War Office staff, still geared to the administration of a small army in the opening weeks of the war, could not hope to supervise the whole programme in detail, so it was decided to adopt the policy of utilising the resources and knowledge of the major armament firms to the utmost, and to rely upon them not only to arrange for the allocation of work among inexperienced firms but also to co-ordinate the flow of manufacture. The expansion of output, from October onwards, was therefore left largely to the personal drive and initiative of the directors of the private firms and to the Chief Superintendent of the Ordnance Factories.

During the late autumn and winter, changes were made in the scale of equipment to be issued to New Army divisions. In November, mainly as a result of the lessons learned on the Western Front, the number of machine-guns per infantry battalion was doubled to four, and early in January four-gun artillery batteries were adopted as the standard in place of the six-gun units with which Britain had entered the war.[14]

The effect of this latter modification on the total artillery armament of a division was in fact slight, since the number of batteries in a brigade was simultaneously increased from three to four, the net reductions in guns per division being thus only eight, from seventy-two to sixty-four. Demands for machine guns, however, continued to climb. In May 1915, General Headquarters in France asked for four Lewis guns for each cavalry and infantry unit in addition to the four Maxim or Vickers guns already laid down, and by the close of 1915 the War Office estimates of machine-gun requirements were based on the establishment of sixty-four guns per brigade, or sixteen for each battalion.[15]

In spite of the huge programmes of armament production set in motion by the War Office and the Cabinet Committee on Munitions, supply always fell well short of demand in the opening year of the war, and because the troops at the fighting fronts inevitably had first call on any available weapons and ammunition, the new formations suffered from acute shortages of rifles, machine guns, artillery pieces and ammunition for several months. It was understood, of course, that the armaments industry would take some time to reach maximum output but many contractors, both at home and abroad, failed to meet their promised production targets. For example, of the 29,986,005 rounds of eighteen-pounder high-explosive and shrapnel ammunition ordered by 29 May 1915, only 1,487,501 had actually been delivered. Even allowing for the fact that the majority of these orders were intended for delivery in 1916, the contractors were still 2,437,567 rounds in arrears of the total promised by June 1915.[16]

The shortage of artillery ammunition was the primary reason for the 'Shells Scandal' of May 1915, which in turn brought about the creation of a separate Ministry of Munitions. Nevertheless, the supply problems in other areas were just as severe. Of the 1,792 Vickers machine guns due to be delivered by July 1915, only 1,022 were received by the War Office in that time. The Birmingham Small Arms Company had hoped to be producing 100 Lewis guns a week by May, but their deliveries during that month averaged thirty-six a week.[17] The number of eighteen-pounder field guns scheduled for delivery by 30 June was 2,338; barely 800 had been issued to the War Office when that date arrived.[18]

On the surface, the position with regard to rifles looked slightly more encouraging in the summer of 1915. On 1 June 1,153,000 service rifles were in the hands of the army, as well as some 410,000 foreign or drill-pattern weapons which could be used for training purposes. New rifles were coming in at the rate of 11,531 per week, together with 6,946 which had been resighted or repaired. The total number of rifles issued weekly was 18,477, as compared with 8,409 in September 1914 and 13,919 in March 1915. Deliveries were at the rate of 82 per cent of contract promises from the Birmingham Small Arms Company and 62 per cent from the London Small Arms Company, although the Royal Small Arms Factory was now exceeding its agreed targets. Yet, of the overall total of 1,153,000 service rifles, a mere 172,000 had so far been allocated to the New Armies, as against 538,000 to the expeditionary forces in France and the Dardanelles, most of the remainder being divided among the Territorials, reserve units and depots. Thus, as late as June 1915, once the First New Army was equipped there were still only some 70,000 modern rifles available for all the other Kitchener divisions.[19]

Full-scale manufacture of trench warfare weapons took even longer to organise, largely because Britain had to start almost from scratch in this field. For several months the soldiers at the front were compelled to make improvised grenades by filling jam tins with explosives and attaching a short length of time fuse, while some production of experimental types was carried out at home. In many of these emergency patterns safety was improved by substituting a friction igniting apparatus for the portfire and Bickford fuse formerly used. In April 1915 orders for loaded Pitcher grenades were placed with two explosives firms. Though such grenades were issued in tens of thousands, accidents with them were so numerous that they earned for the grenade throwers, or 'bombers', the name of 'The Suicide Club'. These were followed by Ball and Oval grenades, which resembled each other in design if not in shape. They consisted of a cast iron body, into which was screwed a plug with a sleeve to take the detonator, fired in the first place by Bickford fuse and a portfire, and later by a friction igniter. Supply of the Ball grenade began in July 1915 and output reached 500,000 weekly in mid-November. Manufacture of the Oval grenade commenced in October 1915 and reached 300,000 weekly within three months.[20] Large quantities of the Ball grenade were issued to the BEF in time for the Battle of Loos in September, where they failed completely, owing to wet weather, for which the first method of ignition was unsuitable. The troops lost confidence in this pattern and, although the subsequent friction igniter was more effective, about a million were withdrawn from service.

The turn of the tide came with the introduction of the really efficient and safe time-fused Mills hand grenade, which was adapted later for use with a rifle. It had a cast iron barrel-shaped body, fitted with an aluminium tube or centre-piece, which was linked to a cylindrical chamber, for the detonator. A five-second fuse, inserted in the central tube, was attached to the detonator, and ended in a rim-fire percussion cap. The cap was fired by means of a steel plunger or striker, held back by an external lever secured by a safety pin. Developed and patented from a Belgian idea by William Mills of Birmingham, the pattern was submitted in January 1915 and experimental work was completed by 21 April, when tenders were invited for 150,000. Production was pushed ahead under the new Ministry of Munitions, and by the end of the war over 50 million Mills grenades had been manufactured. Four and a half million were made during the last quarter of 1915 alone. The Ordnance Factories and the one monopolist of 1914 were replaced by over 200 contractors in the metal trades. Production on the group system was organised among Birmingham firms, including textile machinery makers, motor engineers, cycle factories, and manufacturers of bedsteads, fenders, gas meters, toys, fishing tackle and dental instruments.[21]

The story was much the same in the case of trench mortars. Towards the end of 1914 the Chief Superintendent of the Ordnance Factories initiated experiments which led to the development of a light 4 in. mortar, improvised by boring out a 6 in. shell. By January twelve of these weapons and 545 rounds of ammunition had been issued to the BEF, with a score of 3·7 in. mortars of a pattern devised by the Indian Corps. That month the War Office approved a design of a 1·57 in. trench howitzer introduced by Vickers. This fired a cast iron bomb filled with permite, a perchlorate explosive. A hundred and twenty-seven were delivered to the BEF in France before July.[22] The Ordnance Factories also produced a fourth pattern, the 2 in. medium mortar, firing a spherical 50 lb cast iron bomb with a steel tail, but fewer than thirty had been sent to France by July. At this time, therefore, the army was supplied with small numbers of four different types, and there was very little ammunition for them, as nearly every design authorised by the War Office involved the use of fuses more urgently needed for artillery ammunition. What was required was a weapon which could be produced easily without adding to the work of the already overburdened specialist ordnance firms.

The answer was found in a proposal made by Mr Wilfred Stokes in January 1915. He suggested projecting a cast iron bomb from a steel tube using, as a means of propulsion, a sporting cartridge, inserted in the bomb itself or, later, in a container fixed to the base of the bomb. When the projectile was dropped down the tube of the mortar the percussion cap was fired on impact with a striker fitted in the base of the barrel. This method of loading gave great rapidity of fire. Again it was the Trench Warfare Supply Department under the Ministry of Munitions which provided the necessary drive to standardise design and press the 3 in. Stokes mortar into large-scale production. The advantage of the Stokes mortar was that, apart from the steel tube for the barrel, its manufacture was within the capacity of any small engineering firm possessing suitable lathes, drilling machines and mechanics of average ability. More than 300 Stokes 3 in. mortars were produced by 12 January 1916 and in February a new call was made for 2,400, with ammunition at the rate of 176,000 rounds weekly. The New Armies, however, saw few Mills grenades or Stokes mortars before they went overseas, for while such weapons were in limited supply the troops in the field were naturally accorded priority in all deliveries.[23]

There is some truth in the argument that, even allowing for the lack of efficient patterns of trench warfare equipment in August 1914, the War Office was slow to appreciate the qualities of the Mills grenade and Stokes mortar. As late as 5 June 1915, after six months of trying to satisfy the Ordnance Board of the advantages of his mortar, Stokes was told that the War Office would not approve the weapon for manufacture because it was thought that any addition to the patterns of trench guns then being made would only complicate the supply position.[24] As no order could be officially placed or paid for without a definite demand from the War Office, Lloyd George, as Minister of Munitions, decided to issue contracts in August for the first 100,000 Stokes mortars, meeting the cost from funds provided for munition purposes by a wealthy Indian maharajah.[25] In fact, final approval of the weapon by the Ordnance Board was not granted until 18 September 1915, and delays in deliveries would have been much longer if Lloyd George had not taken his gamble earlier in the summer.

The shortage of skilled labour resulting from indiscriminate recruiting was another factor which contributed to the hold-ups in the production of all types of munitions during the first year of the war. Even so, the War Office was not responsible for all the problems experienced before the creation of the Ministry of Munitions. For example, the provision of machine tools required for the expansion of output soon became a matter of concern and, owing to the limited capacity of the home industry and the massive scale of the new programmes, machine tools had to be ordered from the United States. The inability of American firms to deliver this machinery on time was a prime cause of the breakdown of the production schedules arranged by the War Office. Deliveries of shells from Canadian and American factories were also considerably behind the contract dates. At home the performance of many sub-contractors was similarly disappointing. The principal armament firms tended to attract the available labour, not only because it was believed that they would pay higher wages but also because they appeared to offer better protection from the attentions of recruiting sergeants. It was a common complaint that while the big firms, as direct contractors, had *carte blanche* in questions of expenditure and could name their own price, the contracts that were sub-let, often confined to the easier and cheaper processes, were given on terms that left a very moderate margin of profit. Sub-contractors were further hindered by difficulties in securing machinery and, as most of them were new to the work and did not fully understand the standards of precision called for in shell manufacture or the strictness of inspection, their products frequently failed to pass the tests.

The workers themselves needed to adjust their attitudes and habits, as Kitchener observed in a speech in the House of Lords on 15 March 1915, when he admitted that supplies were not coming up to expectations:

The progress in equipping our New Armies and also in supplying the necessary war material for our forces in the field has been seriously hampered by the failure to obtain sufficient labour and by delays in the production of the necessary plant . . . While the workmen generally . . . have worked loyally and well, there have, I regret to say, been instances where absence, irregular timekeeping, and slack work have led to a marked diminution in the output of our factories. In some cases the temptations of drink account for this failure to work up to the high standard expected. It has been brought to my notice on more than one occasion that the restrictions of trade unions have undoubtedly added to our difficulties, not so much in obtaining sufficient labour as in making the best use of that labour.[26]

Drink certainly contributed to poor timekeeping and absenteeism in the munition factories in the first year of the war, for beer and spirits could more easily be purchased by men enjoying full employment and high wages.[27] By no means everyone followed the King's lead in 'taking the pledge' in April 1915. Nevertheless, the Defence of the Realm (Amendment No. 3) Act on 19 May 1915 and the ensuing Defence of the Realm (Liquor Control) Regulations on 10 June resulted in the establishment of a Central Control Board to regulate the sale of alcohol, particularly in areas where drink was thought to be affecting production. By the beginning of October, fourteen areas of the country were subject to such controls, with a general order prohibiting sale for consumption on or off the premises before noon or during the afternoon after 2.30 p.m., and limiting sales in the evening to two or three hours.[28]

It also took time for the government to whittle away the system of trade union rules and restrictions built up in the years before the war. The first major move in this direction was in November 1914, when a meeting between the unions and the Engineering Employers' Federation produced the so-called Crayford Agreement, which laid down that, although women workers were not to be employed instead of skilled men, they could operate purely automatic machines once the latter had been set up by recognised mechanics.[29] A further step towards 'dilution', or the use of semi-skilled, unskilled or female labour in jobs which had hitherto been the province of skilled craftsmen, was made on 5 March 1915 in the private Shells and Fuses Agreement between the Engineering Employers' Federation and the engineering unions. This agreement determined that the unions would accept some dilution for the duration of the war as long as the employers undertook to avoid any long-term substitution of semi-skilled or female labour for skilled craftsmen and promised that the temporary workers would be the first to be dismissed at the end of the war.[30] A fortnight later, at Lloyd George's initiative, a conference was held at the Treasury, attended by the President of the Board of Trade together with Arthur Henderson and a number of trade union leaders. The unions engaged on essential war work agreed to recommend to their members that they should forgo the right to strike and relax demarcation restrictions during the war on the understanding that disputes would go to arbitration and that the government would ensure that trade union rules would not permanently be endangered. None of these agreements, however, was legally binding, and it was not until the Munitions of War Act of July 1915 that strikes and lock-outs were prohibited and restrictive practices suspended in factories concerned with munitions production.

II

Owing to the general lack of rifles in the first year of the war, New Army and second-line Territorial infantry battalions were forced to carry out much of their arms and musketry training with obsolete or dummy weapons. At the end of November 1914 it was calculated that, to date, the battalions of the First New Army possessed only 30 per cent of the required number of modern service rifles, the remaining 70 per cent being made up of old Lee-Enfields and wooden drill-purpose (DP) rifles. With the exception of the 36th (Ulster) Division, which had a similar proportion of SMLEs, the Second and Third New Armies and the locally raised battalions were equipped almost exclusively with long training rifles, many of which were considered unsafe to fire.[31] Even these training rifles were in extremely short supply.

In the early weeks the absence of rifles was not too worrying, for it enabled battalion commanders to concentrate on teaching their men elementary squad and company drill and on hardening them up by means of route marches and physical exercises. Once the new units had gained some semblance of military discipline, however, the shortage of proper weapons began to have serious effects on the progress of training. Initially, the majority of battalions improvised by using broomsticks and poles to represent rifles. During the late autumn of 1914 sufficient quantities of drill-purpose and dummy wooden rifles were issued to help the men with at least the rudiments of arms drill and the handling of weapons, but recruits frequently treated these substitutes with contempt. As the chaplain to the 10th Green Howards remarked, 'How can one feel like a soldier with a wooden toy to carry about with you, knowing that before parade it has already poked the fire, cleaned the kitchen sink, beaten the dog, or proved of domestic utility in other ways?'[32] At Shoreham men of the 7th Northamptonshire Regiment found that their dummy rifles made ideal supports for clothes lines between the rows of tents.[33]

Almost to the end of the training period, there were comparatively few battalions which possessed a complete set of rifles of any type. For instance, the 7th York and Lancaster Regiment, part of the 17th Division, still had only 200 rifles as late as June 1915. The 8th Battalion of the regiment, which was attached to the 23rd Division, received 100 obsolete Lee-Metford rifles in October 1914 and, though some Short Lee-Enfields were issued the following month, only eight were available for more than 1,000 men. The 12th York and Lancaster Regiment (Sheffield City Battalion), a locally raised unit in the 31st Division, took delivery of 600 long drill-purpose rifles during the last week of October 1914 and a further 1,000 on 21 January 1915. Five hundred had to be returned between 9 May and 10 June, leaving the battalion with 1,100 weapons, of which many were in poor condition and unfit to be fired. On 17 June eighty Short Lee-Enfields were issued for instructional use and allocated to the NCOs. Not until 30 November 1915 did the unit receive its full complement of new service rifles, and it sailed for Egypt just one week later.[34]

As long as limited stocks of rifles had to be shared out between battalions in this fashion it was hard for a recruit to develop any real sense of pride or confidence in his weapon. An officer of the 16th Sherwood Foresters wrote:

In ordinary circumstances each man has his own rifle, and he is responsible for its care, its cleanliness, its very existence. He is taught to regard it as his own peculiar charge, his friend, even his child. With 167 rifles among 250 men, each rifle belonged to no one in particular, it had no guardian, no one wanted to clean it, no one wanted to take a pride in it, no one wanted to father it – the proprietary principle had given way to communism.[35]

Foreign rifles purchased by the War Office were issued to some New Army and Territorial units, yet were often disliked by the troops. John Nettleton recalled the idiosyncracies of the Japanese weapons handed over to the 2/28th London Regiment (Artists Rifles) in 1915:

They had a bolt action like ours, but it was all enclosed. When you twisted a metal rose at the back of the action, the whole thing came adrift and dozens of tiny springs and odd bits of metal shot out at you. It took about five seconds to take the thing to pieces and about five hours to re-assemble it – more if you had not taken the precaution to spread a towel or a piece of paper on the ground to catch the bits and pieces that sprang out. They were beautiful toys, but quite useless under war conditions.[36]

The experience of the 10th Cameronians was fairly typical of the struggle which New Army battalions had to complete their preliminary training. In the words of one of the battalion's officers:

The 9th lent us a few SMLEs which served for exhibition purposes, otherwise the DP long rifles had to do for instruction, a purpose for which they were not intended – and indeed it was difficult to practise aiming from a rest with rifles whose foresights were burred or smashed almost quite away . . . There were many trials, but eventually – early in January '15 – we did have the battalion on its first musketry course. The range was still unfinished, and consisted mainly of water and soft Hampshire sand. We had a hundred service rifles; men fired their five rounds and grounded arms, and the next detail took up arms and carried on . . . The battalion came out with the best shooting average in the Brigade, but musketry was a weariness to everyone for many months.[37]

Supplies of small arms ammunition were similarly restricted. In December 1914 the Hull Commercials were in a hutted camp adjacent to a rifle range on the north-east coast and had been issued with some ammunition, though it was only to be used against the enemy in the event of an invasion. Since the battalion had not yet fired a single shot from its stock of long rifles, Colonel Richardson, the commanding officer, submitted a number of requests to his immediate superiors, pointing out the need for his men to use ammunition for training so that they could at least acquire a little practical knowledge of musketry before any German raid or invasion occurred. The replies were unsatisfactory, but Richardson persisted, and, with Christmas only a week away, he received a telegram from the War Office asking him to report on the efficiency of the battalion's rifles. Characteristically he retorted, 'Reference your telegram. Rifles will certainly go off, doubtful which end.' Soon after this laconic message had been sent to the War Office the battalion was given authority to fire a proportion of its precious ammunition and spent Christmas Day on the range as a result.[38]

Much of the ammunition issued to battalions was found to be defective. According to Private R. F. E. Evans of the 7th Duke of Cornwall's Light Infantry, it was somewhat discouraging, on squeezing the trigger of one's rifle, 'to see the bullet trickle out of the barrel and fall to the ground ten yards further on'.[39] I. L. Read, who was a private in the 8th Leicestershire Regiment in the spring of 1915, wrote:

Our ammunition was American-made, and was so bad that when I was one of a party marking in the butts, bullets repeatedly went through the targets sideways. Really, apart from experience gained in holding our rifles correctly and getting used to the recoil, our firing course was a complete waste of time.[40]

The delays in the production of Vickers and Lewis guns prevented most battalions from beginning realistic machine-gun training for several months. In February 1915 men of the 6th Oxfordshire and Buckinghamshire Light Infantry were still using a policeman's rattle to simulate the noise of a machine gun during mock battles.[41] Private Tom Macdonald was in the Machine Gun Section of the 9th Royal Sussex Regiment at the time: 'We had an old Maxim gun first for instruction, and for training a wooden gun with a tin drain-pipe. We were the laughing-stock of the troops – running around carrying this contraption doing our gun drill, and villagers laughing.'[42] The 9th Northumberland Fusiliers, in the 17th Division, first received Lewis guns in mid-June 1915, about a month prior to the battalion's departure for France.[43] The 8th Leicesters too were allowed only a brief period in which to familiarise themselves with the new weapons, as I. L. Read relates:

As a potential machine-gunner, I, with other enthusiasts, had learned the Vickers gun by means of lectures and wooden models for months past, but, until some real weapons were forthcoming, the Machine Gun Section was not taken seriously by the battalion . . . About six weeks before we left for France, we were issued with four Lewis guns, the like of which we had never seen before, with all their attendant paraphernalia – including heavy Vickers pattern tripod stands on which to mount them. These we learnt feverishly; they were real guns at last and we loved them.[44]

If the lack of weapons and ammunition hampered the training of the infantry battalions, the technical branches of the New Army divisions, particularly the artillery, were in an even worse plight. In the autumn of 1914 many divisional gunners of the First New Army had to learn their complex duties without actually seeing an eighteen-pounder or 4·5 in. howitzer for weeks on end. Two months after the outbreak of war the First New Army had an average of six eighteen pounders per division instead of the required fifty-four. Throughout the New Army and Territorial divisions all sorts of improvised methods were employed to teach the men basic gun drill. In one unit the outline of a gun was drawn on the ground and the recruits drilled around the drawing.[45] At Bordon the artillery of the 15th (Scottish) Division began training with a dummy gun made from a log of wood mounted on a funeral gun carriage. An ancient nine-pounder brass muzzle-loader was also obtained from the Ordnance officers' mess.[46] An officer of A Battery of the 84th Brigade, Royal Field Artillery, which formed part of the 18th Division at Colchester, later described how his unit drilled with wooden guns and shells:

If the 'gun' was loaded smartly, the wooden shell was sent several feet from the muzzle ... by the impetus given to it by the No. 4! We also began to learn field movements on the Abbey Fields. Six men, marching in half sections, with a red flag, represented a gun team, and six men with a white flag pretended to be a wagon team.[47]

One Royal Field Artillery unit in London possessed a dummy gun which consisted of a length of guttering attached to a dung cart of the type that was a common sight in the streets in the days of horse-drawn traffic. Driver Leslie Crofts remembered pulling this cart by ropes to a field off the Fulham Palace Road:

Arriving there we would be met by a young pink-faced officer, so very conscious of his immaculate new uniform. He knew as much as we did about artillery training, but he had a little book and after perusing its pages he would give a word of command which would set us off cavorting around the field with our 'gun'. At a second command we would swing into action and kneel down in the approved manner. Then 'fire,' he would say, whereupon one of us would slam hard on the little tailboard, spring to his feet, give a magnificent salute, and exclaim 'No. 1 gun fired, Sir!'[48]

By such means recruits were taught the rudiments of loading and firing, but without technical aids like rangefinders and dial sights it became almost impossible to move on to the more advanced training. Until these were issued, wooden sights, with the degrees marked roughly upon them, were used by most artillery units. The situation improved slightly at the start of 1915 although deliveries of essential equipment remained frustratingly slow. It was not until February that one eighteen-pounder gun could be issued to each battery of the 20th (Light) Division.[49] The 84th Brigade, Royal Field Artillery, was still short of eighteen-pounders in May 1915, eight months after formation, while the gunners of the 15th Division received proper sights a mere three weeks before crossing to France.[50] In the 34th Division, the 176th Brigade acquired its first 4·5 in. howitzer on 13 August 1915, and the full quota was not available until 24th November. The unit had only three days' gun practice prior to embarkation.[51] For the gunners of the 15th Division the first training shoots with live ammunition made everyone nervous: 'Shells burst at all ranges, and onlookers speculated somewhat uneasily on the fate of infantry in action supported by such artillery.'[52] In fact the artillery brigades of several New Army divisions fell badly behind in their training and were unable to accompany the infantry when the latter went overseas. The 31st Division left for Egypt with the 32nd Division's artillery, which, for a variety of reasons, had progressed more rapidly than its own, and the 33rd Division embarked for France with Territorial gunners of the 54th (East Anglian) Division. Going into battle with gunners whom they had never met before was not the best introduction to active service for the infantry of such divisions.

Notes

1   *History of the Ministry of Munitions*, HMSO, London, 1922, Vol. I, Part I, p. 92.
2   *Ibid.*, Vol. XI, Part IV, p. 2.
3   Note on the production of small arms and small arms ammunition, 1867–1914, MUN 5/341/170/5; *Statistics of the Military Effort of the British Empire*, p. 30.
4   *History of the Ministry of Munitions*, Vol. I, Part I, p. 91; Vol. XI, Part V, pp. 1–2, 9–13.
5   Notes on the development of weapons used in trench warfare, MUN 5/383/1600/14.
6   Notes on the scale of pre-war munitions output, MUN 5/341/170/7; *History of the Ministry of Munitions*, Vol. X, Part I, pp. 1–3.
7   *History of the Ministry of Munitions*, Vol. I, Part I, pp. 81–2.
8   *Ibid.*, Vol. XI, Part IV, p. 4.
9   Papers on War Office machine-gun requirements, MUN 5/123/1000/19; Birmingham Small Arms Co. Ltd: Rifle contracts for 1914 and 1915, MUN 5/377/1420/2.
10 *History of the Ministry of Munitions*, Vol. I, Part I, pp. 84–5.
11 *Ibid.*, pp. 91–2.
12 *Ibid.*, pp. 93–5.
13 *Ibid.*, Vol. I, Part I, pp. 97–8, Vol. XI, Part IV, pp. 10–12.
14 *Ibid.*, Vol. I, Part I, p. 15; Note by Major-General H. M. Lawson on the supply of machine-guns for the New Armies, 24 November 1914, WO 161/22; War Office letter, No. 20/Artillery/3818 A. G. 6, 6 January 1915, see Becke, *Order of Battle of Divisions*, Part 3A, p. i.
15 *History of the Ministry of Munitions*, Vol. XI, Part V, pp. 3–5; Report and statistical tables on munitions for the Army on 1 June 1915 and 1 January 1916, MUN 5/122/100/1.
16 *History of the Ministry of Munitions*, Vol. I, Part I, Appendix III, pp. 146–9.
17 *Ibid.*, Vol. I, Part I, p. 92; Vol. XI, Part V, p. 10.
18 Tables of issue of land service guns from August 1914 to March 1918, MUN 5/373/1200/7.
19 Papers of Lieutenant-Colonel S. C. Halse, Deputy Superintendent, Royal Small Arms Factory, Enfield, on rifle supply, MUN 5/190/1420/20; Reports on deliveries of machine guns, rifles, transport vehicles, etc., November 1915, MUN 5/188/1400/3; Memorandum on munitions supply, 13 April–31 May 1915, with statistical tables, MUN 5/8/172/17.
20 History of trench warfare research from August 1914 to May 1915, MUN 5/382/1600/8; Note on the development of weapons used in trench warfare, MUN 5/383/1600/14.
21 *Ibid.*, MUN 5/382/1600/8 and MUN 5/383/1600/14; Note on the work of the Grenade Section to January 1917, MUN 5/385/1640/1.
22 *History of the Ministry of Munitions*, Vol. XI, Part I, p. 35.
23 Notes on Stokes gun invention from January 1915 to March 1916, MUN 5/384/1611/1; *Ministry of Munitions Journal*, No. 6, May 1917, pp. 165–7.

24 Notes on Stokes gun invention from January 1915 to March 1916, MUN 5/384/1611/1.

25 *Ibid.*, MUN 5/384/1611/1; Lloyd George, *War Memoirs*, II, p. 79.

26 *Parliamentary Debates, House of Lords, 1915*, XVIII, cols. 721–4.

27 *Report and Statistics of Bad Time kept in Shipbuilding, Munitions and Transport Areas*, PP, 1914–1916, LV, 220, pp. 3, 24.

28 *First Report of the Central Control Board*, PP, 1914–16, XXV, Cd 8117, p. 4; *Second Report of the Central Control Board*, PP, 1916, XII, Cd 8243, pp. 1–29.

29 G. D. H. Cole, *Trade Unionism and Munitions*, Oxford University Press, 1923, pp. 53–4.

30 *History of the Ministry of Munitions*, Vol. I, Part II, p. 110.

31 Note by Major-General H. M. Lawson on the supply of rifles for the New Armies, 24 November 1914, WO 161/22.

32 Account by the Rev. O. B. Parsons in *The Green Howards Gazette*, XXIV, No. 277, April 1916, p. 9.

33 H. B. King, *The 7th (Service) Battalion Northamptonshire Regiment, 1914–1919*, Gale & Polden, Aldershot, 1919, p. 5.

34 Colonel H. C. Wylly, *The York and Lancaster Regiment, 1785–1919;* Vol. II (Territorial and Service Battalions), privately published, 1930, pp. 143, 165–6; Richard A. Sparling, *History of the 12th (Service) Battalion York and Lancaster Regiment*, pp. 13–17.

35 Lieutenant-Colonel R. F. Truscott, *A Short History of the 16th Battalion the Sherwood Foresters (Chatsworth Rifles)*, privately published, 1928, pp. 1–19.

36 John Nettleton, *The Anger of the Guns*, Kimber, London, 1979, p. 27.

37 Anon., *The Tenth Battalion the Cameronians (Scottish Rifles): a record and Memorial, 1914–1918*, Edinburgh Press, 1923, p. 9.

38 Captain C. I. Hadrill, *A History of the 10th (Service) Battalion the East Yorkshire Regiment (Hull Commercials) 1914–1919*, pp. 9–10.

39 R. F. E. Evans, *Some Wartime Experiences*, unpublished account, post–1945, IWM PP/MCR/75.

40 I. L. Read, *A Narrative: 1914–1919*, unpublished account, 1968, IWM DS/MISC/68.

41 D. C. Burn, *Peregrinations Pro Patria*, unpublished account, 1919, IWM PP/MCR/73.

42 T. Macdonald, *Kitchener's Man*, unpublished account, n.d., IWM 76/213/1.

43 Captain C. H. Cooke, *Historical Records of the 9th (Service) Battalion Northumberland Fusiliers, p. 13.*

44 I. L. Read, *op. cit.*, IWM DS/MISC/68.

45 P. J. Sale, letter of 2 October 1963, IWM BBC/GW.

46 Lieutenant-Colonel J. Stewart and John Buchan, *The Fifteenth (Scottish) Division, 1914–1919*, pp. 14–15.

47 D. F. Grant, *The History of 'A' Battery, 84th Army Brigade, Royal Field Artillery, 1914–1919*, Marshall, London, 1922, pp. 14–15.

48 Leslie Crofts, letter of 1 November 1963, IWM BBC/GW.

49 Captain V. E. Inglefield, *The History of the Twentieth (Light) Division*, Nisbet, London, 1921, p. 5.

50 Grant, *op. cit.*, p. 16; Stewart and Buchan, *op. cit.*, p. 15.

51 Lieutenant-Colonel J. Shakespear, *The Thirty-fourth Division, 1915–1919*, Witherby, London, 1921, p. 6.

52 Stewart and Buchan, *op. cit.*, p. 15.

12

Preparing for the front

I

The Army Order which officially brought the First New Army into existence on 21 August 1914 also laid down a six-month syllabus of training for men in the infantry, artillery and engineers. Recruit training for the infantry was to cover a period of ten weeks at an average of eight hours a day. In the first fortnight recruits were to receive preliminary instruction in musketry and elementary squad drill and would start to learn such basic military procedures as saluting, standing to attention, forming a straight line on parade, turning by numbers and wheeling from line into a column of fours for route-marching on the roads. Extended order drill and night work would be introduced in the third week, route marching in the fourth week, outpost duties in the fifth week and entrenching and bayonet fighting in the seventh and ninth weeks respectively. Platoon drill would begin in the tenth week. Six hours each week were to be devoted to physical training. After three months, during which the men were expected to complete the recruits' musketry course, company training was to commence and continue for another five weeks. At this juncture some men were to be selected for specialist training as machine-gunners, grenade-throwers ('bombers') and scouts, or in signalling and transport duties. By the fifth month the troops were to have graduated to training at battalion and brigade strength, with field days, entrenching schemes and extended route marches comprising a major part of the syllabus. The final stages of the programme included the completion of the trained soldiers' musketry course, field firing with artillery support, and divisional exercises and route marches lasting two or three days at a time.

In the case of the artillery, the period of recruit training was much shorter, covering only six weeks. Like the infantry, gunners and drivers were to spend time performing dismounted drill and physical exercises, but the gunners also had to learn gun drill and the techniques of loading, laying, fuse-setting and firing, while the drivers were taught how to ride and to look after horses and stables. From the seventh week onwards the gunners would be given special instruction in signalling and rangefinding, with the drivers beginning mounted drill as soon as they were sufficiently good riders. Mounted parades and manoeuvres at battery strength, as well as practice shoots on a miniature range, were to start after thirteen weeks, brigade drills and exercises in the nineteenth week and divisional artillery training in the sixth and final month. For recruits in the field companies of the Royal Engineers there was a three-month programme of basic training which, in addition to squad drill, signalling and musketry, embraced instruction in field fortifications and demolition work. In the fourth month the sappers progressed to bridging and combined training with the infantry and artillery.[1]

These programmes were adequate enough in theory, but in practice they proved impossible to implement. The lack of experienced officers and NCOs was a serious handicap to most New Army and Territorial battalions, particularly during the early weeks of training while vast numbers of recruits and recently commissioned subalterns were struggling to come to terms with their strange new environment and required detailed guidance in almost every aspect of military routine. Even when they had acquired a reasonable knowledge of drill and discipline, recruits were plagued by shortages of vital equipment at each successive stage in their training. Further disruption to the timetables was caused by the atrocious weather in the late autumn of 1914 and the consequent need to move the men out of their unfinished camps into scattered billets. This in turn delayed the concentration of units for brigade and divisional exercises and made it hard for the War Office and the regional commands to supervise and co-ordinate the training of the larger formations. Standards therefore tended to vary, with some divisions reaching the desired level of efficiency much more rapidly than others, a lot depending on the ability and initiative of their individual commanding officers. Whereas they were originally expected to be fit for active service after six months, most New Army divisions remained at home for at least nine months, and in a few instances it was a year or more before they were considered ready to proceed overseas.

The main problem at the beginning was the military ignorance of the majority of recruits and junior officers alike. Some young subalterns were fortunate enough to start their military service with a brief period of attachment to the Inns of Court Officers' Training Corps or a university OTC, while others attended a course of instruction at Sandhurst or the Staff College at Camberley. Those who were given even a limited amount of preliminary training in this way generally found it of immense value. Ivone Kirkpatrick was granted a commission in the 8th Royal Inniskilling Fusiliers in November 1914, but was told to report first to the Staff College at Camberley with full kit:

On my arrival I found that 200 officers had been divided into three companies, 'O', 'P' and 'Q', and that the course was to last a month, i.e. till Christmas. I was posted to 'P' Company under Captain Wheatley of the Argyll and Sutherland Highlanders. The course included instruction in squad drill, company drill, physical training,

entrenching and topography, practical and theoretical. We were kept hard at work. First parade was at 6.30 a.m. and no respite was given till 10 p.m. when we all went cheerfully to bed. Most of us picked up a great deal of knowledge at Camberley and I shudder to think what we should have been without the course.[2]

For J. H. Allen the ten weeks spent with the Inns of Court OTC, prior to receiving a commission in the 13th Worcestershire Regiment, enabled him to overcome much of his self-doubt about his capacity for command:

It was at this time that there was born in my mind a lasting fellow-feeling, or at any rate an understanding sympathy, with the man who has difficulties with his apparently simple duties in the ranks. I found it harder to grasp forming fours than I did later on to explain, say, aiming off the target for wind . . . The terror of a mistake haunted me as it has never done since I have been an officer. After a week or so the maze of drill straightened itself out into something fairly simple. I procured a drill-book, and interest took the place of alarm . . . But I felt no confidence until one afternoon, in Lincoln's Inn Fields, Warner told me to come out and drill the company – I had thought that was a feat I should never achieve. I saw persons of even less than ordinary ability do it with enjoyment and success, and I could only suppose that some deficiency in my brain made it impossible for me. As it happened, Warner missed me out. But I thought, now or never, and in the most horrible funk I asked a sergeant to tell Warner he had overlooked me. I was called out, and my alarm vanished . . . I put the company through a few movements I knew, and shouted out the orders with confidence. When I was getting to the end of what I knew, Warner said: 'That will do. I didn't know you had such a good voice.' I returned to my place in the ranks radiant with relief and happiness.[3]

In 1914, however, many officers were sent straight to their battalions without any training whatsoever and had to learn as they went along. Junior subalterns would often stay up late, preparing their work for the following day, and consistently defied the age-old taboo of 'talking shop' in the officers' mess. Long after the war Guy Chapman recalled the dedication of the young officers of the 13th Royal Fusiliers:

Even now I am amazed at the zeal which induced some of us after dinner to push matches representing platoons about the table, uttering words of command in hoarse whispers, or on Sunday mornings climb the frosty, wind-cropped downs to practise map-reading and marching by the compass . . . We had to get our text-books by heart before we could impart a crumb of information to our platoons. We seized on and devoured every fragment of practical experience which came our way, gobbled whole the advice contained in those little buff pamphlets entitled 'Notes from the Front', advice, alas, out of date before it was published. We listened hopefully to the lectures of general officers who seemed happier talking of Jubbulpore than of Ypres . . . We were in fact amateurs, and though we should stoutly have denied it, in our hearts amateurs we knew ourselves to be, pathetically anxious to achieve the status of the professional.[4]

According to Geoffry Christie-Miller of the 2/1st Buckinghamshire Battalion, it was a major incentive to learn during an afternoon instruction parade for officers if one knew that, next morning, one would have to teach the same thing to a batch of keen-witted and critical recruits:

This was one of the principal factors in the rapidity with which the new officers fitted themselves to instruct and command. There was no chance of the new, inexperienced and sometimes nervous officer being able to . . . shout out 'Sergeant-Major, you take them for a bit', because he knew only too well that whatever misgivings he might have of his own ability to instruct in the military art, these misgivings were multiplied tenfold in the case of his raw and inexperienced NCOs.[5]

Happily for the untrained officers and NCOs, the men shared their desire to equip themselves as quickly as possible for active service. The extraordinary goodwill which prevailed on both sides enabled most units to complete their basic training much sooner than expected, considering the many obstacles they encountered. The task of the officers was also made easier by the high standards of education of a large proportion of the recruits. 'It is interesting work drilling them', wrote Second Lieutenant C. C. Aston of the 4th Battalion of the Bedfordshire Regiment in September 1914. 'Of course they know *nothing* – absolutely – of drill but they're keen and those I've handled so far have been far above the average intelligence of the Tommy.'[6] Nevertheless, it took some weeks for the recruits to shake off the attitudes of civilian life. A private in the 7th King's Shropshire Light Infantry, checked by a sergeant for failing to salute the adjutant, replied indignantly, 'Why, I 'ardly knows 'im!'[7] An officer of the 7th East Lancashire Regiment recounted an amusing incident during the first route march of one of the battalion's four companies:

After 50 minutes' marching, the company was halted and ordered to fall out on the side of the road; the company commander had taken the precaution of halting some 300 yards past the Ram Hotel; but no sooner had the order to fall out . . . been given than almost the whole company rushed in a body to the inn, to the amazement of the officers and the furious indignation of the reservist non-commissioned officers.[8]

The historian of the Newcastle Commercials described the attitude of the recruits in the early days of that battalion as being a blend of earnestness and levity.[9] Humorous incidents at least afforded a little light relief from the drudgery of interminable drill, and recruits were sometimes only too glad to take full advantage of the fumblings of inexperienced officers, as A. E. Perriman of the 11th South Wales Borderers relates:

We soon learned the rudimentary movements of turning to the left, right, and about turn. When it came to 'At the halt on the left or right form platoons,' instructions as to the mass movements were so vague that anything could happen, and did. The biggest laugh was Company drill. Officers in turn took over this parade and were, I'm afraid, not too conversant with the drill book . . . Almost from the first word of command there was chaos. Before the OC realised, he had us herded up like a flock of sheep in a corner of the parade ground. Time and time again this happened . . . To be fair, the lads so enjoyed the mess-up that they went out of their way to add to the confusion.[10]

Shortly after joining the 9th Sherwood Foresters, Second Lieutenant T. H. Barnes found himself in an embarrassing situation when asked by his company commander to take church parade:

I had to form my men of C Company in the third formation of the battalion in mass. Unfortunately untrained troops, as we all were in Kitchener's Army, always spread out when marching. I was watching the company marker for the moment when the last file passed him to give the next order . . . To my utter consternation the three leading files instead of marking time when they reached the fence at the edge of the field, just climbed over it and were marching away across the next field into the blue! I looked towards Major Fielden and he was absolutely doubled up with laughter. He hurried over and said 'They have been a bit too quick for you, Barnes, I will take over.' He roared out 'Files in the field, halt!' He then completed the orders to the rest of the company to bring them into line. He then gave the order to the twelve men in the field, 'About turn, quick, march! . . . Lieutenant-Colonel Bosanquet did not look at all amused!'[11]

The first few weeks of training provided a severe test of the resolution and stamina of all ranks, for the hours were long and hard. Private A. K. Aston, of the 8th Norfolk Regiment, wrote home from Shorncliffe in September 1914:

. . . they are working us like the devil and a lot of chaps are crocking up owing I think chiefly to the rations not being of the best. Personally I never felt better than a slack one. Just listen to this for a day's work, especially to put chaps to who are soft and untrained. Reveille goes at 3.30 a.m., then we have squad drill until about 5.30, then we have a ten minute break. After that we march three miles down to the sea and bathe, come back and have about half an hour for breakfast, and then parade again until 12.30, then one hour for lunch and drill again until 4.30 when we stop for the day and clean up . . . We are allowed out from 7 to 9.30 when all lights have to be put out.[12]

At Aldershot Second Lieutenant Gerard Clauson of the 6th Somerset Light Infantry faithfully recorded the details of each day's training in his diary. 'Swedish drill' (or physical training) was a regular part of the battalion's daily routine. Clauson noted that the work carried out on 5 October was 'more than usually strenuous', having lasted for some sixteen hours:

Rose 5.50. Route march 6.25. Paraded again 8.50, and marched to Horsell Common, where we spent the rest of the morning in extended order drill, attack practice etc., terminating with a fine charge and so home to lunch. 1.50 Parade, Swedish and platoon drill, Swedish drill 5.30, dinner 7 o'clock. Night operations 8.20 to 10.35 and so to bed . . . Have started a rather bad cold and cough on account of the shouting and the dust.[13]

Self-respect, comradeship and patriotism all helped to keep the recruits going during this stringent basic training, as Emlyn Davies of the 17th Royal Welsh Fusiliers lated recalled:

Arms and legs and feet and back reacted too unkindly at first. As days followed days, and weeks followed weeks, the story was rather different . . . Acceptance of the King's shilling brooked neither legitimate nor possible protest. So naturally and not unwillingly, we 'soldiered on'. Might I add 'happily' too. A new comradeship and unity blossomed into our young lives. So we just soldiered on, For God, For King and For Country, as we were each and all convinced.[14]

Boring and arduous it may have been, but the recruit training had the effect of weeding out the unfit from the new battalions and of bringing about a noticeable change in the physique and bearing of many of the men. Fresh air, regular meals and plenty of exercise did wonders for the health of recruits from industrial areas. Robert Roberts was astonished at the appearance of those returning to Salford on leave: 'Pounds – sometimes stones – heavier, taller, confident, clean and straight, they were hardly recognisable as the men who went away. Others, seeing the transformation, hurried off to barracks.'[15]

The growing fitness of the men was reflected in the progressive increases in the length of the route marches they undertook. Initially the marches were for about five or six miles, with a halt of ten minutes every hour, and they served to get the recruits into condition while introducing the officers to such elementary duties as the care of the men's feet. Gradually, however, the marches were extended to twelve or thirteen miles and then to more than twenty. For all the technology of modern war and the widespread use of mechanical transport in everyday life, the army was desperately short of motor transport in 1914 and the ability to march long distances was still considered to be a requirement of paramount importance for the infantryman. The misery of some of these marches is a recurring theme in the diaries, letters and memoirs of the officers and men of Kitchener's army. M. J. H. Drummond describes one such march in July 1915, when he was a subaltern in the 10th Lancashire Fusiliers:

The last seven miles were done without a halt, as the CO thought we were nearly home when we weren't, and went on without the usual rest, with the result that we fell out like flies. Pickering (a 2. Lt. of my Company) and I, being at the back of the battalion, tried to encourage those who fell out to come on, by carrying their rifles etc. I carried three rifles for at least a mile, and two for another two miles, as well as my own equipment and pack. I got into camp about 100 yds. behind the battalion, just able to crawl, having put a bone out of place in my foot . . . I was unable to walk for a day or two, was excused parades, and sent home for a fortnight.[16]

Occasionally men died from over-exertion. Percy Croney of the 12th Essex Regiment has related how after a trying march on a hot day in 1915 seventy-three men were taken to hospital, with three dying from sunstroke:

It is a crime to fall out on a march, nor would any man do so for very honour's sake. One, exhausted, steps to the verge from his file. One there, consciousness gone, drops on the road, and the man behind stumbles against him. The battalion re-forms 'line of companies' in close 'column of platoon' on the parade ground only minutes later than schedule, though much under strength. In the evening, feet having been bathed in cold water and much tea drunk, we lie on our cots twiddling bare toes, and filled with pride, for has not an old 2nd Battalion man, re-joined for the duration, but disdaining promotion, told us, 'You Kitchener's men did tidy well!' . . .[17]

There were other searching examinations of the spirit and discipline of the New Armies. Men of the 18th Durham Light Infantry were on coast defence duties near the Lighthouse Battery at Hartlepool when German warships bombarded the town on 16 December 1914. Five men were killed and eleven wounded, one of whom died later. Two NCOs of the battalion distinguished themselves by running down to the beach in the thick of the shelling to rescue a wounded fisherman.[18] Then, on 22 January 1915, troops of the 9th, 14th, 15th, 20th and 23rd Divisions were inspected in the Epsom–Aldershot–Frensham area by Kitchener and M. Millerand, the French Minister of War.

Most of the men involved had to march several miles to the review in a steady downpour of sleet and snow, and were obliged to wait for two hours or more in a biting wind before Kitchener's party arrived. The ground was a morass of ice, mud and cold water and the majority of bandsmen, suffering from numbed fingers and lips, were unable to play. Lord Midleton, who accompanied the official party, observed that men in the rear ranks of the 14th Division were playing leap-frog to keep warm at the moment when Kitchener and Millerand got out of their car.[19] For the 6th Oxfordshire and Buckinghamshire Light Infantry, part of the 20th Division, the inspection, according to D. C. Burn, merely consisted of a 'string of cars, containing Kitchener and Co., driving slowly along a road, some 300 yards away from the front rank of our division—and that was all. We didn't even see the man for whom 20,000 men had waited, standing shivering in deep thawing snow, for three hours!'[20] Second Lieutenant Ian Melhuish of the 7th Somerset Light Infantry, in the same division, related his experiences in a letter to his mother:

We left Barracks at 11 a.m. for the Review ground. Of course the roads were awful, thick slush and mud, and naturally everyone had their boots full of water. Long before we had completed the seven miles to the ground most of us were wet to the skin in spite of macks and coats. Well, we got to the parade ground at 1.30 p.m. Kitchener did not turn up till 4 p.m. and then he only went by in a closed car and we did not see him. Those two and a half hours standing in water and slush over our ankles, wet through with a biting wind, driving sleet and heavy rain against you all the time, was about the nearest attempt at hell I have so far experienced. We could not move about much as we were in review order. The only recreation and amusement we had was to count the people who fainted and had to be carried out. The engineers won with thirty-two, our company had eight only.

The scandal was that 12,000 men had been brought out seven miles from home with one small ambulance wagon to hold six. The remainder had to lie in the slush, some almost covered, until help arrived. Of course some suffered from exposure, fortunately only two died.

Having been through this ordeal, Melhuish, like many others, had no further doubts about the quality of the troops:

'It is an ill wind' etc., and it has shown that the men are splendid. They held the most splendid discipline worthy of the best trained soldiers, laughing and singing though they were too cold to move their hands. I don't think Germany will win.[21]

Incidents such as the bombardment of the Hartlepools and the Kitchener-Millerand review clearly showed that the New Armies possessed at least some potential for the field and that the units raised in August and September were ready to graduate to more advanced tactical training. The tragedy was that for several months, and through no fault of their own, the men were trained for a type of open warfare which bore little or no resemblance to the conditions they would meet on the western front and elsewhere.

The main feature of the prescribed tactics for the attack and counter-attack, as laid down in the 1914 manual *Infantry Training*, was the combination of fire and movement. Major-General J. M. L. Grover, who went to

Sandhurst just after the outbreak of the Great War, subsequently commented:

The conception of infantry tactics in 1914 was very different from that at the beginning of the Second World War. It was really based on the lessons of the Boer War superimposed on the Crimea . . . One of the main lessons of the Boer War was the immense value of the rifle handled by experts, so that the basic infantry training was to develop a very proficient rifleman with a bolt-operated weapon which he was trained to fire up to fifteen rounds a minute rapid. But we only had two machine-guns in a battalion . . . and they were not even taught at Sandhurst. The idea was, you built up a firing line by advancing in small rushes of detachments, then by the volume of your fire you attempted to overcome the people who were either advancing against you or were shooting at you . . .[22]

In these tactics, the portions of a battalion or platoon gaining ground by a series of rushes would be supported by covering fire from the remainder of the unit and from the artillery. By this procedure a strong firing line would be built up between 200 and 400 yards from the enemy. The leading lines would be reinforced during the ensuing fire-fight and then, according to the manual:

. . . as the enemy's fire is gradually subdued, further progress will be made by bounds from place to place, the movement gathering renewed force at each pause until the enemy can be assaulted with the bayonet.[23]

An attacking force was divided into firing line and supports, with local reserves, and the advance was often made in parallel lines in extended order, but the form was elastic and adapted to the ground with the definite objects of maintaining control, utilising such cover as was available and presenting as difficult a target as possible to the enemy. Against frontal artillery fire, or direct long-range infantry fire, it was recommended that small shallow columns, each on a narrow front, would offer a more difficult target and could usefully be employed during the earlier stages of an attack. On open ground swept by effective rifle fire, an extended line was regarded as the least vulnerable formation. However:

A formation in small columns should be retained as long as it is applicable to the situation, for, when, once extended, a unit loses its power of manoeuvre. As a general principle deployment is necessary when fire is to be opened, the amount of extension then depending on the volume of fire which it is required to produce, and upon the effect of the enemy's fire. The greater the extension of a line, the fewer will be the casualties, but the less will be its fire effect.[24]

The soundness of the principle of fire and movement was proved during the war, but insufficient attention was paid during the training of Kitchener's army to its adaption to the special conditions of trench warfare and the domination of the open ground by machine guns and artillery. Until more machine guns became available, the strengthening of the firing line meant providing reinforcements at the rate of one man for each rifle, and consequently a packed firing line suffered heavily from artillery and machine-gun fire even before the assault phase began. Furthermore, the system of attacking in waves, with supports and reserves following at intervals behind the assault, produced casualties in the rear, where the men were unable to contribute to the fire-fight.

As experience was obtained the hard way on the Western Front it was found that there was no role for supports of the kind suggested in the pre-war manuals. Reinforcing a line already halted by casualties simply resulted in even greater losses without any corresponding advance. It also became apparent that the proper employment of local reserves was to exploit local successes, or, defensively, to fill gaps in the attacking line that had been brought to a standstill.

If some of these lessons were being learned by the spring of 1915, there is little evidence that they were incorporated into the training as a whole until the late summer and autumn of that year, though in individual cases officers returning from the Western Front were able to pass on their knowledge. A few commanding officers, like the CO of the 3rd (Special Reserve) Battalion of the Leinster Regiment, corresponded regularly with officers in France, and were therefore in a position to give training a more practical bias, down to such basic questions as the right and wrong way to fill a sandbag.[25] In general, however, there was a yawning gap between the evolving tactical doctrine of the forces in the field and those in training at home. Only in mid–1915 did it become more customary for officers, NCOs and men of the New Armies to attend special courses of instruction in bombing, musketry, signalling, transport duties and the care and use of machine guns. Not until June 1918 was an Inspector-General of Training appointed. As a result, progress towards a common doctrine was extremely slow, and in the meantime the commanding officers of the New Army formations, guided by the various manuals issued by the War Office, tended to carry the main responsibility for tactical training.

The consequences of leaving much of the training to the resources and imagination of individual commanding officers were not necessarily disastrous in all cases. Major-General Maxse of the 18th Division, for instance, proved an outstanding trainer of troops. Harold Hemming, who served under him in 1915, having transferred from the infantry to the 84th Brigade, Royal Field Artillery, wrote, 'Attending his fortnightly conference, listening hard and taking notes, was like a university course on how to make a fine fighting division out of 20,000 semi-trained, albeit enthusiastic soldiers.'[26] An officer of the 10th Essex Regiment remarked:

As the parade ground gave way to field training, so we began to see more of our great man, General Maxse, and his personality commenced to infuse itself visibly into the corporate consciousness of what we were beginning to know as the 18th Division . . . And one remembers with marvelling the feat he used to perform when he would pass the Battalion, Brigade and later the Division in review on the line of march, and greet by name every subaltern that passed. It went right home, for you felt you were working for a chief who knew you, and not merely for an abstraction in a brass hat.[27]

In contrast, I. L. Read, while training with the 37th Division, saw his divisional commander only once, and then 'from a dusty distance'.[28] Other young officers found that initiative was stifled by their superiors. On a night training exercise Second Lieutenant Arthur Bliss of the 13th Royal Fusiliers was ordered to take a patrol through 'enemy' outposts and report on their positions:

It happened to be a full moon that night which made secrecy difficult; so I commandeered a hay-cart that was moving in the direction we had to take and hid my men in it. To make the disguise even securer, caps were exchanged with the farmer and his son. In this way I was able to make a good get-away and a fairly accurate report. To my surprise I was given to understand that if I played the fool in this way I had better go elsewhere . . . As all of us realised, we were simply wasting these early months in play acting – no proper uniforms, no proper rifles, elderly retired officers instructing us in methods long discarded . . . It required a lot of imagination and confidence to remember that we were training to face the gigantic German war machine.[29]

The lack of general supervision and co-ordination of training, the delays in revising existing tactical doctrine, and the consequent over-dependence of commanding officers on out-of-date manuals all conspired to give field training an air of unreality and amateurishness which began to disappear only when the first New Armies had already gone overseas. Reginald Cockburn remembered field exercises with the 10th King's Royal Rifle Corps:

Those were the happy days when you could capture a village by merely marching into it; when you could hold up a Battalion by pointing a dummy machine-gun at it, and refusing to budge; when you usually had lunch with the enemy, each side claiming the victory, over cheese sandwiches, chocolate, apples and water.[30]

Men of the Newcastle Commercials found it equally hard to take a serious view of tactical schemes:

One had to visualise the hostile enemy marching, say, from Berwick to storm the Town Hall of Gateshead. If the eager defending force did not realise where the hostile troops had reached, there would be an amazing and amusing medley . . . In the famous Battle of Warkworth, 'A' Company marched in column of route up the main street, which, according to the narrative, was swept by a number of machine-guns posted on the top of the hill! Annihilation was often a twice hourly occurrence. The nine lives of a cat were negligible to the number possessed by each man on a tactical scheme.[31]

As late as June 1915, one month before crossing to France, brigades in the 37th Division were performing field exercises which, judging from the following account by the CO of the 10th Royal Fusiliers, would have been more relevant to tactical conditions in the Franco-Prussian War than those prevailing on the western front:

Reveille at 6 a.m. I commanded Rear Guard, i.e. 10th Fusiliers and eight squadrons Cavalry. Force retiring from Vernham's Dean by Conholt and Chute on Ludgershall, A and B Co. in front. C Co. in central secondary position. D Co. in reserve. Fought backwards on a line Fosbury Hill, Oxhill Wood, hence covered by cavalry on to Chute

Causeway. Succeeded in holding enemy until noon, and so enabled main body to retire.[32]

Infantry battalions were expected to devote a fair amount of time to training in night operations, the object of which was to accustom the soldier to moving in the dark, so that individuals and units could act with the same freedom by night as by day. The soldiers were often in the dark in more senses than one. J. L. Stewart-Moore recounts that, in the summer of 1915, the whole of the 36th (Ulster) Division carried out a night exercise in the Eastbourne–Lewes area of Sussex though the overall purpose of the scheme was not revealed to the officers, at least not to those of Stewart-Moore's own battalion, the 15th Royal Irish Rifles.[33] Many night manoeuvres ended in hopeless confusion, like the one described by Captain R. Ede England of the 12th King's Own Yorkshire Light Infantry (Miners' Battalion). This took place in the grounds of Farnley Hall in the winter of 1914–15:

> The scene of action was the Park and its immediate vicinity, which was held by A and D Companies, whose dispositions, it appeared afterwards, were somewhat erratic. A Company, under Captain Prothero, was to force a way through the armed cordon, and had marched out of camp early in the evening. It was a dark and miserable night, and the slightly nervous defending troops waited patiently for a sign of the enemy. Not a sound was heard save the moaning of the wind in the trees. Suddenly an unearthly yell was succeeded by a terrific fusilade of 'blank' and followed by a wild chorus of victory. The defenders, however, remained quite unmoved and unshaken, for it became clear that the attackers had 'captured' a sewage farm which was quite unoccupied by any garrison, and, moreover, was on the wrong side of the river![34]

Even the preparation for the three critical phases of the attack under the old tactics – the advance by detachments, the fire-fight, and the final assault with the bayonet – was not always as thorough as it might have been. The absence of modern weapons and the shortage of small arms ammunition robbed musketry training of much of its value, while troops sometimes found it hard to appreciate the benefits of skirmishing practice. James Pratt, who trained at Bedford as a company sergeant-major with a Territorial battalion, the 1/4th Gordon Highlanders, said:

> You advanced by rushes of twenty, thirty yards, flopped down behind a bit of cover and were then supposed to go on firing from there. But it wasn't very popular, particularly when you had to do it over a ploughed field in the winter time, when you got your clothing and your rifle all thoroughly messed up.[35]

Contrary to popular belief, large numbers of men in Kitchener or Territorial battalions received only a few hours' training in bayonet fighting. For example, from 22 March 1915, when he joined the 19th Royal Fusiliers (2nd Public Schools Battalion), to 14 November 1915, when he crossed to France, Private Leonard Salter spent one morning and parts of three other mornings in bayonet practice, less time than he spent undergoing kit and hut inspections (six mornings and four afternoons).[36] In the 17th Royal Welsh

Fusiliers, Emlyn Davies was instructed in bayonet fighting only once in five months:

Straw-filled sacks were suspended from a cross-bar fixed to two upright posts about six feet high ... From a distance of about thirty yards the assailants rushed at the double with a rile and bayonet firmly grasped at the ready. On reaching the target a short sharp prod in the sack was aimed at the victim's tummy; a sharp withdrawal ensured that the opponent would be unable to return the compliment, then followed a rush forward to the next opponent and so on. Actually I myself crossed the English Channel with only one such practice to rely upon in meeting the enemy. I felt naked.[37]

II

From the end of 1914 onwards, changes in the organisation of the New Armies, coupled with the government's belated recognition of the problems caused by the unrestricted enlistment of skilled manpower—particularly from the munitions industry—began to have serious effects on both the form and continuity of training for many infantry battalions.

In December 1914, with the pattern of trench warfare clearly established on the Western Front, the War Office decided to add a Pioneer battalion on the Indian Army model to each division of the New Armies. These battalions were to be equipped and trained as infantry units but were also to be issued with technical stores and to receive extra instruction in entrenching, road-making, bridging and demolition work. As Pioneer battalions were likely to undertake a great deal of digging, it was decreed that:

... at least 50 per cent of the Non-commissioned officers and men should have been miners or accustomed to work with pick and shovel in civil life. Of the remaining 50 per cent, as many as possible, having due regard to their physique, should be men who were employed or who were learning the trades of carpenter, joiner, mason, bricklayer, blacksmith or other metal worker, but they must all be subsequently instructed in and capable of dealing with earth excavation.

Battalions to be converted into Pioneers were to be those containing the largest proportion of men with such qualifications, although not necessarily from the same division. Thus if a division had more than one suitable battalion it could switch units with a division unable to furnish its own Pioneer battalion.[38] The Pioneers were not incorporated into the Royal Engineers' structure but were intended to supplement Royal Engineers labour and to be associated much more closely with the RE field companies than normal infantry. The North Eastern Railway Battalion (17th Northumberland Fusiliers) and the Miners' Battalion (12th King's Own Yorkshire Light Infantry) had obvious potential as Pioneer units and were converted in January and April 1915 respectively. Some battalions, like the Severn Valley Pioneers (14th Worcestershire Regiment), were specially raised after the War Office decision, but for others conversion meant that soldiers without a recognised trade had to be exchanged for men who did possess the required skills. The 8th Welsh Regiment lost nearly one-sixth of its original officers and men in this way.[39]

The New Armies suffered additional disruption in 1915 as a result of the efforts of the Ministry of Munitions to recover skilled workers from the army. As early as January 1915 Kitchener and the Army Council, who were only too aware of the urgency of army contracts for war material, accepted in principle that it might well prove necessary to let certain highly skilled men return to their old jobs in industry, and over the next few months two different methods were adopted to facilitate the process. One, known as 'individual release', permitted an employer to apply for the release of a skilled man who had worked for him before enlisting. The value of this method was that a soldier who went back to work for his former employer was generally found to be more efficient than a stranger to the firm. The alternative scheme, referred to as 'bulk release', enabled the soldier himself to declare his willingness to return to his old trade, though he had to agree to work wherever he was sent. If his industrial skills seemed likely to be useful in munitions production, he might then be released to an appropriate firm to help meet its demand for that kind of labour. Under the individual release method the names of eligible soldiers were obtained from the employers' applications, but the bulk release scheme required staff officers and representatives of the munition firms to visit units in order to interview the men and arrange terms. In both cases, however, released men continued to be soldiers and remained subject to military discipline. They received the wage prevailing in the area to which they were transferred, or their army pay and allowances, whichever was the higher, and were liable for recall to the colours if and when they were no longer needed for munitions work.

In the first half of 1915 the flow of released men amounted to no more than a trickle. Before the Ministry of Munitions came into existence about 3,000 men had left their units to go back into armaments factories and by the beginning of July the total had reached only 5,025 of whom 4,184 had been released under the bulk scheme and 841 in response to direct applications for individual men.[40] It was not until 4 July that the first significant step was taken towards solving this aspect of the overall manpower problem on a more systematic basis. On that day Major F. J. Scott was appointed to organise a Release from the Colours Section within the Labour Supply Department of the Ministry of Munitions. Nevertheless, as Scott quickly appreciated, there were still several obstacles to overcome before his work would bear fruit. For example, while the War Office was, on the whole, sympathetic to the principle of releasing men, Kitchener argued, not unreasonably, that certain units should be barred to investigators acting on behalf of the Ministry of Munitions. As he explained to Lloyd George on 3 July, the day before Scott's appointment, '. . . I am sure we should do well to begin by taking those serving in the units which have not yet completed their training, and that until we have exhausted this source of supply we should leave alone those which are abroad or are standing ready to go abroad.'[41] Lloyd George agreed to

Kitchener's proposal that, initially at least, the Ministry of Munitions should steer clear of 'barred' units. In short, the First, Second and Third New Armies and first-line Territorial units would not be approached by Scott and his colleagues although men could be taken from depots, reserve units, the Fourth and Fifth New Armies and the second and third lines of the Territorial Force.

The main drawback to these restrictions from the Ministry's standpoint was that many of the most highly skilled workers had enlisted in the first weeks of the war and were therefore in precisely those formations which were now 'barred'. Even when they were not in 'barred' units, recruits were often extremely reluctant to leave their comrades to return to the factory floor. Hence Scott's first attempt to extend the bulk scheme, in July and August 1915, was not a great success, securing the release of just over 2,000 men.[42] When recounting some of these difficulties, in a speech in the House of Commons on 20 December 1915, Lloyd George described efforts to win men back from the colours as a 'great rearguard action' which was like 'getting through barbed wire entanglements without heavy guns'. He went on to say, 'There are entrenchments behind entrenchments. You have not merely the army, the corps, the division, the brigade, the battalion, and the company, but the platoon, and even the squad – everybody fighting to prevent men from coming away.'[43]

By mid-August Major Scott had realised that it would be necessary to wring further concessions from the War Office before a really worthwhile number of skilled men could be obtained from the army. Specifically, Scott wished to make a thorough search for skilled men in *all* units that had not yet gone overseas, including those of the Third New Army. On 9 September, after three weeks of negotiations between the Ministry of Munitions and the War Office, Sclater, the Adjutant-General, at last gave an assurance that any units of the Third New Army which were not under orders to embark would be open to inspection. Then, on 16 September, the Adjutant-General's Department instructed commanding officers that all skilled men 'at present serving with His Majesty's forces in the United Kingdom should, as far as possible, be placed at once at the disposal of the Ministry of Munitions for the purpose of expediting and increasing the supply of munitions'. A register of all suitable men was to be drawn up, excluding only those who were serving in the Royal Flying Corps or who were artificers in cavalry units, the Royal Artillery, Royal Engineers, Army Service Corps or Army Ordnance Corps. In the meantime it had been decided that the task of interviewing the soldiers in question to assess their capabilities would be performed by special investigators selected by the Labour Exchange Department of the Board of Trade. On their visits to units these investigators would be accompanied by expert registration clerks as well as representatives of the Ministry of Munitions and the War Office.[44]

The tours of inspection began on 23 September but did not get off to an auspicious start. When the investigating team arrived at Aldershot to inspect units of the Third New Army, the commander of the 25th Division, Major-General B. J. C. Doran, told them that he had not received the War Office instructions of 16 September and so had made no arrangements for the visit. Indeed, some of his battalions were leaving for the front that very evening while the rest were scheduled to depart in a day or two. The GOC Aldershot Command, Major-General A. Hamilton Gordon, admitted that he had been informed that a representative of the Ministry of Munitions would be coming but said that he had telegraphed to prevent the latter from having a wasted journey. Whatever the true explanation may have been, the inspectors were unable to carry out that part of their programme which related to Third New Army units still in the United Kingdom.[45]

After this, however, the tours of inspection became more effective. Between 23 September and 15 November 1915 some 1,500,000 men were paraded before, and addressed by, the inspectors and nearly 45,000 were assessed as suitable for transfer. In the event, 20,529 of these were actually released for munitions work as a result of this second bulk trawl of units at home. By the time the Release from the Colours programme came to an end in the late autumn of 1916, the total number of soldiers recorded as having started work in munition factories was 51,781, including 30,893 released under one or other of the bulk schemes and 20,888 on direct application from manufacturers.[46]

Despite the need for skilled men, the Ministry of Munitions tried to minimise the disruption to New Army formations, and in October 1915 the Ministry agreed not to seek the release of non commissioned officers of the Fourth New Army, then in the final stages of training. All the same, the sudden descents of the Ministry's inspectors caused some alarm in units about to leave for the front. For instance, some fifty men were earmarked for release from the Sheffield City Battalion (12th York and Lancaster Regiment) when an investigating team visited Hurdcott Camp on Salisbury Plain. Although the unit managed to keep a number of these men by claiming that they were trained specialists (i.e. machine-gunners, transport men and bombers) the problem was one which the battalion could well have done without on the eve of embarkation.[47]

Most New Army infantry battalions, indeed, saw considerable changes in their personnel during the training period, and not only because of the Release from the Colours programme or the conversion of the unit to Pioneer status. Deaths, discharges of under-age or unfit soldiers, desertions, the granting of commissions and transfers to other formations all played their part in altering the composition of a battalion. By 30 June 1915, for example, the 14th Royal Welsh Fusiliers had lost 377 men for various reasons since the battalion's inception in November the previous year. Two hundred and twenty-four of these men had been discharged, six had deserted, two had died and 105 had been transferred to other units. Thus, although the battalion's strength stood at 1,195 on 30 June, 1,532 men had in fact passed through its ranks during these months.[48] The Leeds Pals (15th West Yorkshire Regiment) saw even more men leave. Of the 1,028 officers and men on the battalion's nominal roll shortly before the unit's departure for Egypt in December 1915, only six officers and 534 other ranks were original volunteers who had joined the battalion in the first few days of September 1914.[49]

Within three or four months of the outbreak of war it also became apparent that the New Armies might well suffer heavy losses when they went into battle and would therefore need their own system of reinforcement from home. In December 1914 the locally raised battalions were ordered to form depot companies, and in 1915 these companies were grouped to form local reserve battalions to feed the necessary drafts to the parent units.[50] The original Fourth New Army, which had been organised from the surplus men posted to the Special Reserve battalions in the opening months of the war, was broken up in April 1915 to provide reserve battalions for the first three New Armies (9th to 26th Divisions).[51] The eventual Fourth and Fifth New Armies (30th to 41st Divisions) were composed largely of the Pals and Bantam units raised by cities, towns, private committees and individuals. The Special Reserve battalions continued to feed the Regular divisions of the BEF, while the third-line Territorial battalions fulfilled the same role for their own first and second-line units. Many men who joined the army in 1914 and 1915 were, in fact, sent straight into a Reserve unit rather than one of the new Service battalions and only joined a field unit at the front itself. The 3rd (Special Reserve) Battalion of the Cameron Highlanders alone provided 3,815 officers and men in drafts for battalions on active service during the first year of the war, and reinforcements and replacements on a similar scale were furnished by almost every Reserve battalion throughout the army in that period.[52]

As the Service battalions of the New Armies began to proceed overseas the reserve units took over the major share of the responsibility for training recruits after mid–1915. The length of time needed to prepare a man for a draft was gradually reduced until, by the end of the year, it was set at about twelve to fourteen weeks. For some nine weeks a volunteer would undergo the usual recruit training, including squad and company drill, and would then start preliminary musketry on a miniature range. In the tenth and eleventh weeks he might fire the full musketry course before receiving five days' instruction in bombing. When the short bombing course was over he was entitled to embarkation leave. On his return from this leave he would be taught how to use field dressings and anti-gas helmets and received final training in bayonet fighting, wire entanglements, and rapid loading and firing. The issue of new boots, which took about a fortnight to wear in, was a signal that he would be detailed for a draft in some fourteen days' time.

The training of officers was also placed on a more systematic footing, the practice of posting recently commissioned subalterns to their unit without any previous instruction being discontinued. During the summer of 1915 Young Officer Companies were established and attached to the reserve training brigades so that junior officers could be given an adequate grounding in their duties before being posted to Service battalions. In February 1916 a new method was introduced with the formation of Officer Cadet Battalions, in which candidates for a commission underwent a course of training lasting four months. Henceforth temporary commissions were granted only to those who had passed through the ranks of a cadet unit.[53]

The majority of these measures came too late to be of much immediate benefit to the existing New Army formations, although an attempt was made to provide more realistic training in trench warfare for those units still at home in the latter half of 1915. Practice in entrenching had, indeed, formed part of the training from the very beginning, and many battalions had helped to dig an elaborate system of defensive fortifications around London in the spring of 1915. Now, however, a greater proportion of the training programme was spent in manning and relieving trenches and in trench attacks. An officer of the 7th Royal Inniskilling Fusiliers in the 16th (Irish) Division described the belated steps taken at Bordon in December 1915 to give the men a foretaste of active service conditions:

Peculiar as it may seem, we had up to this time had very little instruction in trench life, and the established routine of 'manning and relieving'. True, we had many lectures about the life and routine of stationary warfare in France, but we needed some practical work in this branch to appreciate it thoroughly. This was all put into execution during our stay at Bordon. At least twice a week, companies would be detailed to dig, and improve the model trenches on the training area . . . By the end of December quite a fair system of trenches and redoubts had been completed, and it became part of the weekly programme to hold an all-night scheme in the vicinity. As a general rule these operations took the form of inter-company trench reliefs, and during the few hours that companies held the front line the men were kept busy widening and improving the trenches . . .[54]

At the end of August the Newcastle Commercials had a two-night exercise in trenches at Codford on the edge of Salisbury Plain: 'All the irritating restrictions were enforced; no movement except under cover; no field kitchens or rations allowed up before dark; communication by telephone; and the trenches improved or dug during the hours of darkness.'[55] Men in other units complained that their trench warfare training was both brief and unsatisfactory. A scheme involving the whole of the 24th Division was mounted on Chobham Common in August when it was intended that the troops should occupy trenches for several days with regular reliefs throughout and a trench-to-trench attack at the end of the exercise. 'It happened that the weather was very bad and the scheme was abandoned on the second day,' recorded the historians of the 8th Royal West Kent Regiment.[56] Second Lieutenant F. G. V. Beard of the 9th Worcesters told a young friend about a practice trench attack carried out just over a month before the battalion sailed for Gallipoli:

We had live bombs and mines to make it a little more realistic than it usually is. However it is rather rot. The enemy is imaginary, there is not even barbed wire, and everyone walks about outside and sits on top of the trenches in a most casual way. I guess we shall keep down all right on the other side.[57]

Since deliveries of special trench warfare equipment were usually made to Service battalions only a month or so before departure, the value of training in trench attacks was minimal. Godfrey Drage tried to give his company of the 7th Royal Munster Fusiliers some bombing instruction, using an improvised grenade made from a condensed milk tin filled with nails: 'I stood down in a trench and threw it as far as I could and most of the contents came whistling back and hit the bank behind my head. If I couldn't toss the infernal machine a safe distance I knew that no one else in my company could, and so I called the practice off.'[58] Second Lieutenant C. B. Leather of the 18th King's (Liverpool) Regiment (2nd City Battalion) also had a lucky escape on 3 September:

I nearly blew up the entire class yesterday. I made a bomb out of two sticks of gelatine dynamite attached to a piece of wood about a foot long. Unfortunately when I threw it the explosive came off the stick and landed about three yards outside the trench we were in . . . We all crouched in the trench and of course were all right.[59]

Similarly, the trained soldiers' musketry course often had to be rushed because of the late deliveries of SMLE service rifles. Buckmaster relates how men of the 7th Duke of Cornwall's Light Infantry faked the results of their final musketry practice:

At last came the great day when we were issued with the new short rifle, though we were limited to a ridiculously small amount of ammunition. Yet the battalion had to reach a certain standard of musketry before being passed for service overseas. Many of the men were naturally bad shots, and as they would only be able to fire a few rounds, it was unlikely that they would learn to shoot, which might even mean that the whole battalion would be held back. However, we found a simple way out of our problem. When the battalion was firing on the range, the Regimental Sergeant Major, who was a crack shot, would keep his eyes open for anyone missing the target or scoring nothing but outers. He would order them to stop firing, telling them that their rifles needed testing. He would then take the place of one of these bad shots, and put enough bulls on the target to bring the score on the man's card up to the figure needed.[60]

For all the shortcomings of certain aspects of their training, the men of the New Armies were impatient to proceed on active service. Having volunteered in a spirit of intense enthusiasm, many felt that they were in danger of becoming stale after months of arduous, if frequently irrelevant, preparation. Charles Sorley, writing in May 1915, told a friend of 'the undisguised boredom' of the officers of his battalion, the 7th Suffolk Regiment: 'We hate our general, our CO and men; we do not hate the Germans. In short we are nearing the attitude of Regular soldiers to the Army.'[61] Second Lieutenant Arthur Heath of the 6th Royal West Kents commented that 'any increase to our efficiency would be more than counterbalanced by the growing staleness the men will suffer from if we are kept back much longer. They have done in eight months what the ordinary Regulars take three years for, and nothing could keep them going but the expectation of battle soon.'[62] As early as February 1915 F. G. V. Beard was 'sick of messing about' in England:

. . . not that I am at all thinking I shall enjoy the front, but it is a duty one has to do and may as well make the best of. I never believe anyone who says he *really wants* to go – very few are ignorant enough to say so. Everyone in the army would be very glad to get out of it if they could, but only by beating them thoroughly first, which there is no doubt we shall – and soon. K.'s Army are simply magnificent material – and wonderfully fit.[63]

The previous autumn Major-General Henry Wilson, now the Deputy Chief of Staff of the British Expeditionary Force, had written of Kitchener's 'ridiculous and preposterous army' as 'the laughing stock of every soldier in Europe', declaring that 'under no circumstances could these mobs take the field for two years'. He also remarked that 'It took the Germans 40 years of incessant work to make an army of 25 Corps with the aid of conscription; it will take us to all eternity to do the same by voluntary effort.'[64] As Wilson wrote these comments in France in mid-September 1914, when even the divisions of the First New Army were under a month old, his judgement could be described as premature. Certainly some of his senior colleagues did not wholly agree with him. A much more realistic assessment was that of Major-General Ivor Maxse a few weeks later. Maxse, who had commanded the 1st (Guards) Brigade since 1910 and had returned from France at the beginning of October 1914 to take command of the 18th (Eastern) Division, was able to evaluate the strengths and weaknesses of New Army units at first hand and was therefore much better placed than Wilson to compare them directly with pre-war Regular formations. Early in November 1914, after he had been in command of the 18th Division for about a month, Maxse compiled some preliminary notes on the New Armies, sending copies to Kitchener and to Lieutenant-General Sir Archibald Murray, who, as Chief of the General Staff at GHQ in France, was senior to Wilson. In his notes Maxse emphasised that he had already formed a good impression of the junior officers of the New Armies:

They have tackled the job of commanding war strength platoons with a zest and a fearlessness which augurs well. They spend eight hours a day with their platoons and identify themselves with the men's interests both on and off parade. Their keenness to learn the work of training men to fight makes some think that after six months' service they will be as good platoon commanders as the average subaltern of the old Army. This also is the opinion of several Commanding Officers.

Maxse was no less impressed with the other ranks:

The quality of the men is undoubtedly of a higher standard than that of the average men we usually recruited in the old Army. Everyone I have spoken to holds the same opinion. Having discussed the matter with ex-NC Officers who have re-enlisted, I find they hold the opinion that they never had better men in their old Regiments.

Then, following some remarks about the training area allotted to the 18th Division, Maxse made a few more revealing points of comparison between the New Armies and pre-war units:

As every battalion is about 1,150 strong and as each platoon has more than one subaltern *permanently* employed in its training, progress has been more rapid than it was in the old Army, owing to the latter's absurdly low peace establishment and its paucity of officers actually present. At Aldershot last July more than half the platoons were commanded by NCOs instead of Officers. Moreover, every individual officer and NCO is thoroughly aware of the fact that he is now training himself and his men to fight a definite enemy within a few months. He also knows that the unit he commands will not be swamped 'on mobilisation' by 60 per cent of reservists. His time is therefore spent in trying to make his own particular unit handy for fighting . . .
. . . For the above reasons I am convinced that the sections and platoons of the 1st and 2nd New Armies will be better trained for fighting than is generally expected.[65]

After another three months in command of the 18th Division, Maxse again recorded his thoughts about the New Armies, concentrating in particular upon his own division. This time he drew up a list of the weapons and items of clothing and equipment which the division still lacked, adding ruefully that his recital of these pressing needs 'indicates sufficiently the difficulties of training all ranks and all arms in any nation unprepared in peace for a big war'. Yet, for all his frustration over the shortages of equipment, Maxse's views about the junior officers and men were largely unchanged:

My previous notes emphasised the good quality and hearty keenness of the rank and file and of the subaltern officers of all arms. I am now more than ever convinced of this.[66]

Maxse had correctly identified one of the most important characteristics of the New Armies, namely their social cohesion, which gave them their own distinctive *esprit de corps*. This was partly the result of the manner in which they were raised, from which many units derived a powerful sense of local rather than purely national identity, and was partly governed, too, by the special circumstances of their training. In a vast number of battalions the men ate, slept and worked in the sections and platoons in which they were to fight in France or elsewhere. The officers not only knew their men by sight and name, and each individual's level of proficiency, but also knew many of the details of their private affairs, in some cases even their families. Thus, whatever the weaknesses of their training, there was an understanding and sympathy between all ranks in the New Armies which was to stand them in good stead when they came to be tested in the crucible of battle. Reginald Cockburn wrote:

Our discipline was a discipline founded more on friendship; mutual support between officers and men; a recognition of the fact that we had all got to carry on as best we could, mistakes or no mistakes; an appreciation of the very humour of the situation; and perhaps most important of all, the discovery by the officers that these men, and by the men that these young officers, were not such bad fellows after all.[67]

A month before the 9th (Scottish) Division left Britain to join the BEF in France, Sir Archibald Murray, now Deputy Chief of the Imperial General Staff with special responsibility for supervising the training of the New Armies, sent Sir John French a summary of his views on the standards attained by the divisions of the First New Army. Several of Murray's comments echoed the opinions expressed by Maxse. Murray himself noted:

Speaking generally, and looking at them on parade and on the march, they are finer Divisions than we have ever seen in peacetime; march discipline good, and the men capable of marching twenty miles a day for any number of consecutive days. The shooting of the infantry is of course only fair, and that of the artillery is an unknown quantity . . .
. . . I think the Brigadiers and Battalion Commanders will mostly do, but now it is only war which will find out the unfits. The Platoon Commanders are a keen, hardworking lot, and if taken quietly at first will be useful men. They are full of theoretical knowledge quickly acquired which has not become instinctive. Between the Battalion Commanders and the Platoon Commanders some, not all, battalions are weak. Perhaps the best characteristic of these Divisions is that, should the ring of trenches in Flanders be broken, they are capable at once, covered by our Cavalry, of long sustained efforts in marching.[68]

The 9th (Scottish) Division, which left for France on 9 May 1915, was the first New Army division numerically and the first to go to the front. It was followed on 29 May by the 12th (Eastern) Division. The 13th (Western), 11th (Northern) and 10th (Irish) Divisions sailed for the Dardanelles on 13 June, 1 July and 7 July respectively, and the 14th (Light) Division embarked for France on 18 June. All thirty New Army divisions had gone overseas by 1 June 1916. Henry Wilson had been proved wrong. That Britain had been able to create a mass citizen army almost from scratch and place thirty New Army and seven second-line Territorial divisions in the field within two and a half years was, in itself, a national achievement of colossal proportions.

Notes

1   Army Order I of 21 August 1914 (AO 324 of 1914), Appendix C.
2   Sir Ivone Kirkpatrick, *The War, 1914–1918*, unpublished account, *c.* 1920, IWM 79/50/1.
3   J. H. Allen to his father, 12 May 1915, quoted in Ina Montgomery, *John Hugh Allen of the Gallant Company: a Memoir*, Arnold, London, 1919, pp. 190–1.
4   Guy Chapman, *A Passionate Prodigality*, Nicholson & Watson, London, 1933, pp. 5–6.
5   Colonel Sir Geoffry Christie-Miller, *Memoirs*, IWM 80/32/1.
6   C. C. Aston to his mother, 9 September 1914, IWM CON/CCA.
7   Major W. de B. Wood, *The History of the King's Shropshire Light Infantry in the Great War*, p. 206.
8   Account by Major H. W. House in Nicholson and MacMullen, *History of the East Lancashire Regiment in the Great War*, p. 358.
9   Captain C. H. Cooke, *Historical Records of the 16th (Service) Battalion Northumberland Fusiliers*, p. 4.
10 A. E. Perriman, unpublished account, 1976, IWM 80/43/1.
11 T. H. Barnes, *Learning to be a Soldier*, privately published *c.* 1969, p. 3.

12 A. K. Aston to his mother, undated letter, probably early September 1914, IWM CON/CCA.
13 Diary of Second Lieutenant G. L. M. Clauson, entry of 5 October 1914, papers of Sir Gerard Clauson, IWM 75/51/1.
14 Emlyn Davies, *Taffy went to War*, privately published, *c.* 1968, p. 2.
15 Robert Robertson, *The Classic Slum*, Manchester University Press, 1971 (Pelican edition, 1973), p. 189.
16 M. J. H. Drummond, unpublished account, *c.* 1963, IWM DS/MISC/29.
17 Percy Croney, *Soldier's Luck*, pp. 23–4.
18 Lieutenant-Colonel W. D. Lowe, *War History of the 18th (Service) Battalion Durham Light Infantry*, p. 7; Frederick Miller, *The Hartlepools and the Great War*, Sage, West Hartlepool, 1920, p. 78.
19 Note by Lord Midleton on the Kitchener-Millerand Inspection of the New Armies on 22 January 1915, undated, Midleton papers, PRO 30/67/25.
20 D. C. Burn, *Peregrinations Pro Patria*, 1919 IWM PP/MCR/173.
21 I. V. B. Melhuish to his mother, 24 January 1915, IWM PP/MCR/69.
22 Interview with Major-General J. M. L. Grover, IWM Department of Sound Records, 000046/08.
23 *Infantry Training*, HMSO, London, 1914, p. 134.
24 *Ibid.*, pp. 127–8.
25 Lieutenant-Colonel F. E. Whitton (ed.), *The History of the Prince of Wales's Leinster Regiment*, II, pp. 169–70.
26 Lieutenant-Colonel H. H. Hemming, *Preparing for War*, unpublished account, 1976, IWM PP/MCR/155.
27 Lieutenant-Colonel T. M. Banks and Captain R. A. Chell, *With the 10th Essex in France*, pp. 21–2.
28 I. L. Read, *A Narrative: 1914–1919*, IWM DS/MISC/69.
29 Sir Arthur Bliss, *As I Remember*, p. 31.
30 R. S. Cockburn, *First World War Diary and Recollections*, unpublished account, 1965, IWM p. 258.
31 Captain C. H. Cooke, *Historical Records of the 16th (Service) Battalion Northumberland Fusiliers*, p. 11.
32 *Extracts from the Diary of Brigadier-General the Hon. Robert White*, Dimbleby, Richmond, n.d., p. 13.
33 J. L. Stewart-Moore, *Random Recollections*, Part II, *The Great War 1914–1918*, unpublished account, 1976, IWM 77/39/1.
34 Captain R. Ede England, *A Brief History of the 12th King's Own Yorkshire Light Infantry (Pioneers): the Miners' Battalion*, p. 23.
35 Interview with J. D. Pratt, IWM Department of Sound Records, 000495/06.
36 Diary of Private Leonard Salter, 18 March 1915–6 December 1916, IWM 76/95/1.
37 Emlyn Davies, *op. cit.*, p. 3.
38 Adjutant-General's Department to GOCs-in-C of Commands, 3 December 1914, WO 162/3.
39 Major-General Sir Thomas Marden, *The History of the Welsh Regiment*, Part II, 1914–1918, Western Mail, Cardiff, 1932, p. 283.
40 R. J. Q. Adams, *Arms and the Wizard: Lloyd George and the Ministry of Munitions, 1915–1916*, Cassell, London, 1978, pp. 95–7; *History of the Ministry of Munitions*, Vol. IV, Part I, pp. 17–18.
41 Kitchener to Lloyd George, 3 July 1915, quoted in *History of the Ministry of Munitions*, Vol. IV, Part I, p. 18.
42 Adams, *Arms and the Wizard*, p. 96.
43 *Parliamentary Debates, House of Commons, 1914–15*, LXXVII, col. 119.

44 *History of the Ministry of Munitions*, Vol. IV, Part I, pp. 24–8.
45 *Ibid.*, pp. 29–30.
46 *Ibid.*, p. 30, and Vol. IV, Part IV, pp. 35, 56.
47 Sparling, *History of the 12th (Service) Battalion York and Lancaster Regiment*, p. 16; *History of the Ministry of Munitions*, Vol. IV, Part IV, p. 37.
48 Strengths and total losses of the 13th to 19th Battalions, Royal Welsh Fusiliers, on 30 June 1915, 'Memoranda' file, NLW/WAC; see also Clive Hughes, 'Army Recruitment in Gwynedd, 1914–1916', unpublished M. A. thesis, University of Wales, 1983, p. 215. I am most grateful to Clive Hughes for making this information available to me.
49 These figures have been compiled by comparing the names and regimental numbers of the men listed on the battalion's Nominal Roll in late 1915 with the names of the original volunteers which were published in the *Yorkshire Post* on 6, 7, 8 and 9 September 1914. A copy of the Nominal Roll, printed by John T. Turner of Pontefract in 1915, can be found in the Local History Department of the Leeds City Library. I am greatly indebted to my colleague Laurie Milner for pointing these sources out to me.
50 Army Council Instruction, 13 December 1914; Army Council Instruction 109, July 1915.
51 Army Council Instruction 96, April 1915.
52 *Historical Records of the Queen's Own Cameron Highlanders*, Vol. III, Blackwood, Edinburgh, 1931, p. 390.
53 Army Council Instruction 357, February 1916.
54 G. A. Cooper-Walker, *The Book of the Seventh (Service) Battalion the Royal Inniskilling Fusiliers*, p. 16.
55 Captain C. H. Cooke, *op. cit.*, p. 19.
56 Captain H. J. Wenyon and Major H. S. Brown, *The History of the Eighth Battalion The Queen's Own Royal West Kent Regiment*, p. 12.
57 F. G. V. Beard to C. S. B. Swinley, 1 June 1915, IWM 77/188/1.
58 Commander Charles Drage, *Chindwin to Criccieth: the life of Godfrey Drage*, p. 103.
59 C. B. Leather to his mother, 4 September 1915, IWM 74/44/1.
60 Viscount Buckmaster, *Roundabout*, p. 126.
61 Charles Sorley to Arthur Watts, 23 May 1915, see *The Letters of Charles Sorley*, p. 265.
62 Arthur Heath to Ernest Barker, (?) April 1915, see *Letters of Arthur George Heath*, Blackwell, Oxford, 1917, pp. 58–9.
63 F. G. V. Beard to C. S. B. Swinley, 17 February 1915, IWM 77/188/1.
64 Major-General Sir C. E. Callwell, *Field-Marshal Sir Henry Wilson: his life and Diaries*, Cassell, London, 1927, I, p. 178.
65 Major-General Ivor Maxse, 'Notes on the New Armies by a Divisional Commander, No. 1', early November 1914, Maxse papers, IWM 69/53/5.
66 Maxse, 'Notes on the New Armies by a Divisional Commander, No. 2', 3 February 1915, Maxse papers, IWM 69/53/5. Copies of these notes were sent to Kitchener and to Lieutenant-General Sir William Robertson, Murray's successor as Chief of the General Staff at GHQ in France.
67 R. S. Cockburn, *op. cit.*, IWM P. 258.
68 Murray to French, 3 April 1915, French papers, IWM 75/46/13.

Conclusion

Kitchener, the architect of the New Armies, died on 5 June 1916. Having accepted an invitation to head a mission to Russia to investigate how Britain might most usefully render military and financial aid to her ally, he sailed from Scapa Flow in the cruiser HMS *Hampshire* at 4.45 p.m. that day. Shortly before 8.00 p.m. the *Hampshire* struck a mine off the Orkneys and sank within fifteen minutes. Kitchener was not among the handful of survivors and his body was never found. When the news of his death reached the public around noon on 6 June, it was greeted by many people with a mixture of stunned disbelief and despair. The big London stores closed for the rest of the day, the blinds were drawn at the War Office and the Admiralty, and all over the country flags were lowered to half-mast. In some respects the moment of Kitchener's passing may be regarded as almost symbolic, for it came at a critical point in the war, less than a fortnight after the second Military Service Act had received the Royal Assent and less than a month before the ranks of the New Armies were decimated in the slaughter of the first day of the Battle of the Somme.

It was fitting that the New Armies popularly bore Kitchener's name, for it was his energy and foresight in the first weeks of the war that had planted the seeds from which they grew. His conviction that the war would last at least three years had caused the government and the people to revise most of their earlier ideas about the scale on which the national resources should be marshalled to meet the situation. Moreover, the shortages of military power in 1918 appear, in retrospect, to underline the wisdom of his belief that these resources, once mobilised, should be husbanded until the decisive blow could be administered.

Although he professed ignorance of political and social conditions, Kitchener interpreted the national mood more accurately than many of his more politically experienced colleagues in August 1914. The link between Kitchener and the people, founded partly on myth and legend, was one of instinct on both sides, not of deep mutual knowledge. Had Kitchener spent

...ever commit...
...Stocking Story of his mole...
8.K. The line between Kar-
...form and legend, was one of
...knowledge. Had Kitchener know

more time in Britain before the war, it is unlikely that his reputation would have remained so massive as it was in 1914. In his case, distance certainly lent enchantment to the view. Yet, even if his prestige owed a great deal to his remoteness and was higher than his actual military or administrative ability warranted, he gave the people the same sort of confidence in August 1914 as Churchill was able to provide in the summer of 1940. It must be stressed that, at the outbreak of the First World War, Britain had already experienced several years of growing industrial and social malaise, and while the greater crisis of a European conflict pushed domestic problems into the background, it did not entirely dispel doubts about the quality of leadership which Asquith's Cabinet could offer. In contrast, Kitchener was seen as a talisman of victory and as a symbol of unity who spoke and acted for King and country and stood aloof from party or sectional interests. The extraordinary hold which he maintained on the public was the bedrock on which the New Armies were built.

However, if Kitchener had visualised the end, he did not always prove so successful in organising the means. Lloyd George likened him to 'one of those revolving lighthouses which radiate momentary gleams of revealing light far out into the surrounding gloom and then suddenly relapse into complete darkness'.[1] Leo Amery described him as 'a great improviser, but also a great disorganiser'.[2] There is some truth in both these statements. Having decided to create the New Armies, a task which few of his contemporaries either wished or were prepared to undertake so early in the war, Kitchener unquestionably tried to do too much too soon. The muddle and confusion at the recruiting offices, depots and training centres, and the longer-term effects of unrestricted enlistment on industry, were all consequences of his failure to regulate the rate of expansion of the army in the opening months, before the proper machinery had been established. On the other hand, the difficulties encountered on the industrial front were compounded by his reluctance to relinquish War Office authority in the vital area of munitions production. Similarly, his delay in backing universal conscription only made it harder for the government to plan ahead and prepare the necessary machinery for the systematic mobilisation of the nation's manpower reserves. His record on each of the three key issues involved in the creation of a mass army were therefore erratic. In the case of recruiting he lost control at an early stage and, after September 1914, the real work of raising the New Armies was very largely performed by the Parliamentary Recruiting Committee and civilian bodies up and down the country. In the matter of munitions production he tried to keep too firm a grip, with the result that, in the end, control was taken out of his hands by the politicians. On the third issue, that of compulsory service, he was strangely indecisive and ultimately bowed to external pressures and advice.

Kitchener was not responsible for all the problems which Britain faced in expanding her army. His predecessors at the War Office, and the Liberal government as a whole, had permitted the country to enter a major war without any blueprint for industrial mobilisation or even any clear idea about the degree of military and technological effort which might be required. It was for this reason, above all, that Asquith and the Cabinet placed an almost crushing load on Kitchener's shoulders in 1914. As well as assuming the routine burdens of his department, he was also allowed to raise, equip and train the biggest land force Britain had ever put into the field; to direct the initial expansion of armaments production; and to supervise the conduct of British military operations in all theatres. Not surprisingly, all this proved beyond the capacity of one man to handle. Precisely because Kitchener was a symbol of unity and success in 1914, he inevitably became the chief target of criticism when attacks on the government's handling of the war began, though he was by no means solely to blame for its mistakes. Furthermore, since the increased authority of the Secretary of State for War in 1914 was uniquely dependent on Kitchener's personal prestige, the lessening of his influence in the Cabinet meant that, by the end of the following year, the office itself had declined to a status not unlike that of the old Secretary at War.

Even in the sphere of munitions, Kitchener's achievements have been underrated by the majority of historians. If the moment was ripe in May 1915 for industrial mobilisation on the lines advocated by Lloyd George, it is doubtful whether it could have been successfully implemented the previous autumn. The policy of expanding output through the existing armament firms had much to commend it at the beginning of the war, because those firms alone had experience of munitions manufacture. Ordinary engineering firms could not take up such work at once, and it was the knowledge of shell-making which they acquired gradually as sub-contractors that later helped them to organise themselves effectively on a wider and more independent basis under the Ministry of Munitions. Indeed, the time needed for the creation of new capacity in 1914 differed little from that which the Ministry of Munitions later found necessary for the development of bulk output from totally fresh sources of supply. The shortages of weapons and ammunition in the spring of 1915 were brought about by arrears of deliveries rather than lack of orders. The real achievement of Kitchener and the War Office was in providing the impetus for industry to meet the needs of the thirty divisions envisaged in 1914, and the fruits of their labours are more fairly judged by the supply position in December 1915 than in May that year. Between December 1914 and December 1915 the output of small arms ammunition increased tenfold, and the production of shells rose from 871,700 to 23,663,186. As early as May 1915 the War Office was obtaining in three days the same amount of ammunition normally produced in one year in time of peace.[3] These figures might well have been much higher if Kitchener had not fought so long to keep munitions production under War Office control, but, given the severe problems he had inherited, the totals are not unimpressive.

One may also question whether the government could have successfully introduced compulsory military service in 1914. The level of public hostility to conscription, once the war had started, was probably overestimated by the Liberals, for, immediately following the Battle of Mons, national and local newspapers were bombarded with letters calling for some form of compulsory service. It is conceivable, therefore, that the public would have accepted conscription at this point, particularly if Kitchener had asked for it. In the atmosphere of August and September 1914 almost anything seemed possible, as the story of the raising of the New Armies graphically illustrates. When conscription came at last in 1916, comparatively few people actively protested against it. Nevertheless, at the beginning of the war Britain had no administrative apparatus for registration and compulsory enlistment, and had Kitchener postponed the expansion of the army until this was in being, the strategic consequences might have proved extremely serious, if not fatal. Controlled enlistment under a compulsory scheme would have eliminated many of the hardships caused by over-hasty and indiscriminate voluntary recruiting, but, by the time such a system could have been put into operation, the immense public enthusiasm for recruiting which prevailed in the first two months would almost certainly have evaporated. As one of Kitchener's most recent biographers has commented, 'The high quality of the forces placed in the field during Kitchener's tenure was possible only because they were made up of keen and ardent volunteers rather than unwilling conscripts.'[4] The recruiting figures for the whole of the war tend to support this view. More men joined the army voluntarily between August 1914 and December 1915 than were conscripted in 1916 and 1917 combined, while the number of recruits attested in September 1914 alone (462,901) was only 30,000 less than the total of conscripts obtained in 1918.[5]

Well over a decade after the armistice Lloyd George asserted that it was the overwhelming response to Kitchener's appeals for volunteers in 1914 that caused the government to incline towards a much greater participation in the war on land.[6] Again, there is some justification for this claim. Possession of a mass army made it correspondingly difficult for Britain to avoid being drawn into the huge battles of attrition on the Western Front; without one, the government would have been forced to adopt a different strategic posture. However, what Lloyd George appeared to overlook was that a Liberal government of which he was a member had already acquiesced in a Continental commitment for the army long before Kitchener took office, accepting that the BEF would fight alongside the French army on the European mainland. From the moment this commitment was made, there was always a strong possibility that, in the event of war, Britain would be compelled to increase the scale of her contribution to the land campaign. Kitchener's policy at least ensured that Britain could meet these obligations when the need arose.

The expansion of the army in 1914 and 1915 had far-reaching effects throughout society. The growing role of women in industry, the extension of the power of organised labour and the trade unions, and the increase of government involvement in every aspect of national life were all greatly accelerated by the creation of a mass army and the mobilisation of the manufacturing resources necessary to sustain such a force in the field. Once the decision to expand the army had been taken, and the requirements of a decisive victory on land had been acknowledged, increased State control of industry and manpower was bound to follow. Many of the problems which arose during the raising of the New Armies stemmed from the Liberal government's collective, if not individual, failure to accept that fact. In the end, Asquith's attempts to conduct the war along 'business as usual' lines, and to delay State control for as long as possible, caused a split within the Liberal Party and destroyed it as an effective political force. The New Armies, which were largely formed under the old voluntary methods, may thus be seen as one of the last major manifestations of Edwardian Liberalism before Britain became fully adjusted to the demands of total war and the other challenges of the twentieth century. They were the unique product of a particular combination of political, social, economic and military factors which existed only in 1914 and 1915 and could not have been conceived or raised in the same form at any other time before or since.

If Kitchener provided the inspiration for the British people to create a vastly expanded army despite all the previous deficiencies in experience and preparation, it was, in the final analysis, essentially a *national* effort. In the sense that it was raised for the most part by civilian committees and *ad hoc* voluntary organisations in all corners of the country, Kitchener's army was the closest thing to a true citizen army that Britain has ever produced. Without the support and enthusiasm of the majority of the population no administration could have secured nearly 2,500,000 men by purely voluntary methods in less than seventeen months from the outbreak of war.

Notes

1 Lloyd George, *War Memoirs*, II, p. 751.
2 Amery, *My Political Life*, II, p. 23.
3 *Statistics of the Military Effort of the British Empire*, p. 477; *History of the Ministry of Munitions*, Vol. I, Part I, Appendices III and IV, pp. 146–50.
4 George H. Cassar, *Kitchener: Architect of Victory*, William Kimber, London, 1977, p. 444.
5 *Statistics of the Military Effort of the British Empire*, p. 364.
6 Lloyd George, *op. cit.*, II, p. 709.

Sources and bibliography

Manuscript sources

Unpublished official papers

British Library. Minutes of the Parliamentary Recruiting Committee, 1914–16.
Minutes of the Executive Committee of the War Emergency Workers' National
Committee, 1914–16.
Labour Party Archives, Transport House, London. War Emergency Workers'
National Committee Papers, 1914–16.
Public Record Office. Admiralty Papers, Board of Trade Papers. Cabinet Papers.
Committee of Imperial Defence Papers. Foreign Office Papers. Ministry of Health
Papers. Ministry of Munitions Papers. Ministry of National Service Papers. Min-
istry of Reconstruction Papers. War Office Papers.

Unpublished private papers

Bodleian Library, Oxford. Asquith Papers. Selborne Papers.
British Library. Balfour Papers. Midleton Papers. C. P. Scott Papers.
Churchill College, Cambridge. Esher Papers.
House of Lords Record Office. Bonar Law Papers. Lloyd George Papers. St Loe
Strachey Papers.
Imperial War Museum. Creedy Papers. French Papers. Maxse Papers. von Donop
Papers. Wilson Papers.
Liddell Hart Centre for Military Archives. Hamilton Papers. Robertson Papers. Spicer
Papers.
Liverpool Record Office. Derby Papers.
National Army Museum. Roberts Papers.
National Library of Ireland. Redmond Papers.
National Library of Scotland. Haig Papers. Haldane Papers.
Nuffield College, Oxford. Emmott Papers. Mottistone Papers.
Public Record Office. Grey Papers. Kitchener Papers. Midleton Papers. Roberts
Papers.
University of Birmingham Library. Austen Chamberlain Papers.
University of Newcastle-upon-Tyne Library. Runciman Papers.

Unpublished local collections

Bristol Central Library. Minutes of the Bristol Citizens' Recruiting Committee, 1914–20.

Bristol Record Office. Minutes of the Meetings Sub-committee of the Bristol Citizens' Recruiting Committee, 1915.

Essex Record Office, Chelmsford. Notes on Recruiting kept by the Rev. E. H. L. Reeve, Rector of Stondon Massey, 1914–16.

Imperial War Museum. Tyneside Scottish Dependants' Aid Committee, Case Register, 1914–15.

National Library of Wales. Welsh Army Corps Papers.

Westminster City Libraries, Marylebone. Minutes of the Recruiting Committee of the Metropolitan Borough of St Marylebone, 1915.

Diaries, letters and unpublished memoirs in the collections of the Imperial War Museum

Colonel C. B. Arnold; Lieutenant-Colonel C. C. Aston; Captain A. G. Bartlett; Lieutenant F. G. V. Beard (in the papers of Captain C. S. B. Swinley, RN); J. Beeken; Major H. P. Berney-Ficklin (in the papers of Major C. F. Ashdown); Lieutenant R. C. F. Besch; T. A. Bickerton; Lieutenant D. C. Burn; Lieutenant C. P. Burnley; C. A. Cain; Lieutenant-Colonel Charles Carrington; Colonel Sir Geoffry Christie-Miller; Sir Gerard Clauson; Major R. S. Cockburn; Captain W. N. Collins; Captain W. T. Colyer; Captain W. G. Cook; W. Cook; Lieutenant H. V. Drinkwater; Captain M. J. H. Drummond; J. N. Dykes; N. F. Ellison; R. F. E. Evans; Captain L. I. L. Ferguson; A. Gaunt; F. L. Goldthorpe; Captain Graham Greenwell; Lieutenant-Colonel H. H. Hemming; A. E. Henderson; E. Herd; H. F. Hooton; H. E. Hunt; C. Jones; P. H. Jones; Sir Ivone Kirkpatrick; Lieutenant C. B. Leather; Lieutenant-Colonel R. M. Lester; T. Macdonald; Lieutenant A. E. MacGregor; Captain W. C. D. Maile; Second Lieutenant I. V. B. Melhuish; F. T. Mullins; Lieutenant R. W. Murphy; G. Nash; Captain H. U. S. Nisbet; C. K. Ogden; Major R. D. Oliver; R. S. Patston; A. E. Perriman; Major P. H. Pilditch; E. W. Prosser; J. Ramsden; Lieutenant I. L. Read; E. J. Robinson; A. Runcie; L. S. Salter; E. Scullin; Captain P. M. Sharp; E. Sheard; T. A. Silver; Captain J. H. M. Staniforth; J. W. Stephenson; Lieutenant J. L. Stewart-Moore; W. R. Thomas; Lieutenant A. Thompson; Captain R. J. Thompson; R. H. Turner; A. Winstanley.

BBC-TV Great War series correspondence (Imperial War Museum)

Alfred G. Allen; Harold Aylott; E. J. O. Bird; C. J. Butler; Charles Cameron; Basil H. Chase; Francis T. Cowing; Leslie Crofts; William Day; James H. Ellis; G. W. Evans; William Fraser; Bertram Glover; J. G. Gordon; Ernest Goulden; E. C. Haddrell; I. P. James; A. R. Kennewell; E. Lugg; T. H. Merrifield; W. R. Owen; Thomas Peers; Leonard Preuss; the Rev. Lewis E. Roberts; E. Robinson; G. Eric Rutherford; P. J. Sale; H. Sargent; Thomas Sloan; Oswald Sturdy; H. Sullivan; H. Symonds; C. W. G. Taylor; G. F. Taylor; W. S. Tremain; Mrs J. Upjohn; J. Eric Wainwright; G. T. Walton; Carl Wehner.

Unpublished theses

Allison, M. J., 'The National Service Issue, 1899–1914', Ph.D., London, 1975.

Blanch, M. D., 'Nation, Empire and the Birmingham Working Class, 1899–1914', Ph.D., Birmingham, 1975.

Hughes, Clive, 'Army Recruitment in Gwynedd, 1914–1916', M.A., Wales, 1983.

Moon, H. R., 'The Invasion of the United Kingdom: Public Controversy and Official Planning, 1888–1918', Ph.D., London, 1968.

Otley, C. B., 'The Origins and Recruitment of the British Army Elite, 1870–1939', Ph.D., Hull, 1965.

Perry, F. W., 'Manpower and Organisational Problems in the Expansion of the British and other Commonwealth Armies during the two World Wars', Ph.D., London, 1982.

Summerton, N. W., 'The Development of British Military Planning for a War against Germany, 1904–1914', Ph.D., London, 1970.

Printed sources

British Parliamentary Papers

Census of England and Wales, 1901: General Report, with Appendices, (1904) CVIII, Cd 2174.

Memorandum by the Secretary of State for War on Army Reorganisation: dated 30 July 1906, (1906) LXVII, Cd 2993.

Interim Report of the War Office Committee on the provision of officers (a) for service with the Regular Army in war, and (b) for the Auxiliary Forces, (1907) XLIX, Cd 3294.

The Annual Return of the Territorial Force for the Year 1910, (1911) XLVI, Cd 5482.

The General Annual Report on the British Army for the Year ending 30 September 1913, (1914) LII, Cd 7252.

The Annual Return of the Territorial Force for the Year 1913, (1914) LII, Cd 7254.

Increased Rates of Separation Allowances for the Wives and Children of Soldiers, (1914–1916) XXXIX, Cd 7623.

Report of the Military Court of Enquiry, constituted by the Army Council for the purpose of investigating certain matters connected with the British Empire Committee, (1914–1916) XXXIX, Cd 7681.

Report of the Board of Trade on the State of Employment in the United Kingdom in October 1914, (1914–1916) XXI, Cd 7703.

Report of the Board of Trade on the State of Employment in the United Kingdom in December 1914, (1914–1916) XXI, Cd 7755.

Report of the Board of Trade on the State of Employment in the United Kingdom in February 1915, (1914–1916) XXI, Cd 7850.

Report of the Departmental Committee Appointed to Enquire into Conditions prevailing in the Coal Mining Industry due to the War, (1914–1916) XXVIII, Cd 7939.

First Report of the Central Control Board (Liquor Traffic) appointed under the Defence of the Realm (Amendment) (No. 3) Act, 1915, (1914–1916) XXV, Cd 8117.

Second General Report of the Departmental Committee appointed to Enquire into Conditions prevailing in the Coal Mining Industry due to the War, (1914–1916) XXVIII, Cd 8147.

Report on Recruiting by the Earl of Derby, Director-General of Recruiting, (1914–1916) XXXIX, Cd 8149.

Report on Recruiting in Ireland, (1914–1916), XXXIX, Cd 8168.

Report and Statistics of Bad Time kept in Shipbuilding, Munitions and Transport Areas, (1914–1916) LV, 220.

Return showing the approximate cost of the Hutting provided for the accommodation of Troops and Horses in the United Kingdom in the years 1914 to 1916, (1916) XVII, Cd 8193.

Second Report of the Central Control Board (Liquor Traffic) appointed under the Defence of the Realm (Amendment) (No. 3) Act, 1915, (1916) XII, Cd 8243.

Annual Report of the Registrar-General of Births, Deaths and Marriages in England and Wales, 1915, (1917–1918) V, Cd 8484.

Dardanelles Commission: First Report and Supplement, HMSO, 1917, Cd 8490.

Census of 1911: General Report, with Appendices, (1917–1918) XXXV, Cd 8491.

Annual Report of the Registrar-General of Births, Deaths and Marriages in England and Wales, 1916, (1917–1918), VI, Cd 8869.

Dardanelles Commission: Final Report and Appendices, HMSO, 1919, Cmd 371.

Other official publications

Army Council Instructions.
Army Debates.
Army Orders.
Board of Trade *Labour Gazette.*
Field Service Pocket Book, 1914.
Infantry Training, HMSO, London, 1914.
Parliamentary Debates.
Royal Warrant for Pay, Appointment and Non-effective Pay of the Army, 1914.
Report of the War Office Committee of Enquiry into Shell shock, HMSO, London, 1922.
Statistics of the Military Effort of the British Empire during the Great War, 1914–1920, HMSO, London, 1922.
War Office, *List of Changes in War Matériel and of Patterns of Military Stores*, December 1914.
War Office, *Locally raised Units. List of Units raised by Communities and Individuals, who undertook to clothe, house, and feed them at the public expense until such time as the military authorities were prepared to assume these duties*, London, 1916.
War Office, *History of the Development and Work of the Directorate of Organisation, August 1914–December 1918*, London, 1919.

Official histories

Becke, Major A. F.; *History of the Great War: Order of Battle of Divisions, Parts 1–4*, HMSO, London, 1935–45.

Edmonds, Brigadier-General Sir J. E. (ed.), *History of the Great War: Military Operations, France and Belgium*, 14 vols., Macmillan and HMSO, London, 1922–49.

History of the Ministry of Munitions, 12 vols., HMSO, London, 1920–22.

Macpherson, Major-General Sir W. G. (ed.), *History of the Great War: Medical Service*, 12 vols., HMSO, London, 1928–31.

Miscellaneous reports, etc.

Mac Giolla Choille, Brendan (ed.), *Intelligence Notes, 1913–1916*, State Paper Office, Dublin, 1966.

Soldier's and Sailors' Families Association: Annual Report, 1914–1915, London, 1915.

Tyneside Scottish Brigade Committee: First Report of the Honorary Secretaries, September 1914–December 1915, Newcastle, 1915.

Welsh Army Corps: Report of the Executive Committee, Cardiff, 1921.

Published diaries, memoirs and biographies

Amery, L. S., *My Political Life*, 3 vols., Hutchinson, London, 1953–55.

Arthur, Sir George, *Life of Lord Kitchener:* 3 vols., Macmillan, London, 1920.

Asquith, Earl of Oxford and, *Memories and Reflections, 1852–1927*, 2 vols., Cassell, London, 1928.

Bacon, Admiral Sir R. H., *The Life of Lord Fisher of Kilverstone*, Hodder & Stoughton, London, 1929.

Balfour, A. J. (First Earl of), *Chapters of Autobiography*, Cassell, London, 1930.

Bickersteth, Rev. Samuel, *Morris Bickersteth, 1891–1916*, Cambridge University Press, 1931.

Blake, Robert (ed.), *The Private Papers of Douglas Haig, 1914–1919*, Eyre & Spottiswoode, London, 1952.

Bliss, Sir Arthur, *As I Remember*, Faber, London, 1970.

Bonham-Carter, Violet, *Winston Churchill as I knew him*, Eyre Spottiswoode and Collins, London, 1965.

Brett, M. V., and Viscount Esher (eds.), *Journals and Letters of Reginald Viscount Esher*, 4 vols., Nicholson & Watson, London, 1934–38.

Brock, Michael and Eleanor (eds.), *H. H. Asquith: Letters to Venetia Stanley*, Oxford University Press, 1982.

Buckmaster, Viscount, *Roundabout*, Witherby, London, 1969.

Butterworth, George, *Extracts from Diary and Letters*, Delittle & Fenwick, London, 1918.

Callwell, Major-General Sir C. E. *Field-Marshal Sir Henry Wilson: his Life and Diaries*, 2 vols., Cassell, London, 1927.

Cassar, George H., *Kitchener: Architect of Victory*, Kimber, London, 1977.

—*The Tragedy of Sir John French*, Associated University Presses, London, 1985,

Chamberlain, Sir Austen, *Down the Years*, Cassell, London, 1935.

—*Politics from the Inside*, Cassell, London, 1936.

Chapman-Huston, Major Desmond, and Major Owen Rutter, *General Sir John Cowans: the Quartermaster-General of the Great War*, 2 vols., Hutchinson, London, 1924.

Charteris, Brigadier-General John, *Field-Marshal Earl Haig*, Cassell, London, 1929.

Churchill, Randolph, *Lord Derby*, Heinemann, London, 1960.

Churchill, Winston S., *The World Crisis, 1911–1914*, Thornton Butterworth, London, 1923.

Colvin, Ian, *The Life of Lord Carson*, 3 vols., Gollancz, London, 1934–36.

Cooper, A Duff, *Haig*, 2 vols., Faber, London, 1935.

Crow, Duncan, *A Man of Push and Go: the life of George Macaulay Booth*, Hart-Davis, London, 1965.

Crozier, Brigadier-General F. P., *Impressions and Recollections*, T. Werner Laurie, London, 1930.

David, Edward (ed.), *Inside Asquith's Cabinet: from the Diaries of Charles Hobhouse*, Murray, London, 1977.

Drage, Commander Charles, *Chindwin to Criccieth: the Life of Godfrey Drage*, Evans, Caernarvon, 1956.

Dugdale, Blanche E. C., *Arthur James Balfour*, 2 vols., Hutchinson, London, 1936.

Eden, Anthony, *Another World, 1897–1917*, Allen Lane, London, 1976.

Eyston, George, *Safety Last*, Vincent, London, 1975.

Farrar-Hockley, Anthony, *Goughie: the Life of General Sir Hubert Gough*, Hart-Davis MacGibbon, London, 1975.

Fife, Lieutenant-Colonel Ronald, *Mosaic of Memories*, Heath Cranton, London, 1943.

Fisher, Admiral of the Fleet Lord, *Memories*, Hodder & Stoughton, London, 1919.

—*Records,* Hodder & Stoughton, London, 1929.

Fitzroy, Sir Almeric, *Memoirs*, 2 vols., Hutchinson, London, 1925.

Fraser, Peter, *Lord Esher: a Political Biography*, Hart-Davis MacGibbon, London, 1973.

French, Field-Marshal Lord, *1914*, Constable, London, 1919.

Gilbert, Martin, *Winston S. Churchill*, III, 1914–1916, Heinemann, London, 1971.

Grey, Viscount (of Fallodon), *Twenty-five Years, 1892–1916*, 2 vols., Hodder & Stoughton, London, 1926.

Grigg, John, *Lloyd George: from Peace to War, 1912–1916*, Methuen, London, 1985.

Gwynn, Denis, *The Life of John Redmond*, Harrap, London, 1932.

Haldane, R. B. *Before the War*, Cassell, London, 1920.

—*An Autobiography*, Hodder & Stoughton, London, 1929.

Hamilton, Ian B. M., *The Happy Warrior: a Life of General Sir Ian Hamilton*, Cassell, London, 1966.

Hankey, Lord, *The Supreme Command, 1914–1918*, 2 vols., Allen & Unwin, London, 1961.

Heath, Arthur George, *Letters*, Blackwell, Oxford, 1917.

Holmes, Richard, *The Little Field-Marshal: Sir John French*, Cape, London, 1981.

Jenkins, Roy, *Asquith*, Collins, London, 1964.

Jourdain, Lieutenant-Colonel H. F. N., *Ranging Memories*, Oxford University Press, 1934.

Kelly, Sir David, *The Ruling Few*, Hollis & Carter, London, 1952.

Koss, Stephen, *Lord Haldane: Scapegoat for Liberalism*, Columbia University Press, New York, 1969.

—*Asquith*, Allen Lane, London, 1976.

Lloyd George, David, *War Memoirs*, 6 vols., Nicholson & Watson, London, 1933–36.

Long, Viscount, *Memories*, Hutchinson, London, 1923.

Mackay, Ruddock F., *Fisher of Kilverstone*, Oxford University Press, 1973.

—*Balfour: Intellectual Statesman*, Oxford University Press, 1985.

Macmillan, Harold, *Winds of Change, 1914–1939*, Macmillan, London, 1966.

Magnus, Sir Philip, *Kitchener: Portrait of an Imperialist*, Murray, London, 1958.

Marder, Arthur J. (ed.), *Fear God and Dread Nought: Correspondence of Admiral of the Fleet Lord Fisher of Kilverstone*, 3 vols., Cape, London, 1952–59.

Maurice, Major-General Sir Frederick, *The Life of General Lord Rawlinson of Trent*, Cassell, London, 1928.

—*Haldane: the Life of Viscount Haldane of Cloan*, 2 vols., Faber, London, 1937–39.

Midleton, Earl of, *Records and Reactions, 1856–1939*, Murray, London, 1939.

Miller, Edward (ed.), *Letters of Donald Hankey*, Melrose, London, 1919.

Montgomery, Ina, *John Hugh Allen of the Gallant Company: a Memoir*, Arnold, London, 1919.

Morgan, Kenneth O. (ed.), *Lloyd George Family Letters, 1885–1936*, University of Wales Press, Cardiff, 1973.

Mottistone, Lord (J. E. B. Seely), *Adventure*, Heinemann, London, 1930.

Nicholson, Sir Harold, *King George V: his Life and Reign*, Constable, London, 1952.

O'Broin, Leon, *The Chief Secretary: Augustine Birrell in Ireland*, Chatto & Windus, London, 1969.

Petrie, Sir Charles, *The Life and Letters of the Rt. Hon. Sir Austen Chamberlain*, 2 vols., Cassell, London, 1939–40.

Riddell, Lord, *War Diary, 1914–1918*, Nicholson & Watson, London, 1933.
Robertson, Field-Marshal Sir William, *From Private to Field-Marshal*, Constable, London, 1921.
—*Soldiers and Statesmen, 1914–1918*, 2 vols., Cassell, London, 1926.
Roskill, Stephen, *Hankey: Man of Secrets*, 3 vols., Collins, London, 1970–1974.
Rowland, Peter, *Lloyd George*, Barrie & Jenkins, London, 1975.
Royle, Trevor, *The Kitchener Enigma*, Michael Joseph, London, 1985.
Samuel, Viscount, *Memoirs*, Cresset, London, 1945.
Slater, G. (ed.), *My Warrior Sons: the Borton Family Diary, 1914–1918*. Peter Davies, London 1973.
Sommer, Dudley, *Haldane of Cloan: his life and Times, 1856–1928*, Allen & Unwin, London, 1960.
Sorley, W. R. (ed.), *The Letters of Charles Sorley*, Cambridge University Press, 1919.
Spender, J. A., *Life, Journalism and Politics*, 2 vols., Cassell, London, 1927.
—and Cyril Asquith, *Life of Herbert Henry Asquith, Lord Oxford and Asquith*, Hutchinson, London, 1932.
Spiers, Edward M., *Haldane: an Army Reformer*, Edinburgh University Press, 1980.
Taylor, A. J. P. (ed.), *Lloyd George: a Diary by Frances Stevenson*, Hutchinson, London, 1971.
Terraine, John, *Douglas Haig: the Educated Soldier*, Hutchinson, London, 1963.
Woods, Edward S. (ed.), *Andrew R. Buxton: a Memoir*, Scott, London, 1918.
Wilson, Trevor (ed.), *The Political Diaries of C. P. Scott, 1911–1928*, Collins, London, 1970.

Personal experiences

Andrews, William Linton, *Haunting Years: the Commentaries of a War Territorial*, Hutchinson, London, n.d.
Barnes, T. H., *Learning to be a Soldier*, privately published, 1969.
Behrend, Arthur, *Make me a Soldier*, Eyre & Spottiswoode, London, 1961.
Callwell, Major-General Sir C. E., *Experiences of a Dug-out, 1914–1918*, Constable, London, 1920.
Carrington, Charles E., *Soldier from the Wars Returning*, Hutchinson, London, 1964.
Cartmell, H. *For Remembrance: an Account of some Fateful Years*, Toulmin, Preston, 1919.
Casson, Stanley, *Steady Drummer*, Bell, London, 1935.
Chapman, Guy, *A Passionate Prodigality*, Nicholson & Watson, London, 1933.
Coppard, George, *With a Machine Gun to Cambrai*, Imperial War Museum/ HMSO, London, 1969.
Croney, Percy, *Soldier's Luck: Memoirs of a Soldier of the Great War*, Stockwell, Ilfracombe, 1965.
Crozier, Brigadier-General F. P., *A Brass Hat in No Man's Land*, Cape, London, 1930.
Davies, Emlyn, *Taffy went to War*, privately published, *c.* 1968.
Douie, Charles, *The Weary Road: Recollections of a Subaltern of Infantry*, Murray, London, 1929.
Extracts from the Diary of Brigadier-General the Hon. Robert White, Dimbleby, Richmond, n.d.
Graves, Robert, *Good-bye to all That*, Cape, London, 1929.
Hargrave, John, *At Suvla Bay*, Constable, London, 1916.
Kernahan, Coulson, *The Experiences of a Recruiting Officer*, Hodder & Stoughton, London, 1915.
Mellersh, H. E. L., *Schoolboy into War*, Kimber, London, 1978.

Nettleton, John, *The Anger of the Guns*, Kimber, London, 1979.
Parker, Ernest, *Into Battle, 1914–1918: a Seventeen-year-old Boy enlists in Kitchener's Army*, Longmans, London, 1964.
Rogerson, Sidney, *Twelve Days*, Barker, London, 1933.
Tucker, John F., *Johnny get your gun: a Personal Narrative of the Somme, Ypres and Arras*, Kimber, London, 1978.
Tucker, W. A., *The Lousier War*, New English Library, London, 1974.
Wheatley, Dennis, *Officer and Temporary Gentleman, 1914–1919*, Hutchinson, London, 1978.

Corps and regimental histories

Anon., *Historical Records of the Queen's Own Cameron Highlanders*, IV, Blackwood, Edinburgh, 1931.
Atkinson, C. T. *The Devonshire Regiment, 1914–1918*, Eland, Exeter, 1926.
—*The History of the South Wales Borderers, 1914–1918*, Medici Society, London, 1931.
Berkeley, Reginald, *The History of the Rifle Brigade in the War of 1914–1918*, I, Rifle Brigade Club, London, 1927.
Bond, Lieutenant-Colonel R. C., *History of the King's Own Yorkshire Light Infantry in the Great War, 1914–1918*, Lund Humphries, London, 1929.
Burrows, J. W., *Essex Units in the War, 1914–1919: 6, Service Battalions*, Burrows, Southend, 1935.
Crookenden, Arthur, *The History of the Cheshire Regiment in the Great War*, Evans, Chester, n.d.
Falls, Cyril, *The Life of a Regiment*, IV, *The Gordon Highlanders in the First World War, 1914–1919*, Aberdeen University Press, 1958.
Fisher, W. G., *The History of Somerset Yeomanry, Volunteer and Territorial Units*, Goodman, Taunton, 1924.
Harris, Henry, *The Irish Regiments in the First World War*; Mercier Press, Cork, 1968.
Kenrick, Colonel N. C. E., *The Story of the Wiltshire Regiment (Duke of Edinburgh's), 1756–1959*, Gale & Polden, Aldershot, 1963.
Latter, Major-General J. C., *The History of the Lancashire Fusiliers, 1914–1918*, I, Gale & Polden, Aldershot, 1949.
Marden, Major-General Sir Thomas, *The History of the Welsh Regiment*, II, *1914–1918*, Western Mail and Echo, Cardiff, 1932.
Mockler-Ferryman, Lieutenant-Colonel A. F. (ed.), *The Oxfordshire and Buckinghamshire Light Infantry Chronicle*, XXIV, 4 August 1914–31 July 1915, Eyre & Spottiswoode, London, *c.* 1916.
Moody, Colonel R. S. H., *Historical Records of the Buffs (East Kent Regiment), 1914–1919*, Medici Society, London, 1922.
Nicholson, Major-General Sir C. Lothian, and Major H. T. MacMullen, *History of the East Lancashire Regiment in the Great War, 1914–1918*, Littlebury, Liverpool, 1936.
O'Neill, H. C., *The Royal Fusiliers in the Great War*, Heinemann, London, 1922.
Petre, F. Loraine, *The Royal Berkshire Regiment (Princess Charlotte of Wales's)* II, *1914–1918*, The Barracks, Reading, 1925.
—*The History of the Norfolk Regiment, 1685–1918*, II, *4 August 1914 to 31 December 1918*, Jarrold, Norwich, n.d.
Pritchard, Major-General H. L. (ed.), *History of the Corps of Royal Engineers*, V, The Home Front, France, Flanders and Italy in the First World War, Institution of Royal Engineers, Chatham, 1952.

Simpson, Major-General C. R. (ed.), *The History of the Lincolnshire Regiment, 1914–1918*, Medici Society, London, 1931.

Story, Colonel H. H. *History of the Cameronians (Scottish Rifles), 1910–1933*, Hazell Watson & Viney, Aylesbury, 1961.

Wauchope, Major-General A. G. (ed.), *A History of the Black Watch (Royal Highlanders) in the Great War, 1914–1918*, III, *New Army*, Medici Society, London, 1926.

Whalley-Kelly, Captain H., *Ich Dien: the Prince of Wales's Volunteers (South Lancashire), 1914–1934*, Gale & Polden, Aldershot, 1935.

Whitton, Lieutenant-Colonel F. E. (ed.), *The History of the Prince of Wales's Leinster Regiment (Royal Canadians)*, II, *The Great War and the Disbandment of the Regiment*, Gale & Polden, Aldershot, 1924.

Wood, Major W. de B., *The History of the King's Shropshire Light Infantry in the Great War, 1914–1918*, Medici Society, London, 1925.

Wylly, Colonel H. C., *The Border Regiment in the Great War*, Gale & Polden, Aldershot, 1924.

—*The Green Howards in the Great War*, privately published, Richmond, Yorks., 1926.

—*The York and Lancaster Regiment, 1785–1919*, II (*Territorial and Service Battalions*), privately published, 1930.

Divisional and brigade histories

Anon., *The History of the Royal Fusiliers 'UPS': University and Public Schools Brigade (Formation and Training)*, Times Publishing Company, London, 1917.

Atteridge, A. Hilliard, *History of the 17th (Northern) Division*, University Press, Glasgow, 1929.

Barlow, Sir C. A. Montague, *The Lancashire Fusiliers: the Roll of Honour of the Salford Brigade*, Sherratt & Hughes, Manchester, 1920.

Buchan, John and Lieutenant-Colonel J. Stewart, *The Fifteenth (Scottish) Division, 1914–1919*, Blackwood, Edinburgh, 1926.

Cooper, Major Bryan, *The Tenth (Irish) Division in Gallipoli*, Jenkins, London, 1918.

Davson, Lieutenant-Colonel H. M., *The History of the 35th Division in the Great War*, Sifton Praed, London, 1926.

Ewing, John, *The History of the 9th (Scottish) Division, 1914–1919*, Murray, London, 1921.

Falls, Cyril, *The History of the 36th (Ulster) Division*, M'Caw Stevenson & Orr, Belfast, 1922.

Hughes, Colin, *Mametz: Lloyd George's 'Welsh Army' at the Battle of the Somme*, Orion Press, Gerrards Cross, 1982.

Inglefield, Captain V. E., *The History of the Twentieth (Light) Division*, Nisbet, London, 1921.

Munby, Lieutenant-Colonel J. E., *A History of the 38th (Welsh) Division*, Rees, London, 1920.

Nichols, Captain G. H. F., *The 18th Division in the Great War*, Blackwood, London, 1922.

Sandilands, Lieutenant-Colonel H. R., *The Twenty-third Division, 1914–1919*, Blackwood, London, 1925.

Scott, Major-General Sir Arthur, and P. Middleton Brumwell, *History of the 12th (Eastern) Division in the Great War, 1914–1918*, Nisbet, London, 1923.

Shakespear, Lieutenant-Colonel J., *The Thirty-fourth Division, 1915–1919: the Story of its Career from Ripon to the Rhine*, Witherby, London, 1921.

Stanley, Brigadier-General F. C., *The History of the 89th Brigade, 1914–1918*, Liverpool Daily Post, 1919.

Ternan, Brigadier-General Trevor, *The Story of the Tyneside Scottish*, Northumberland Press, Newcastle, n.d.

Whitton, Lieutenant-Colonel F. E., *History of the 40th Division:* Gale & Polden, Aldershot, 1926.

Wyrall, Everard, *The History of the 19th Division, 1914–1918*, Arnold, London, n.d.

Battalion and other unit histories

Anon., *A Short Diary of the 11th (Service) Battalion, East Yorkshire Regiment, 1914–1919*, Goddard Walker & Brown, Hull, 1921.

Anon., *The Tenth Battalion the Cameronians (Scottish Rifles): a Record and Memorial, 1914–1918*, privately published, Edinburgh, 1923.

Arthur, J. W., and I. S. Munro, *The Seventeenth Highland Light Infantry (Glasgow Chamber of Commerce Battalion): Record of War Service, 1914–1918*, Clark, Glasgow, 1920.

Ashcroft, Major A. H. (ed.), *The History of the Seventh South Staffordshire Regiment*, Boyle & Watchurst, London, 1919.

Aston, J. and L. M. Duggan, *The History of the 12th (Bermondsey) Battalion, East Surrey Regiment*, Union Press, London, 1936.

Banks, Lieutenant-Colonel T. M., and Captain R. A. Chell, *With the 10th Essex in France*, Gay & Hancock, London, 1921.

Bowater, Sir William (ed.), *Birmingham City Battalions: Book of Honour*, Sherratt & Hughes, London, 1919.

Burton, Lieutenant-Colonel F. N. (ed.), *The War Diary of the 10th (Service) Battalion, Royal Welsh Fusiliers*, Brendon, Plymouth, 1926.

Chalmers, Thomas (ed.), *An Epic of Glasgow: History of the 15th Battalion the Highland Light Infantry (City of Glasgow Regiment)*, McCallum, Glasgow, 1934.

—*History of the 16th Battalion the Highland Light Infantry*, McCallum, Glasgow, 1930.

Cooke, Captain C. H., *Historical Records of the 9th (Service) Battalion, Northumberland Fusiliers*, Newcastle and Gateshead Incorporated Chamber of Commerce, 1928.

—*Historical Records of the 16th (Service) Battalion, Northumberland Fusiliers*, Newcastle and Gateshead Incorporated Chamber of Commerce, 1923.

Cooksey, Jon, *Pals: the 13th and 14th Battalions York and Lancaster Regiment: a History of the two Battalions raised by Barnsley in World War One*, Barnsley Chronicle, 1986.

Cooper-Walker, G. A., *The Book of the Seventh Service Battalion the Royal Inniskilling Fusiliers: from Tipperary to Ypres*, Brindley, Dublin, 1920.

England, Captain R. Ede, *A Brief History of the 12th Battalion King's Own Yorkshire Light Infantry (Pioneers): the Miners' Battalion*, Borough Press, Wakefield, n.d.

Fairclough, J. E. B., *The First Birmingham Battalion in the Great War, 1914–1919*, Cornish, Birmingham, 1933.

Fryer, Percy, *The Men from the Greenwood: the War History of the 11th (Service) Battalion, Sherwood Foresters*, Cresswell & Oaksford, Nottingham, 1920.

Grain, H. W. Wallis, *The 16th (Public Schools) Service Battalion (the Duke of Cambridge's Own) Middlesex Regiment and the Great War, 1914–1918*, Lewington, London, n.d.

Grant, D. F., *The History of 'A' Battery, 84th Army Brigade, Royal Field Artillery, 1914–1919*, Marshall, London, 1922.

Grave, L. W. de, *The War History of the Fifth Battalion the Sherwood Foresters, Notts and Derby Regiment, 1914–1918*, Bemrose, Derby, 1930.

Hadrill, Captain C. I. (ed.), *A History of the 10th (Service) Battalion the East*

Yorkshire Regiment (Hull Commercials), 1914–1919, Brown, London, 1937.

Hall, W. G., *The Green Triangle: the History of the 2/5th Battalion the Sherwood Foresters in the Great European War, 1914–1918*, Garden City Press, Letchworth, 1920.

Hanna, Henry, *The Pals at Suvla Bay: being the Record of 'D' Company of the 7th Royal Dublin Fusiliers*, Ponsonby, Dublin, 1916.

Hudson, R. N., *The Bradford Pals: a Short History of the 16th and 18th (Service) Battalions of the Prince of Wales's Own West Yorkshire Regiment*, privately published, Bradford, 1977.

Jackson, Peter, *The Glorious Sixth (Northamptonshire Regiment): a day to day history recording the movements of the 6th Battalion Northamptonshire Regiment in the Great War*, privately published, 1975.

James, Lieutenant-Colonel H. L. (ed.), *Sixteenth, Seventeenth, Eighteenth, Nineteenth Battalions, the Manchester Regiment: a record, 1914–1918*, Sherratt & Hughes, Manchester, 1923.

Kempster, Brigadier-General F., and Brigadier-General H. C. E. Westropp, *Manchester City Battalions: Book of Honour*, Sherratt & Hughes, Manchester, 1917.

King, H. B., *The 7th (Service) Battalion, Northamptonshire Regiment, 1914–1919*, Gale & Polden, Aldershot, 1919.

Lowe, Lieutenant-Colonel W. D., *War History of the 18th (Service) Battalion, Durham Light Infantry*, Oxford University Press, 1920.

MacLeod, Lieutenant-Colonel Norman, *War History of the 6th (Service) Battalion Queen's Own Cameron Highlanders*, Blackwood, Edinburgh, 1934.

Midwinter, C., *Memories of the 32nd Field Ambulance, 10th (Irish) Division, 1914–1919*, Fougler, Bexleyheath, 1933.

Montague, J. B., *A History of the 9th (Service) Battalion, the York and Lancaster Regiment, 1914–1919*, privately published, n.d.

Neave, Captain E. W. J., *History of the 11th Battalion, 'The Queen's*, Brixton Free Press, London, 1931.

Paget, Captain Guy, *History of the Raising of the 7th (Service) Battalion Northamptonshire Regiment, 14 September 1914–31 August 1915*, Gale & Polden, Aldershot, 1915.

Potter, Captain C. H. and Captain A. S. C. Fothergill, *The History of the 2/6th Lancashire Fusiliers*, privately published, Rochdale, 1927.

Rowlands, D. H., *For the Duration: the Story of the Thirteenth Battalion, the Rifle Brigade*, Simpkin Marshall, London, 1932.

Russell, Captain R. O., *The History of the 11th (Lewisham) Battalion the Queen's Own Royal West Kent Regiment*, Lewisham Newspaper Company, 1934.

Rutter, Owen (ed.), *The History of the Seventh (Service) Battalion, the Royal Sussex Regiment*, Times Publishing Company, London, 1934.

Sandilands, Colonel J. W., and Lieutenant-Colonel Norman MacLeod, *The History of the 7th Battalion Queen's Own Cameron Highlanders*, Mackay, Stirling, 1922.

Shakespear, Lieutenant-Colonel J., *A Record of the 17th and 32nd (Service) Battalions Northumberland Fusiliers (NER) Pioneers, 1914–1919*, Northumberland Press, Newcastle, 1926.

Sparling, Richard A., *History of the 12th (Service) Battalion York and Lancaster Regiment*, J. W. Northend, Sheffield, 1920.

Stone, Major Christopher Stone (ed.), *A History of the 22nd (Service) Battalion Royal Fusiliers (Kensington)*, privately published, London, 1923.

Swann, Major-General, J. C., *The 2nd Bucks Battalion, 1914–1918*, Aylesbury, 1926.

Truscott, Lieutenant-Colonel R. F., *A Short History of the 16th Battalion the*

Sherwood Foresters (Chatsworth Rifles), privately published, 1928.

Various authors, *The History of the 2/6th Battalion the Royal Warwickshire Regiment, 1914–1919*, Cornish, Birmingham, 1929.

—A Border Battalion, *The History of the 7/8th (Service) Battalion King's Own Scottish Borderers*, Foulis, Edinburgh, 1920.

—*The History of the Locally Raised 20th (Service) Battalion Durham Light Infantry*, Youll, Sunderland, 1920.

'V.M.', *Record of the XIth (Service) Battalion Border Regiment (Lonsdale) from September 1914 to July 1st 1916*, Whitehead, Appleby, n.d.

Ward, F. W., *The 23rd (Service) Battalion Royal Fusiliers (First Sportsman's): a Record of its Services in the Great War, 1914–1919*, Sidgwick & Jackson, London, 1920.

'W.D.R.' (ed.), *Souvenir Booklet of the Sixth Cameron Highlanders*, Glasgow Herald, 1916.

Wenyon, Lieutenant-Colonel H. J., and Major H. S. Brown, *The History of the Eighth Battalion the Queen's Own Royal West Kent Regiment, 1914–1919*, Hazell Watson & Viney, London, 1921.

Wheeler, Lieutenant-Colonel C. (ed.), *Memorial Record of the Seventh (Service) Battalion, the Oxfordshire and Buckinghamshire Light Infantry*, Blackwell, Oxford, 1921.

Wheeler-Holohan, Captain A. V., and Captain G. M. G. Wyatt, *The Rangers' Historical Records: from 1859 to the Conclusion of the Great War*, Harrison, London, 1921.

Wilde, Herbert (ed.), *The Oldham Battalion of Comrades: Book of Honour*, Sherratt & Hughes, Manchester, 1920.

Wurtzburg, Captain C. E., *The History of the 2/6th (Rifle) Battalion, the King's (Liverpool) Regiment, 1914–1919*, Gale & Polden, Aldershot, 1920.

Wyrall, Everard, *The 17th (Service) Battalion Royal Fusiliers*, Methuen, London, 1920.

Local histories

Anon., *The 'Leader' Local War Record, 1914–1915*, Coulton, Nelson, 1915.

Armitage, F. P., *Leicester, 1914–1918*, Backus, Leicester, 1933.

Bavin, W. D., *Swindon's War Record*, Drew, Swindon, 1922.

Cole, Lieutenant-Colonel Howard N., *The Story of Catterick Camp, 1915–1972*, Forces Press, Aldershot, 1972.

Field, the Rev. Lawrence P., *The Souvenir Book of Eye, 1914–1919*, Eye Patriotic Association, 1920.

Gates, William G., *Portsmouth and the Great War*, Portsmouth Evening News, 1919.

Kennedy, Major J. H., *Attleborough in War Time*, London and Norwich Press, 1920.

Lee, John A., *Todmorden and the Great War: a Local Record*, Waddington, Todmorden, 1922.

MacDonagh, Michael, *In London during the Great War*, Eyre & Spottiswoode, London, 1935.

Middlebrook, Martin, *Boston at War*, Kay, Boston, 1974.

Miller, Frederick, *The Hartlepools and the Great War*, Sage, West Hartlepool, 1920.

Oakley, William H., *Guildford in the Great War*, Billing, Guildford, 1934.

Pain, E. C., *History of Deal, 1914–1953*, Pain, Deal, 1953.

Perfect, Charles, *Hornchurch during the Great War*, Benham, Colchester, 1920.

Robertson, William (ed.), *Middlesbrough's Effort in the Great War*, Jordison, Middlesbrough, n.d.

Scott, W. H., *Leeds in the Great War, 1914–1918*, Libraries and Arts Committee,

Leeds, 1923.

Sidebotham, Randal, *Hyde in Wartime: Soldiers', Sailors' and Civilians' Deeds*, North Cheshire Herald, 1916.

Stone, George F., and Charles Wells (eds.), *Bristol and the Great War*, Arrowsmith, Bristol, 1920.

General works

Adams, R. J. Q.: *Arms and the Wizard: Lloyd George and the Ministry of Munitions, 1915–1916:* Cassell, London, 1978.

—and Philip P. Poirier, *The Conscription Controversy in Great Britain, 1900–1918*, Macmillan, London, 1987.

Allinson, Sidney, *The Bantams: the Untold Story of World War I*, Baker, London, 1981.

Amery, L. S. (ed.), *The Times History of the War in South Africa, 1899–1902*, 7 vols., London, 1900–09.

Arnold-Forster, H. O., *The Army in 1906: a Policy and a Vindication*, Murray, London, 1906.

Arnot, R. Page, *The Miners, Years of Struggle: a History of the Miners' Federation of Great Britain from 1910 onwards*, Allen & Unwin, London, 1960.

Baker, Harold, *The Territorial Force: a Manual of its Law, Organisation and Administration*, Murray, London, 1909.

Barnett, Correlli, *Britain and her Army, 1509–1970: a Military, Political and Social Survey*, Allen Lane, London, 1970.

Beckett, Ian F. W., and John Gooch (eds.), *Politicians and Defence: Studies in the Formulation of British Defence Policy, 1845–1970*, Manchester University Press, 1981.

Beckett, Ian F. W., *Riflemen Form: a Study of the Rifle Volunteer Movement, 1859–1908*, Ogilby Trusts, Aldershot, 1982.

Beckett, Ian F. W., and Keith Simpson (eds.), *A Nation in Arms: a Social Study of the British Army in the First World War*, Manchester University Press, 1985.

Beckett, Ian F. W. (ed.), *The Army and the Curragh Incident, 1914*, Bodley Head for the Army Record Society, London, 1986.

Best, Geoffrey, and A. Wheatcroft (eds.), *War, Economy and the Military Mind*, Croom Helm, London, 1976.

Biddulph, General Sir Robert, *Lord Cardwell at the War Office*, Murray, London, 1904.

Bidwell, Shelford, and Dominick Graham, *Fire-power: British Army Weapons and Theories of War, 1904–1945*, Allen & Unwin, London, 1982.

Bond, Brian (ed.), *Victorian Military Campaigns*, Hutchinson, London, 1967.

Bond, Brian, *The Victorian Army and the Staff College, 1854–1914*, Eyre Methuen, London, 1972.

Bowley, A. L., *Prices and Wages in the United Kingdom, 1914–1920*, Clarendon Press, Oxford, 1921.

Brown, Malcolm, *Tommy goes to War*, Dent, London, 1978.

Burk, Kathleen (ed.), *War and the State: the Transformation of British Government, 1914–1919*, Allen & Unwin, London, 1982.

Clarke, J., C. Critcher and R. Johnson (eds.), *Working Class Culture*, Hutchinson, London, 1979.

Cole, G. D. H., *Trade Unionism and Munitions*, Oxford University Press, 1923.

Cousins, Geoffrey, *The Defenders: a history of the British Volunteer*, Muller, London, 1968.

Cunningham, Hugh, *The Volunteer Force: a Social and Political History, 1859–1908*,

Croom Helm, London, 1975.

Dangerfield, George, *The Strange Death of Liberal England*, Constable, London, 1935.

—*The Damnable Question: a Study in Anglo-Irish Relations*, Constable, London, 1977.

D'Ombrain, Nicholas, *War Machinery and High Policy: Defence Administration in Peacetime Britain, 1902–1914*, Oxford University Press, 1973.

Douglas, Roy, *The History of the Liberal Party, 1895–1970*, Sidgwick & Jackson, London, 1971.

Dunlop, Colonel John K., *The Development of the British Army, 1899–1914*, Methuen, London, 1938.

Ehrman, John, *Cabinet Government and War, 1890–1940*, Cambridge University Press, 1958.

Ensor, Sir Robert, *England, 1870–1914*, Clarendon Press, Oxford, 1936.

Fergusson, Sir James, *The Curragh Incident*, Faber, London, 1964.

Field, Eric, *Advertising: the Forgotten Years*, Benn, London, 1959.

French, David, *British Economic and Strategic Planning, 1905–1915*, Allen & Unwin, London, 1982.

Fussell, Paul, *The Great War and Modern Memory*, Oxford University Press, 1975.

Germains, V. W., *The Kitchener Armies*, Peter Davies, London, 1930.

Gooch, John, *The Plans of War: the General Staff and British Military Strategy, c. 1900–1916*, Routledge & Kegan Paul, London, 1974.

—*The Prospect of War: Studies in British Defence Policy, 1847–1942*, Cass, London, 1981.

Gordon, Hampden, *The War Office*, Putnam, London, 1935.

Graham, John W., *Conscription and Conscience*, Allen & Unwin, London, 1922.

Guinn, Paul, *British Strategy and Politics, 1914–1918*, Clarendon Press, Oxford, 1965.

Haig-Brown, Captain A. R., *The OTC and the Great War*, Country Life, London, 1915.

Hamer, W. S., *The British Army: Civil–Military Relations, 1885–1905*, Clarendon Press, Oxford, 1970.

Hay, Ian (John Hay Beith), *The First Hundred Thousand*, Blackwood, London, 1916.

Hayes, Denis, *Conscription Conflict*, Sheppard, London, 1949.

Hazlehurst, Cameron, *Politicians at War, July 1914 to May 1915: a Prologue to the Triumph of Lloyd George*, Cape, London, 1971.

Higenbottam, S., *Our Society's History*, Amalgamated Society of Woodworkers, Manchester, 1939.

Howard, Michael, *Studies in War and Peace*, Temple Smith, London, 1970.

Hunt, B., and A. Preston (eds.), *War Aims and Strategic Policy in the Great War, 1914–1918*, Croom Helm, London, 1978.

Hyam, R., *Britain's Imperial Century, 1815–1914*, Batsford, London, 1976.

Hynes, S., *The Edwardian Turn of Mind*, Princeton University Press, 1968.

Jalland, Patricia, *The Liberals and Ireland: the Ulster Question and British Politics to 1914*, Harvester, Brighton, 1980.

James, Brigadier E. A., *British Regiments, 1914–1918*, Samson, London, 1978.

Johnson, Franklyn A., *Defence by Committee: the British Committee of Imperial Defence, 1885–1959*, Oxford University Press, 1960.

Kee, Robert, *The Green Flag*, Weidenfeld & Nicolson, London, 1972.

Kennedy, Paul M., *The Rise of the Anglo-German Antagonism, 1860–1914*, Allen & Unwin, London, 1980.

Kennedy, T. C., *The Hound of Conscience: a History of the No Conscription Fellowship, 1914–1919*, Arkansas University Press, 1981.

Kipling, Rudyard, *The New Army in Training*, Macmillan, London, 1915.
Koch, H. W. (ed.), *The Origins of the First World War*, Macmillan, London, 1972.
Krieger, Leonard, and Fritz Stern (eds.), *The Responsibility of Power*, Macmillan, London, 1968.
Lavery, Felix (ed.), *Irish Heroes in the War*, Everett, London, 1917.
Liddell Hart, B. H., *A History of the World War, 1914–1918*, Faber, London, 1934.
—*Through the Fog of War*, Faber, London, 1938.
Luvaas, Jay, *The Education of an Army: British Military Thought, 1815–1940*, Cassell, London, 1965.
Macdonald, Lyn, *Somme*, Joseph, London, 1983.
MacLean, A. H. H., *Public Schools and the War in South Africa*, Simpson & Marshall, London, 1902.
Marder, Arthur J., *From the Dreadnought to Scapa Flow: the Royal Navy in the Fisher Era, 1904–1919*, 5 vols., Oxford University Press, 1961–70.
—*The Anatomy of British Sea Power: a History of British Naval Policy in the pre-Dreadnought Era, 1880–1905*, Cass, London, 1964.
Marwick, Arthur, *The Deluge: British Society and the First World War*, Bodley Head, London, 1965.
—*Women at War, 1914–1918*, Fontana, London, 1977.
Meakin, A. M. B., *Enlistment or Conscription?* Routledge, London, 1915.
Middlebrook, Martin, *The First Day on the Somme*, Allen Lane, London, 1971.
Monger, George, *The End of Isolation: British Foreign Policy, 1900–1907*, Nelson, London, 1963.
Morris, A. J. A., *Radicalism against War, 1906–1914: the Advocacy of Peace and Retrenchment*, Longman, London, 1972.
—*Edwardian Radicalism, 1900–1914: some Aspects of British Radicalism*: Routledge & Kegan Paul, London, 1974.
O'Day, Alan (ed.), *The Edwardian Age: Conflict and Stability, 1900–1914*, Macmillan, London, 1979.
Omond, Lieutenant-Colonel J. S., *Parliament and the Army, 1624–1904*, Cambridge University Press, 1933.
Osborne, J. M., *The Voluntary Recruiting Movement in Britain, 1914–1916*, Garland, New York, 1982.
Petrie, Sir Charles, *Scenes of Edwardian Life*, Eyre & Spottiswoode, London, 1965.
Playne, Caroline E., *Society at War, 1914–1916*, Allen & Unwin, London, 1931.
Pound, Reginald, *The Lost Generation*, Constable, London, 1964.
Pratt, E. A., *British Railways and the Great War*, 2 vols., Selwyn & Blount, London, 1921.
Price, R., *An Imperial War and the British Working Class*, Routledge & Kegan Paul, London, 1972.
Rae, John, *Conscience and Politics: the British Government and the Conscientious Objector to Military Service, 1916–1919*, Oxford University Press, 1970.
Repington, Lieutenant-Colonel Charles à Court, *The First World War, 1914–1918*, 2 vols., Constable, London, 1920.
Roberts, Robert, *The Classic Slum*, Manchester University Press, 1971.
Ryan, A. P., *Mutiny at the Curragh*, Macmillan, London, 1956.
Searle, G. R., *The Quest for National Efficiency*, Blackwell, Oxford, 1971.
—*Eugenics and Politics in Britain, 1900–1914*, Sijthoff, The Hague, 1976.
Simon, B., and I. Bradley (eds.), *The Victorian Public School*, Gill & Macmillan, London, 1975.
Spiers, Edward M., *The Army and Society, 1815–1914*, Longman, London, 1980.
Springhall, John, *Youth, Empire and Society: British Youth Movements, 1883–1940*, Croom Helm, London, 1977.

Steiner, Zara, S., *Britain and the Origins of the First World War*, Macmillan, London, 1977.

Stewart, A. T. Q., *The Ulster Crisis: Resistance to Home Rule, 1912–14*, Faber, London, 1967.

Turner, E. S., *Gallant Gentlemen: a Portrait of the British Officer, 1660–1956*, Joseph, London, 1956.

Tyler, J. E., *The British Army and the Continent, 1904–1914*, Arnold, London, 1938.

Wallace, Edgar, *Kitchener's Army and the Territorial Forces*, Newnes, London, 1916.

Wilkinson, Alan, *The Church of England and the First World War*, SPCK, London, 1978.

Williams, Captain B., *Raising and Training the New Armies*, Constable, London, 1918.

Williamson, Samuel R., *The Politics of Grand Strategy: British and France prepare for War, 1904–1914*, Harvard University Press, Cambridge, Mass., 1969.

Wilson, Trevor, *The Downfall of the Liberal Party, 1914–1935*, Collins, London, 1966.

—*The Myriad Faces of War: Britain and the Great War, 1914–1918*, Polity Press, Cambridge, 1986.

Winter, Denis, *Death's Men: Soldiers of the Great War*, Allen Lane, London, 1978.

Winter, J. M., *Socialism and the Challenge of War: Ideas and Politics in Britain, 1912–1918*, Routledge & Kegan Paul, London, 1974.

—*The Great War and the British People*, Macmillan, London, 1986.

Wohl, Robert, *The Generation of 1914*, Weidenfeld & Nicolson, London, 1980.

Wolfe, Humbert, *Labour Supply and Regulation*, Oxford University Press, 1923.

Woodward, Sir Llewellyn, *Great Britain and the War of 1914–1918*, Metheun, London, 1967.

Articles

Bond, Brian, 'Richard Burdon Haldane at the War Office, 1905–1912', *Army Quarterly*, LXXXVI, 1, 1963.

Callan, Patrick, 'British recruitment in Ireland, 1914–1918', *Revue Internationale d'Histoire Militaire*, 63, 1985.

Dewey, P. E., 'Military recruiting and the British labour force during the First World War', *Historical Journal*, XXVII, 1, 1984.

Douglas, Roy, 'Voluntary enlistment in the First World War and the work of the Parliamentary Recruiting Committee', *Journal of Modern History*, 42, 4, 1970.

Englander, D., and J., Osborne, 'Jack, Tommy and Henry Dubb: the armed forces and the working class', *Historical Journal*, 21, 3, 1978.

Esher, Lord, 'The voluntary principle', *National Review*, LVI, 331, 1910.

—'Lord K.', *National Review*, LXVII, 401, 1916.

Farrar, Peter N., 'Hull's New Army, 1914', *Journal of Local Studies*, 1, 2, 1981.

Fraser, Peter, 'The British "Shells Scandal" of 1915', *Canadian Journal of History*, XVIII, 1, 1983.

French, David, 'Spy fever in Britain, 1900–1915', *Historical Journal*, 21, 2, 1978.

Haggie, Paul, 'The Royal Navy and war planning in the Fisher era', *Journal of Contemporary History*, 8, 3, 1973.

Hazlehurst, Cameron, 'Asquith as Prime Minister, 1908–1916', *English Historical Review*, 85, 336, 1970.

Howard, Michael, 'Empire, race and war', *History Today*, 31, 12, 1981.

McDermott, John, 'The revolution in British military thinking from the Boer War to the Moroccan crisis', *Canadian Journal of History*, IX, 2, 1974.

McEwen, John M., 'The national press during the First World War: ownership and circulation', *Journal of Contemporary History*, 17, 3, 1982.

Morris, A. J. Anthony, 'Haldane's army reforms, 1906–1908: the deception of the radicals', *History*, 56, 186, 1971.

Neilson, Keith, 'Kitchener: a reputation refurbished', *Canadian Journal of History*, XV, 2, 1980.

Ropp, Theodore, 'Conscription in Great Britain, 1900–1914: a failure in civil-military communications?', *Military Affairs*, XX, 2, 1956.

Scott-Moncrieff, Major-General Sir George, 'The hutting problem in the war', *Royal Engineers Journal*, XXXVIII, 3, 1924.

Springhall, John, 'The Boy Scouts, class and militarism in relation to British youth movements, 1908–1930', *International Review of Social History*, 16, 2, 1971.

Summers, Anne, 'Militarism in Britain before the Great War', *History Workshop*, 2, 1976.

Teagarden, E. M., 'Lord Haldane and the origins of the Officer Training Corps', *Journal of the Society for Army Historical Research*, XLV, 182, 1967.

Travers, T. H. E., 'The hidden army: structural problems in the British officer corps, 1900–1918', *Journal of Contemporary History*, 17, 3, 1982.

Wilkinson, P., 'English youth movements, 1908–1930', *Journal of Contemporary History*, 4, 2, 1969.

Williams, Orlo, 'The War Office from the inside', *National Review*, LXXIII, 437, 1919.

Winter, J. M., 'Britain's lost generation of the First World War', *Population Studies*, 31, 3, 1977.

Worthington, Ian, 'Antecedent education and officer recruitment: the origins and early development of the public school – Army relationship', *Military Affairs*, XLI, 4, 1977.

Newspapers and periodicals

Birmingham Daily Post. Brighton Gazette. Brighton Herald. Bristol Times and Mirror. Daily Express. Daily Mail. Daily Mirror. Daily News. Daily Telegraph. Dumfries Standard. Freeman's Journal. Glasgow Herald. Hull Daily Mail. Irish Independent. Labour Leader. Leeds and District Weekly Citizen. Liverpool Daily Courier. Liverpool Daily Post. London Opinion. Manchester Guardian. Morning Post. Nation. Observer. Punch. South Wales Daily News. Stroud News. Sunday Pictorial. The Scotsman. The Tatler. The Times. Western Daily Press. Western Mail. Y Goleuad. Yorkshire Observer. Yorkshire Post.

Regimental journals

The Back Badge (journal of the Gloucestershire Regiment).
The Green Howards Gazette.
The Oak Tree (journal of the Cheshire Regiment).
The Snapper (journal of the East Yorkshire Regiment).

Oral history interviews

Chelmsford and Essex Museum. O. I. Dickson.
Imperial War Museum. B. G. Buxton. Major-General J. M. L. Grover. Thomas McIndoe. J. D. Pratt. Charles R. Quinnell. Perry Webb.

General Index

Index of units